2005 | LITTLE GREEN
DATA BOOK

The World Bank

ISBN 0-8213-6076-0

The Little Green Data Book 2005 is a joint product of the
Group and Environment Department of the World Bank.

Contents

Acknowledgments

The Little Green Data Book 2005 is based on World Development Indicators 2005 and its accompanying CD-ROM. Defining, gathering, and disseminating international statistics is a collective effort of many people and organizations. The indicators presented in World Development Indicators are the fruit of decades of work at many levels, from the field workers who administer censuses and household surveys to the committees and working parties of the national and international statistical agencies that develop the nomenclature, classifications, and standards fundamental to the international statistical system. Nongovernmental organizations have also made important contributions. We are indebted to the World Development Indicators network of partners, as detailed in World Development Indicators 2005. The financial assistance of the Government of Sweden is gratefully acknowledged.

The Little Green Data Book is the result of close collaboration between the staff of the Environment Department and the Development Economics Data Group. Mehdi Akhlaghi, Mahyar Eshragh-Tabary, Richard Fix, Kirk Hamilton, Saeed Ordoubadi, Giovanni Ruta, and Alexandra Sears contributed to its preparation. Jim Cantrell designed the cover. Cover photographs are from Kirk Hamilton and the World Bank photo archives. The book was edited, designed, and laid out by Meta de Coquereaumont, Christopher Trott, and Elaine Wilson of Communications Development Incorporated in Washington, D.C.

Foreword

The 2005 edition of *The Little Green Data Book* coincides with important transformations linked to sustainable development. This year will be remembered for the entry into force of the Kyoto Protocol. It also marked a renewed commitment by the G-8 countries to foster development in Africa. Finally, this year will witness the reconstruction efforts following the tsunami disaster in South and East Asia.

Development and poverty alleviation—the World Bank's mission—call for a long-term vision. Enhancing environmental quality, improving natural resource management, and maintaining global ecosystems are all important steps toward this goal. Better environmental management can improve people's livelihoods, health, and security today and in the future.

To achieve these lasting results we need to start from a sound base of information that helps us set priorities and measure progress toward environmental sustainability goals. *The Little Green Data Book* is a step in this direction, with key indicators of the environment and its relationship to people for more than 200 countries. This year's edition includes new indicators for fish catch, in the agriculture and fisheries section, and biomass fuel use, in the energy section. While there are gaps and shortcomings in the data, we hope this book will inspire decisionmakers at all levels to use this information and to seek to fill the gaps for their own countries. We welcome your suggestions on how future editions can be improved and made more useful.

Shaida Badiee   James Warren Evans
Director,   Director,
Development Data Group   Environment Department

Data notes

The data in this book are for the most recent year for which data are available between 1999 and 2003, unless otherwise noted in the glossary. Regional aggregates include data for low- and middle-income economies only. Aggregates for regions and income groups are shown only if data are available for 66 percent of the economies in that group.

Symbols used:

      ..   means that data are not available or that aggregates cannot be calculated because of missing data.

0 or 0.0   means zero or less than half the unit shown.

      $ means current U.S. dollars.

Data are shown for economies with populations greater than 30,000 and for smaller economies if they are members of the World Bank. The term *country* (used interchangeably with *economy*) does not imply political independence or official recognition by the World Bank but refers to any economy for which the authorities report separate social or economic statistics.

In keeping with *World Development Indicators 2005, The Little Green Data Book 2005* uses terminology in line with the 1993 System of National Accounts (SNA). In particular, gross national income (GNI) is used in place of gross national product (GNP).

Regional tables

The country composition of regions is based on the World Bank's analytical regions and may differ from common geographic usage.

East Asia and Pacific

American Samoa, Cambodia, China, Fiji, Indonesia, Kiribati, Korea, Dem. Rep., Lao PDR, Malaysia, Marshall Islands, Micronesia, Fed. Sts., Mongolia, Myanmar, Northern Mariana Islands, Palau, Papua New Guinea, Philippines, Samoa, Solomon Islands, Thailand, Timor-Leste, Tonga, Vanuatu, Vietnam

Europe and Central Asia

Albania, Armenia, Azerbaijan, Belarus, Bosnia and Herzegovina, Bulgaria, Croatia, Czech Republic, Estonia, Georgia, Hungary, Kazakhstan, Kyrgyz Republic, Latvia, Lithuania, Macedonia, FYR, Moldova, Poland, Romania, Russian Federation, Serbia and Montenegro, Slovak Republic, Tajikistan, Turkey, Turkmenistan, Ukraine, Uzbekistan

Latin America and Caribbean

Antigua and Barbuda, Argentina, Aruba, Barbados, Belize, Bolivia, Brazil, Chile, Colombia, Costa Rica, Cuba, Dominica, Dominican Republic, Ecuador, El Salvador, Grenada, Guatemala, Guyana, Haiti, Honduras, Jamaica, Mexico, Nicaragua, Panama, Paraguay, Peru, St. Kitts and Nevis, St. Lucia, St. Vincent and the Grenadines, Suriname, Trinidad and Tobago, Uruguay, Venezuela, RB

Middle East and North Africa

Algeria, Djibouti, Egypt, Arab Rep., Iran, Islamic Rep., Iraq, Jordan, Lebanon, Libya, Morocco, Oman, Saudi Arabia, Syrian Arab Republic, Tunisia, West Bank and Gaza, Yemen, Rep.

South Asia

Afghanistan, Bangladesh, Bhutan, India, Maldives, Nepal, Pakistan, Sri Lanka

Sub-Saharan Africa

Angola, Benin, Botswana, Burkina Faso, Burundi, Cameroon, Cape Verde, Central African Republic, Chad, Comoros, Congo, Dem. Rep., Congo, Rep., Côte d'Ivoire, Equatorial Guinea, Eritrea, Ethiopia, Gabon, The Gambia, Ghana, Guinea, Guinea-Bissau, Kenya, Lesotho, Liberia, Madagascar, Malawi, Mali, Mauritania, Mauritius, Mayotte, Mozambique, Namibia, Niger, Nigeria, Rwanda, São Tomé and Principe, Senegal, Seychelles, Sierra Leone, Somalia, South Africa, Sudan, Swaziland, Tanzania, Togo, Uganda, Zambia, Zimbabwe

World

Population (millions)	6,272.5
Urban population (% of total)	48.7
GDP ($ billions)	36,461
GNI per capita, *Atlas* method ($)	5,510

Agriculture and fisheries

Land area (1,000 sq. km)	130,331
Agricultural land (% of land area)	38
Irrigated land (% of crop land)	19.8
Fertilizer consumption (100 grams/ha arable land)	1,008
Population density, rural (people/sq. km arable land)	477
Fish catch, total (1,000 metric tons)	129,611

Forests

Forest area (1,000 sq. km)	38,611
Forest area share of total land area (%)	29.7
Annual deforestation (% change, 1990–2000)	0.2

Biodiversity

Mammal species, total known	
Mammal species, threatened	
Bird species, total breeding	
Bird species, threatened	
Nationally protected area (% of land area)	10.7

Energy

GDP per unit of energy use (2000 PPP$/kg oil equiv)	4.6
Energy use per capita (kg oil equiv)	1,699
Energy from biomass products and waste (% of total)	10.6
Energy imports, net (% of energy use)	–1
Electric power consumption per capita (kWh)	2,225
Electricity generated by coal (% of total)	39.1

Emissions and pollution

CO_2 emissions per unit of GDP (kg/2000 PPP$ GDP)	0.5
CO_2 emissions per capita (metric tons)	3.8
Particulate matter (pop. weighted average, µg/cu. m)	44
Passenger cars (per 1,000 people)	105

Water and sanitation

Internal freshwater resources per capita (cu. m)	6,895
Freshwater withdrawal	
Total (% of internal resources)	7.8
Agriculture (% of total freshwater withdrawal)	71
Access to improved water source (% of total population)	82
Rural (% of rural population)	72
Urban (% of urban population)	94
Access to sanitation (% of total population)	54
Rural (% of rural population)	35
Urban (% of urban population)	79
Under-five mortality rate (per 1,000)	86

National accounting aggregates, 2003

Gross national savings (% of GNI)	20.6
Consumption of fixed capital (% of GNI)	12.6
Education expenditure (% of GNI)	4.4
Energy depletion (% of GNI)	2.3
Mineral depletion (% of GNI)	0.1
Net forest depletion (% of GNI)	0.0
CO_2 damage (% of GNI)	0.5
Particulate emission damage (% of GNI)	0.3
Adjusted net savings (% of GNI)	9.3

East Asia & Pacific

Population (millions)	1,854.6
Urban population (% of total)	39.1
GDP ($ billions)	2,033
GNI per capita, *Atlas* method ($)	1,070

Agriculture and fisheries

Land area (1,000 sq. km)	15,886
Agricultural land (% of land area)	50
Irrigated land (% of crop land)	..
Fertilizer consumption (100 grams/ha arable land)	2,297
Population density, rural (people/sq. km arable land)	565
Fish catch, total (1,000 metric tons)	60,812

Forests

Forest area (1,000 sq. km)	4,284
Forest area share of total land area (%)	27.0
Annual deforestation (% change, 1990–2000)	0.2

Biodiversity

Mammal species, total known	
Mammal species, threatened	
Bird species, total breeding	
Bird species, threatened	
Nationally protected area (% of land area)	9.2

Energy

GDP per unit of energy use (2000 PPP$/kg oil equiv)	4.6
Energy use per capita (kg oil equiv)	904
Energy from biomass products and waste (% of total)	19.6
Energy imports, net (% of energy use)	−4
Electric power consumption per capita (kWh)	891
Electricity generated by coal (% of total)	66.8

Emissions and pollution

CO_2 emissions per unit of GDP (kg/2000 PPP$ GDP)	0.5
CO_2 emissions per capita (metric tons)	2.1
Particulate matter (pop. weighted average, µg/cu. m)	69
Passenger cars (per 1,000 people)	10

Water and sanitation

Internal freshwater resources per capita (cu. m)	5,103
Freshwater withdrawal	
Total (% of internal resources)	8.2
Agriculture (% of total freshwater withdrawal)	81
Access to improved water source (% of total population)	78
Rural (% of rural population)	69
Urban (% of urban population)	92
Access to sanitation (% of total population)	49
Rural (% of rural population)	35
Urban (% of urban population)	71
Under-five mortality rate (per 1,000)	41

National accounting aggregates, 2003

Gross national savings (% of GNI)	41.7
Consumption of fixed capital (% of GNI)	9.2
Education expenditure (% of GNI)	2.3
Energy depletion (% of GNI)	3.9
Mineral depletion (% of GNI)	0.3
Net forest depletion (% of GNI)	0.1
CO_2 damage (% of GNI)	1.8
Particulate emission damage (% of GNI)	0.8
Adjusted net savings (% of GNI)	27.9

Europe & Central Asia

Population (millions)	472.2
Urban population (% of total)	63.8
GDP ($ billions)	1,403
GNI per capita, *Atlas* method ($)	2,580

Agriculture and fisheries
Land area (1,000 sq. km)	23,868
Agricultural land (% of land area)	28
Irrigated land (% of crop land)	10.9
Fertilizer consumption (100 grams/ha arable land)	344
Population density, rural (people/sq. km arable land)	122
Fish catch, total (1,000 metric tons)	5,527

Forests
Forest area (1,000 sq. km)	9,463
Forest area share of total land area (%)	39.6
Annual deforestation (% change, 1990–2000)	–0.1

Biodiversity
Mammal species, total known	
Mammal species, threatened	
Bird species, total breeding	
Bird species, threatened	
Nationally protected area (% of land area)	6.8

Energy
GDP per unit of energy use (2000 PPP$/kg oil equiv)	2.5
Energy use per capita (kg oil equiv)	2,697
Energy from biomass products and waste (% of total)	2.3
Energy imports, net (% of energy use)	–23
Electric power consumption per capita (kWh)	2,808
Electricity generated by coal (% of total)	29.4

Emissions and pollution
CO_2 emissions per unit of GDP (kg/2000 PPP$ GDP)	1.1
CO_2 emissions per capita (metric tons)	6.7
Particulate matter (pop. weighted average, μg/cu. m)	33
Passenger cars (per 1,000 people)	138

Water and sanitation
Internal freshwater resources per capita (cu. m)	11,128
Freshwater withdrawal	
Total (% of internal resources)	7.4
Agriculture (% of total freshwater withdrawal)	57
Access to improved water source (% of total population)	91
Rural (% of rural population)	80
Urban (% of urban population)	98
Access to sanitation (% of total population)	82
Rural (% of rural population)	64
Urban (% of urban population)	93
Under-five mortality rate (per 1,000)	36

National accounting aggregates, 2003
Gross national savings (% of GNI)	21.9
Consumption of fixed capital (% of GNI)	10.7
Education expenditure (% of GNI)	4.1
Energy depletion (% of GNI)	11.6
Mineral depletion (% of GNI)	0.1
Net forest depletion (% of GNI)	0.0
CO_2 damage (% of GNI)	1.9
Particulate emission damage (% of GNI)	0.6
Adjusted net savings (% of GNI)	1.1

Latin America & Caribbean

Population (millions)	532.7
Urban population (% of total)	76.6
GDP ($ billions)	1,741
GNI per capita, *Atlas* method ($)	3,280

Agriculture and fisheries

Land area (1,000 sq. km)	20,057
Agricultural land (% of land area)	39
Irrigated land (% of crop land)	12.5
Fertilizer consumption (100 grams/ha arable land)	892
Population density, rural (people/sq. km arable land)	210
Fish catch, total (1,000 metric tons)	17,804

Forests

Forest area (1,000 sq. km)	9,552
Forest area share of total land area (%)	47.6
Annual deforestation (% change, 1990–2000)	0.5

Biodiversity

Mammal species, total known	
Mammal species, threatened	
Bird species, total breeding	
Bird species, threatened	
Nationally protected area (% of land area)	11.2

Energy

GDP per unit of energy use (2000 PPP$/kg oil equiv)	6.1
Energy use per capita (kg oil equiv)	1,156
Energy from biomass products and waste (% of total)	14.6
Energy imports, net (% of energy use)	−42
Electric power consumption per capita (kWh)	1,506
Electricity generated by coal (% of total)	5.0

Emissions and pollution

CO_2 emissions per unit of GDP (kg/2000 PPP$ GDP)	0.4
CO_2 emissions per capita (metric tons)	2.7
Particulate matter (pop. weighted average, μg/cu. m)	40
Passenger cars (per 1,000 people)	..

Water and sanitation

Internal freshwater resources per capita (cu. m)	25,245
Freshwater withdrawal	
Total (% of internal resources)	2.0
Agriculture (% of total freshwater withdrawal)	74
Access to improved water source (% of total population)	89
Rural (% of rural population)	69
Urban (% of urban population)	96
Access to sanitation (% of total population)	74
Rural (% of rural population)	44
Urban (% of urban population)	84
Under-five mortality rate (per 1,000)	33

National accounting aggregates, 2003

Gross national savings (% of GNI)	19.5
Consumption of fixed capital (% of GNI)	10.3
Education expenditure (% of GNI)	4.2
Energy depletion (% of GNI)	6.4
Mineral depletion (% of GNI)	0.7
Net forest depletion (% of GNI)	0.0
CO_2 damage (% of GNI)	0.5
Particulate emission damage (% of GNI)	0.5
Adjusted net savings (% of GNI)	5.3

Middle East & North Africa

Population (millions)	311.6
Urban population (% of total)	59.0
GDP ($ billions)	745
GNI per capita, *Atlas* method ($)	2,390

Agriculture and fisheries	
Land area (1,000 sq. km)	11,111
Agricultural land (% of land area)	34
Irrigated land (% of crop land)	38.3
Fertilizer consumption (100 grams/ha arable land)	854
Population density, rural (people/sq. km arable land)	603
Fish catch, total (1,000 metric tons)	2,840

Forests	
Forest area (1,000 sq. km)	168
Forest area share of total land area (%)	1.5
Annual deforestation (% change, 1990–2000)	−0.1

Biodiversity	
Mammal species, total known	
Mammal species, threatened	
Bird species, total breeding	
Bird species, threatened	
Nationally protected area (% of land area)	11.3

Energy	
GDP per unit of energy use (2000 PPP$/kg oil equiv)	3.5
Energy use per capita (kg oil equiv)	1,504
Energy from biomass products and waste (% of total)	1.0
Energy imports, net (% of energy use)	−168
Electric power consumption per capita (kWh)	1,412
Electricity generated by coal (% of total)	2.3

Emissions and pollution	
CO_2 emissions per unit of GDP (kg/2000 PPP$ GDP)	0.8
CO_2 emissions per capita (metric tons)	4.2
Particulate matter (pop. weighted average, µg/cu. m)	87
Passenger cars (per 1,000 people)	..

Water and sanitation	
Internal freshwater resources per capita (cu. m)	761
Freshwater withdrawal	
Total (% of internal resources)	101.7
Agriculture (% of total freshwater withdrawal)	88
Access to improved water source (% of total population)	88
Rural (% of rural population)	78
Urban (% of urban population)	96
Access to sanitation (% of total population)	75
Rural (% of rural population)	56
Urban (% of urban population)	90
Under-five mortality rate (per 1,000)	53

National accounting aggregates, 2003	
Gross national savings (% of GNI)	31.2
Consumption of fixed capital (% of GNI)	10.0
Education expenditure (% of GNI)	5.5
Energy depletion (% of GNI)	30.7
Mineral depletion (% of GNI)	0.1
Net forest depletion (% of GNI)	0.0
CO_2 damage (% of GNI)	1.2
Particulate emission damage (% of GNI)	0.8
Adjusted net savings (% of GNI)	−6.2

South Asia

Population (millions)	1,424.7
Urban population (% of total)	28.3
GDP ($ billions)	765
GNI per capita, *Atlas* method ($)	510

Agriculture and fisheries

Land area (1,000 sq. km)	4,781
Agricultural land (% of land area)	55
Irrigated land (% of crop land)	41.2
Fertilizer consumption (100 grams/ha arable land)	1,027
Population density, rural (people/sq. km arable land)	559
Fish catch, total (1,000 metric tons)	8,724

Forests

Forest area (1,000 sq. km)	780
Forest area share of total land area (%)	16.3
Annual deforestation (% change, 1990–2000)	0.1

Biodiversity

Mammal species, total known	
Mammal species, threatened	
Bird species, total breeding	
Bird species, threatened	
Nationally protected area (% of land area)	4.8

Energy

GDP per unit of energy use (2000 PPP$/kg oil equiv)	5.1
Energy use per capita (kg oil equiv)	468
Energy from biomass products and waste (% of total)	39.3
Energy imports, net (% of energy use)	19
Electric power consumption per capita (kWh)	344
Electricity generated by coal (% of total)	59.8

Emissions and pollution

CO_2 emissions per unit of GDP (kg/2000 PPP$ GDP)	0.4
CO_2 emissions per capita (metric tons)	0.9
Particulate matter (pop. weighted average, µg/cu. m)	69
Passenger cars (per 1,000 people)	6

Water and sanitation

Internal freshwater resources per capita (cu. m)	1,275
Freshwater withdrawal	
Total (% of internal resources)	40.5
Agriculture (% of total freshwater withdrawal)	94
Access to improved water source (% of total population)	84
Rural (% of rural population)	80
Urban (% of urban population)	93
Access to sanitation (% of total population)	35
Rural (% of rural population)	23
Urban (% of urban population)	64
Under-five mortality rate (per 1,000)	92

National accounting aggregates, 2003

Gross national savings (% of GNI)	24.9
Consumption of fixed capital (% of GNI)	9.0
Education expenditure (% of GNI)	3.5
Energy depletion (% of GNI)	2.4
Mineral depletion (% of GNI)	0.3
Net forest depletion (% of GNI)	0.7
CO_2 damage (% of GNI)	1.3
Particulate emission damage (% of GNI)	0.7
Adjusted net savings (% of GNI)	14.0

Sub-Saharan Africa

Population (millions)	704.5
Urban population (% of total)	36.5
GDP ($ billions)	439
GNI per capita, *Atlas* method ($)	500

Agriculture and fisheries	
Land area (1,000 sq. km)	23,596
Agricultural land (% of land area)	43
Irrigated land (% of crop land)	4.2
Fertilizer consumption (100 grams/ha arable land)	145
Population density, rural (people/sq. km arable land)	352
Fish catch, total (1,000 metric tons)	5,191

Forests	
Forest area (1,000 sq. km)	6,435
Forest area share of total land area (%)	27.3
Annual deforestation (% change, 1990–2000)	0.8

Biodiversity	
Mammal species, total known	
Mammal species, threatened	
Bird species, total breeding	
Bird species, threatened	
Nationally protected area (% of land area)	8.7

Energy	
GDP per unit of energy use (2000 PPP$/kg oil equiv)	2.8
Energy use per capita (kg oil equiv)	667
Energy from biomass products and waste (% of total)	57.5
Energy imports, net (% of energy use)	–56
Electric power consumption per capita (kWh)	457
Electricity generated by coal (% of total)	68.2

Emissions and pollution	
CO_2 emissions per unit of GDP (kg/2000 PPP$ GDP)	0.4
CO_2 emissions per capita (metric tons)	0.7
Particulate matter (pop. weighted average, µg/cu. m)	54
Passenger cars (per 1,000 people)	..

Water and sanitation	
Internal freshwater resources per capita (cu. m)	5,546
Freshwater withdrawal	
Total (% of internal resources)	1.8
Agriculture (% of total freshwater withdrawal)	85
Access to improved water source (% of total population)	58
Rural (% of rural population)	46
Urban (% of urban population)	82
Access to sanitation (% of total population)	36
Rural (% of rural population)	26
Urban (% of urban population)	55
Under-five mortality rate (per 1,000)	171

National accounting aggregates, 2003	
Gross national savings (% of GNI)	16.9
Consumption of fixed capital (% of GNI)	10.6
Education expenditure (% of GNI)	4.7
Energy depletion (% of GNI)	8.0
Mineral depletion (% of GNI)	0.5
Net forest depletion (% of GNI)	0.7
CO_2 damage (% of GNI)	0.9
Particulate emission damage (% of GNI)	0.4
Adjusted net savings (% of GNI)	0.6

Income group tables

For operational and analytical purposes the World Bank's main criterion for classifying economies is gross national income (GNI) per capita. Every economy is classified as low income, middle income (subdivided into lower middle and upper middle), or high income. Low- and middle-income economies are sometimes referred to as developing economies. The use of the term is convenient; it is not intended to imply that all economies in the group are experiencing similar development or that other economies have reached a preferred or final stage of development. Note that classification by income does not necessarily reflect development status.

Low-income economies are those with a GNI per capita of $765 or less in 2003.

Middle-income economies are those with a GNI per capita of more than $765 but less than $9,386.

Lower-middle-income and **upper-middle-income** economies are separated at a GNI per capita of $3,035.

High-income economies are those with a GNI per capita of $9,386 or more.

The 12 participating member countries of the **European Monetary Union** are Austria, Belgium, Finland, France, Germany, Greece, Ireland, Italy, Luxembourg, Netherlands, Portugal, and Spain.

Low income

Population (millions)	2,311.9
Urban population (% of total)	30.4
GDP ($ billions)	1,103
GNI per capita, *Atlas* method ($)	440

Agriculture and fisheries

Land area (1,000 sq. km)	30,456
Agricultural land (% of land area)	43
Irrigated land (% of crop land)	26.7
Fertilizer consumption (100 grams/ha arable land)	654
Population density, rural (people/sq. km arable land)	509
Fish catch, total (1,000 metric tons)	16,410

Forests

Forest area (1,000 sq. km)	7,939
Forest area share of total land area (%)	26.1
Annual deforestation (% change, 1990–2000)	0.7

Biodiversity

Mammal species, total known	
Mammal species, threatened	
Bird species, total breeding	
Bird species, threatened	
Nationally protected area (% of land area)	7.7

Energy

GDP per unit of energy use (2000 PPP$/kg oil equiv)	4.1
Energy use per capita (kg oil equiv)	493
Energy from biomass products and waste (% of total)	49.4
Energy imports, net (% of energy use)	–6
Electric power consumption per capita (kWh)	312
Electricity generated by coal (% of total)	47.4

Emissions and pollution

CO_2 emissions per unit of GDP (kg/2000 PPP$ GDP)	0.4
CO_2 emissions per capita (metric tons)	0.8
Particulate matter (pop. weighted average, µg/cu. m)	63
Passenger cars (per 1,000 people)	..

Water and sanitation

Internal freshwater resources per capita (cu. m)	3,583
Freshwater withdrawal	
Total (% of internal resources)	11.5
Agriculture (% of total freshwater withdrawal)	92
Access to improved water source (% of total population)	75
Rural (% of rural population)	70
Urban (% of urban population)	89
Access to sanitation (% of total population)	36
Rural (% of rural population)	24
Urban (% of urban population)	61
Under-five mortality rate (per 1,000)	123

National accounting aggregates, 2003

Gross national savings (% of GNI)	23.1
Consumption of fixed capital (% of GNI)	8.9
Education expenditure (% of GNI)	3.4
Energy depletion (% of GNI)	5.8
Mineral depletion (% of GNI)	0.3
Net forest depletion (% of GNI)	0.8
CO_2 damage (% of GNI)	1.2
Particulate emission damage (% of GNI)	0.6
Adjusted net savings (% of GNI)	8.9

Middle income

Population (millions)	2,988.6
Urban population (% of total)	52.6
GDP ($ billions)	6,023
GNI per capita, *Atlas* method ($)	1,930

Agriculture and fisheries

Land area (1,000 sq. km)	68,844
Agricultural land (% of land area)	38
Irrigated land (% of crop land)	19.7
Fertilizer consumption (100 grams/ha arable land)	1,113
Population density, rural (people/sq. km arable land)	480
Fish catch, total (1,000 metric tons)	84,489

Forests

Forest area (1,000 sq. km)	22,743
Forest area share of total land area (%)	33.0
Annual deforestation (% change, 1990–2000)	0.2

Biodiversity

Mammal species, total known	
Mammal species, threatened	
Bird species, total breeding	
Bird species, threatened	
Nationally protected area (% of land area)	9.4

Energy

GDP per unit of energy use (2000 PPP$/kg oil equiv)	4.1
Energy use per capita (kg oil equiv)	1,338
Energy from biomass products and waste (% of total)	10.8
Energy imports, net (% of energy use)	−35
Electric power consumption per capita (kWh)	1,422
Electricity generated by coal (% of total)	39.2

Emissions and pollution

CO_2 emissions per unit of GDP (kg/2000 PPP$ GDP)	0.6
CO_2 emissions per capita (metric tons)	3.2
Particulate matter (pop. weighted average, µg/cu. m)	40
Passenger cars (per 1,000 people)	42

Water and sanitation

Internal freshwater resources per capita (cu. m)	8,657
Freshwater withdrawal	
Total (% of internal resources)	5.9
Agriculture (% of total freshwater withdrawal)	74
Access to improved water source (% of total population)	83
Rural (% of rural population)	71
Urban (% of urban population)	94
Access to sanitation (% of total population)	61
Rural (% of rural population)	41
Urban (% of urban population)	81
Under-five mortality rate (per 1,000)	37

National accounting aggregates, 2003

Gross national savings (% of GNI)	27.8
Consumption of fixed capital (% of GNI)	10.1
Education expenditure (% of GNI)	3.7
Energy depletion (% of GNI)	9.1
Mineral depletion (% of GNI)	0.4
Net forest depletion (% of GNI)	0.0
CO_2 damage (% of GNI)	1.4
Particulate emission damage (% of GNI)	0.7
Adjusted net savings (% of GNI)	10.0

Lower middle income

Population (millions)	2,655.5
Urban population (% of total)	49.8
GDP ($ billions)	4,168
GNI per capita, *Atlas* method ($)	1,490

Agriculture and fisheries
Land area (1,000 sq. km)	56,103
Agricultural land (% of land area)	35
Irrigated land (% of crop land)	20.8
Fertilizer consumption (100 grams/ha arable land)	1,170
Population density, rural (people/sq. km arable land)	497
Fish catch, total (1,000 metric tons)	74,407

Forests
Forest area (1,000 sq. km)	20,316
Forest area share of total land area (%)	36.2
Annual deforestation (% change, 1990–2000)	0.1

Biodiversity
Mammal species, total known	
Mammal species, threatened	
Bird species, total breeding	
Bird species, threatened	
Nationally protected area (% of land area)	7.7

Energy
GDP per unit of energy use (2000 PPP$/kg oil equiv)	4.1
Energy use per capita (kg oil equiv)	1,227
Energy from biomass products and waste (% of total)	12.3
Energy imports, net (% of energy use)	−22
Electric power consumption per capita (kWh)	1,289
Electricity generated by coal (% of total)	42.8

Emissions and pollution
CO_2 emissions per unit of GDP (kg/2000 PPP$ GDP)	0.6
CO_2 emissions per capita (metric tons)	2.9
Particulate matter (pop. weighted average, µg/cu. m)	49
Passenger cars (per 1,000 people)	28

Water and sanitation
Internal freshwater resources per capita (cu. m)	8,397
Freshwater withdrawal	
Total (% of internal resources)	5.9
Agriculture (% of total freshwater withdrawal)	74
Access to improved water source (% of total population)	82
Rural (% of rural population)	71
Urban (% of urban population)	94
Access to sanitation (% of total population)	60
Rural (% of rural population)	41
Urban (% of urban population)	80
Under-five mortality rate (per 1,000)	39

National accounting aggregates, 2003
Gross national savings (% of GNI)	30.6
Consumption of fixed capital (% of GNI)	9.8
Education expenditure (% of GNI)	3.2
Energy depletion (% of GNI)	8.1
Mineral depletion (% of GNI)	0.4
Net forest depletion (% of GNI)	0.1
CO_2 damage (% of GNI)	1.6
Particulate emission damage (% of GNI)	0.7
Adjusted net savings (% of GNI)	13.2

Upper middle income

Population (millions)	333.1
Urban population (% of total)	75.4
GDP ($ billions)	1,856
GNI per capita, *Atlas* method ($)	5,440

Agriculture and fisheries

Land area (1,000 sq. km)	12,741
Agricultural land (% of land area)	48
Irrigated land (% of crop land)	13.5
Fertilizer consumption (100 grams/ha arable land)	796
Population density, rural (people/sq. km arable land)	193
Fish catch, total (1,000 metric tons)	10,082

Forests

Forest area (1,000 sq. km)	2,427
Forest area share of total land area (%)	19.1
Annual deforestation (% change, 1990–2000)	0.6

Biodiversity

Mammal species, total known	
Mammal species, threatened	
Bird species, total breeding	
Bird species, threatened	
Nationally protected area (% of land area)	17.3

Energy

GDP per unit of energy use (2000 PPP$/kg oil equiv)	4.3
Energy use per capita (kg oil equiv)	2,232
Energy from biomass products and waste (% of total)	4.1
Energy imports, net (% of energy use)	–91
Electric power consumption per capita (kWh)	2,496
Electricity generated by coal (% of total)	23.9

Emissions and pollution

CO_2 emissions per unit of GDP (kg/2000 PPP$ GDP)	0.6
CO_2 emissions per capita (metric tons)	6.3
Particulate matter (pop. weighted average, µg/cu. m)	29
Passenger cars (per 1,000 people)	153

Water and sanitation

Internal freshwater resources per capita (cu. m)	10,741
Freshwater withdrawal	
Total (% of internal resources)	5.7
Agriculture (% of total freshwater withdrawal)	71
Access to improved water source (% of total population)	
Rural (% of rural population)	..
Urban (% of urban population)	96
Access to sanitation (% of total population)	
Rural (% of rural population)	..
Urban (% of urban population)	..
Under-five mortality rate (per 1,000)	22

National accounting aggregates, 2003

Gross national savings (% of GNI)	22.1
Consumption of fixed capital (% of GNI)	10.7
Education expenditure (% of GNI)	5.0
Energy depletion (% of GNI)	11.4
Mineral depletion (% of GNI)	0.3
Net forest depletion (% of GNI)	0.0
CO_2 damage (% of GNI)	0.8
Particulate emission damage (% of GNI)	0.6
Adjusted net savings (% of GNI)	3.3

Low and middle income

Population (millions)	5,300.5
Urban population (% of total)	43.0
GDP ($ billions)	7,125
GNI per capita, *Atlas* method ($)	1,280

Agriculture and fisheries
Land area (1,000 sq. km)	99,300
Agricultural land (% of land area)	39
Irrigated land (% of crop land)	22.3
Fertilizer consumption (100 grams/ha arable land)	944
Population density, rural (people/sq. km arable land)	495
Fish catch, total (1,000 metric tons)	100,899

Forests
Forest area (1,000 sq. km)	30,682
Forest area share of total land area (%)	30.9
Annual deforestation (% change, 1990–2000)	0.3

Biodiversity
Mammal species, total known	
Mammal species, threatened	
Bird species, total breeding	
Bird species, threatened	
Nationally protected area (% of land area)	8.9

Energy
GDP per unit of energy use (2000 PPP$/kg oil equiv)	4.1
Energy use per capita (kg oil equiv)	990
Energy from biomass products and waste (% of total)	18.4
Energy imports, net (% of energy use)	−29
Electric power consumption per capita (kWh)	970
Electricity generated by coal (% of total)	40.4

Emissions and pollution
CO_2 emissions per unit of GDP (kg/2000 PPP$ GDP)	0.6
CO_2 emissions per capita (metric tons)	2.2
Particulate matter (pop. weighted average, µg/cu. m)	49
Passenger cars (per 1,000 people)	27

Water and sanitation
Internal freshwater resources per capita (cu. m)	6,441
Freshwater withdrawal	
Total (% of internal resources)	7.3
Agriculture (% of total freshwater withdrawal)	81
Access to improved water source (% of total population)	79
Rural (% of rural population)	70
Urban (% of urban population)	93
Access to sanitation (% of total population)	50
Rural (% of rural population)	32
Urban (% of urban population)	75
Under-five mortality rate (per 1,000)	87

National accounting aggregates, 2003
Gross national savings (% of GNI)	27.2
Consumption of fixed capital (% of GNI)	9.9
Education expenditure (% of GNI)	3.7
Energy depletion (% of GNI)	8.6
Mineral depletion (% of GNI)	0.4
Net forest depletion (% of GNI)	0.1
CO_2 damage (% of GNI)	1.3
Particulate emission damage (% of GNI)	0.6
Adjusted net savings (% of GNI)	9.9

Population (millions)	306.9
Urban population (% of total)	77.9
GDP ($ billions)	8,196
GNI per capita, *Atlas* method ($)	22,810

Agriculture and fisheries

Land area (1,000 sq. km)	2,436
Agricultural land (% of land area)	48
Irrigated land (% of crop land)	19.9
Fertilizer consumption (100 grams/ha arable land)	1,968
Population density, rural (people/sq. km arable land)	138
Fish catch, total (1,000 metric tons)	4,596

Forests

Forest area (1,000 sq. km)	853
Forest area share of total land area (%)	35.1
Annual deforestation (% change, 1990–2000)	–0.4

Biodiversity

Mammal species, total known	
Mammal species, threatened	
Bird species, total breeding	
Bird species, threatened	
Nationally protected area (% of land area)	13.5

Energy

GDP per unit of energy use (2000 PPP$/kg oil equiv)	6.4
Energy use per capita (kg oil equiv)	3,895
Energy from biomass products and waste (% of total)	3.7
Energy imports, net (% of energy use)	63
Electric power consumption per capita (kWh)	5,912
Electricity generated by coal (% of total)	27.1

Emissions and pollution

CO_2 emissions per unit of GDP (kg/2000 PPP$ GDP)	0.3
CO_2 emissions per capita (metric tons)	7.9
Particulate matter (pop. weighted average, µg/cu. m)	30
Passenger cars (per 1,000 people)	483

Water and sanitation

Internal freshwater resources per capita (cu. m)	2,970
Freshwater withdrawal	
Total (% of internal resources)	20.6
Agriculture (% of total freshwater withdrawal)	38
Access to improved water source (% of total population)	..
Rural (% of rural population)	..
Urban (% of urban population)	100
Access to sanitation (% of total population)	..
Rural (% of rural population)	..
Urban (% of urban population)	..
Under-five mortality rate (per 1,000)	..

National accounting aggregates, 2003

Gross national savings (% of GNI)	20.8
Consumption of fixed capital (% of GNI)	13.9
Education expenditure (% of GNI)	4.6
Energy depletion (% of GNI)	0.1
Mineral depletion (% of GNI)	0.0
Net forest depletion (% of GNI)	0.0
CO_2 damage (% of GNI)	0.2
Particulate emission damage (% of GNI)	0.2
Adjusted net savings (% of GNI)	11.1

High income

Population (millions)	972.1
Urban population (% of total)	79.9
GDP ($ billions)	29,341
GNI per capita, *Atlas* method ($)	28,600

Agriculture and fisheries

Land area (1,000 sq. km)	31,030
Agricultural land (% of land area)	36
Irrigated land (% of crop land)	12.3
Fertilizer consumption (100 grams/ha arable land)	1,198
Population density, rural (people/sq. km arable land)	202
Fish catch, total (1,000 metric tons)	28,712

Forests

Forest area (1,000 sq. km)	7,929
Forest area share of total land area (%)	25.9
Annual deforestation (% change, 1990–2000)	–0.1

Biodiversity

Mammal species, total known	
Mammal species, threatened	
Bird species, total breeding	
Bird species, threatened	
Nationally protected area (% of land area)	19.5

Energy

GDP per unit of energy use (2000 PPP$/kg oil equiv)	5.2
Energy use per capita (kg oil equiv)	5,395
Energy from biomass products and waste (% of total)	3.1
Energy imports, net (% of energy use)	26
Electric power consumption per capita (kWh)	8,693
Electricity generated by coal (% of total)	38.2

Emissions and pollution

CO_2 emissions per unit of GDP (kg/2000 PPP$ GDP)	0.5
CO_2 emissions per capita (metric tons)	12.4
Particulate matter (pop. weighted average, µg/cu. m)	33
Passenger cars (per 1,000 people)	436

Water and sanitation

Internal freshwater resources per capita (cu. m)	9,479
Freshwater withdrawal	
Total (% of internal resources)	9.7
Agriculture (% of total freshwater withdrawal)	42
Access to improved water source (% of total population)	99
Rural (% of rural population)	98
Urban (% of urban population)	100
Access to sanitation (% of total population)	..
Rural (% of rural population)	..
Urban (% of urban population)	..
Under-five mortality rate (per 1,000)	7

National accounting aggregates, 2003

Gross national savings (% of GNI)	19.1
Consumption of fixed capital (% of GNI)	13.2
Education expenditure (% of GNI)	4.6
Energy depletion (% of GNI)	0.8
Mineral depletion (% of GNI)	0.0
Net forest depletion (% of GNI)	0.0
CO_2 damage (% of GNI)	0.3
Particulate emission damage (% of GNI)	0.3
Adjusted net savings (% of GNI)	9.2

Country tables

China. On July 1, 1997, China resumed its exercise of sovereignty over Hong Kong, and on December 20, 1999, it resumed its exercise of sovereignty over Macao. Unless otherwise noted, data for China do not include data for Hong Kong, China; Taiwan, China; or Macao, China.

Democratic Republic of Congo. Data for the Democratic Republic of Congo (Congo, Dem. Rep., in the table listings) refer to the former Zaire. (The Republic of Congo is referred to as Congo, Rep., in the table listings.)

Czech Republic and Slovak Republic. Data are shown whenever possible for the individual countries formed from the former Czechoslovakia—the Czech Republic and the Slovak Republic.

Eritrea. Data are shown for Eritrea whenever possible, but in most cases before 1992 Eritrea is included in the data for Ethiopia.

Germany. Data for Germany refer to the unified Germany unless otherwise noted.

Serbia and Montenegro. On February 4, 2003, the Federal Republic of Yugoslavia changed its name to Serbia and Montenegro.

Timor-Leste. On May 20, 2002, Timor-Leste became an independent country. Data for Indonesia include Timor-Leste through 1999 unless otherwise noted.

Union of Soviet Socialist Republics. In 1991 the Union of Soviet Socialist Republics came to an end. Available data are shown for the individual countries now existing on its former territory (Armenia, Azerbaijan, Belarus, Estonia, Georgia, Kazakhstan, Kyrgyz Republic, Latvia, Lithuania, Moldova, Russian Federation, Tajikistan, Turkmenistan, Ukraine, and Uzbekistan).

República Bolivariana de Venezuela. In December 1999 the official name of Venezuela was changed to República Bolivariana de Venezuela (Venezuela, RB, in the table listings).

Republic of Yemen. Data for the Republic of Yemen refer to that country from 1990 onward; data for previous years refer to aggregated data for the former People's Democratic Republic of Yemen and the former Yemen Arab Republic unless otherwise noted.

Afghanistan

Environmental strategy/action plan prepared in ..

	Country data	Group data South Asia	Lower middle income
Population (millions)	..	1,425	2,655
Urban population (% of total)	..	28.3	49.8
GDP ($ billions)	4.7	765	4,168
GNI per capita, *Atlas* method ($)	..	510	1,490
Agriculture and fisheries			
Land area (1,000 sq. km)	652	4,781	56,103
Agricultural land (% of land area)	58	55	35
Irrigated land (% of crop land)	29.6	41.2	20.8
Fertilizer consumption (100 grams/ha arable land)	26	1,027	1,170
Population density, rural (people/sq. km arable land)	273	559	497
Fish catch, total (1,000 metric tons)	1	8,724	74,407
Forests			
Forest area (1,000 sq. km)	14	780	20,316
Forest area share of total land area (%)	2.1	16.3	36.2
Annual deforestation (% change, 1990–2000)	0.0	0.1	0.1
Biodiversity			
Mammal species, total known	119		
Mammal species, threatened	13		
Bird species, total breeding	181		
Bird species, threatened	11		
Nationally protected area (% of land area)	0.3	4.8	7.7
Energy			
GDP per unit of energy use (2000 PPP$/kg oil equiv)	..	5.1	4.1
Energy use per capita (kg oil equiv)	..	468	1,227
Energy from biomass products and waste (% of total)	..	39.3	12.3
Energy imports, net (% of energy use)	..	19	-22
Electric power consumption per capita (kWh)	..	344	1,289
Electricity generated by coal (% of total)	..	59.8	42.8
Emissions and pollution			
CO_2 emissions per unit of GDP (kg/2000 PPP$ GDP)	..	0.4	0.6
CO_2 emissions per capita (metric tons)	0.0	0.9	2.9
Particulate matter (pop. weighted average, µg/cu. m)	47	69	49
Passenger cars (per 1,000 people)	..	6	28
Water and sanitation			
Internal freshwater resources per capita (cu. m)	1,912	1,275	8,397
Freshwater withdrawal			
Total (% of internal resources)	47.5	40.5	5.9
Agriculture (% of total freshwater withdrawal)	99	94	74
Access to improved water source (% of total population)	13	84	82
Rural (% of rural population)	11	80	71
Urban (% of urban population)	19	93	94
Access to sanitation (% of total population)	8	35	60
Rural (% of rural population)	5	23	41
Urban (% of urban population)	16	64	80
Under-five mortality rate (per 1,000)	..	92	39
National accounting aggregates, 2003			
Gross national savings (% of GNI)	..	24.9	30.6
Consumption of fixed capital (% of GNI)	..	9.0	9.8
Education expenditure (% of GNI)	..	3.5	3.2
Energy depletion (% of GNI)	..	2.4	8.1
Mineral depletion (% of GNI)	..	0.3	0.4
Net forest depletion (% of GNI)	..	0.7	0.1
CO_2 damage (% of GNI)	..	1.3	1.6
Particulate emission damage (% of GNI)	..	0.7	0.7
Adjusted net savings (% of GNI)	..	14.0	13.2

Albania

Environmental strategy/action plan prepared in **1993**

	Country data	Group data Europe & Central Asia	Lower middle income
Population (millions)	3.2	472	2,655
Urban population (% of total)	44.2	63.8	49.8
GDP ($ billions)	6.1	1,403	4,168
GNI per capita, *Atlas* method ($)	1,740	2,580	1,490
Agriculture and fisheries			
Land area (1,000 sq. km)	27	23,868	56,103
Agricultural land (% of land area)	42	28	35
Irrigated land (% of crop land)	48.6	10.9	20.8
Fertilizer consumption (100 grams/ha arable land)	612	344	1,170
Population density, rural (people/sq. km arable land)	307	122	497
Fish catch, total (1,000 metric tons)	4	5,527	74,407
Forests			
Forest area (1,000 sq. km)	10	9,463	20,316
Forest area share of total land area (%)	36.2	39.6	36.2
Annual deforestation (% change, 1990–2000)	0.8	–0.1	0.1
Biodiversity			
Mammal species, total known	68		
Mammal species, threatened	3		
Bird species, total breeding	193		
Bird species, threatened	3		
Nationally protected area (% of land area)	3.8	6.8	7.7
Energy			
GDP per unit of energy use (2000 PPP$/kg oil equiv)	6.7	2.5	4.1
Energy use per capita (kg oil equiv)	617	2,697	1,227
Energy from biomass products and waste (% of total)	6.9	2.3	12.3
Energy imports, net (% of energy use)	60	–23	–22
Electric power consumption per capita (kWh)	1,390	2,808	1,289
Electricity generated by coal (% of total)	..	29.4	42.8
Emissions and pollution			
CO_2 emissions per unit of GDP (kg/2000 PPP$ GDP)	0.2	1.1	0.6
CO_2 emissions per capita (metric tons)	0.9	6.7	2.9
Particulate matter (pop. weighted average, µg/cu. m)	32	33	49
Passenger cars (per 1,000 people)	43	138	28
Water and sanitation			
Internal freshwater resources per capita (cu. m)	8,520	11,128	8,397
Freshwater withdrawal			
Total (% of internal resources)	5.2	7.4	5.9
Agriculture (% of total freshwater withdrawal)	71	57	74
Access to improved water source (% of total population)	97	91	82
Rural (% of rural population)	95	80	71
Urban (% of urban population)	99	98	94
Access to sanitation (% of total population)	89	82	60
Rural (% of rural population)	81	64	41
Urban (% of urban population)	99	93	80
Under-five mortality rate (per 1,000)	21	36	39
National accounting aggregates, 2003			
Gross national savings (% of GNI)	18.2	21.9	30.6
Consumption of fixed capital (% of GNI)	9.6	10.7	9.8
Education expenditure (% of GNI)	2.8	4.1	3.2
Energy depletion (% of GNI)	0.9	11.6	8.1
Mineral depletion (% of GNI)	0.0	0.1	0.4
Net forest depletion (% of GNI)	0.0	0.0	0.1
CO_2 damage (% of GNI)	0.3	1.9	1.6
Particulate emission damage (% of GNI)	0.1	0.6	0.7
Adjusted net savings (% of GNI)	10.2	1.1	13.2

Algeria

Environmental strategy/action plan prepared in **1993**

	Country data	Middle East & North Africa	Lower middle Income
Population (millions)	31.8	312	2,655
Urban population (% of total)	58.8	59.0	49.8
GDP ($ billions)	66.5	745	4,168
GNI per capita, *Atlas* method ($)	1,930	2,390	1,490
Agriculture and fisheries			
Land area (1,000 sq. km)	2,382	11,111	56,103
Agricultural land (% of land area)	17	34	35
Irrigated land (% of crop land)	6.8	38.3	20.8
Fertilizer consumption (100 grams/ha arable land)	128	854	1,170
Population density, rural (people/sq. km arable land)	171	603	497
Fish catch, total (1,000 metric tons)	100	2,840	74,407
Forests			
Forest area (1,000 sq. km)	21	168	20,316
Forest area share of total land area (%)	0.9	1.5	36.2
Annual deforestation (% change, 1990–2000)	−1.3	−0.1	0.1
Biodiversity			
Mammal species, total known	92		
Mammal species, threatened	13		
Bird species, total breeding	183		
Bird species, threatened	6		
Nationally protected area (% of land area)	5.0	11.3	7.7
Energy			
GDP per unit of energy use (2000 PPP$/kg oil equiv)	5.6	3.5	4.1
Energy use per capita (kg oil equiv)	985	1,504	1,227
Energy from biomass products and waste (% of total)	0.2	1.0	12.3
Energy imports, net (% of energy use)	−387	−168	−22
Electric power consumption per capita (kWh)	662	1,412	1,289
Electricity generated by coal (% of total)	..	2.3	42.8
Emissions and pollution			
CO_2 emissions per unit of GDP (kg/2000 PPP$ GDP)	0.5	0.8	0.6
CO_2 emissions per capita (metric tons)	2.9	4.2	2.9
Particulate matter (pop. weighted average, µg/cu. m)	76	87	49
Passenger cars (per 1,000 people)	..	..	28
Water and sanitation			
Internal freshwater resources per capita (cu. m)	440	761	8,397
Freshwater withdrawal			
Total (% of internal resources)	35.7	101.7	5.9
Agriculture (% of total freshwater withdrawal)	52	88	74
Access to improved water source (% of total population)	87	88	82
Rural (% of rural population)	80	78	71
Urban (% of urban population)	92	96	94
Access to sanitation (% of total population)	92	75	60
Rural (% of rural population)	82	56	41
Urban (% of urban population)	99	90	80
Under-five mortality rate (per 1,000)	41	53	39
National accounting aggregates, 2003			
Gross national savings (% of GNI)	43.1	31.2	30.6
Consumption of fixed capital (% of GNI)	11.0	10.0	9.8
Education expenditure (% of GNI)	4.5	5.5	3.2
Energy depletion (% of GNI)	37.5	30.7	8.1
Mineral depletion (% of GNI)	0.0	0.1	0.4
Net forest depletion (% of GNI)	0.1	0.0	0.1
CO_2 damage (% of GNI)	1.2	1.2	1.6
Particulate emission damage (% of GNI)	0.7	0.8	0.7
Adjusted net savings (% of GNI)	−2.9	−6.2	13.2

American Samoa

Environmental strategy/action plan prepared in **2001**

	Country data	East Asia & Pacific	Upper middle income
		Group data	
Population (millions)	0.1	1,855	333
Urban population (% of total)	54.2	39.1	75.4
GDP ($ billions)	..	2,033	1,856
GNI per capita, *Atlas* method ($)	..	1,070	5,440
Agriculture and fisheries			
Land area (1,000 sq. km)	0	15,886	12,741
Agricultural land (% of land area)	25	50	48
Irrigated land (% of crop land)	..	..	13.5
Fertilizer consumption (100 grams/ha arable land)	..	2,297	796
Population density, rural (people/sq. km arable land)	..	565	193
Fish catch, total (1,000 metric tons)	4	60,812	10,082
Forests			
Forest area (1,000 sq. km)	0	4,284	2,427
Forest area share of total land area (%)	60.0	27.0	19.1
Annual deforestation (% change, 1990–2000)	0.0	0.2	0.6
Biodiversity			
Mammal species, total known	..		
Mammal species, threatened	3		
Bird species, total breeding	..		
Bird species, threatened	2		
Nationally protected area (% of land area)	..	9.2	17.3
Energy			
GDP per unit of energy use (2000 PPP$/kg oil equiv)	..	4.6	4.3
Energy use per capita (kg oil equiv)	..	904	2,232
Energy from biomass products and waste (% of total)	..	19.6	4.1
Energy imports, net (% of energy use)	..	−4	−91
Electric power consumption per capita (kWh)	..	891	2,496
Electricity generated by coal (% of total)	..	66.8	23.9
Emissions and pollution			
CO_2 emissions per unit of GDP (kg/2000 PPP$ GDP)	..	0.5	0.6
CO_2 emissions per capita (metric tons)	..	2.1	6.3
Particulate matter (pop. weighted average, µg/cu. m)	..	69	29
Passenger cars (per 1,000 people)	..	10	153
Water and sanitation			
Internal freshwater resources per capita (cu. m)	..	5,103	10,741
Freshwater withdrawal			
Total (% of internal resources)	..	8.2	5.7
Agriculture (% of total freshwater withdrawal)	..	81	71
Access to improved water source (% of total population)	..	78	..
Rural (% of rural population)	..	69	..
Urban (% of urban population)	..	92	96
Access to sanitation (% of total population)	..	49	..
Rural (% of rural population)	..	35	..
Urban (% of urban population)	..	71	..
Under-five mortality rate (per 1,000)	..	41	22
National accounting aggregates, 2003			
Gross national savings (% of GNI)	..	41.7	22.1
Consumption of fixed capital (% of GNI)	..	9.2	10.7
Education expenditure (% of GNI)	..	2.3	5.0
Energy depletion (% of GNI)	..	3.9	11.4
Mineral depletion (% of GNI)	..	0.3	0.3
Net forest depletion (% of GNI)	..	0.1	0.0
CO_2 damage (% of GNI)	..	1.8	0.8
Particulate emission damage (% of GNI)	..	0.8	0.6
Adjusted net savings (% of GNI)	..	27.9	3.3

Andorra

Environmental strategy/action plan prepared in ..

	Country data	Group data High Income
Population (millions)	0.1	972
Urban population (% of total)	91.7	79.9
GDP ($ billions)	..	29,341
GNI per capita, *Atlas* method ($)	..	28,600

Agriculture and fisheries

Land area (1,000 sq. km)	0	31,030
Agricultural land (% of land area)	58	36
Irrigated land (% of crop land)	..	12.3
Fertilizer consumption (100 grams/ha arable land)	..	1,198
Population density, rural (people/sq. km arable land)	..	202
Fish catch, total (1,000 metric tons)	..	28,712

Forests

Forest area (1,000 sq. km)	..	7,929
Forest area share of total land area (%)	..	25.9
Annual deforestation (% change, 1990–2000)	..	–0.1

Biodiversity

Mammal species, total known	..	
Mammal species, threatened	3	
Bird species, total breeding	..	
Bird species, threatened	0	
Nationally protected area (% of land area)	..	19.5

Energy

GDP per unit of energy use (2000 PPP$/kg oil equiv)	..	5.2
Energy use per capita (kg oil equiv)	..	5,395
Energy from biomass products and waste (% of total)	..	3.1
Energy imports, net (% of energy use)	..	26
Electric power consumption per capita (kWh)	..	8,693
Electricity generated by coal (% of total)	..	38.2

Emissions and pollution

CO_2 emissions per unit of GDP (kg/2000 PPP$ GDP)	..	0.5
CO_2 emissions per capita (metric tons)	..	12.4
Particulate matter (pop. weighted average, µg/cu. m)	33	33
Passenger cars (per 1,000 people)	..	436

Water and sanitation

Internal freshwater resources per capita (cu. m)	..	9,479
Freshwater withdrawal		
Total (% of internal resources)	..	9.7
Agriculture (% of total freshwater withdrawal)	..	42
Access to improved water source (% of total population)	100	99
Rural (% of rural population)	100	98
Urban (% of urban population)	100	100
Access to sanitation (% of total population)	100	..
Rural (% of rural population)	100	..
Urban (% of urban population)	100	..
Under-five mortality rate (per 1,000)	7	7

National accounting aggregates, 2003

Gross national savings (% of GNI)	..	19.1
Consumption of fixed capital (% of GNI)	..	13.2
Education expenditure (% of GNI)	..	4.6
Energy depletion (% of GNI)	..	0.8
Mineral depletion (% of GNI)	..	0.0
Net forest depletion (% of GNI)	..	0.0
CO_2 damage (% of GNI)	..	0.3
Particulate emission damage (% of GNI)	..	0.3
Adjusted net savings (% of GNI)	..	9.2

Angola

Environmental strategy/action plan prepared in ..

	Country data	Group data Sub-Saharan Africa	Group data Low Income
Population (millions)	13.5	705	2,312
Urban population (% of total)	36.2	36.5	30.4
GDP ($ billions)	13.2	439	1,103
GNI per capita, *Atlas* method ($)	740	500	440
Agriculture and fisheries			
Land area (1,000 sq. km)	1,247	23,596	30,456
Agricultural land (% of land area)	46	43	43
Irrigated land (% of crop land)	2.3	4.2	26.7
Fertilizer consumption (100 grams/ha arable land)	..	145	654
Population density, rural (people/sq. km arable land)	282	352	509
Fish catch, total (1,000 metric tons)	253	5,191	16,410
Forests			
Forest area (1,000 sq. km)	698	6,435	7,939
Forest area share of total land area (%)	56.0	27.3	26.1
Annual deforestation (% change, 1990–2000)	0.2	0.8	0.7
Biodiversity			
Mammal species, total known	276		
Mammal species, threatened	19		
Bird species, total breeding	265		
Bird species, threatened	15		
Nationally protected area (% of land area)	6.6	8.7	7.7
Energy			
GDP per unit of energy use (2000 PPP$/kg oil equiv)	3.2	2.8	4.1
Energy use per capita (kg oil equiv)	672	667	493
Energy from biomass products and waste (% of total)	67.8	57.5	49.4
Energy imports, net (% of energy use)	−485	−56	−6
Electric power consumption per capita (kWh)	109	457	312
Electricity generated by coal (% of total)	..	68.2	47.4
Emissions and pollution			
CO_2 emissions per unit of GDP (kg/2000 PPP$ GDP)	0.3	0.4	0.4
CO_2 emissions per capita (metric tons)	0.5	0.7	0.8
Particulate matter (pop. weighted average, µg/cu. m)	125	54	63
Passenger cars (per 1,000 people)	..	..	..
Water and sanitation			
Internal freshwater resources per capita (cu. m)	13,607	5,546	3,583
Freshwater withdrawal			
Total (% of internal resources)	0.3	1.8	11.5
Agriculture (% of total freshwater withdrawal)	76	85	92
Access to improved water source (% of total population)	50	58	75
Rural (% of rural population)	40	46	70
Urban (% of urban population)	70	82	89
Access to sanitation (% of total population)	30	36	36
Rural (% of rural population)	16	26	24
Urban (% of urban population)	56	55	61
Under-five mortality rate (per 1,000)	260	171	123
National accounting aggregates, 2003			
Gross national savings (% of GNI)	22.2	16.9	23.1
Consumption of fixed capital (% of GNI)	11.0	10.6	8.9
Education expenditure (% of GNI)	4.4	4.7	3.4
Energy depletion (% of GNI)	43.6	8.0	5.8
Mineral depletion (% of GNI)	0.0	0.5	0.3
Net forest depletion (% of GNI)	0.0	0.7	0.8
CO_2 damage (% of GNI)	0.5	0.9	1.2
Particulate emission damage (% of GNI)	..	0.4	0.6
Adjusted net savings (% of GNI)	−28.5	0.6	8.9

Antigua and Barbuda

Environmental strategy/action plan prepared in ..

	Country data	Latin America & Caribbean	Upper middle income
Population (millions)	0.1	533	333
Urban population (% of total)	37.8	76.6	75.4
GDP ($ billions)	0.8	1,741	1,856
GNI per capita, *Atlas* method ($)	9,160	3,280	5,440
Agriculture and fisheries			
Land area (1,000 sq. km)	0	20,057	12,741
Agricultural land (% of land area)	32	39	48
Irrigated land (% of crop land)	..	12.5	13.5
Fertilizer consumption (100 grams/ha arable land)	..	892	796
Population density, rural (people/sq. km arable land)	598	210	193
Fish catch, total (1,000 metric tons)	2	17,804	10,082
Forests			
Forest area (1,000 sq. km)	0	9,552	2,427
Forest area share of total land area (%)	20.5	47.6	19.1
Annual deforestation (% change, 1990–2000)	0.0	0.5	0.6
Biodiversity			
Mammal species, total known	..		
Mammal species, threatened	0		
Bird species, total breeding	..		
Bird species, threatened	1		
Nationally protected area (% of land area)	..	11.2	17.3
Energy			
GDP per unit of energy use (2000 PPP$/kg oil equiv)	..	6.1	4.3
Energy use per capita (kg oil equiv)	..	1,156	2,232
Energy from biomass products and waste (% of total)	..	14.6	4.1
Energy imports, net (% of energy use)	..	–42	–91
Electric power consumption per capita (kWh)	..	1,506	2,496
Electricity generated by coal (% of total)	..	5.0	23.9
Emissions and pollution			
CO_2 emissions per unit of GDP (kg/2000 PPP$ GDP)	0.5	0.4	0.6
CO_2 emissions per capita (metric tons)	4.9	2.7	6.3
Particulate matter (pop. weighted average, µg/cu. m)	16	40	29
Passenger cars (per 1,000 people)	..	..	153
Water and sanitation			
Internal freshwater resources per capita (cu. m)	1,307	25,245	10,741
Freshwater withdrawal			
Total (% of internal resources)	..	2.0	5.7
Agriculture (% of total freshwater withdrawal)	20	74	71
Access to improved water source (% of total population)	91	89	..
Rural (% of rural population)	89	69	..
Urban (% of urban population)	95	96	96
Access to sanitation (% of total population)	95	74	..
Rural (% of rural population)	94	44	..
Urban (% of urban population)	98	84	..
Under-five mortality rate (per 1,000)	12	33	22
National accounting aggregates, 2003			
Gross national savings (% of GNI)	..	19.5	22.1
Consumption of fixed capital (% of GNI)	12.7	10.3	10.7
Education expenditure (% of GNI)	3.7	4.2	5.0
Energy depletion (% of GNI)	0.0	6.4	11.4
Mineral depletion (% of GNI)	0.0	0.7	0.3
Net forest depletion (% of GNI)	0.0	0.0	0.0
CO_2 damage (% of GNI)	0.4	0.5	0.8
Particulate emission damage (% of GNI)	..	0.5	0.6
Adjusted net savings (% of GNI)	..	5.3	3.3

Argentina

Environmental strategy/action plan prepared in **1992**

	Country data	Latin America & Caribbean	Upper middle income
		Group data	
Population (millions)	36.8	533	333
Urban population (% of total)	88.6	76.6	75.4
GDP ($ billions)	129.6	1,741	1,856
GNI per capita, *Atlas* method ($)	3,810	3,280	5,440
Agriculture and fisheries			
Land area (1,000 sq. km)	2,737	20,057	12,741
Agricultural land (% of land area)	65	39	48
Irrigated land (% of crop land)	4.5	12.5	13.5
Fertilizer consumption (100 grams/ha arable land)	219	892	796
Population density, rural (people/sq. km arable land)	12	210	193
Fish catch, total (1,000 metric tons)	925	17,804	10,082
Forests			
Forest area (1,000 sq. km)	346	9,552	2,427
Forest area share of total land area (%)	12.7	47.6	19.1
Annual deforestation (% change, 1990–2000)	0.8	0.5	0.6
Biodiversity			
Mammal species, total known	320		
Mammal species, threatened	34		
Bird species, total breeding	362		
Bird species, threatened	39		
Nationally protected area (% of land area)	6.6	11.2	17.3
Energy			
GDP per unit of energy use (2000 PPP$/kg oil equiv)	6.9	6.1	4.3
Energy use per capita (kg oil equiv)	1,543	1,156	2,232
Energy from biomass products and waste (% of total)	5.3	14.6	4.1
Energy imports, net (% of energy use)	–45	–42	–91
Electric power consumption per capita (kWh)	2,024	1,506	2,496
Electricity generated by coal (% of total)	1.4	5.0	23.9
Emissions and pollution			
CO_2 emissions per unit of GDP (kg/2000 PPP$ GDP)	0.3	0.4	0.6
CO_2 emissions per capita (metric tons)	3.9	2.7	6.3
Particulate matter (pop. weighted average, µg/cu. m)	71	40	29
Passenger cars (per 1,000 people)	140	..	153
Water and sanitation			
Internal freshwater resources per capita (cu. m)	7,506	25,245	10,741
Freshwater withdrawal			
Total (% of internal resources)	10.4	2.0	5.7
Agriculture (% of total freshwater withdrawal)	75	74	71
Access to improved water source (% of total population)	..	89	..
Rural (% of rural population)	..	69	..
Urban (% of urban population)	97	96	96
Access to sanitation (% of total population)	..	74	..
Rural (% of rural population)	..	44	..
Urban (% of urban population)	..	84	..
Under-five mortality rate (per 1,000)	20	33	22
National accounting aggregates, 2003			
Gross national savings (% of GNI)	21.9	19.5	22.1
Consumption of fixed capital (% of GNI)	11.3	10.3	10.7
Education expenditure (% of GNI)	3.2	4.2	5.0
Energy depletion (% of GNI)	6.3	6.4	11.4
Mineral depletion (% of GNI)	0.1	0.7	0.3
Net forest depletion (% of GNI)	0.0	0.0	0.0
CO_2 damage (% of GNI)	0.6	0.5	0.8
Particulate emission damage (% of GNI)	1.6	0.5	0.6
Adjusted net savings (% of GNI)	5.2	5.3	3.3

Armenia

Environmental strategy/action plan prepared in ..

	Country data	Europe & Central Asia	Lower middle income
		Group data	
Population (millions)	3.1	472	2,655
Urban population (% of total)	67.5	63.8	49.8
GDP ($ billions)	2.8	1,403	4,168
GNI per capita, *Atlas* method ($)	950	2,580	1,490
Agriculture and fisheries			
Land area (1,000 sq. km)	28	23,868	56,103
Agricultural land (% of land area)	48	28	35
Irrigated land (% of crop land)	50.0	10.9	20.8
Fertilizer consumption (100 grams/ha arable land)	228	344	1,170
Population density, rural (people/sq. km arable land)	202	122	497
Fish catch, total (1,000 metric tons)	2	5,527	74,407
Forests			
Forest area (1,000 sq. km)	4	9,463	20,316
Forest area share of total land area (%)	12.4	39.6	36.2
Annual deforestation (% change, 1990–2000)	−1.3	−0.1	0.1
Biodiversity			
Mammal species, total known	84		
Mammal species, threatened	11		
Bird species, total breeding	236		
Bird species, threatened	4		
Nationally protected area (% of land area)	7.6	6.8	7.7
Energy			
GDP per unit of energy use (2000 PPP$/kg oil equiv)	4.8	2.5	4.1
Energy use per capita (kg oil equiv)	632	2,697	1,227
Energy from biomass products and waste (% of total)	0.1	2.3	12.3
Energy imports, net (% of energy use)	62	−23	−22
Electric power consumption per capita (kWh)	1,113	2,808	1,289
Electricity generated by coal (% of total)	..	29.4	42.8
Emissions and pollution			
CO_2 emissions per unit of GDP (kg/2000 PPP$ GDP)	0.5	1.1	0.6
CO_2 emissions per capita (metric tons)	1.1	6.7	2.9
Particulate matter (pop. weighted average, µg/cu. m)	85	33	49
Passenger cars (per 1,000 people)	..	138	28
Water and sanitation			
Internal freshwater resources per capita (cu. m)	2,945	11,128	8,397
Freshwater withdrawal			
Total (% of internal resources)	32.2	7.4	5.9
Agriculture (% of total freshwater withdrawal)	66	57	74
Access to improved water source (% of total population)	92	91	82
Rural (% of rural population)	80	80	71
Urban (% of urban population)	99	98	94
Access to sanitation (% of total population)	84	82	60
Rural (% of rural population)	61	64	41
Urban (% of urban population)	96	93	80
Under-five mortality rate (per 1,000)	33	36	39
National accounting aggregates, 2003			
Gross national savings (% of GNI)	17.2	21.9	30.6
Consumption of fixed capital (% of GNI)	8.6	10.7	9.8
Education expenditure (% of GNI)	1.8	4.1	3.2
Energy depletion (% of GNI)	0.0	11.6	8.1
Mineral depletion (% of GNI)	0.1	0.1	0.4
Net forest depletion (% of GNI)	0.0	0.0	0.1
CO_2 damage (% of GNI)	1.1	1.9	1.6
Particulate emission damage (% of GNI)	2.0	0.6	0.7
Adjusted net savings (% of GNI)	7.2	1.1	13.2

Aruba

Environmental strategy/action plan prepared in **1992**

	Country data	Group data High Income
Population (millions)	0.1	972
Urban population (% of total)	51.5	79.9
GDP ($ billions)	2	29,341
GNI per capita, *Atlas* method ($)	..	28,600
Agriculture and fisheries		
Land area (1,000 sq. km)	0	31,030
Agricultural land (% of land area)	11	36
Irrigated land (% of crop land)	..	12.3
Fertilizer consumption (100 grams/ha arable land)	..	1,198
Population density, rural (people/sq. km arable land)	..	202
Fish catch, total (1,000 metric tons)	0	28,712
Forests		
Forest area (1,000 sq. km)	..	7,929
Forest area share of total land area (%)	..	25.9
Annual deforestation (% change, 1990–2000)	..	–0.1
Biodiversity		
Mammal species, total known	..	
Mammal species, threatened	1	
Bird species, total breeding	..	
Bird species, threatened	0	
Nationally protected area (% of land area)	..	19.5
Energy		
GDP per unit of energy use (2000 PPP$/kg oil equiv)	..	5.2
Energy use per capita (kg oil equiv)	..	5,395
Energy from biomass products and waste (% of total)	..	3.1
Energy imports, net (% of energy use)	..	26
Electric power consumption per capita (kWh)	..	8,693
Electricity generated by coal (% of total)	..	38.2
Emissions and pollution		
CO_2 emissions per unit of GDP (kg/2000 PPP$ GDP)	..	0.5
CO_2 emissions per capita (metric tons)	..	12.4
Particulate matter (pop. weighted average, µg/cu. m)	..	33
Passenger cars (per 1,000 people)	..	436
Water and sanitation		
Internal freshwater resources per capita (cu. m)	..	9,479
Freshwater withdrawal		
Total (% of internal resources)	..	9.7
Agriculture (% of total freshwater withdrawal)	..	42
Access to improved water source (% of total population)	100	99
Rural (% of rural population)	100	98
Urban (% of urban population)	100	100
Access to sanitation (% of total population)	..	..
Rural (% of rural population)	..	..
Urban (% of urban population)	..	..
Under-five mortality rate (per 1,000)	..	7
National accounting aggregates, 2003		
Gross national savings (% of GNI)	..	19.1
Consumption of fixed capital (% of GNI)	..	13.2
Education expenditure (% of GNI)	..	4.6
Energy depletion (% of GNI)	..	0.8
Mineral depletion (% of GNI)	..	0.0
Net forest depletion (% of GNI)	..	0.0
CO_2 damage (% of GNI)	..	0.3
Particulate emission damage (% of GNI)	..	0.3
Adjusted net savings (% of GNI)	..	9.2

Australia

Environmental strategy/action plan prepared in **1992**

	Country data	High income
		Group data
Population (millions)	19.9	972
Urban population (% of total)	91.9	79.9
GDP ($ billions)	522	29,341
GNI per capita, *Atlas* method ($)	21,950	28,600
Agriculture and fisheries		
Land area (1,000 sq. km)	7,682	31,030
Agricultural land (% of land area)	59	36
Irrigated land (% of crop land)	5.2	12.3
Fertilizer consumption (100 grams/ha arable land)	472	1,198
Population density, rural (people/sq. km arable land)	3	202
Fish catch, total (1,000 metric tons)	236	28,712
Forests		
Forest area (1,000 sq. km)	1,545	7,929
Forest area share of total land area (%)	20.1	25.9
Annual deforestation (% change, 1990–2000)	0.2	–0.1
Biodiversity		
Mammal species, total known	252	
Mammal species, threatened	63	
Bird species, total breeding	497	
Bird species, threatened	37	
Nationally protected area (% of land area)	13.4	19.5
Energy		
GDP per unit of energy use (2000 PPP$/kg oil equiv)	4.8	5.2
Energy use per capita (kg oil equiv)	5,732	5,395
Energy from biomass products and waste (% of total)	6.2	3.1
Energy imports, net (% of energy use)	-126	26
Electric power consumption per capita (kWh)	9,663	8,693
Electricity generated by coal (% of total)	78.3	38.2
Emissions and pollution		
CO_2 emissions per unit of GDP (kg/2000 PPP$ GDP)	0.7	0.5
CO_2 emissions per capita (metric tons)	18.0	12.4
Particulate matter (pop. weighted average, μg/cu. m)	19	33
Passenger cars (per 1,000 people)	..	436
Water and sanitation		
Internal freshwater resources per capita (cu. m)	24,747	9,479
Freshwater withdrawal		
Total (% of internal resources)	3.0	9.7
Agriculture (% of total freshwater withdrawal)	33	42
Access to improved water source (% of total population)	100	99
Rural (% of rural population)	100	98
Urban (% of urban population)	100	100
Access to sanitation (% of total population)	100	..
Rural (% of rural population)	100	..
Urban (% of urban population)	100	..
Under-five mortality rate (per 1,000)	6	7
National accounting aggregates, 2003		
Gross national savings (% of GNI)	19.7	19.1
Consumption of fixed capital (% of GNI)	16.1	13.2
Education expenditure (% of GNI)	4.5	4.6
Energy depletion (% of GNI)	1.3	0.8
Mineral depletion (% of GNI)	1.3	0.0
Net forest depletion (% of GNI)	0.0	0.0
CO_2 damage (% of GNI)	0.5	0.3
Particulate emission damage (% of GNI)	0.1	0.3
Adjusted net savings (% of GNI)	4.9	9.2

Austria

Environmental strategy/action plan prepared in ..

	Group data	
	Country data	High income
Population (millions)	8.1	972
Urban population (% of total)	67.8	79.9
GDP ($ billions)	253	29,341
GNI per capita, *Atlas* method ($)	26,810	28,600
Agriculture and fisheries		
Land area (1,000 sq. km)	83	31,030
Agricultural land (% of land area)	41	36
Irrigated land (% of crop land)	0.3	12.3
Fertilizer consumption (100 grams/ha arable land)	1,497	1,198
Population density, rural (people/sq. km arable land)	188	202
Fish catch, total (1,000 metric tons)	3	28,712
Forests		
Forest area (1,000 sq. km)	39	7,929
Forest area share of total land area (%)	47.0	25.9
Annual deforestation (% change, 1990–2000)	–0.2	–0.1
Biodiversity		
Mammal species, total known	83	
Mammal species, threatened	7	
Bird species, total breeding	230	
Bird species, threatened	3	
Nationally protected area (% of land area)	33.0	19.5
Energy		
GDP per unit of energy use (2000 PPP$/kg oil equiv)	7.5	5.2
Energy use per capita (kg oil equiv)	3,774	5,395
Energy from biomass products and waste (% of total)	11.1	3.1
Energy imports, net (% of energy use)	67	26
Electric power consumption per capita (kWh)	6,838	8,693
Electricity generated by coal (% of total)	12.3	38.2
Emissions and pollution		
CO_2 emissions per unit of GDP (kg/2000 PPP$ GDP)	0.3	0.5
CO_2 emissions per capita (metric tons)	7.6	12.4
Particulate matter (pop. weighted average, µg/cu. m)	33	33
Passenger cars (per 1,000 people)	494	436
Water and sanitation		
Internal freshwater resources per capita (cu. m)	6,799	9,479
Freshwater withdrawal		
Total (% of internal resources)	4.4	9.7
Agriculture (% of total freshwater withdrawal)	9	42
Access to improved water source (% of total population)	100	99
Rural (% of rural population)	100	98
Urban (% of urban population)	100	100
Access to sanitation (% of total population)	100	..
Rural (% of rural population)	100	..
Urban (% of urban population)	100	..
Under-five mortality rate (per 1,000)	6	7
National accounting aggregates, 2003		
Gross national savings (% of GNI)	22.7	19.1
Consumption of fixed capital (% of GNI)	14.5	13.2
Education expenditure (% of GNI)	5.6	4.6
Energy depletion (% of GNI)	0.1	0.8
Mineral depletion (% of GNI)	0.0	0.0
Net forest depletion (% of GNI)	0.0	0.0
CO_2 damage (% of GNI)	0.2	0.3
Particulate emission damage (% of GNI)	0.2	0.3
Adjusted net savings (% of GNI)	13.3	9.2

Azerbaijan

Environmental strategy/action plan prepared in **1998**

	Country data	Europe & Central Asia	Lower middle income
		Group data	
Population (millions)	8.2	472	2,655
Urban population (% of total)	51.9	63.8	49.8
GDP ($ billions)	7.1	1,403	4,168
GNI per capita, *Atlas* method ($)	820	2,580	1,490
Agriculture and fisheries			
Land area (1,000 sq. km)	83	23,868	56,103
Agricultural land (% of land area)	52	28	35
Irrigated land (% of crop land)	72.4	10.9	20.8
Fertilizer consumption (100 grams/ha arable land)	99	344	1,170
Population density, rural (people/sq. km arable land)	220	122	497
Fish catch, total (1,000 metric tons)	11	5,527	74,407
Forests			
Forest area (1,000 sq. km)	11	9,463	20,316
Forest area share of total land area (%)	13.2	39.6	36.2
Annual deforestation (% change, 1990–2000)	−1.3	−0.1	0.1
Biodiversity			
Mammal species, total known	99		
Mammal species, threatened	13		
Bird species, total breeding	229		
Bird species, threatened	8		
Nationally protected area (% of land area)	6.1	6.8	7.7
Energy			
GDP per unit of energy use (2000 PPP$/kg oil equiv)	2.2	2.5	4.1
Energy use per capita (kg oil equiv)	1,435	2,697	1,227
Energy from biomass products and waste (% of total)	0.0	2.3	12.3
Energy imports, net (% of energy use)	-68	−23	−22
Electric power consumption per capita (kWh)	1,878	2,808	1,289
Electricity generated by coal (% of total)	..	29.4	42.8
Emissions and pollution			
CO_2 emissions per unit of GDP (kg/2000 PPP$ GDP)	1.4	1.1	0.6
CO_2 emissions per capita (metric tons)	3.6	6.7	2.9
Particulate matter (pop. weighted average, µg/cu. m)	99	33	49
Passenger cars (per 1,000 people)	43	138	28
Water and sanitation			
Internal freshwater resources per capita (cu. m)	972	11,128	8,397
Freshwater withdrawal			
Total (% of internal resources)	206.3	7.4	5.9
Agriculture (% of total freshwater withdrawal)	70	57	74
Access to improved water source (% of total population)	77	91	82
Rural (% of rural population)	59	80	71
Urban (% of urban population)	95	98	94
Access to sanitation (% of total population)	55	82	60
Rural (% of rural population)	36	64	41
Urban (% of urban population)	73	93	80
Under-five mortality rate (per 1,000)	91	36	39
National accounting aggregates, 2003			
Gross national savings (% of GNI)	22.2	21.9	30.6
Consumption of fixed capital (% of GNI)	15.0	10.7	9.8
Education expenditure (% of GNI)	3.0	4.1	3.2
Energy depletion (% of GNI)	45.4	11.6	8.1
Mineral depletion (% of GNI)	0.0	0.1	0.4
Net forest depletion (% of GNI)	0.0	0.0	0.1
CO_2 damage (% of GNI)	5.0	1.9	1.6
Particulate emission damage (% of GNI)	1.0	0.6	0.7
Adjusted net savings (% of GNI)	−41.2	1.1	13.2

Bahamas, The

Environmental strategy/action plan prepared in ..

	Country data	Group data High income
Population (millions)	0.3	972
Urban population (% of total)	89.4	79.9
GDP ($ billions)	5	29,341
GNI per capita, *Atlas* method ($)	14,920	28,600
Agriculture and fisheries		
Land area (1,000 sq. km)	10	31,030
Agricultural land (% of land area)	1	36
Irrigated land (% of crop land)	8.3	12.3
Fertilizer consumption (100 grams/ha arable land)	1,000	1,198
Population density, rural (people/sq. km arable land)	428	202
Fish catch, total (1,000 metric tons)	9	28,712
Forests		
Forest area (1,000 sq. km)	8	7,929
Forest area share of total land area (%)	84.1	25.9
Annual deforestation (% change, 1990–2000)	0.0	–0.1
Biodiversity		
Mammal species, total known	..	
Mammal species, threatened	5	
Bird species, total breeding	..	
Bird species, threatened	4	
Nationally protected area (% of land area)	..	19.5
Energy		
GDP per unit of energy use (2000 PPP$/kg oil equiv)	..	5.2
Energy use per capita (kg oil equiv)	..	5,395
Energy from biomass products and waste (% of total)	..	3.1
Energy imports, net (% of energy use)	..	26
Electric power consumption per capita (kWh)	..	8,693
Electricity generated by coal (% of total)	..	38.2
Emissions and pollution		
CO_2 emissions per unit of GDP (kg/2000 PPP$ GDP)	0.4	0.5
CO_2 emissions per capita (metric tons)	5.9	12.4
Particulate matter (pop. weighted average, µg/cu. m)	43	33
Passenger cars (per 1,000 people)	..	436
Water and sanitation		
Internal freshwater resources per capita (cu. m)	..	9,479
Freshwater withdrawal		
Total (% of internal resources)	..	9.7
Agriculture (% of total freshwater withdrawal)	..	42
Access to improved water source (% of total population)	97	99
Rural (% of rural population)	86	98
Urban (% of urban population)	98	100
Access to sanitation (% of total population)	100	..
Rural (% of rural population)	100	..
Urban (% of urban population)	100	..
Under-five mortality rate (per 1,000)	14	7
National accounting aggregates, 2003		
Gross national savings (% of GNI)	..	19.1
Consumption of fixed capital (% of GNI)	..	13.2
Education expenditure (% of GNI)	3.8	4.6
Energy depletion (% of GNI)	..	0.8
Mineral depletion (% of GNI)	..	0.0
Net forest depletion (% of GNI)	..	0.0
CO_2 damage (% of GNI)	..	0.3
Particulate emission damage (% of GNI)	..	0.3
Adjusted net savings (% of GNI)	..	9.2

Bahrain

Environmental strategy/action plan prepared in ..

	Country data	Group data High income
Population (millions)	0.7	972
Urban population (% of total)	93.0	79.9
GDP ($ billions)	8	29,341
GNI per capita, *Atlas* method ($)	10,850	28,600
Agriculture and fisheries		
Land area (1,000 sq. km)	1	31,030
Agricultural land (% of land area)	14	36
Irrigated land (% of crop land)	66.7	12.3
Fertilizer consumption (100 grams/ha arable land)	500	1,198
Population density, rural (people/sq. km arable land)	2,525	202
Fish catch, total (1,000 metric tons)	11	28,712
Forests		
Forest area (1,000 sq. km)	..	7,929
Forest area share of total land area (%)	..	25.9
Annual deforestation (% change, 1990–2000)	..	–0.1
Biodiversity		
Mammal species, total known	..	
Mammal species, threatened	1	
Bird species, total breeding	..	
Bird species, threatened	6	
Nationally protected area (% of land area)	..	19.5
Energy		
GDP per unit of energy use (2000 PPP$/kg oil equiv)	1.7	5.2
Energy use per capita (kg oil equiv)	9,837	5,395
Energy from biomass products and waste (% of total)	..	3.1
Energy imports, net (% of energy use)	–122	26
Electric power consumption per capita (kWh)	9,248	8,693
Electricity generated by coal (% of total)	..	38.2
Emissions and pollution		
CO_2 emissions per unit of GDP (kg/2000 PPP$ GDP)	1.8	0.5
CO_2 emissions per capita (metric tons)	29.1	12.4
Particulate matter (pop. weighted average, µg/cu. m)	70	33
Passenger cars (per 1,000 people)	307	436
Water and sanitation		
Internal freshwater resources per capita (cu. m)	0	9,479
Freshwater withdrawal		
Total (% of internal resources)	..	9.7
Agriculture (% of total freshwater withdrawal)	57	42
Access to improved water source (% of total population)	..	99
Rural (% of rural population)	..	98
Urban (% of urban population)	100	100
Access to sanitation (% of total population)	..	..
Rural (% of rural population)	..	..
Urban (% of urban population)	100	..
Under-five mortality rate (per 1,000)	15	7
National accounting aggregates, 2003		
Gross national savings (% of GNI)	..	19.1
Consumption of fixed capital (% of GNI)	..	13.2
Education expenditure (% of GNI)	4.4	4.6
Energy depletion (% of GNI)	..	0.8
Mineral depletion (% of GNI)	..	0.0
Net forest depletion (% of GNI)	..	0.0
CO_2 damage (% of GNI)	..	0.3
Particulate emission damage (% of GNI)	..	0.3
Adjusted net savings (% of GNI)	..	9.2

Bangladesh

Environmental strategy/action plan prepared in **1991**

	Country data	South Asia	Low income
		Group data	
Population (millions)	138.1	1,425	2,312
Urban population (% of total)	26.8	28.3	30.4
GDP ($ billions)	51.9	765	1,103
GNI per capita, *Atlas* method ($)	400	510	440
Agriculture and fisheries			
Land area (1,000 sq. km)	130	4,781	30,456
Agricultural land (% of land area)	70	55	43
Irrigated land (% of crop land)	54.5	41.2	26.7
Fertilizer consumption (100 grams/ha arable land)	1,775	1,027	654
Population density, rural (people/sq. km arable land)	1,249	559	509
Fish catch, total (1,000 metric tons)	1,687	8,724	16,410
Forests			
Forest area (1,000 sq. km)	13	780	7,939
Forest area share of total land area (%)	10.2	16.3	26.1
Annual deforestation (% change, 1990–2000)	–1.3	0.1	0.7
Biodiversity			
Mammal species, total known	125		
Mammal species, threatened	23		
Bird species, total breeding	166		
Bird species, threatened	23		
Nationally protected area (% of land area)	0.8	4.8	7.7
Energy			
GDP per unit of energy use (2000 PPP$/kg oil equiv)	10.5	5.1	4.1
Energy use per capita (kg oil equiv)	155	468	493
Energy from biomass products and waste (% of total)	37.5	39.3	49.4
Energy imports, net (% of energy use)	20	19	-6
Electric power consumption per capita (kWh)	100	344	312
Electricity generated by coal (% of total)	..	59.8	47.4
Emissions and pollution			
CO_2 emissions per unit of GDP (kg/2000 PPP$ GDP)	0.1	0.4	0.4
CO_2 emissions per capita (metric tons)	0.2	0.9	0.8
Particulate matter (pop. weighted average, µg/cu. m)	147	69	63
Passenger cars (per 1,000 people)	0	6	..
Water and sanitation			
Internal freshwater resources per capita (cu. m)	761	1,275	3,583
Freshwater withdrawal			
Total (% of internal resources)	13.9	40.5	11.5
Agriculture (% of total freshwater withdrawal)	86	94	92
Access to improved water source (% of total population)	75	84	75
Rural (% of rural population)	72	80	70
Urban (% of urban population)	82	93	89
Access to sanitation (% of total population)	48	35	36
Rural (% of rural population)	39	23	24
Urban (% of urban population)	75	64	61
Under-five mortality rate (per 1,000)	69	92	123
National accounting aggregates, 2003			
Gross national savings (% of GNI)	28.4	24.9	23.1
Consumption of fixed capital (% of GNI)	5.8	9.0	8.9
Education expenditure (% of GNI)	1.3	3.5	3.4
Energy depletion (% of GNI)	2.0	2.4	5.8
Mineral depletion (% of GNI)	0.0	0.3	0.3
Net forest depletion (% of GNI)	0.7	0.7	0.8
CO_2 damage (% of GNI)	0.4	1.3	1.2
Particulate emission damage (% of GNI)	0.3	0.7	0.6
Adjusted net savings (% of GNI)	20.6	14.0	8.9

Barbados

Environmental strategy/action plan prepared in ..

	Country data	Latin America & Caribbean	Upper middle income
		Group data	
Population (millions)	0.3	533	333
Urban population (% of total)	51.7	76.6	75.4
GDP ($ billions)	2.6	1,741	1,856
GNI per capita, *Atlas* method ($)	9,260	3,280	5,440
Agriculture and fisheries			
Land area (1,000 sq. km)	0	20,057	12,741
Agricultural land (% of land area)	44	39	48
Irrigated land (% of crop land)	5.9	12.5	13.5
Fertilizer consumption (100 grams/ha arable land)	507	892	796
Population density, rural (people/sq. km arable land)	823	210	193
Fish catch, total (1,000 metric tons)	3	17,804	10,082
Forests			
Forest area (1,000 sq. km)	0	9,552	2,427
Forest area share of total land area (%)	4.7	47.6	19.1
Annual deforestation (% change, 1990–2000)	0.0	0.5	0.6
Biodiversity			
Mammal species, total known	..		
Mammal species, threatened	0		
Bird species, total breeding	..		
Bird species, threatened	1		
Nationally protected area (% of land area)	..	11.2	17.3
Energy			
GDP per unit of energy use (2000 PPP$/kg oil equiv)	..	6.1	4.3
Energy use per capita (kg oil equiv)	..	1,156	2,232
Energy from biomass products and waste (% of total)	..	14.6	4.1
Energy imports, net (% of energy use)	..	–42	–91
Electric power consumption per capita (kWh)	..	1,506	2,496
Electricity generated by coal (% of total)	..	5.0	23.9
Emissions and pollution			
CO_2 emissions per unit of GDP (kg/2000 PPP$ GDP)	0.3	0.4	0.6
CO_2 emissions per capita (metric tons)	4.4	2.7	6.3
Particulate matter (pop. weighted average, µg/cu. m)	41	40	29
Passenger cars (per 1,000 people)	3	..	153
Water and sanitation			
Internal freshwater resources per capita (cu. m)	371	25,245	10,741
Freshwater withdrawal			
Total (% of internal resources)	..	2.0	5.7
Agriculture (% of total freshwater withdrawal)	24	74	71
Access to improved water source (% of total population)	100	89	..
Rural (% of rural population)	100	69	..
Urban (% of urban population)	100	96	96
Access to sanitation (% of total population)	99	74	..
Rural (% of rural population)	100	44	..
Urban (% of urban population)	99	84	..
Under-five mortality rate (per 1,000)	13	33	22
National accounting aggregates, 2003			
Gross national savings (% of GNI)	..	19.5	22.1
Consumption of fixed capital (% of GNI)	12.6	10.3	10.7
Education expenditure (% of GNI)	5.8	4.2	5.0
Energy depletion (% of GNI)	0.0	6.4	11.4
Mineral depletion (% of GNI)	0.0	0.7	0.3
Net forest depletion (% of GNI)	0.0	0.0	0.0
CO_2 damage (% of GNI)	0.3	0.5	0.8
Particulate emission damage (% of GNI)	..	0.5	0.6
Adjusted net savings (% of GNI)	..	5.3	3.3

Belarus

Environmental strategy/action plan prepared in ..

	Country data	Europe & Central Asia	Lower middle income
		Group data	
Population (millions)	9.9	472	2,655
Urban population (% of total)	69.9	63.8	49.8
GDP ($ billions)	17.5	1,403	4,168
GNI per capita, *Atlas* method ($)	1,600	2,580	1,490
Agriculture and fisheries			
Land area (1,000 sq. km)	207	23,868	56,103
Agricultural land (% of land area)	45	28	35
Irrigated land (% of crop land)	2.3	10.9	20.8
Fertilizer consumption (100 grams/ha arable land)	1,334	344	1,170
Population density, rural (people/sq. km arable land)	54	122	497
Fish catch, total (1,000 metric tons)	6	5,527	74,407
Forests			
Forest area (1,000 sq. km)	94	9,463	20,316
Forest area share of total land area (%)	45.3	39.6	36.2
Annual deforestation (% change, 1990–2000)	–3.2	–0.1	0.1
Biodiversity			
Mammal species, total known	74		
Mammal species, threatened	7		
Bird species, total breeding	194		
Bird species, threatened	3		
Nationally protected area (% of land area)	6.3	6.8	7.7
Energy			
GDP per unit of energy use (2000 PPP$/kg oil equiv)	2.1	2.5	4.1
Energy use per capita (kg oil equiv)	2,496	2,697	1,227
Energy from biomass products and waste (% of total)	4.4	2.3	12.3
Energy imports, net (% of energy use)	86	–23	–22
Electric power consumption per capita (kWh)	2,657	2,808	1,289
Electricity generated by coal (% of total)	..	29.4	42.8
Emissions and pollution			
CO_2 emissions per unit of GDP (kg/2000 PPP$ GDP)	1.2	1.1	0.6
CO_2 emissions per capita (metric tons)	5.9	6.7	2.9
Particulate matter (pop. weighted average, µg/cu. m)	15	33	49
Passenger cars (per 1,000 people)	156	138	28
Water and sanitation			
Internal freshwater resources per capita (cu. m)	3,745	11,128	8,397
Freshwater withdrawal			
Total (% of internal resources)	7.3	7.4	5.9
Agriculture (% of total freshwater withdrawal)	35	57	74
Access to improved water source (% of total population)	100	91	82
Rural (% of rural population)	100	80	71
Urban (% of urban population)	100	98	94
Access to sanitation (% of total population)	..	82	60
Rural (% of rural population)	..	64	41
Urban (% of urban population)	..	93	80
Under-five mortality rate (per 1,000)	17	36	39
National accounting aggregates, 2003			
Gross national savings (% of GNI)	21.2	21.9	30.6
Consumption of fixed capital (% of GNI)	9.3	10.7	9.8
Education expenditure (% of GNI)	5.4	4.1	3.2
Energy depletion (% of GNI)	2.0	11.6	8.1
Mineral depletion (% of GNI)	0.0	0.1	0.4
Net forest depletion (% of GNI)	0.0	0.0	0.1
CO_2 damage (% of GNI)	3.0	1.9	1.6
Particulate emission damage (% of GNI)	0.0	0.6	0.7
Adjusted net savings (% of GNI)	12.4	1.1	13.2

Belgium

Environmental strategy/action plan prepared in ..

	Country data	Group data High Income
Population (millions)	10.4	972
Urban population (% of total)	97.5	79.9
GDP ($ billions)	302	29,341
GNI per capita, *Atlas* method ($)	25,760	28,600

Agriculture and fisheries

Land area (1,000 sq. km)	30	31,030
Agricultural land (% of land area)	46	36
Irrigated land (% of crop land)	..	12.3
Fertilizer consumption (100 grams/ha arable land)	..	1,198
Population density, rural (people/sq. km arable land)	..	202
Fish catch, total (1,000 metric tons)	..	28,712

Forests

Forest area (1,000 sq. km)	7	7,929
Forest area share of total land area (%)	..	25.9
Annual deforestation (% change, 1990–2000)	0.2	–0.1

Biodiversity

Mammal species, total known	58	
Mammal species, threatened	11	
Bird species, total breeding	191	
Bird species, threatened	2	
Nationally protected area (% of land area)	..	19.5

Energy

GDP per unit of energy use (2000 PPP$/kg oil equiv)	4.8	5.2
Energy use per capita (kg oil equiv)	5,505	5,395
Energy from biomass products and waste (% of total)	1.6	3.1
Energy imports, net (% of energy use)	77	26
Electric power consumption per capita (kWh)	7,592	8,693
Electricity generated by coal (% of total)	15.6	38.2

Emissions and pollution

CO_2 emissions per unit of GDP (kg/2000 PPP$ GDP)	0.4	0.5
CO_2 emissions per capita (metric tons)	10.0	12.4
Particulate matter (pop. weighted average, µg/cu. m)	28	33
Passenger cars (per 1,000 people)	464	436

Water and sanitation

Internal freshwater resources per capita (cu. m)	1,157	9,479
Freshwater withdrawal		
Total (% of internal resources)	..	9.7
Agriculture (% of total freshwater withdrawal)	..	42
Access to improved water source (% of total population)	..	99
Rural (% of rural population)	..	98
Urban (% of urban population)	100	100
Access to sanitation (% of total population)	..	..
Rural (% of rural population)	..	..
Urban (% of urban population)	..	..
Under-five mortality rate (per 1,000)	5	7

National accounting aggregates, 2003

Gross national savings (% of GNI)	24.0	19.1
Consumption of fixed capital (% of GNI)	14.4	13.2
Education expenditure (% of GNI)	3.0	4.6
Energy depletion (% of GNI)	0.0	0.8
Mineral depletion (% of GNI)	0.0	0.0
Net forest depletion (% of GNI)	0.0	0.0
CO_2 damage (% of GNI)	0.2	0.3
Particulate emission damage (% of GNI)	0.2	0.3
Adjusted net savings (% of GNI)	12.2	9.2

Belize

Environmental strategy/action plan prepared in ..

	Country data	Group data Latin America & Caribbean	Upper middle income
Population (millions)	0.3	533	333
Urban population (% of total)	48.4	76.6	75.4
GDP ($ billions)	1.0	1,741	1,856
GNI per capita, *Atlas* method ($)	3,370	3,280	5,440
Agriculture and fisheries			
Land area (1,000 sq. km)	23	20,057	12,741
Agricultural land (% of land area)	7	39	48
Irrigated land (% of crop land)	2.9	12.5	13.5
Fertilizer consumption (100 grams/ha arable land)	671	892	796
Population density, rural (people/sq. km arable land)	196	210	193
Fish catch, total (1,000 metric tons)	19	17,804	10,082
Forests			
Forest area (1,000 sq. km)	13	9,552	2,427
Forest area share of total land area (%)	59.1	47.6	19.1
Annual deforestation (% change, 1990–2000)	2.3	0.5	0.6
Biodiversity			
Mammal species, total known	125		
Mammal species, threatened	4		
Bird species, total breeding	161		
Bird species, threatened	2		
Nationally protected area (% of land area)	..	11.2	17.3
Energy			
GDP per unit of energy use (2000 PPP$/kg oil equiv)	..	6.1	4.3
Energy use per capita (kg oil equiv)	..	1,156	2,232
Energy from biomass products and waste (% of total)	..	14.6	4.1
Energy imports, net (% of energy use)	..	−42	−91
Electric power consumption per capita (kWh)	..	1,506	2,496
Electricity generated by coal (% of total)	..	5.0	23.9
Emissions and pollution			
CO_2 emissions per unit of GDP (kg/2000 PPP$ GDP)	0.5	0.4	0.6
CO_2 emissions per capita (metric tons)	3.1	2.7	6.3
Particulate matter (pop. weighted average, µg/cu. m)	23	40	29
Passenger cars (per 1,000 people)	42	..	153
Water and sanitation			
Internal freshwater resources per capita (cu. m)	58,458	25,245	10,741
Freshwater withdrawal			
Total (% of internal resources)	0.6	2.0	5.7
Agriculture (% of total freshwater withdrawal)	0	74	71
Access to improved water source (% of total population)	91	89	..
Rural (% of rural population)	82	69	..
Urban (% of urban population)	100	96	96
Access to sanitation (% of total population)	47	74	..
Rural (% of rural population)	25	44	..
Urban (% of urban population)	71	84	..
Under-five mortality rate (per 1,000)	39	33	22
National accounting aggregates, 2003			
Gross national savings (% of GNI)	2.4	19.5	22.1
Consumption of fixed capital (% of GNI)	6.1	10.3	10.7
Education expenditure (% of GNI)	6.2	4.2	5.0
Energy depletion (% of GNI)	0.0	6.4	11.4
Mineral depletion (% of GNI)	0.0	0.7	0.3
Net forest depletion (% of GNI)	0.0	0.0	0.0
CO_2 damage (% of GNI)	0.5	0.5	0.8
Particulate emission damage (% of GNI)	..	0.5	0.6
Adjusted net savings (% of GNI)	2.0	5.3	3.3

Benin

	Country data	Sub-Saharan Africa	Low income
		Group data	
Population (millions)	6.7	705	2,312
Urban population (% of total)	44.5	36.5	30.4
GDP ($ billions)	3.5	439	1,103
GNI per capita, *Atlas* method ($)	440	500	440
Agriculture and fisheries			
Land area (1,000 sq. km)	111	23,596	30,456
Agricultural land (% of land area)	25	43	43
Irrigated land (% of crop land)	0.4	4.2	26.7
Fertilizer consumption (100 grams/ha arable land)	188	145	654
Population density, rural (people/sq. km arable land)	144	352	509
Fish catch, total (1,000 metric tons)	38	5,191	16,410
Forests			
Forest area (1,000 sq. km)	27	6,435	7,939
Forest area share of total land area (%)	24.0	27.3	26.1
Annual deforestation (% change, 1990–2000)	2.3	0.8	0.7
Biodiversity			
Mammal species, total known	188		
Mammal species, threatened	8		
Bird species, total breeding	112		
Bird species, threatened	2		
Nationally protected area (% of land area)	11.4	8.7	7.7
Energy			
GDP per unit of energy use (2000 PPP$/kg oil equiv)	3.0	2.8	4.1
Energy use per capita (kg oil equiv)	340	667	493
Energy from biomass products and waste (% of total)	69.3	57.5	49.4
Energy imports, net (% of energy use)	31	−56	−6
Electric power consumption per capita (kWh)	76	457	312
Electricity generated by coal (% of total)	..	68.2	47.4
Emissions and pollution			
CO_2 emissions per unit of GDP (kg/2000 PPP$ GDP)	0.3	0.4	0.4
CO_2 emissions per capita (metric tons)	0.3	0.7	0.8
Particulate matter (pop. weighted average, μg/cu. m)	47	54	63
Passenger cars per 1,000 people	..	..	..
Water and sanitation			
Internal freshwater resources per capita (cu. m)	1,488	5,546	3,583
Freshwater withdrawal			
Total (% of internal resources)	1.0	1.8	11.5
Agriculture (% of total freshwater withdrawal)	67	85	92
Access to improved water source (% of total population)	68	58	75
Rural (% of rural population)	60	46	70
Urban (% of urban population)	79	82	89
Access to sanitation (% of total population)	32	36	36
Rural (% of rural population)	12	26	24
Urban (% of urban population)	58	55	61
Under-five mortality rate (per 1,000)	154	171	123
National accounting aggregates, 2003			
Gross national savings (% of GNI)	4.8	16.9	23.1
Consumption of fixed capital (% of GNI)	8.2	10.6	8.9
Education expenditure (% of GNI)	2.7	4.7	3.4
Energy depletion (% of GNI)	0.0	8.0	5.8
Mineral depletion (% of GNI)	0.0	0.5	0.3
Net forest depletion (% of GNI)	1.1	0.7	0.8
CO_2 damage (% of GNI)	0.3	0.9	1.2
Particulate emission damage (% of GNI)	0.3	0.4	0.6
Adjusted net savings (% of GNI)	−2.4	0.6	8.9

Bermuda

Environmental strategy/action plan prepared in ..

	Country data	Group data High income
Population (millions)	0.1	972
Urban population (% of total)	100.0	79.9
GDP ($ billions)	..	29,341
GNI per capita, *Atlas* method ($)	..	28,600

Agriculture and fisheries

Land area (1,000 sq. km)	0	31,030
Agricultural land (% of land area)	20	36
Irrigated land (% of crop land)	..	12.3
Fertilizer consumption (100 grams/ha arable land)	1,000	1,198
Population density, rural (people/sq. km arable land)	0	202
Fish catch, total (1,000 metric tons)	0	28,712

Forests

Forest area (1,000 sq. km)	..	7,929
Forest area share of total land area (%)	..	25.9
Annual deforestation (% change, 1990–2000)	..	–0.1

Biodiversity

Mammal species, total known	..	
Mammal species, threatened	2	
Bird species, total breeding	..	
Bird species, threatened	2	
Nationally protected area (% of land area)	..	19.5

Energy

GDP per unit of energy use (2000 PPP$/kg oil equiv)	..	5.2
Energy use per capita (kg oil equiv)	..	5,395
Energy from biomass products and waste (% of total)	..	3.1
Energy imports, net (% of energy use)	..	26
Electric power consumption per capita (kWh)	..	8,693
Electricity generated by coal (% of total)	..	38.2

Emissions and pollution

CO_2 emissions per unit of GDP (kg/2000 PPP$ GDP)	..	0.5
CO_2 emissions per capita (metric tons)	7.2	12.4
Particulate matter (pop. weighted average, μg/cu. m)	..	33
Passenger cars (per 1,000 people)	..	436

Water and sanitation

Internal freshwater resources per capita (cu. m)	..	9,479
Freshwater withdrawal		
Total (% of internal resources)	..	9.7
Agriculture (% of total freshwater withdrawal)	..	42
Access to improved water source (% of total population)	..	99
Rural (% of rural population)	..	98
Urban (% of urban population)	..	100
Access to sanitation (% of total population)	..	..
Rural (% of rural population)	..	..
Urban (% of urban population)	..	..
Under-five mortality rate (per 1,000)	..	7

National accounting aggregates, 2003

Gross national savings (% of GNI)	..	19.1
Consumption of fixed capital (% of GNI)	..	13.2
Education expenditure (% of GNI)	3.3	4.6
Energy depletion (% of GNI)	..	0.8
Mineral depletion (% of GNI)	..	0.0
Net forest depletion (% of GNI)	..	0.0
CO_2 damage (% of GNI)	..	0.3
Particulate emission damage (% of GNI)	..	0.3
Adjusted net savings (% of GNI)	..	9.2

Bhutan

Environmental strategy/action plan prepared in ..

	Country data	Group data South Asia	Group data Low Income
Population (millions)	0.9	1,425	2,312
Urban population (% of total)	7.9	28.3	30.4
GDP ($ billions)	0.7	765	1,103
GNI per capita, *Atlas* method ($)	630	510	440
Agriculture and fisheries			
Land area (1,000 sq. km)	47	4,781	30,456
Agricultural land (% of land area)	12	55	43
Irrigated land (% of crop land)	24.2	41.2	26.7
Fertilizer consumption (100 grams/ha arable land)	..	1,027	654
Population density, rural (people/sq. km arable land)	542	559	509
Fish catch, total (1,000 metric tons)	0	8,724	16,410
Forests			
Forest area (1,000 sq. km)	30	780	7,939
Forest area share of total land area (%)	64.2	16.3	26.1
Annual deforestation (% change, 1990–2000)	0.0	0.1	0.7
Biodiversity			
Mammal species, total known	160		
Mammal species, threatened	22		
Bird species, total breeding	209		
Bird species, threatened	12		
Nationally protected area (% of land area)	25.1	4.8	7.7
Energy			
GDP per unit of energy use (2000 PPP$/kg oil equiv)	..	5.1	4.1
Energy use per capita (kg oil equiv)	..	468	493
Energy from biomass products and waste (% of total)	..	39.3	49.4
Energy imports, net (% of energy use)	..	19	-6
Electric power consumption per capita (kWh)	..	344	312
Electricity generated by coal (% of total)	..	59.8	47.4
Emissions and pollution			
CO_2 emissions per unit of GDP (kg/2000 PPP$ GDP)	..	0.4	0.4
CO_2 emissions per capita (metric tons)	0.5	0.9	0.8
Particulate matter (pop. weighted average, µg/cu. m)	41	69	63
Passenger cars (per 1,000 people)	..	6	..
Water and sanitation			
Internal freshwater resources per capita (cu. m)	108,738	1,275	3,583
Freshwater withdrawal			
Total (% of internal resources)	0.0	40.5	11.5
Agriculture (% of total freshwater withdrawal)	54	94	92
Access to improved water source (% of total population)	62	84	75
Rural (% of rural population)	60	80	70
Urban (% of urban population)	86	93	89
Access to sanitation (% of total population)	70	35	36
Rural (% of rural population)	70	23	24
Urban (% of urban population)	65	64	61
Under-five mortality rate (per 1,000)	85	92	123
National accounting aggregates, 2003			
Gross national savings (% of GNI)	..	24.9	23.1
Consumption of fixed capital (% of GNI)	9.7	9.0	8.9
Education expenditure (% of GNI)	2.4	3.5	3.4
Energy depletion (% of GNI)	0.0	2.4	5.8
Mineral depletion (% of GNI)	0.0	0.3	0.3
Net forest depletion (% of GNI)	4.3	0.7	0.8
CO_2 damage (% of GNI)	0.6	1.3	1.2
Particulate emission damage (% of GNI)	..	0.7	0.6
Adjusted net savings (% of GNI)	..	14.0	8.9

Bolivia

Environmental strategy/action plan prepared in **1994**

	Country data	Group data	
		Latin America & Caribbean	Lower middle income
Population (millions)	8.8	533	2,655
Urban population (% of total)	64.0	76.6	49.8
GDP ($ billions)	7.9	1,741	4,168
GNI per capita, *Atlas* method ($)	900	3,280	1,490
Agriculture and fisheries			
Land area (1,000 sq. km)	1,084	20,057	56,103
Agricultural land (% of land area)	34	39	35
Irrigated land (% of crop land)	4.2	12.5	20.8
Fertilizer consumption (100 grams/ha arable land)	47	892	1,170
Population density, rural (people/sq. km arable land)	109	210	497
Fish catch, total (1,000 metric tons)	6	17,804	74,407
Forests			
Forest area (1,000 sq. km)	531	9,552	20,316
Forest area share of total land area (%)	48.9	47.6	36.2
Annual deforestation (% change, 1990–2000)	0.3	0.5	0.1
Biodiversity			
Mammal species, total known	316		
Mammal species, threatened	24		
Bird species, total breeding	504		
Bird species, threatened	28		
Nationally protected area (% of land area)	13.4	11.2	7.7
Energy			
GDP per unit of energy use (2000 PPP$/kg oil equiv)	4.8	6.1	4.1
Energy use per capita (kg oil equiv)	499	1,156	1,227
Energy from biomass products and waste (% of total)	16.8	14.6	12.3
Energy imports, net (% of energy use)	–89	–42	–22
Electric power consumption per capita (kWh)	419	1,506	1,289
Electricity generated by coal (% of total)	..	5.0	42.8
Emissions and pollution			
CO_2 emissions per unit of GDP (kg/2000 PPP$ GDP)	0.6	0.4	0.6
CO_2 emissions per capita (metric tons)	1.3	2.7	2.9
Particulate matter (pop. weighted average, µg/cu. m)	106	40	49
Passenger cars (per 1,000 people)	..	..	28
Water and sanitation			
Internal freshwater resources per capita (cu. m)	34,490	25,245	8,397
Freshwater withdrawal			
Total (% of internal resources)	0.4	2.0	5.9
Agriculture (% of total freshwater withdrawal)	87	74	74
Access to improved water source (% of total population)	85	89	82
Rural (% of rural population)	68	69	71
Urban (% of urban population)	95	96	94
Access to sanitation (% of total population)	45	74	60
Rural (% of rural population)	23	44	41
Urban (% of urban population)	58	84	80
Under-five mortality rate (per 1,000)	66	33	39
National accounting aggregates, 2003			
Gross national savings (% of GNI)	12.0	19.5	30.6
Consumption of fixed capital (% of GNI)	9.2	10.3	9.8
Education expenditure (% of GNI)	4.8	4.2	3.2
Energy depletion (% of GNI)	8.7	6.4	8.1
Mineral depletion (% of GNI)	0.8	0.7	0.4
Net forest depletion (% of GNI)	0.0	0.0	0.1
CO_2 damage (% of GNI)	1.2	0.5	1.6
Particulate emission damage (% of GNI)	0.7	0.5	0.7
Adjusted net savings (% of GNI)	–3.8	5.3	13.2

Bosnia and Herzegovina

Environmental strategy/action plan prepared in ..

	Country data	Group data Europe & Central Asia	Group data Lower middle income
Population (millions)	4.1	472	2,655
Urban population (% of total)	44.4	63.8	49.8
GDP ($ billions)	7.0	1,403	4,168
GNI per capita, *Atlas* method ($)	1,530	2,580	1,490
Agriculture and fisheries			
Land area (1,000 sq. km)	51	23,868	56,103
Agricultural land (% of land area)	36	28	35
Irrigated land (% of crop land)	0.3	10.9	20.8
Fertilizer consumption (100 grams/ha arable land)	327	344	1,170
Population density, rural (people/sq. km arable land)	231	122	497
Fish catch, total (1,000 metric tons)	3	5,527	74,407
Forests			
Forest area (1,000 sq. km)	23	9,463	20,316
Forest area share of total land area (%)	44.4	39.6	36.2
Annual deforestation (% change, 1990–2000)	0.0	–0.1	0.1
Biodiversity			
Mammal species, total known	72		
Mammal species, threatened	10		
Bird species, total breeding	205		
Bird species, threatened	3		
Nationally protected area (% of land area)	0.5	6.8	7.7
Energy			
GDP per unit of energy use (2000 PPP$/kg oil equiv)	5.3	2.5	4.1
Energy use per capita (kg oil equiv)	1,052	2,697	1,227
Energy from biomass products and waste (% of total)	4.2	2.3	12.3
Energy imports, net (% of energy use)	23	–23	–22
Electric power consumption per capita (kWh)	1,633	2,808	1,289
Electricity generated by coal (% of total)	49.9	29.4	42.8
Emissions and pollution			
CO_2 emissions per unit of GDP (kg/2000 PPP$ GDP)	0.9	1.1	0.6
CO_2 emissions per capita (metric tons)	4.8	6.7	2.9
Particulate matter (pop. weighted average, µg/cu. m)	30	33	49
Passenger cars (per 1,000 people)	..	138	28
Water and sanitation			
Internal freshwater resources per capita (cu. m)	8,696	11,128	8,397
Freshwater withdrawal			
Total (% of internal resources)	2.8	7.4	5.9
Agriculture (% of total freshwater withdrawal)	60	57	74
Access to improved water source (% of total population)	98	91	82
Rural (% of rural population)	96	80	71
Urban (% of urban population)	100	98	94
Access to sanitation (% of total population)	93	82	60
Rural (% of rural population)	88	64	41
Urban (% of urban population)	99	93	80
Under-five mortality rate (per 1,000)	17	36	39
National accounting aggregates, 2003			
Gross national savings (% of GNI)	10.3	21.9	30.6
Consumption of fixed capital (% of GNI)	9.3	10.7	9.8
Education expenditure (% of GNI)	..	4.1	3.2
Energy depletion (% of GNI)	0.1	11.6	8.1
Mineral depletion (% of GNI)	0.0	0.1	0.4
Net forest depletion (% of GNI)	0.0	0.0	0.1
CO_2 damage (% of GNI)	2.0	1.9	1.6
Particulate emission damage (% of GNI)	0.4	0.6	0.7
Adjusted net savings (% of GNI)	..	1.1	13.2

Botswana

Environmental strategy/action plan prepared in **1990**

	Country data	Group data Sub-Saharan Africa	Group data Upper middle income
Population (millions)	1.7	705	333
Urban population (% of total)	50.3	36.5	75.4
GDP ($ billions)	7.5	439	1,856
GNI per capita, *Atlas* method ($)	3,530	500	5,440
Agriculture and fisheries			
Land area (1,000 sq. km)	567	23,596	12,741
Agricultural land (% of land area)	46	43	48
Irrigated land (% of crop land)	0.3	4.2	13.5
Fertilizer consumption (100 grams/ha arable land)	124	145	796
Population density, rural (people/sq. km arable land)	232	352	193
Fish catch, total (1,000 metric tons)	0	5,191	10,082
Forests			
Forest area (1,000 sq. km)	124	6,435	2,427
Forest area share of total land area (%)	21.9	27.3	19.1
Annual deforestation (% change, 1990–2000)	0.9	0.8	0.6
Biodiversity			
Mammal species, total known	164		
Mammal species, threatened	6		
Bird species, total breeding	184		
Bird species, threatened	7		
Nationally protected area (% of land area)	18.5	8.7	17.3
Energy			
GDP per unit of energy use (2000 PPP$/kg oil equiv)	..	2.8	4.3
Energy use per capita (kg oil equiv)	..	667	2,232
Energy from biomass products and waste (% of total)	..	57.5	4.1
Energy imports, net (% of energy use)	..	−56	−91
Electric power consumption per capita (kWh)	..	457	2,496
Electricity generated by coal (% of total)	..	68.2	23.9
Emissions and pollution			
CO_2 emissions per unit of GDP (kg/2000 PPP$ GDP)	0.3	0.4	0.6
CO_2 emissions per capita (metric tons)	2.3	0.7	6.3
Particulate matter (pop. weighted average, µg/cu. m)	..	54	29
Passenger cars (per 1,000 people)	30	..	153
Water and sanitation			
Internal freshwater resources per capita (cu. m)	1,742	5,546	10,741
Freshwater withdrawal			
Total (% of internal resources)	3.3	1.8	5.7
Agriculture (% of total freshwater withdrawal)	48	85	71
Access to improved water source (% of total population)	95	58	..
Rural (% of rural population)	90	46	..
Urban (% of urban population)	100	82	96
Access to sanitation (% of total population)	41	36	..
Rural (% of rural population)	25	26	..
Urban (% of urban population)	57	55	..
Under-five mortality rate (per 1,000)	112	171	22
National accounting aggregates, 2003			
Gross national savings (% of GNI)	35.6	16.9	22.1
Consumption of fixed capital (% of GNI)	11.8	10.6	10.7
Education expenditure (% of GNI)	5.6	4.7	5.0
Energy depletion (% of GNI)	0.0	8.0	11.4
Mineral depletion (% of GNI)	0.2	0.5	0.3
Net forest depletion (% of GNI)	0.0	0.7	0.0
CO_2 damage (% of GNI)	0.4	0.9	0.8
Particulate emission damage (% of GNI)	..	0.4	0.6
Adjusted net savings (% of GNI)	28.8	0.6	3.3

Brazil

Environmental strategy/action plan prepared in ..

	Country data	Group data Latin America & Caribbean	Group data Lower middle income
Population (millions)	176.6	533	2,655
Urban population (% of total)	82.8	76.6	49.8
GDP ($ billions)	492.3	1,741	4,168
GNI per capita, *Atlas* method ($)	2,720	3,280	1,490
Agriculture and fisheries			
Land area (1,000 sq. km)	8,459	20,057	56,103
Agricultural land (% of land area)	31	39	35
Irrigated land (% of crop land)	4.4	12.5	20.8
Fertilizer consumption (100 grams/ha arable land)	1,302	892	1,170
Population density, rural (people/sq. km arable land)	53	210	497
Fish catch, total (1,000 metric tons)	980	17,804	74,407
Forests			
Forest area (1,000 sq. km)	5,439	9,552	20,316
Forest area share of total land area (%)	64.3	47.6	36.2
Annual deforestation (% change, 1990–2000)	0.4	0.5	0.1
Biodiversity			
Mammal species, total known	394		
Mammal species, threatened	81		
Bird species, total breeding	686		
Bird species, threatened	114		
Nationally protected area (% of land area)	6.7	11.2	7.7
Energy			
GDP per unit of energy use (2000 PPP$/kg oil equiv)	6.8	6.1	4.1
Energy use per capita (kg oil equiv)	1,093	1,156	1,227
Energy from biomass products and waste (% of total)	24.3	14.6	12.3
Energy imports, net (% of energy use)	15	−42	−22
Electric power consumption per capita (kWh)	1,776	1,506	1,289
Electricity generated by coal (% of total)	2.4	5.0	42.8
Emissions and pollution			
CO_2 emissions per unit of GDP (kg/2000 PPP$ GDP)	0.2	0.4	0.6
CO_2 emissions per capita (metric tons)	1.8	2.7	2.9
Particulate matter (pop. weighted average, µg/cu. m)	33	40	49
Passenger cars (per 1,000 people)	..	..	28
Water and sanitation			
Internal freshwater resources per capita (cu. m)	30,680	25,245	8,397
Freshwater withdrawal			
Total (% of internal resources)	1.0	2.0	5.9
Agriculture (% of total freshwater withdrawal)	61	74	74
Access to improved water source (% of total population)	89	89	82
Rural (% of rural population)	58	69	71
Urban (% of urban population)	96	96	94
Access to sanitation (% of total population)	75	74	60
Rural (% of rural population)	35	44	41
Urban (% of urban population)	83	84	80
Under-five mortality rate (per 1,000)	35	33	39
National accounting aggregates, 2003			
Gross national savings (% of GNI)	19.1	19.5	30.6
Consumption of fixed capital (% of GNI)	10.8	10.3	9.8
Education expenditure (% of GNI)	3.9	4.2	3.2
Energy depletion (% of GNI)	3.1	6.4	8.1
Mineral depletion (% of GNI)	1.1	0.7	0.4
Net forest depletion (% of GNI)	0.0	0.0	0.1
CO_2 damage (% of GNI)	0.4	0.5	1.6
Particulate emission damage (% of GNI)	0.2	0.5	0.7
Adjusted net savings (% of GNI)	7.4	5.3	13.2

Brunei

Environmental strategy/action plan prepared in ..

	Country data	Group data High income
Population (millions)	0.4	972
Urban population (% of total)	73.8	79.9
GDP ($ billions)	..	29,341
GNI per capita, *Atlas* method ($)	..	28,600
Agriculture and fisheries		
Land area (1,000 sq. km)	5	31,030
Agricultural land (% of land area)	2	36
Irrigated land (% of crop land)	7.7	12.3
Fertilizer consumption (100 grams/ha arable land)	..	1,198
Population density, rural (people/sq. km arable land)	1,042	202
Fish catch, total (1,000 metric tons)	2	28,712
Forests		
Forest area (1,000 sq. km)	4	7,929
Forest area share of total land area (%)	83.9	25.9
Annual deforestation (% change, 1990–2000)	0.2	–0.1
Biodiversity		
Mammal species, total known	..	
Mammal species, threatened	11	
Bird species, total breeding	..	
Bird species, threatened	14	
Nationally protected area (% of land area)	..	19.5
Energy		
GDP per unit of energy use (2000 PPP$/kg oil equiv)	..	5.2
Energy use per capita (kg oil equiv)	6,149	5,395
Energy from biomass products and waste (% of total)	0.8	3.1
Energy imports, net (% of energy use)	–833	26
Electric power consumption per capita (kWh)	6,563	8,693
Electricity generated by coal (% of total)	..	38.2
Emissions and pollution		
CO_2 emissions per unit of GDP (kg/2000 PPP$ GDP)	..	0.5
CO_2 emissions per capita (metric tons)	14.2	12.4
Particulate matter (pop. weighted average, µg/cu. m)	38	33
Passenger cars (per 1,000 people)	..	436
Water and sanitation		
Internal freshwater resources per capita (cu. m)	24,242	9,479
Freshwater withdrawal		
Total (% of internal resources)	..	9.7
Agriculture (% of total freshwater withdrawal)	..	42
Access to improved water source (% of total population)	..	99
Rural (% of rural population)	..	98
Urban (% of urban population)	..	100
Access to sanitation (% of total population)	..	..
Rural (% of rural population)	..	..
Urban (% of urban population)	..	..
Under-five mortality rate (per 1,000)	6	7
National accounting aggregates, 2003		
Gross national savings (% of GNI)	..	19.1
Consumption of fixed capital (% of GNI)	..	13.2
Education expenditure (% of GNI)	2.9	4.6
Energy depletion (% of GNI)	..	0.8
Mineral depletion (% of GNI)	..	0.0
Net forest depletion (% of GNI)	..	0.0
CO_2 damage (% of GNI)	..	0.3
Particulate emission damage (% of GNI)	..	0.3
Adjusted net savings (% of GNI)	..	9.2

Bulgaria

Environmental strategy/action plan prepared in ..

	Country data	Europe & Central Asia	Lower middle income
		Group data	
Population (millions)	7.8	472	2,655
Urban population (% of total)	67.5	63.8	49.8
GDP ($ billions)	19.9	1,403	4,168
GNI per capita, *Atlas* method ($)	2,130	2,580	1,490
Agriculture and fisheries			
Land area (1,000 sq. km)	111	23,868	56,103
Agricultural land (% of land area)	57	28	35
Irrigated land (% of crop land)	16.5	10.9	20.8
Fertilizer consumption (100 grams/ha arable land)	495	344	1,170
Population density, rural (people/sq. km arable land)	76	122	497
Fish catch, total (1,000 metric tons)	8	5,527	74,407
Forests			
Forest area (1,000 sq. km)	37	9,463	20,316
Forest area share of total land area (%)	33.4	39.6	36.2
Annual deforestation (% change, 1990–2000)	−0.6	−0.1	0.1
Biodiversity			
Mammal species, total known	81		
Mammal species, threatened	14		
Bird species, total breeding	248		
Bird species, threatened	10		
Nationally protected area (% of land area)	4.5	6.8	7.7
Energy			
GDP per unit of energy use (2000 PPP$/kg oil equiv)	2.9	2.5	4.1
Energy use per capita (kg oil equiv)	2,417	2,697	1,227
Energy from biomass products and waste (% of total)	3.4	2.3	12.3
Energy imports, net (% of energy use)	45	−23	−22
Electric power consumption per capita (kWh)	3,060	2,808	1,289
Electricity generated by coal (% of total)	41.2	29.4	42.8
Emissions and pollution			
CO_2 emissions per unit of GDP (kg/2000 PPP$ GDP)	0.8	1.1	0.6
CO_2 emissions per capita (metric tons)	5.3	6.7	2.9
Particulate matter (pop. weighted average, μg/cu. m)	75	33	49
Passenger cars (per 1,000 people)	287	138	28
Water and sanitation			
Internal freshwater resources per capita (cu. m)	2,684	11,128	8,397
Freshwater withdrawal			
Total (% of internal resources)	66.2	7.4	5.9
Agriculture (% of total freshwater withdrawal)	22	57	74
Access to improved water source (% of total population)	100	91	82
Rural (% of rural population)	100	80	71
Urban (% of urban population)	100	98	94
Access to sanitation (% of total population)	100	82	60
Rural (% of rural population)	100	64	41
Urban (% of urban population)	100	93	80
Under-five mortality rate (per 1,000)	17	36	39
National accounting aggregates, 2003			
Gross national savings (% of GNI)	13.3	21.9	30.6
Consumption of fixed capital (% of GNI)	10.5	10.7	9.8
Education expenditure (% of GNI)	3.0	4.1	3.2
Energy depletion (% of GNI)	0.1	11.6	8.1
Mineral depletion (% of GNI)	0.4	0.1	0.4
Net forest depletion (% of GNI)	0.0	0.0	0.1
CO_2 damage (% of GNI)	1.8	1.9	1.6
Particulate emission damage (% of GNI)	2.1	0.6	0.7
Adjusted net savings (% of GNI)	1.3	1.1	13.2

Burkina Faso

Environmental strategy/action plan prepared in **1993**

	Country data	Sub-Saharan Africa	Low income
		Group data	
Population (millions)	12.1	705	2,312
Urban population (% of total)	17.6	36.5	30.4
GDP ($ billions)	4.2	439	1,103
GNI per capita, *Atlas* method ($)	300	500	440
Agriculture and fisheries			
Land area (1,000 sq. km)	274	23,596	30,456
Agricultural land (% of land area)	37	43	43
Irrigated land (% of crop land)	0.6	4.2	26.7
Fertilizer consumption (100 grams/ha arable land)	4	145	654
Population density, rural (people/sq. km arable land)	225	352	509
Fish catch, total (1,000 metric tons)	9	5,191	16,410
Forests			
Forest area (1,000 sq. km)	71	6,435	7,939
Forest area share of total land area (%)	25.9	27.3	26.1
Annual deforestation (% change, 1990–2000)	0.2	0.8	0.7
Biodiversity			
Mammal species, total known	147		
Mammal species, threatened	7		
Bird species, total breeding	138		
Bird species, threatened	2		
Nationally protected area (% of land area)	11.5	8.7	7.7
Energy			
GDP per unit of energy use (2000 PPP$/kg oil equiv)	..	2.8	4.1
Energy use per capita (kg oil equiv)	..	667	493
Energy from biomass products and waste (% of total)	..	57.5	49.4
Energy imports, net (% of energy use)	..	−56	−6
Electric power consumption per capita (kWh)	..	457	312
Electricity generated by coal (% of total)	..	68.2	47.4
Emissions and pollution			
CO_2 emissions per unit of GDP (kg/2000 PPP$ GDP)	0.1	0.4	0.4
CO_2 emissions per capita (metric tons)	0.1	0.7	0.8
Particulate matter (pop. weighted average, µg/cu. m)	108	54	63
Passenger cars (per 1,000 people)	..	..	..
Water and sanitation			
Internal freshwater resources per capita (cu. m)	1,074	5,546	3,583
Freshwater withdrawal			
Total (% of internal resources)	3.1	1.8	11.5
Agriculture (% of total freshwater withdrawal)	81	85	92
Access to improved water source (% of total population)	51	58	75
Rural (% of rural population)	44	46	70
Urban (% of urban population)	82	82	89
Access to sanitation (% of total population)	12	36	36
Rural (% of rural population)	5	26	24
Urban (% of urban population)	45	55	61
Under-five mortality rate (per 1,000)	207	171	123
National accounting aggregates, 2003			
Gross national savings (% of GNI)	6.6	16.9	23.1
Consumption of fixed capital (% of GNI)	7.6	10.6	8.9
Education expenditure (% of GNI)	2.4	4.7	3.4
Energy depletion (% of GNI)	0.0	8.0	5.8
Mineral depletion (% of GNI)	0.0	0.5	0.3
Net forest depletion (% of GNI)	1.0	0.7	0.8
CO_2 damage (% of GNI)	0.2	0.9	1.2
Particulate emission damage (% of GNI)	0.5	0.4	0.6
Adjusted net savings (% of GNI)	−0.2	0.6	8.9

Burundi

Environmental strategy/action plan prepared in **1994**

	Country data	Sub-Saharan Africa	Low income
		Group data	
Population (millions)	7.2	705	2,312
Urban population (% of total)	9.9	36.5	30.4
GDP ($ billions)	0.6	439	1,103
GNI per capita, *Atlas* method ($)	90	500	440
Agriculture and fisheries			
Land area (1,000 sq. km)	26	23,596	30,456
Agricultural land (% of land area)	85	43	43
Irrigated land (% of crop land)	5.5	4.2	26.7
Fertilizer consumption (100 grams/ha arable land)	26	145	654
Population density, rural (people/sq. km arable land)	648	352	509
Fish catch, total (1,000 metric tons)	9	5,191	16,410
Forests			
Forest area (1,000 sq. km)	1	6,435	7,939
Forest area share of total land area (%)	3.7	27.3	26.1
Annual deforestation (% change, 1990–2000)	9.0	0.8	0.7
Biodiversity			
Mammal species, total known	107		
Mammal species, threatened	6		
Bird species, total breeding	145		
Bird species, threatened	7		
Nationally protected area (% of land area)	5.7	8.7	7.7
Energy			
GDP per unit of energy use (2000 PPP$/kg oil equiv)	..	2.8	4.1
Energy use per capita (kg oil equiv)	..	667	493
Energy from biomass products and waste (% of total)	..	57.5	49.4
Energy imports, net (% of energy use)	..	−56	−6
Electric power consumption per capita (kWh)	..	457	312
Electricity generated by coal (% of total)	..	68.2	47.4
Emissions and pollution			
CO_2 emissions per unit of GDP (kg/2000 PPP$ GDP)	0.1	0.4	0.4
CO_2 emissions per capita (metric tons)	0.0	0.7	0.8
Particulate matter (pop. weighted average, µg/cu. m)	36	54	63
Passenger cars (per 1,000 people)	..	..	..
Water and sanitation			
Internal freshwater resources per capita (cu. m)	555	5,546	3,583
Freshwater withdrawal			
Total (% of internal resources)	2.5	1.8	11.5
Agriculture (% of total freshwater withdrawal)	64	85	92
Access to improved water source (% of total population)	79	58	75
Rural (% of rural population)	78	46	70
Urban (% of urban population)	90	82	89
Access to sanitation (% of total population)	36	36	36
Rural (% of rural population)	35	26	24
Urban (% of urban population)	47	55	61
Under-five mortality rate (per 1,000)	190	171	123
National accounting aggregates, 2003			
Gross national savings (% of GNI)	22.4	16.9	23.1
Consumption of fixed capital (% of GNI)	5.9	10.6	8.9
Education expenditure (% of GNI)	4.1	4.7	3.4
Energy depletion (% of GNI)	0.0	8.0	5.8
Mineral depletion (% of GNI)	0.1	0.5	0.3
Net forest depletion (% of GNI)	15.2	0.7	0.8
CO_2 damage (% of GNI)	0.3	0.9	1.2
Particulate emission damage (% of GNI)	0.1	0.4	0.6
Adjusted net savings (% of GNI)	5.0	0.6	8.9

Cambodia

Environmental strategy/action plan prepared in **1999**

	Country data	Group data East Asia & Pacific	Low income
Population (millions)	13.4	1,855	2,312
Urban population (% of total)	18.6	39.1	30.4
GDP ($ billions)	4.2	2,033	1,103
GNI per capita, *Atlas* method ($)	300	1,070	440
Agriculture and fisheries			
Land area (1,000 sq. km)	177	15,886	30,456
Agricultural land (% of land area)	30	50	43
Irrigated land (% of crop land)	7.1	..	26.7
Fertilizer consumption (100 grams/ha arable land)	..	2,297	654
Population density, rural (people/sq. km arable land)	292	565	509
Fish catch, total (1,000 metric tons)	413	60,812	16,410
Forests			
Forest area (1,000 sq. km)	93	4,284	7,939
Forest area share of total land area (%)	52.9	27.0	26.1
Annual deforestation (% change, 1990–2000)	0.6	0.2	0.7
Biodiversity			
Mammal species, total known	123		
Mammal species, threatened	24		
Bird species, total breeding	183		
Bird species, threatened	19		
Nationally protected area (% of land area)	18.5	9.2	7.7
Energy			
GDP per unit of energy use (2000 PPP$/kg oil equiv)	..	4.6	4.1
Energy use per capita (kg oil equiv)	..	904	493
Energy from biomass products and waste (% of total)	..	19.6	49.4
Energy imports, net (% of energy use)	..	–4	–6
Electric power consumption per capita (kWh)	..	891	312
Electricity generated by coal (% of total)	..	66.8	47.4
Emissions and pollution			
CO_2 emissions per unit of GDP (kg/2000 PPP$ GDP)	0.0	0.5	0.4
CO_2 emissions per capita (metric tons)	0.0	2.1	0.8
Particulate matter (pop. weighted average, µg/cu. m)	69	69	63
Passenger cars (per 1,000 people)	312	10	..
Water and sanitation			
Internal freshwater resources per capita (cu. m)	9,027	5,103	3,583
Freshwater withdrawal			
Total (% of internal resources)	0.4	8.2	11.5
Agriculture (% of total freshwater withdrawal)	94	81	92
Access to improved water source (% of total population)	34	78	75
Rural (% of rural population)	29	69	70
Urban (% of urban population)	58	92	89
Access to sanitation (% of total population)	16	49	36
Rural (% of rural population)	8	35	24
Urban (% of urban population)	53	71	61
Under-five mortality rate (per 1,000)	140	41	123
National accounting aggregates, 2003			
Gross national savings (% of GNI)	21.0	41.7	23.1
Consumption of fixed capital (% of GNI)	7.8	9.2	8.9
Education expenditure (% of GNI)	2.0	2.3	3.4
Energy depletion (% of GNI)	0.0	3.9	5.8
Mineral depletion (% of GNI)	0.0	0.3	0.3
Net forest depletion (% of GNI)	0.9	0.1	0.8
CO_2 damage (% of GNI)	0.1	1.8	1.2
Particulate emission damage (% of GNI)	0.1	0.8	0.6
Adjusted net savings (% of GNI)	14.2	27.9	8.9

Cameroon

Environmental strategy/action plan prepared in ..

	Country data	Group data Sub-Saharan Africa	Low Income
Population (millions)	16.1	705	2,312
Urban population (% of total)	51.2	36.5	30.4
GDP ($ billions)	12.5	439	1,103
GNI per capita, *Atlas* method ($)	630	500	440
Agriculture and fisheries			
Land area (1,000 sq. km)	465	23,596	30,456
Agricultural land (% of land area)	20	43	43
Irrigated land (% of crop land)	0.5	4.2	26.7
Fertilizer consumption (100 grams/ha arable land)	59	145	654
Population density, rural (people/sq. km arable land)	131	352	509
Fish catch, total (1,000 metric tons)	111	5,191	16,410
Forests			
Forest area (1,000 sq. km)	239	6,435	7,939
Forest area share of total land area (%)	51.3	27.3	26.1
Annual deforestation (% change, 1990–2000)	0.9	0.8	0.7
Biodiversity			
Mammal species, total known	409		
Mammal species, threatened	40		
Bird species, total breeding	165		
Bird species, threatened	15		
Nationally protected area (% of land area)	4.5	8.7	7.7
Energy			
GDP per unit of energy use (2000 PPP$/kg oil equiv)	4.7	2.8	4.1
Energy use per capita (kg oil equiv)	417	667	493
Energy from biomass products and waste (% of total)	79.2	57.5	49.4
Energy imports, net (% of energy use)	–83	–56	–6
Electric power consumption per capita (kWh)	161	457	312
Electricity generated by coal (% of total)	..	68.2	47.4
Emissions and pollution			
CO_2 emissions per unit of GDP (kg/2000 PPP$ GDP)	0.2	0.4	0.4
CO_2 emissions per capita (metric tons)	0.4	0.7	0.8
Particulate matter (pop. weighted average, µg/cu. m)	85	54	63
Passenger cars (per 1,000 people)	..	..	..
Water and sanitation			
Internal freshwater resources per capita (cu. m)	16,970	5,546	3,583
Freshwater withdrawal			
Total (% of internal resources)	0.1	1.8	11.5
Agriculture (% of total freshwater withdrawal)	35	85	92
Access to improved water source (% of total population)	63	58	75
Rural (% of rural population)	41	46	70
Urban (% of urban population)	84	82	89
Access to sanitation (% of total population)	48	36	36
Rural (% of rural population)	33	26	24
Urban (% of urban population)	63	55	61
Under-five mortality rate (per 1,000)	166	171	123
National accounting aggregates, 2003			
Gross national savings (% of GNI)	11.9	16.9	23.1
Consumption of fixed capital (% of GNI)	9.2	10.6	8.9
Education expenditure (% of GNI)	2.3	4.7	3.4
Energy depletion (% of GNI)	5.2	8.0	5.8
Mineral depletion (% of GNI)	0.0	0.5	0.3
Net forest depletion (% of GNI)	0.0	0.7	0.8
CO_2 damage (% of GNI)	0.5	0.9	1.2
Particulate emission damage (% of GNI)	0.7	0.4	0.6
Adjusted net savings (% of GNI)	–1.4	0.6	8.9

Canada

Environmental strategy/action plan prepared in **1990**

	Country data	High income
		Group data
Population (millions)	31.6	972
Urban population (% of total)	79.3	79.9
GDP ($ billions)	857	29,341
GNI per capita, *Atlas* method ($)	24,470	28,600
Agriculture and fisheries		
Land area (1,000 sq. km)	9,221	31,030
Agricultural land (% of land area)	8	36
Irrigated land (% of crop land)	1.7	12.3
Fertilizer consumption (100 grams/ha arable land)	571	1,198
Population density, rural (people/sq. km arable land)	14	202
Fish catch, total (1,000 metric tons)	1,202	28,712
Forests		
Forest area (1,000 sq. km)	2,446	7,929
Forest area share of total land area (%)	26.5	25.9
Annual deforestation (% change, 1990–2000)	0.0	–0.1
Biodiversity		
Mammal species, total known	193	
Mammal species, threatened	14	
Bird species, total breeding	310	
Bird species, threatened	8	
Nationally protected area (% of land area)	11.1	19.5
Energy		
GDP per unit of energy use (2000 PPP$/kg oil equiv)	3.6	5.2
Energy use per capita (kg oil equiv)	7,973	5,395
Energy from biomass products and waste (% of total)	4.5	3.1
Energy imports, net (% of energy use)	–54	26
Electric power consumption per capita (kWh)	15,613	8,693
Electricity generated by coal (% of total)	19.5	38.2
Emissions and pollution		
CO_2 emissions per unit of GDP (kg/2000 PPP$ GDP)	0.5	0.5
CO_2 emissions per capita (metric tons)	14.2	12.4
Particulate matter (pop. weighted average, µg/cu. m)	22	33
Passenger cars (per 1,000 people)	559	436
Water and sanitation		
Internal freshwater resources per capita (cu. m)	90,104	9,479
Freshwater withdrawal		
Total (% of internal resources)	1.6	9.7
Agriculture (% of total freshwater withdrawal)	12	42
Access to improved water source (% of total population)	100	99
Rural (% of rural population)	99	98
Urban (% of urban population)	100	100
Access to sanitation (% of total population)	100	..
Rural (% of rural population)	99	..
Urban (% of urban population)	100	..
Under-five mortality rate (per 1,000)	7	7
National accounting aggregates, 2003		
Gross national savings (% of GNI)	20.5	19.1
Consumption of fixed capital (% of GNI)	13.0	13.2
Education expenditure (% of GNI)	6.9	4.6
Energy depletion (% of GNI)	4.7	0.8
Mineral depletion (% of GNI)	0.1	0.0
Net forest depletion (% of GNI)	0.0	0.0
CO_2 damage (% of GNI)	0.4	0.3
Particulate emission damage (% of GNI)	0.2	0.3
Adjusted net savings (% of GNI)	9.0	9.2

Cape Verde

Environmental strategy/action plan prepared in ..

	Country data	Group data	
		Sub-Saharan Africa	Lower middle income
Population (millions)	0.5	705	2,655
Urban population (% of total)	65.7	36.5	49.8
GDP ($ billions)	0.8	439	4,168
GNI per capita, *Atlas* method ($)	1,440	500	1,490
Agriculture and fisheries			
Land area (1,000 sq. km)	4	23,596	56,103
Agricultural land (% of land area)	16	43	35
Irrigated land (% of crop land)	6.7	4.2	20.8
Fertilizer consumption (100 grams/ha arable land)	52	145	1,170
Population density, rural (people/sq. km arable land)	387	352	497
Fish catch, total (1,000 metric tons)	10	5,191	74,407
Forests			
Forest area (1,000 sq. km)	1	6,435	20,316
Forest area share of total land area (%)	21.1	27.3	36.2
Annual deforestation (% change, 1990–2000)	–9.3	0.8	0.1
Biodiversity			
Mammal species, total known	..		
Mammal species, threatened	3		
Bird species, total breeding	..		
Bird species, threatened	2		
Nationally protected area (% of land area)	..	8.7	7.7
Energy			
GDP per unit of energy use (2000 PPP$/kg oil equiv)	..	2.8	4.1
Energy use per capita (kg oil equiv)	..	667	1,227
Energy from biomass products and waste (% of total)	..	57.5	12.3
Energy imports, net (% of energy use)	..	–56	–22
Electric power consumption per capita (kWh)	..	457	1,289
Electricity generated by coal (% of total)	..	68.2	42.8
Emissions and pollution			
CO_2 emissions per unit of GDP (kg/2000 PPP$ GDP)	0.1	0.4	0.6
CO_2 emissions per capita (metric tons)	0.3	0.7	2.9
Particulate matter (pop. weighted average, µg/cu. m)	..	54	49
Passenger cars (per 1,000 people)	..	..	28
Water and sanitation			
Internal freshwater resources per capita (cu. m)	655	5,546	8,397
Freshwater withdrawal			
Total (% of internal resources)	..	1.8	5.9
Agriculture (% of total freshwater withdrawal)	88	85	74
Access to improved water source (% of total population)	80	58	82
Rural (% of rural population)	73	46	71
Urban (% of urban population)	86	82	94
Access to sanitation (% of total population)	42	36	60
Rural (% of rural population)	19	26	41
Urban (% of urban population)	61	55	80
Under-five mortality rate (per 1,000)	35	171	39
National accounting aggregates, 2003			
Gross national savings (% of GNI)	8.8	16.9	30.6
Consumption of fixed capital (% of GNI)	9.9	10.6	9.8
Education expenditure (% of GNI)	3.9	4.7	3.2
Energy depletion (% of GNI)	0.0	8.0	8.1
Mineral depletion (% of GNI)	0.0	0.5	0.4
Net forest depletion (% of GNI)	0.0	0.7	0.1
CO_2 damage (% of GNI)	0.1	0.9	1.6
Particulate emission damage (% of GNI)	..	0.4	0.7
Adjusted net savings (% of GNI)	2.7	0.6	13.2

Cayman Islands

Environmental strategy/action plan prepared in **1990**

	Country data	Group data — High income
Population (millions)	0.0	972
Urban population (% of total)	100.0	79.9
GDP ($ billions)	..	29,341
GNI per capita, *Atlas* method ($)	..	28,600
Agriculture and fisheries		
Land area (1,000 sq. km)	0	31,030
Agricultural land (% of land area)	12	36
Irrigated land (% of crop land)	..	12.3
Fertilizer consumption (100 grams/ha arable land)	..	1,198
Population density, rural (people/sq. km arable land)	..	202
Fish catch, total (1,000 metric tons)	0	28,712
Forests		
Forest area (1,000 sq. km)	0	7,929
Forest area share of total land area (%)	50.0	25.9
Annual deforestation (% change, 1990–2000)	0.0	–0.1
Biodiversity		
Mammal species, total known	..	
Mammal species, threatened	0	
Bird species, total breeding	..	
Bird species, threatened	1	
Nationally protected area (% of land area)	..	19.5
Energy		
GDP per unit of energy use (2000 PPP$/kg oil equiv)	..	5.2
Energy use per capita (kg oil equiv)	..	5,395
Energy from biomass products and waste (% of total)	..	3.1
Energy imports, net (% of energy use)	..	26
Electric power consumption per capita (kWh)	..	8,693
Electricity generated by coal (% of total)	..	38.2
Emissions and pollution		
CO_2 emissions per unit of GDP (kg/2000 PPP$ GDP)	..	0.5
CO_2 emissions per capita (metric tons)	..	12.4
Particulate matter (pop. weighted average, µg/cu. m)	33	33
Passenger cars (per 1,000 people)	..	436
Water and sanitation		
Internal freshwater resources per capita (cu. m)	..	9,479
Freshwater withdrawal		
Total (% of internal resources)	..	9.7
Agriculture (% of total freshwater withdrawal)	..	42
Access to improved water source (% of total population)	..	99
Rural (% of rural population)	..	98
Urban (% of urban population)	..	100
Access to sanitation (% of total population)	..	..
Rural (% of rural population)	..	..
Urban (% of urban population)	..	..
Under-five mortality rate (per 1,000)	..	7
National accounting aggregates, 2003		
Gross national savings (% of GNI)	..	19.1
Consumption of fixed capital (% of GNI)	..	13.2
Education expenditure (% of GNI)	..	4.6
Energy depletion (% of GNI)	..	0.8
Mineral depletion (% of GNI)	..	0.0
Net forest depletion (% of GNI)	..	0.0
CO_2 damage (% of GNI)	..	0.3
Particulate emission damage (% of GNI)	..	0.3
Adjusted net savings (% of GNI)	..	9.2

Central African Republic

Environmental strategy/action plan prepared in ..

	Country data	Group data Sub-Saharan Africa	Group data Low Income
Population (millions)	3.9	705	2,312
Urban population (% of total)	42.7	36.5	30.4
GDP ($ billions)	1.2	439	1,103
GNI per capita, *Atlas* method ($)	260	500	440
Agriculture and fisheries			
Land area (1,000 sq. km)	623	23,596	30,456
Agricultural land (% of land area)	8	43	43
Irrigated land (% of crop land)	..	4.2	26.7
Fertilizer consumption (100 grams/ha arable land)	3	145	654
Population density, rural (people/sq. km arable land)	114	352	509
Fish catch, total (1,000 metric tons)	15	5,191	16,410
Forests			
Forest area (1,000 sq. km)	229	6,435	7,939
Forest area share of total land area (%)	36.8	27.3	26.1
Annual deforestation (% change, 1990–2000)	0.1	0.8	0.7
Biodiversity			
Mammal species, total known	209		
Mammal species, threatened	14		
Bird species, total breeding	168		
Bird species, threatened	3		
Nationally protected area (% of land area)	8.7	8.7	7.7
Energy			
GDP per unit of energy use (2000 PPP$/kg oil equiv)	..	2.8	4.1
Energy use per capita (kg oil equiv)	..	667	493
Energy from biomass products and waste (% of total)	..	57.5	49.4
Energy imports, net (% of energy use)	..	−56	−6
Electric power consumption per capita (kWh)	..	457	312
Electricity generated by coal (% of total)	..	68.2	47.4
Emissions and pollution			
CO_2 emissions per unit of GDP (kg/2000 PPP$ GDP)	0.1	0.4	0.4
CO_2 emissions per capita (metric tons)	0.1	0.7	0.8
Particulate matter (pop. weighted average, µg/cu. m)	49	54	63
Passenger cars (per 1,000 people)	..	..	..
Water and sanitation			
Internal freshwater resources per capita (cu. m)	36,332	5,546	3,583
Freshwater withdrawal			
Total (% of internal resources)	0.1	1.8	11.5
Agriculture (% of total freshwater withdrawal)	74	85	92
Access to improved water source (% of total population)	75	58	75
Rural (% of rural population)	61	46	70
Urban (% of urban population)	93	82	89
Access to sanitation (% of total population)	27	36	36
Rural (% of rural population)	12	26	24
Urban (% of urban population)	47	55	61
Under-five mortality rate (per 1,000)	180	171	123
National accounting aggregates, 2003			
Gross national savings (% of GNI)	11.6	16.9	23.1
Consumption of fixed capital (% of GNI)	7.5	10.6	8.9
Education expenditure (% of GNI)	1.6	4.7	3.4
Energy depletion (% of GNI)	0.0	8.0	5.8
Mineral depletion (% of GNI)	0.0	0.5	0.3
Net forest depletion (% of GNI)	0.0	0.7	0.8
CO_2 damage (% of GNI)	0.1	0.9	1.2
Particulate emission damage (% of GNI)	0.4	0.4	0.6
Adjusted net savings (% of GNI)	5.2	0.6	8.9

Chad

Environmental strategy/action plan prepared in **1990**

	Country data	Group data Sub-Saharan Africa	Low Income
Population (millions)	8.6	705	2,312
Urban population (% of total)	25.0	36.5	30.4
GDP ($ billions)	2.6	439	1,103
GNI per capita, *Atlas* method ($)	240	500	440
Agriculture and fisheries			
Land area (1,000 sq. km)	1,259	23,596	30,456
Agricultural land (% of land area)	39	43	43
Irrigated land (% of crop land)	0.6	4.2	26.7
Fertilizer consumption (100 grams/ha arable land)	49	145	654
Population density, rural (people/sq. km arable land)	175	352	509
Fish catch, total (1,000 metric tons)	84	5,191	16,410
Forests			
Forest area (1,000 sq. km)	127	6,435	7,939
Forest area share of total land area (%)	10.1	27.3	26.1
Annual deforestation (% change, 1990–2000)	0.6	0.8	0.7
Biodiversity			
Mammal species, total known	134		
Mammal species, threatened	17		
Bird species, total breeding	141		
Bird species, threatened	5		
Nationally protected area (% of land area)	9.1	8.7	7.7
Energy			
GDP per unit of energy use (2000 PPP$/kg oil equiv)	..	2.8	4.1
Energy use per capita (kg oil equiv)	..	667	493
Energy from biomass products and waste (% of total)	..	57.5	49.4
Energy imports, net (% of energy use)	..	−56	−6
Electric power consumption per capita (kWh)	..	457	312
Electricity generated by coal (% of total)	..	68.2	47.4
Emissions and pollution			
CO_2 emissions per unit of GDP (kg/2000 PPP$ GDP)	0.0	0.4	0.4
CO_2 emissions per capita (metric tons)	0.0	0.7	0.8
Particulate matter (pop. weighted average, μg/cu. m)	161	54	63
Passenger cars (per 1,000 people)	..	..	..
Water and sanitation			
Internal freshwater resources per capita (cu. m)	1,748	5,546	3,583
Freshwater withdrawal			
Total (% of internal resources)	1.3	1.8	11.5
Agriculture (% of total freshwater withdrawal)	82	85	92
Access to improved water source (% of total population)	34	58	75
Rural (% of rural population)	32	46	70
Urban (% of urban population)	40	82	89
Access to sanitation (% of total population)	8	36	36
Rural (% of rural population)	0	26	24
Urban (% of urban population)	30	55	61
Under-five mortality rate (per 1,000)	200	171	123
National accounting aggregates, 2003			
Gross national savings (% of GNI)	11.9	16.9	23.1
Consumption of fixed capital (% of GNI)	8.3	10.6	8.9
Education expenditure (% of GNI)	1.4	4.7	3.4
Energy depletion (% of GNI)	0.0	8.0	5.8
Mineral depletion (% of GNI)	0.0	0.5	0.3
Net forest depletion (% of GNI)	0.0	0.7	0.8
CO_2 damage (% of GNI)	0.0	0.9	1.2
Particulate emission damage (% of GNI)	..	0.4	0.6
Adjusted net savings (% of GNI)	5.1	0.6	8.9

Channel Islands

Environmental strategy/action plan prepared in ..

	Country data	Group data — High Income
Population (millions)	0.1	972
Urban population (% of total)	29.0	79.9
GDP ($ billions)	..	29,341
GNI per capita, *Atlas* method ($)	..	28,600
Agriculture and fisheries		
Land area (1,000 sq. km)	0	31,030
Agricultural land (% of land area)	..	36
Irrigated land (% of crop land)	..	12.3
Fertilizer consumption (100 grams/ha arable land)	..	1,198
Population density, rural (people/sq. km arable land)	..	202
Fish catch, total (1,000 metric tons)	..	28,712
Forests		
Forest area (1,000 sq. km)	..	7,929
Forest area share of total land area (%)	..	25.9
Annual deforestation (% change, 1990–2000)	..	–0.1
Biodiversity		
Mammal species, total known	..	
Mammal species, threatened	..	
Bird species, total breeding	..	
Bird species, threatened	..	
Nationally protected area (% of land area)	..	19.5
Energy		
GDP per unit of energy use (2000 PPP$/kg oil equiv)	..	5.2
Energy use per capita (kg oil equiv)	..	5,395
Energy from biomass products and waste (% of total)	..	3.1
Energy imports, net (% of energy use)	..	26
Electric power consumption per capita (kWh)	..	8,693
Electricity generated by coal (% of total)	..	38.2
Emissions and pollution		
CO_2 emissions per unit of GDP (kg/2000 PPP$ GDP)	..	0.5
CO_2 emissions per capita (metric tons)	..	12.4
Particulate matter (pop. weighted average, µg/cu. m)	..	33
Passenger cars (per 1,000 people)	..	436
Water and sanitation		
Internal freshwater resources per capita (cu. m)		9,479
Freshwater withdrawal		
Total (% of internal resources)	..	9.7
Agriculture (% of total freshwater withdrawal)	..	42
Access to improved water source (% of total population)	..	99
Rural (% of rural population)	..	98
Urban (% of urban population)	..	100
Access to sanitation (% of total population)	..	..
Rural (% of rural population)	..	..
Urban (% of urban population)	..	..
Under-five mortality rate (per 1,000)	..	7
National accounting aggregates, 2003		
Gross national savings (% of GNI)	..	19.1
Consumption of fixed capital (% of GNI)	..	13.2
Education expenditure (% of GNI)	..	4.6
Energy depletion (% of GNI)	..	0.8
Mineral depletion (% of GNI)	..	0.0
Net forest depletion (% of GNI)	..	0.0
CO_2 damage (% of GNI)	..	0.3
Particulate emission damage (% of GNI)	..	0.3
Adjusted net savings (% of GNI)	..	9.2

Chile

Environmental strategy/action plan prepared in ..

	Country data	Group data Latin America & Caribbean	Upper middle income
Population (millions)	15.8	533	333
Urban population (% of total)	86.6	76.6	75.4
GDP ($ billions)	72.4	1,741	1,856
GNI per capita, *Atlas* method ($)	4,360	3,280	5,440
Agriculture and fisheries			
Land area (1,000 sq. km)	749	20,057	12,741
Agricultural land (% of land area)	20	39	48
Irrigated land (% of crop land)	82.4	12.5	13.5
Fertilizer consumption (100 grams/ha arable land)	2,296	892	796
Population density, rural (people/sq. km arable land)	108	210	193
Fish catch, total (1,000 metric tons)	4,363	17,804	10,082
Forests			
Forest area (1,000 sq. km)	155	9,552	2,427
Forest area share of total land area (%)	20.7	47.6	19.1
Annual deforestation (% change, 1990–2000)	0.1	0.5	0.6
Biodiversity			
Mammal species, total known	91		
Mammal species, threatened	21		
Bird species, total breeding	157		
Bird species, threatened	22		
Nationally protected area (% of land area)	18.9	11.2	17.3
Energy			
GDP per unit of energy use (2000 PPP$/kg oil equiv)	6.0	6.1	4.3
Energy use per capita (kg oil equiv)	1,585	1,156	2,232
Energy from biomass products and waste (% of total)	17.4	14.6	4.1
Energy imports, net (% of energy use)	64	–42	–91
Electric power consumption per capita (kWh)	2,617	1,506	2,496
Electricity generated by coal (% of total)	19.0	5.0	23.9
Emissions and pollution			
CO_2 emissions per unit of GDP (kg/2000 PPP$ GDP)	0.4	0.4	0.6
CO_2 emissions per capita (metric tons)	3.9	2.7	6.3
Particulate matter (pop. weighted average, µg/cu. m)	65	40	29
Passenger cars (per 1,000 people)	87	..	153
Water and sanitation			
Internal freshwater resources per capita (cu. m)	56,042	25,245	10,741
Freshwater withdrawal			
Total (% of internal resources)	2.3	2.0	5.7
Agriculture (% of total freshwater withdrawal)	84	74	71
Access to improved water source (% of total population)	95	89	..
Rural (% of rural population)	59	69	..
Urban (% of urban population)	100	96	96
Access to sanitation (% of total population)	92	74	..
Rural (% of rural population)	64	44	..
Urban (% of urban population)	96	84	..
Under-five mortality rate (per 1,000)	9	33	22
National accounting aggregates, 2003			
Gross national savings (% of GNI)	24.5	19.5	22.1
Consumption of fixed capital (% of GNI)	10.1	10.3	10.7
Education expenditure (% of GNI)	3.8	4.2	5.0
Energy depletion (% of GNI)	0.4	6.4	11.4
Mineral depletion (% of GNI)	5.9	0.7	0.3
Net forest depletion (% of GNI)	0.0	0.0	0.0
CO_2 damage (% of GNI)	0.6	0.5	0.8
Particulate emission damage (% of GNI)	1.0	0.5	0.6
Adjusted net savings (% of GNI)	10.3	5.3	3.3

China

Environmental strategy/action plan prepared in **1994**

	Country data	Group data — East Asia & Pacific	Group data — Lower middle income
Population (millions)	1,288.4	1,855	2,655
Urban population (% of total)	38.7	39.1	49.8
GDP ($ billions)	1,417.0	2,033	4,168
GNI per capita, *Atlas* method ($)	1,100	1,070	1,490
Agriculture and fisheries			
Land area (1,000 sq. km)	9,327	15,886	56,103
Agricultural land (% of land area)	60	50	35
Irrigated land (% of crop land)	35.7	..	20.8
Fertilizer consumption (100 grams/ha arable land)	2,777	2,297	1,170
Population density, rural (people/sq. km arable land)	559	565	497
Fish catch, total (1,000 metric tons)	44,100	60,812	74,407
Forests			
Forest area (1,000 sq. km)	1,635	4,284	20,316
Forest area share of total land area (%)	17.5	27.0	36.2
Annual deforestation (% change, 1990–2000)	–1.2	0.2	0.1
Biodiversity			
Mammal species, total known	394		
Mammal species, threatened	79		
Bird species, total breeding	618		
Bird species, threatened	74		
Nationally protected area (% of land area)	7.8	9.2	7.7
Energy			
GDP per unit of energy use (2000 PPP$/kg oil equiv)	4.6	4.6	4.1
Energy use per capita (kg oil equiv)	960	904	1,227
Energy from biomass products and waste (% of total)	17.7	19.6	12.3
Energy imports, net (% of energy use)	1	–4	–22
Electric power consumption per capita (kWh)	987	891	1,289
Electricity generated by coal (% of total)	77.5	66.8	42.8
Emissions and pollution			
CO_2 emissions per unit of GDP (kg/2000 PPP$ GDP)	0.6	0.5	0.6
CO_2 emissions per capita (metric tons)	2.2	2.1	2.9
Particulate matter (pop. weighted average, μg/cu. m)	87	69	49
Passenger cars (per 1,000 people)	7	10	28
Water and sanitation			
Internal freshwater resources per capita (cu. m)	2,183	5,103	8,397
Freshwater withdrawal			
Total (% of internal resources)	18.7	8.2	5.9
Agriculture (% of total freshwater withdrawal)	78	81	74
Access to improved water source (% of total population)	77	78	82
Rural (% of rural population)	68	69	71
Urban (% of urban population)	92	92	94
Access to sanitation (% of total population)	44	49	60
Rural (% of rural population)	29	35	41
Urban (% of urban population)	69	71	80
Under-five mortality rate (per 1,000)	37	41	39
National accounting aggregates, 2003			
Gross national savings (% of GNI)	47.8	41.7	30.6
Consumption of fixed capital (% of GNI)	9.2	9.2	9.8
Education expenditure (% of GNI)	2.0	2.3	3.2
Energy depletion (% of GNI)	2.9	3.9	8.1
Mineral depletion (% of GNI)	0.2	0.3	0.4
Net forest depletion (% of GNI)	0.0	0.1	0.1
CO_2 damage (% of GNI)	2.2	1.8	1.6
Particulate emission damage (% of GNI)	1.0	0.8	0.7
Adjusted net savings (% of GNI)	34.4	27.9	13.2

Colombia

Environmental strategy/action plan prepared in **1998**

	Country data	Group data	
		Latin America & Caribbean	Lower middle income
Population (millions)	44.6	533	2,655
Urban population (% of total)	76.5	76.6	49.8
GDP ($ billions)	78.7	1,741	4,168
GNI per capita, *Atlas* method ($)	1,810	3,280	1,490
Agriculture and fisheries			
Land area (1,000 sq. km)	1,039	20,057	56,103
Agricultural land (% of land area)	44	39	35
Irrigated land (% of crop land)	23.4	12.5	20.8
Fertilizer consumption (100 grams/ha arable land)	3,016	892	1,170
Population density, rural (people/sq. km arable land)	459	210	497
Fish catch, total (1,000 metric tons)	190	17,804	74,407
Forests			
Forest area (1,000 sq. km)	496	9,552	20,316
Forest area share of total land area (%)	47.8	47.6	36.2
Annual deforestation (% change, 1990–2000)	0.4	0.5	0.1
Biodiversity			
Mammal species, total known	359		
Mammal species, threatened	41		
Bird species, total breeding	708		
Bird species, threatened	78		
Nationally protected area (% of land area)	10.2	11.2	7.7
Energy			
GDP per unit of energy use (2000 PPP$/kg oil equiv)	9.8	6.1	4.1
Energy use per capita (kg oil equiv)	625	1,156	1,227
Energy from biomass products and waste (% of total)	18.0	14.6	12.3
Energy imports, net (% of energy use)	–164	–42	–22
Electric power consumption per capita (kWh)	817	1,506	1,289
Electricity generated by coal (% of total)	6.7	5.0	42.8
Emissions and pollution			
CO_2 emissions per unit of GDP (kg/2000 PPP$ GDP)	0.2	0.4	0.6
CO_2 emissions per capita (metric tons)	1.4	2.7	2.9
Particulate matter (pop. weighted average, µg/cu. m)	25	40	49
Passenger cars (per 1,000 people)	43	..	28
Water and sanitation			
Internal freshwater resources per capita (cu. m)	47,371	25,245	8,397
Freshwater withdrawal			
Total (% of internal resources)	0.4	2.0	5.9
Agriculture (% of total freshwater withdrawal)	37	74	74
Access to improved water source (% of total population)	92	89	82
Rural (% of rural population)	71	69	71
Urban (% of urban population)	99	96	94
Access to sanitation (% of total population)	86	74	60
Rural (% of rural population)	54	44	41
Urban (% of urban population)	96	84	80
Under-five mortality rate (per 1,000)	21	33	39
National accounting aggregates, 2003			
Gross national savings (% of GNI)	14.6	19.5	30.6
Consumption of fixed capital (% of GNI)	10.2	10.3	9.8
Education expenditure (% of GNI)	3.1	4.2	3.2
Energy depletion (% of GNI)	7.7	6.4	8.1
Mineral depletion (% of GNI)	0.3	0.7	0.4
Net forest depletion (% of GNI)	0.0	0.0	0.1
CO_2 damage (% of GNI)	0.6	0.5	1.6
Particulate emission damage (% of GNI)	0.1	0.5	0.7
Adjusted net savings (% of GNI)	–1.1	5.3	13.2

Comoros

Environmental strategy/action plan prepared in ..

	Country data	Group data Sub-Saharan Africa	Group data Low Income
Population (millions)	0.6	705	2,312
Urban population (% of total)	35.0	36.5	30.4
GDP ($ billions)	0.3	439	1,103
GNI per capita, *Atlas* method ($)	450	500	440
Agriculture and fisheries			
Land area (1,000 sq. km)	2	23,596	30,456
Agricultural land (% of land area)	66	43	43
Irrigated land (% of crop land)	..	4.2	26.7
Fertilizer consumption (100 grams/ha arable land)	38	145	654
Population density, rural (people/sq. km arable land)	480	352	509
Fish catch, total (1,000 metric tons)	12	5,191	16,410
Forests			
Forest area (1,000 sq. km)	0	6,435	7,939
Forest area share of total land area (%)	3.6	27.3	26.1
Annual deforestation (% change, 1990–2000)	4.0	0.8	0.7
Biodiversity			
Mammal species, total known	..		
Mammal species, threatened	2		
Bird species, total breeding	..		
Bird species, threatened	9		
Nationally protected area (% of land area)	..	8.7	7.7
Energy			
GDP per unit of energy use (2000 PPP$/kg oil equiv)	..	2.8	4.1
Energy use per capita (kg oil equiv)	..	667	493
Energy from biomass products and waste (% of total)	..	57.5	49.4
Energy imports, net (% of energy use)	..	−56	−6
Electric power consumption per capita (kWh)	..	457	312
Electricity generated by coal (% of total)	..	68.2	47.4
Emissions and pollution			
CO_2 emissions per unit of GDP (kg/2000 PPP$ GDP)	0.1	0.4	0.4
CO_2 emissions per capita (metric tons)	0.1	0.7	0.8
Particulate matter (pop. weighted average, µg/cu. m)	51	54	63
Passenger cars (per 1,000 people)	..	..	..
Water and sanitation			
Internal freshwater resources per capita (cu. m)	1,707	5,546	3,583
Freshwater withdrawal			
Total (% of internal resources)	..	1.8	11.5
Agriculture (% of total freshwater withdrawal)	..	85	92
Access to improved water source (% of total population)	94	58	75
Rural (% of rural population)	96	46	70
Urban (% of urban population)	90	82	89
Access to sanitation (% of total population)	23	36	36
Rural (% of rural population)	15	26	24
Urban (% of urban population)	38	55	61
Under-five mortality rate (per 1,000)	73	171	123
National accounting aggregates, 2003			
Gross national savings (% of GNI)	0.7	16.9	23.1
Consumption of fixed capital (% of GNI)	8.2	10.6	8.9
Education expenditure (% of GNI)	4.2	4.7	3.4
Energy depletion (% of GNI)	0.0	8.0	5.8
Mineral depletion (% of GNI)	0.0	0.5	0.3
Net forest depletion (% of GNI)	0.0	0.7	0.8
CO_2 damage (% of GNI)	0.2	0.9	1.2
Particulate emission damage (% of GNI)	..	0.4	0.6
Adjusted net savings (% of GNI)	−3.4	0.6	8.9

Congo, Dem. Rep.

Environmental strategy/action plan prepared in ..

	Country data	Group data		
		Sub-Saharan Africa	Low income	
Population (millions)	53.2	705	2,312
Urban population (% of total)	..	36.5	30.4
GDP ($ billions)	5.7	439	1,103
GNI per capita, *Atlas* method ($)	100	500	440

Agriculture and fisheries

Land area (1,000 sq. km)	2,267	23,596	30,456
Agricultural land (% of land area)	10	43	43
Irrigated land (% of crop land)	0.1	4.2	26.7
Fertilizer consumption (100 grams/ha arable land)	16	145	654
Population density, rural (people/sq. km arable land)	..	352	509
Fish catch, total (1,000 metric tons)	209	5,191	16,410

Forests

Forest area (1,000 sq. km)	1,352	6,435	7,939
Forest area share of total land area (%)	59.6	27.3	26.1
Annual deforestation (% change, 1990–2000)	0.4	0.8	0.7

Biodiversity

Mammal species, total known	200		
Mammal species, threatened	15		
Bird species, total breeding	130		
Bird species, threatened	3		
Nationally protected area (% of land area)	5.0	8.7	7.7

Energy

GDP per unit of energy use (2000 PPP$/kg oil equiv)	2.2	2.8	4.1
Energy use per capita (kg oil equiv)	299	667	493
Energy from biomass products and waste (% of total)	93.6	57.5	49.4
Energy imports, net (% of energy use)	–5	–56	–6
Electric power consumption per capita (kWh)	43	457	312
Electricity generated by coal (% of total)	..	68.2	47.4

Emissions and pollution

CO_2 emissions per unit of GDP (kg/2000 PPP$ GDP)	0.1	0.4	0.4
CO_2 emissions per capita (metric tons)	0.1	0.7	0.8
Particulate matter (pop. weighted average, µg/cu. m)	51	54	63
Passenger cars (per 1,000 people)	..	..	..

Water and sanitation

Internal freshwater resources per capita (cu. m)	16,932	5,546	3,583
Freshwater withdrawal			
Total (% of internal resources)	0.0	1.8	11.5
Agriculture (% of total freshwater withdrawal)	23	85	92
Access to improved water source (% of total population)	46	58	75
Rural (% of rural population)	29	46	70
Urban (% of urban population)	83	82	89
Access to sanitation (% of total population)	29	36	36
Rural (% of rural population)	23	26	24
Urban (% of urban population)	43	55	61
Under-five mortality rate (per 1,000)	205	171	123

National accounting aggregates, 2003

Gross national savings (% of GNI)	..	16.9	23.1
Consumption of fixed capital (% of GNI)	6.6	10.6	8.9
Education expenditure (% of GNI)	0.9	4.7	3.4
Energy depletion (% of GNI)	2.2	8.0	5.8
Mineral depletion (% of GNI)	0.0	0.5	0.3
Net forest depletion (% of GNI)	0.0	0.7	0.8
CO_2 damage (% of GNI)	0.3	0.9	1.2
Particulate emission damage (% of GNI)	0.0	0.4	0.6
Adjusted net savings (% of GNI)	..	0.6	8.9

Congo, Rep.

Environmental strategy/action plan prepared in ..

	Country data	Sub-Saharan Africa	Low Income
		Group data	
Population (millions)	3.8	705	2,312
Urban population (% of total)	67.3	36.5	30.4
GDP ($ billions)	3.6	439	1,103
GNI per capita, *Atlas* method ($)	650	500	440
Agriculture and fisheries			
Land area (1,000 sq. km)	342	23,596	30,456
Agricultural land (% of land area)	30	43	43
Irrigated land (% of crop land)	0.4	4.2	26.7
Fertilizer consumption (100 grams/ha arable land)	12	145	654
Population density, rural (people/sq. km arable land)	642	352	509
Fish catch, total (1,000 metric tons)	42	5,191	16,410
Forests			
Forest area (1,000 sq. km)	221	6,435	7,939
Forest area share of total land area (%)	64.6	27.3	26.1
Annual deforestation (% change, 1990–2000)	0.1	0.8	0.7
Biodiversity			
Mammal species, total known	450		
Mammal species, threatened	40		
Bird species, total breeding	345		
Bird species, threatened	28		
Nationally protected area (% of land area)	6.5	8.7	7.7
Energy			
GDP per unit of energy use (2000 PPP$/kg oil equiv)	3.7	2.8	4.1
Energy use per capita (kg oil equiv)	252	667	493
Energy from biomass products and waste (% of total)	67.3	57.5	49.4
Energy imports, net (% of energy use)	–1,330	–56	–6
Electric power consumption per capita (kWh)	82	457	312
Electricity generated by coal (% of total)	..	68.2	47.4
Emissions and pollution			
CO_2 emissions per unit of GDP (kg/2000 PPP$ GDP)	0.5	0.4	0.4
CO_2 emissions per capita (metric tons)	0.5	0.7	0.8
Particulate matter (pop. weighted average, µg/cu. m)	90	54	63
Passenger cars (per 1,000 people)	..	..	..
Water and sanitation			
Internal freshwater resources per capita (cu. m)	59,086	5,546	3,583
Freshwater withdrawal			
Total (% of internal resources)	0.0	1.8	11.5
Agriculture (% of total freshwater withdrawal)	11	85	92
Access to improved water source (% of total population)	46	58	75
Rural (% of rural population)	17	46	70
Urban (% of urban population)	72	82	89
Access to sanitation (% of total population)	9	36	36
Rural (% of rural population)	2	26	24
Urban (% of urban population)	14	55	61
Under-five mortality rate (per 1,000)	108	171	123
National accounting aggregates, 2003			
Gross national savings (% of GNI)	29.8	16.9	23.1
Consumption of fixed capital (% of GNI)	11.9	10.6	8.9
Education expenditure (% of GNI)	5.9	4.7	3.4
Energy depletion (% of GNI)	49.3	8.0	5.8
Mineral depletion (% of GNI)	0.2	0.5	0.3
Net forest depletion (% of GNI)	0.0	0.7	0.8
CO_2 damage (% of GNI)	0.6	0.9	1.2
Particulate emission damage (% of GNI)	..	0.4	0.6
Adjusted net savings (% of GNI)	–26.3	0.6	8.9

Costa Rica

Environmental strategy/action plan prepared in **1990**

	Country data	Latin America & Caribbean	Upper middle income
		Group data	
Population (millions)	4.0	533	333
Urban population (% of total)	60.6	76.6	75.4
GDP ($ billions)	17.4	1,741	1,856
GNI per capita, *Atlas* method ($)	4,300	3,280	5,440
Agriculture and fisheries			
Land area (1,000 sq. km)	51	20,057	12,741
Agricultural land (% of land area)	56	39	48
Irrigated land (% of crop land)	20.6	12.5	13.5
Fertilizer consumption (100 grams/ha arable land)	6,736	892	796
Population density, rural (people/sq. km arable land)	700	210	193
Fish catch, total (1,000 metric tons)	35	17,804	10,082
Forests			
Forest area (1,000 sq. km)	20	9,552	2,427
Forest area share of total land area (%)	38.5	47.6	19.1
Annual deforestation (% change, 1990–2000)	0.8	0.5	0.6
Biodiversity			
Mammal species, total known	205		
Mammal species, threatened	14		
Bird species, total breeding	279		
Bird species, threatened	13		
Nationally protected area (% of land area)	23.0	11.2	17.3
Energy			
GDP per unit of energy use (2000 PPP$/kg oil equiv)	9.4	6.1	4.3
Energy use per capita (kg oil equiv)	904	1,156	2,232
Energy from biomass products and waste (% of total)	7.5	14.6	4.1
Energy imports, net (% of energy use)	51	−42	−91
Electric power consumption per capita (kWh)	1,611	1,506	2,496
Electricity generated by coal (% of total)	..	5.0	23.9
Emissions and pollution			
CO_2 emissions per unit of GDP (kg/2000 PPP$ GDP)	0.2	0.4	0.6
CO_2 emissions per capita (metric tons)	1.4	2.7	6.3
Particulate matter (pop. weighted average, µg/cu. m)	38	40	29
Passenger cars (per 1,000 people)	..	..	153
Water and sanitation			
Internal freshwater resources per capita (cu. m)	27,967	25,245	10,741
Freshwater withdrawal			
Total (% of internal resources)	5.2	2.0	5.7
Agriculture (% of total freshwater withdrawal)	80	74	71
Access to improved water source (% of total population)	97	89	..
Rural (% of rural population)	92	69	..
Urban (% of urban population)	100	96	96
Access to sanitation (% of total population)	92	74	..
Rural (% of rural population)	97	44	..
Urban (% of urban population)	89	84	..
Under-five mortality rate (per 1,000)	10	33	22
National accounting aggregates, 2003			
Gross national savings (% of GNI)	15.3	19.5	22.1
Consumption of fixed capital (% of GNI)	6.0	10.3	10.7
Education expenditure (% of GNI)	4.9	4.2	5.0
Energy depletion (% of GNI)	0.0	6.4	11.4
Mineral depletion (% of GNI)	0.0	0.7	0.3
Net forest depletion (% of GNI)	0.3	0.0	0.0
CO_2 damage (% of GNI)	0.3	0.5	0.8
Particulate emission damage (% of GNI)	0.3	0.5	0.6
Adjusted net savings (% of GNI)	13.4	5.3	3.3

Côte d'Ivoire

Environmental strategy/action plan prepared in **1994**

	Country data	Group data Sub-Saharan Africa	Group data Low Income
Population (millions)	16.8	705	2,312
Urban population (% of total)	44.9	36.5	30.4
GDP ($ billions)	13.7	439	1,103
GNI per capita, *Atlas* method ($)	660	500	440
Agriculture and fisheries			
Land area (1,000 sq. km)	318	23,596	30,456
Agricultural land (% of land area)	64	43	43
Irrigated land (% of crop land)	1.1	4.2	26.7
Fertilizer consumption (100 grams/ha arable land)	352	145	654
Population density, rural (people/sq. km arable land)	296	352	509
Fish catch, total (1,000 metric tons)	75	5,191	16,410
Forests			
Forest area (1,000 sq. km)	71	6,435	7,939
Forest area share of total land area (%)	22.4	27.3	26.1
Annual deforestation (% change, 1990–2000)	3.1	0.8	0.7
Biodiversity			
Mammal species, total known	230		
Mammal species, threatened	19		
Bird species, total breeding	252		
Bird species, threatened	12		
Nationally protected area (% of land area)	6.0	8.7	7.7
Energy			
GDP per unit of energy use (2000 PPP$/kg oil equiv)	3.7	2.8	4.1
Energy use per capita (kg oil equiv)	397	667	493
Energy from biomass products and waste (% of total)	66.0	57.5	49.4
Energy imports, net (% of energy use)	0	−56	−6
Electric power consumption per capita (kWh)	..	457	312
Electricity generated by coal (% of total)	..	68.2	47.4
Emissions and pollution			
CO_2 emissions per unit of GDP (kg/2000 PPP$ GDP)	0.4	0.4	0.4
CO_2 emissions per capita (metric tons)	0.7	0.7	0.8
Particulate matter (pop. weighted average, μg/cu. m)	64	54	63
Passenger cars (per 1,000 people)	..	..	..
Water and sanitation			
Internal freshwater resources per capita (cu. m)	4,574	5,546	3,583
Freshwater withdrawal			
Total (% of internal resources)	0.9	1.8	11.5
Agriculture (% of total freshwater withdrawal)	67	85	92
Access to improved water source (% of total population)	84	58	75
Rural (% of rural population)	74	46	70
Urban (% of urban population)	98	82	89
Access to sanitation (% of total population)	40	36	36
Rural (% of rural population)	23	26	24
Urban (% of urban population)	61	55	61
Under-five mortality rate (per 1,000)	192	171	123
National accounting aggregates, 2003			
Gross national savings (% of GNI)	14.8	16.9	23.1
Consumption of fixed capital (% of GNI)	9.2	10.6	8.9
Education expenditure (% of GNI)	4.5	4.7	3.4
Energy depletion (% of GNI)	2.6	8.0	5.8
Mineral depletion (% of GNI)	0.0	0.5	0.3
Net forest depletion (% of GNI)	0.6	0.7	0.8
CO_2 damage (% of GNI)	0.4	0.9	1.2
Particulate emission damage (% of GNI)	0.6	0.4	0.6
Adjusted net savings (% of GNI)	5.8	0.6	8.9

Croatia

Environmental strategy/action plan prepared in ..

	Country data	Europe & Central Asia	Upper middle income
		Group data	
Population (millions)	4.4	472	333
Urban population (% of total)	59.0	63.8	75.4
GDP ($ billions)	28.8	1,403	1,856
GNI per capita, *Atlas* method ($)	5,370	2,580	5,440
Agriculture and fisheries			
Land area (1,000 sq. km)	56	23,868	12,741
Agricultural land (% of land area)	56	28	48
Irrigated land (% of crop land)	0.3	10.9	13.5
Fertilizer consumption (100 grams/ha arable land)	1,176	344	796
Population density, rural (people/sq. km arable land)	126	122	193
Fish catch, total (1,000 metric tons)	28	5,527	10,082
Forests			
Forest area (1,000 sq. km)	18	9,463	2,427
Forest area share of total land area (%)	31.9	39.6	19.1
Annual deforestation (% change, 1990–2000)	–0.1	–0.1	0.6
Biodiversity			
Mammal species, total known	76		
Mammal species, threatened	9		
Bird species, total breeding	224		
Bird species, threatened	4		
Nationally protected area (% of land area)	7.5	6.8	17.3
Energy			
GDP per unit of energy use (2000 PPP$/kg oil equiv)	5.3	2.5	4.3
Energy use per capita (kg oil equiv)	1,852	2,697	2,232
Energy from biomass products and waste (% of total)	3.6	2.3	4.1
Energy imports, net (% of energy use)	55	–23	–91
Electric power consumption per capita (kWh)	2,855	2,808	2,496
Electricity generated by coal (% of total)	17.3	29.4	23.9
Emissions and pollution			
CO_2 emissions per unit of GDP (kg/2000 PPP$ GDP)	0.5	1.1	0.6
CO_2 emissions per capita (metric tons)	4.5	6.7	6.3
Particulate matter (pop. weighted average, µg/cu. m)	37	33	29
Passenger cars (per 1,000 people)	280	138	153
Water and sanitation			
Internal freshwater resources per capita (cu. m)	8,550	11,128	10,741
Freshwater withdrawal			
Total (% of internal resources)	2.1	7.4	5.7
Agriculture (% of total freshwater withdrawal)	0	57	71
Access to improved water source (% of total population)	..	91	..
Rural (% of rural population)	..	80	..
Urban (% of urban population)	..	98	96
Access to sanitation (% of total population)	..	82	..
Rural (% of rural population)	..	64	..
Urban (% of urban population)	..	93	..
Under-five mortality rate (per 1,000)	7	36	22
National accounting aggregates, 2003			
Gross national savings (% of GNI)	22.2	21.9	22.1
Consumption of fixed capital (% of GNI)	12.0	10.7	10.7
Education expenditure (% of GNI)	..	4.1	5.0
Energy depletion (% of GNI)	1.1	11.6	11.4
Mineral depletion (% of GNI)	0.0	0.1	0.3
Net forest depletion (% of GNI)	0.0	0.0	0.0
CO_2 damage (% of GNI)	0.6	1.9	0.8
Particulate emission damage (% of GNI)	0.3	0.6	0.6
Adjusted net savings (% of GNI)	..	1.1	3.3

Cuba

Environmental strategy/action plan prepared in ..

	Country data	Group data Latin America & Caribbean	Lower middle income
Population (millions)	11.3	533	2,655
Urban population (% of total)	75.9	76.6	49.8
GDP ($ billions)	..	1,741	4,168
GNI per capita, *Atlas* method ($)	..	3,280	1,490
Agriculture and fisheries			
Land area (1,000 sq. km)	110	20,057	56,103
Agricultural land (% of land area)	61	39	35
Irrigated land (% of crop land)	23.0	12.5	20.8
Fertilizer consumption (100 grams/ha arable land)	457	892	1,170
Population density, rural (people/sq. km arable land)	103	210	497
Fish catch, total (1,000 metric tons)	110	17,804	74,407
Forests			
Forest area (1,000 sq. km)	23	9,552	20,316
Forest area share of total land area (%)	21.4	47.6	36.2
Annual deforestation (% change, 1990–2000)	−1.3	0.5	0.1
Biodiversity			
Mammal species, total known	31		
Mammal species, threatened	11		
Bird species, total breeding	86		
Bird species, threatened	18		
Nationally protected area (% of land area)	69.1	11.2	7.7
Energy			
GDP per unit of energy use (2000 PPP$/kg oil equiv)	..	6.1	4.1
Energy use per capita (kg oil equiv)	1,262	1,156	1,227
Energy from biomass products and waste (% of total)	17.1	14.6	12.3
Energy imports, net (% of energy use)	54	−42	−22
Electric power consumption per capita (kWh)	1,094	1,506	1,289
Electricity generated by coal (% of total)	..	5.0	42.8
Emissions and pollution			
CO_2 emissions per unit of GDP (kg/2000 PPP$ GDP)	..	0.4	0.6
CO_2 emissions per capita (metric tons)	2.8	2.7	2.9
Particulate matter (pop. weighted average, µg/cu. m)	25	40	49
Passenger cars (per 1,000 people)	16	..	28
Water and sanitation			
Internal freshwater resources per capita (cu. m)	3,355	25,245	8,397
Freshwater withdrawal			
Total (% of internal resources)	13.7	2.0	5.9
Agriculture (% of total freshwater withdrawal)	51	74	74
Access to improved water source (% of total population)	91	89	82
Rural (% of rural population)	78	69	71
Urban (% of urban population)	95	96	94
Access to sanitation (% of total population)	98	74	60
Rural (% of rural population)	95	44	41
Urban (% of urban population)	99	84	80
Under-five mortality rate (per 1,000)	8	33	39
National accounting aggregates, 2003			
Gross national savings (% of GNI)	..	19.5	30.6
Consumption of fixed capital (% of GNI)	..	10.3	9.8
Education expenditure (% of GNI)	6.1	4.2	3.2
Energy depletion (% of GNI)	..	6.4	8.1
Mineral depletion (% of GNI)	..	0.7	0.4
Net forest depletion (% of GNI)	..	0.0	0.1
CO_2 damage (% of GNI)	..	0.5	1.6
Particulate emission damage (% of GNI)	..	0.5	0.7
Adjusted net savings (% of GNI)	..	5.3	13.2

Cyprus

Environmental strategy/action plan prepared in ..

	Country data	High income
		Group data
Population (millions)	0.8	972
Urban population (% of total)	70.9	79.9
GDP ($ billions)	11	29,341
GNI per capita, *Atlas* method ($)	..	28,600
Agriculture and fisheries		
Land area (1,000 sq. km)	9	31,030
Agricultural land (% of land area)	13	36
Irrigated land (% of crop land)	35.4	12.3
Fertilizer consumption (100 grams/ha arable land)	2,140	1,198
Population density, rural (people/sq. km arable land)	313	202
Fish catch, total (1,000 metric tons)	78	28,712
Forests		
Forest area (1,000 sq. km)	2	7,929
Forest area share of total land area (%)	18.6	25.9
Annual deforestation (% change, 1990–2000)	–3.8	–0.1
Biodiversity		
Mammal species, total known	..	
Mammal species, threatened	3	
Bird species, total breeding	..	
Bird species, threatened	3	
Nationally protected area (% of land area)	..	19.5
Energy		
GDP per unit of energy use (2000 PPP$/kg oil equiv)	5.5	5.2
Energy use per capita (kg oil equiv)	3,225	5,395
Energy from biomass products and waste (% of total)	0.4	3.1
Energy imports, net (% of energy use)	98	26
Electric power consumption per capita (kWh)	4,425	8,693
Electricity generated by coal (% of total)	..	38.2
Emissions and pollution		
CO_2 emissions per unit of GDP (kg/2000 PPP$ GDP)	0.5	0.5
CO_2 emissions per capita (metric tons)	8.5	12.4
Particulate matter (pop. weighted average, μg/cu. m)	55	33
Passenger cars (per 1,000 people)	404	436
Water and sanitation		
Internal freshwater resources per capita (cu. m)	1,046	9,479
Freshwater withdrawal		
Total (% of internal resources)	..	9.7
Agriculture (% of total freshwater withdrawal)	71	42
Access to improved water source (% of total population)	100	99
Rural (% of rural population)	100	98
Urban (% of urban population)	100	100
Access to sanitation (% of total population)	100	..
Rural (% of rural population)	100	..
Urban (% of urban population)	100	..
Under-five mortality rate (per 1,000)	5	7
National accounting aggregates, 2003		
Gross national savings (% of GNI)	..	19.1
Consumption of fixed capital (% of GNI)	..	13.2
Education expenditure (% of GNI)	5.3	4.6
Energy depletion (% of GNI)	..	0.8
Mineral depletion (% of GNI)	..	0.0
Net forest depletion (% of GNI)	..	0.0
CO_2 damage (% of GNI)	..	0.3
Particulate emission damage (% of GNI)	..	0.3
Adjusted net savings (% of GNI)	..	9.2

Czech Republic

Environmental strategy/action plan prepared in **1994**

	Country data	Group data Europe & Central Asia	Group data Upper middle income
Population (millions)	10.2	472	333
Urban population (% of total)	74.7	63.8	75.4
GDP ($ billions)	89.7	1,403	1,856
GNI per capita, *Atlas* method ($)	7,150	2,580	5,440
Agriculture and fisheries			
Land area (1,000 sq. km)	77	23,868	12,741
Agricultural land (% of land area)	55	28	48
Irrigated land (% of crop land)	0.7	10.9	13.5
Fertilizer consumption (100 grams/ha arable land)	1,202	344	796
Population density, rural (people/sq. km arable land)	84	122	193
Fish catch, total (1,000 metric tons)	25	5,527	10,082
Forests			
Forest area (1,000 sq. km)	26	9,463	2,427
Forest area share of total land area (%)	34.1	39.6	19.1
Annual deforestation (% change, 1990–2000)	0.0	–0.1	0.6
Biodiversity			
Mammal species, total known	81		
Mammal species, threatened	8		
Bird species, total breeding	205		
Bird species, threatened	2		
Nationally protected area (% of land area)	16.1	6.8	17.3
Energy			
GDP per unit of energy use (2000 PPP$/kg oil equiv)	3.7	2.5	4.3
Energy use per capita (kg oil equiv)	4,090	2,697	2,232
Energy from biomass products and waste (% of total)	2.0	2.3	4.1
Energy imports, net (% of energy use)	26	–23	–91
Electric power consumption per capita (kWh)	4,982	2,808	2,496
Electricity generated by coal (% of total)	66.8	29.4	23.9
Emissions and pollution			
CO_2 emissions per unit of GDP (kg/2000 PPP$ GDP)	0.8	1.1	0.6
CO_2 emissions per capita (metric tons)	11.6	6.7	6.3
Particulate matter (pop. weighted average, µg/cu. m)	27	33	29
Passenger cars (per 1,000 people)	356	138	153
Water and sanitation			
Internal freshwater resources per capita (cu. m)	1,274	11,128	10,741
Freshwater withdrawal			
Total (% of internal resources)	20.8	7.4	5.7
Agriculture (% of total freshwater withdrawal)	2	57	71
Access to improved water source (% of total population)	..	91	..
Rural (% of rural population)	..	80	..
Urban (% of urban population)	..	98	96
Access to sanitation (% of total population)	..	82	..
Rural (% of rural population)	..	64	..
Urban (% of urban population)	..	93	..
Under-five mortality rate (per 1,000)	5	36	22
National accounting aggregates, 2003			
Gross national savings (% of GNI)	22.4	21.9	22.1
Consumption of fixed capital (% of GNI)	12.5	10.7	10.7
Education expenditure (% of GNI)	4.0	4.1	5.0
Energy depletion (% of GNI)	0.1	11.6	11.4
Mineral depletion (% of GNI)	0.0	0.1	0.3
Net forest depletion (% of GNI)	0.0	0.0	0.0
CO_2 damage (% of GNI)	1.0	1.9	0.8
Particulate emission damage (% of GNI)	0.1	0.6	0.6
Adjusted net savings (% of GNI)	12.7	1.1	3.3

Denmark

Environmental strategy/action plan prepared in **1994**

	Country data	High income
		Group data
Population (millions)	5.4	972
Urban population (% of total)	85.1	79.9
GDP ($ billions)	212	29,341
GNI per capita, *Atlas* method ($)	33,570	28,600
Agriculture and fisheries		
Land area (1,000 sq. km)	42	31,030
Agricultural land (% of land area)	63	36
Irrigated land (% of crop land)	19.6	12.3
Fertilizer consumption (100 grams/ha arable land)	1,305	1,198
Population density, rural (people/sq. km arable land)	35	202
Fish catch, total (1,000 metric tons)	1,552	28,712
Forests		
Forest area (1,000 sq. km)	5	7,929
Forest area share of total land area (%)	10.7	25.9
Annual deforestation (% change, 1990–2000)	–0.2	–0.1
Biodiversity		
Mammal species, total known	43	
Mammal species, threatened	5	
Bird species, total breeding	196	
Bird species, threatened	1	
Nationally protected area (% of land area)	34.0	19.5
Energy		
GDP per unit of energy use (2000 PPP$/kg oil equiv)	8.1	5.2
Energy use per capita (kg oil equiv)	3,675	5,395
Energy from biomass products and waste (% of total)	10.5	3.1
Energy imports, net (% of energy use)	–46	26
Electric power consumption per capita (kWh)	6,024	8,693
Electricity generated by coal (% of total)	46.5	38.2
Emissions and pollution		
CO_2 emissions per unit of GDP (kg/2000 PPP$ GDP)	0.3	0.5
CO_2 emissions per capita (metric tons)	8.4	12.4
Particulate matter (pop. weighted average, μg/cu. m)	23	33
Passenger cars (per 1,000 people)	360	436
Water and sanitation		
Internal freshwater resources per capita (cu. m)	1,114	9,479
Freshwater withdrawal		
Total (% of internal resources)	20.0	9.7
Agriculture (% of total freshwater withdrawal)	43	42
Access to improved water source (% of total population)	100	99
Rural (% of rural population)	100	98
Urban (% of urban population)	100	100
Access to sanitation (% of total population)	..	..
Rural (% of rural population)	..	..
Urban (% of urban population)	..	..
Under-five mortality rate (per 1,000)	6	7
National accounting aggregates, 2003		
Gross national savings (% of GNI)	23.5	19.1
Consumption of fixed capital (% of GNI)	15.2	13.2
Education expenditure (% of GNI)	7.9	4.6
Energy depletion (% of GNI)	0.7	0.8
Mineral depletion (% of GNI)	0.0	0.0
Net forest depletion (% of GNI)	0.0	0.0
CO_2 damage (% of GNI)	0.2	0.3
Particulate emission damage (% of GNI)	0.1	0.3
Adjusted net savings (% of GNI)	15.2	9.2

Djibouti

Environmental strategy/action plan prepared in ..

	Country data	Middle East & North Africa	Lower middle income
		Group data	
Population (millions)	0.7	312	2,655
Urban population (% of total)	84.6	59.0	49.8
GDP ($ billions)	0.6	745	4,168
GNI per capita, *Atlas* method ($)	910	2,390	1,490
Agriculture and fisheries			
Land area (1,000 sq. km)	23	11,111	56,103
Agricultural land (% of land area)	56	34	35
Irrigated land (% of crop land)	..	38.3	20.8
Fertilizer consumption (100 grams/ha arable land)	..	854	1,170
Population density, rural (people/sq. km arable land)	10,830	603	497
Fish catch, total (1,000 metric tons)	0	2,840	74,407
Forests			
Forest area (1,000 sq. km)	0	168	20,316
Forest area share of total land area (%)	0.3	1.5	36.2
Annual deforestation (% change, 1990–2000)	0.0	–0.1	0.1
Biodiversity			
Mammal species, total known	..		
Mammal species, threatened	4		
Bird species, total breeding	..		
Bird species, threatened	5		
Nationally protected area (% of land area)	..	11.3	7.7
Energy			
GDP per unit of energy use (2000 PPP$/kg oil equiv)	..	3.5	4.1
Energy use per capita (kg oil equiv)	..	1,504	1,227
Energy from biomass products and waste (% of total)	..	1.0	12.3
Energy imports, net (% of energy use)	..	–168	–22
Electric power consumption per capita (kWh)	..	1,412	1,289
Electricity generated by coal (% of total)	..	2.3	42.8
Emissions and pollution			
CO_2 emissions per unit of GDP (kg/2000 PPP$ GDP)	0.3	0.8	0.6
CO_2 emissions per capita (metric tons)	0.6	4.2	2.9
Particulate matter (pop. weighted average, µg/cu. m)	..	87	49
Passenger cars (per 1,000 people)	..	..	28
Water and sanitation			
Internal freshwater resources per capita (cu. m)	433	761	8,397
Freshwater withdrawal			
Total (% of internal resources)	..	101.7	5.9
Agriculture (% of total freshwater withdrawal)	87	88	74
Access to improved water source (% of total population)	80	88	82
Rural (% of rural population)	67	78	71
Urban (% of urban population)	82	96	94
Access to sanitation (% of total population)	50	75	60
Rural (% of rural population)	27	56	41
Urban (% of urban population)	55	90	80
Under-five mortality rate (per 1,000)	138	53	39
National accounting aggregates, 2003			
Gross national savings (% of GNI)	..	31.2	30.6
Consumption of fixed capital (% of GNI)	8.6	10.0	9.8
Education expenditure (% of GNI)	..	5.5	3.2
Energy depletion (% of GNI)	0.0	30.7	8.1
Mineral depletion (% of GNI)	0.0	0.1	0.4
Net forest depletion (% of GNI)	0.0	0.0	0.1
CO_2 damage (% of GNI)	0.4	1.2	1.6
Particulate emission damage (% of GNI)	..	0.8	0.7
Adjusted net savings (% of GNI)	..	–6.2	13.2

Dominica

Environmental strategy/action plan prepared in ..

| | | Group data | |
	Country data	Latin America & Caribbean	Upper middle income
Population (millions)	0.1	533	333
Urban population (% of total)	72.0	76.6	75.4
GDP ($ billions)	0.3	1,741	1,856
GNI per capita, *Atlas* method ($)	3,330	3,280	5,440
Agriculture and fisheries			
Land area (1,000 sq. km)	1	20,057	12,741
Agricultural land (% of land area)	29	39	48
Irrigated land (% of crop land)	..	12.5	13.5
Fertilizer consumption (100 grams/ha arable land)	1,086	892	796
Population density, rural (people/sq. km arable land)	402	210	193
Fish catch, total (1,000 metric tons)	1	17,804	10,082
Forests			
Forest area (1,000 sq. km)	0	9,552	2,427
Forest area share of total land area (%)	61.3	47.6	19.1
Annual deforestation (% change, 1990–2000)	0.8	0.5	0.6
Biodiversity			
Mammal species, total known	..		
Mammal species, threatened	1		
Bird species, total breeding	..		
Bird species, threatened	3		
Nationally protected area (% of land area)	..	11.2	17.3
Energy			
GDP per unit of energy use (2000 PPP$/kg oil equiv)	..	6.1	4.3
Energy use per capita (kg oil equiv)	..	1,156	2,232
Energy from biomass products and waste (% of total)	..	14.6	4.1
Energy imports, net (% of energy use)	..	−42	−91
Electric power consumption per capita (kWh)	..	1,506	2,496
Electricity generated by coal (% of total)	..	5.0	23.9
Emissions and pollution			
CO_2 emissions per unit of GDP (kg/2000 PPP$ GDP)	0.2	0.4	0.6
CO_2 emissions per capita (metric tons)	1.4	2.7	6.3
Particulate matter (pop. weighted average, μg/cu. m)	28	40	29
Passenger cars (per 1,000 people)	..	..	153
Water and sanitation			
Internal freshwater resources per capita (cu. m)	..	25,245	10,741
Freshwater withdrawal			
Total (% of internal resources)	..	2.0	5.7
Agriculture (% of total freshwater withdrawal)	0	74	71
Access to improved water source (% of total population)	97	89	..
Rural (% of rural population)	90	69	..
Urban (% of urban population)	100	96	96
Access to sanitation (% of total population)	83	74	..
Rural (% of rural population)	75	44	..
Urban (% of urban population)	86	84	..
Under-five mortality rate (per 1,000)	14	33	22
National accounting aggregates, 2003			
Gross national savings (% of GNI)	0.5	19.5	22.1
Consumption of fixed capital (% of GNI)	11.6	10.3	10.7
Education expenditure (% of GNI)	5.0	4.2	5.0
Energy depletion (% of GNI)	0.0	6.4	11.4
Mineral depletion (% of GNI)	0.0	0.7	0.3
Net forest depletion (% of GNI)	0.0	0.0	0.0
CO_2 damage (% of GNI)	0.2	0.5	0.8
Particulate emission damage (% of GNI)	..	0.5	0.6
Adjusted net savings (% of GNI)	−6.4	5.3	3.3

Dominican Republic

Environmental strategy/action plan prepared in ..

	Country data	Latin America & Caribbean	Lower middle income
		Group data	
Population (millions)	8.7	533	2,655
Urban population (% of total)	67.1	76.6	49.8
GDP ($ billions)	16.5	1,741	4,168
GNI per capita, *Atlas* method ($)	2,130	3,280	1,490
Agriculture and fisheries			
Land area (1,000 sq. km)	48	20,057	56,103
Agricultural land (% of land area)	76	39	35
Irrigated land (% of crop land)	17.2	12.5	20.8
Fertilizer consumption (100 grams/ha arable land)	818	892	1,170
Population density, rural (people/sq. km arable land)	263	210	497
Fish catch, total (1,000 metric tons)	16	17,804	74,407
Forests			
Forest area (1,000 sq. km)	14	9,552	20,316
Forest area share of total land area (%)	28.4	47.6	36.2
Annual deforestation (% change, 1990–2000)	0.0	0.5	0.1
Biodiversity			
Mammal species, total known	20		
Mammal species, threatened	5		
Bird species, total breeding	79		
Bird species, threatened	15		
Nationally protected area (% of land area)	51.9	11.2	7.7
Energy			
GDP per unit of energy use (2000 PPP$/kg oil equiv)	6.8	6.1	4.1
Energy use per capita (kg oil equiv)	948	1,156	1,227
Energy from biomass products and waste (% of total)	17.6	14.6	12.3
Energy imports, net (% of energy use)	81	–42	–22
Electric power consumption per capita (kWh)	853	1,506	1,289
Electricity generated by coal (% of total)	5.5	5.0	42.8
Emissions and pollution			
CO_2 emissions per unit of GDP (kg/2000 PPP$ GDP)	0.5	0.4	0.6
CO_2 emissions per capita (metric tons)	3.0	2.7	2.9
Particulate matter (pop. weighted average, µg/cu. m)	39	40	49
Passenger cars (per 1,000 people)	..	..	28
Water and sanitation			
Internal freshwater resources per capita (cu. m)	2,403	25,245	8,397
Freshwater withdrawal			
Total (% of internal resources)	39.5	2.0	5.9
Agriculture (% of total freshwater withdrawal)	89	74	74
Access to improved water source (% of total population)	93	89	82
Rural (% of rural population)	85	69	71
Urban (% of urban population)	98	96	94
Access to sanitation (% of total population)	57	74	60
Rural (% of rural population)	43	44	41
Urban (% of urban population)	67	84	80
Under-five mortality rate (per 1,000)	35	33	39
National accounting aggregates, 2003			
Gross national savings (% of GNI)	29.4	19.5	30.6
Consumption of fixed capital (% of GNI)	5.5	10.3	9.8
Education expenditure (% of GNI)	2.3	4.2	3.2
Energy depletion (% of GNI)	0.0	6.4	8.1
Mineral depletion (% of GNI)	0.5	0.7	0.4
Net forest depletion (% of GNI)	0.0	0.0	0.1
CO_2 damage (% of GNI)	1.2	0.5	1.6
Particulate emission damage (% of GNI)	0.2	0.5	0.7
Adjusted net savings (% of GNI)	24.3	5.3	13.2

Ecuador

Environmental strategy/action plan prepared in **1993**

	Country data	Latin America & Caribbean	Lower middle income
		Group data	
Population (millions)	13.0	533	2,655
Urban population (% of total)	64.3	76.6	49.8
GDP ($ billions)	27.2	1,741	4,168
GNI per capita, *Atlas* method ($)	1,830	3,280	1,490
Agriculture and fisheries			
Land area (1,000 sq. km)	277	20,057	56,103
Agricultural land (% of land area)	29	39	35
Irrigated land (% of crop land)	29.0	12.5	20.8
Fertilizer consumption (100 grams/ha arable land)	1,417	892	1,170
Population density, rural (people/sq. km arable land)	286	210	497
Fish catch, total (1,000 metric tons)	655	17,804	74,407
Forests			
Forest area (1,000 sq. km)	106	9,552	20,316
Forest area share of total land area (%)	38.1	47.6	36.2
Annual deforestation (% change, 1990–2000)	1.2	0.5	0.1
Biodiversity			
Mammal species, total known	302		
Mammal species, threatened	33		
Bird species, total breeding	640		
Bird species, threatened	62		
Nationally protected area (% of land area)	18.3	11.2	7.7
Energy			
GDP per unit of energy use (2000 PPP$/kg oil equiv)	4.8	6.1	4.1
Energy use per capita (kg oil equiv)	706	1,156	1,227
Energy from biomass products and waste (% of total)	8.0	14.6	12.3
Energy imports, net (% of energy use)	–145	–42	–22
Electric power consumption per capita (kWh)	665	1,506	1,289
Electricity generated by coal (% of total)	..	5.0	42.8
Emissions and pollution			
CO_2 emissions per unit of GDP (kg/2000 PPP$ GDP)	0.6	0.4	0.6
CO_2 emissions per capita (metric tons)	2.0	2.7	2.9
Particulate matter (pop. weighted average, µg/cu. m)	28	40	49
Passenger cars (per 1,000 people)	44	..	28
Water and sanitation			
Internal freshwater resources per capita (cu. m)	33,210	25,245	8,397
Freshwater withdrawal			
Total (% of internal resources)	3.9	2.0	5.9
Agriculture (% of total freshwater withdrawal)	82	74	74
Access to improved water source (% of total population)	86	89	82
Rural (% of rural population)	77	69	71
Urban (% of urban population)	92	96	94
Access to sanitation (% of total population)	72	74	60
Rural (% of rural population)	59	44	41
Urban (% of urban population)	80	84	80
Under-five mortality rate (per 1,000)	27	33	39
National accounting aggregates, 2003			
Gross national savings (% of GNI)	25.1	19.5	30.6
Consumption of fixed capital (% of GNI)	10.6	10.3	9.8
Education expenditure (% of GNI)	3.2	4.2	3.2
Energy depletion (% of GNI)	15.1	6.4	8.1
Mineral depletion (% of GNI)	0.0	0.7	0.4
Net forest depletion (% of GNI)	0.0	0.0	0.1
CO_2 damage (% of GNI)	0.6	0.5	1.6
Particulate emission damage (% of GNI)	0.1	0.5	0.7
Adjusted net savings (% of GNI)	1.9	5.3	13.2

Egypt, Arab Rep.

Environmental strategy/action plan prepared in **1992**

	Country data	Middle East & North Africa	Lower middle income
		Group data	
Population (millions)	67.6	312	2,655
Urban population (% of total)	42.8	59.0	49.8
GDP ($ billions)	82.4	745	4,168
GNI per capita, *Atlas* method ($)	1,390	2,390	1,490
Agriculture and fisheries			
Land area (1,000 sq. km)	995	11,111	56,103
Agricultural land (% of land area)	3	34	35
Irrigated land (% of crop land)	100.0	38.3	20.8
Fertilizer consumption (100 grams/ha arable land)	4,375	854	1,170
Population density, rural (people/sq. km arable land)	1,309	603	497
Fish catch, total (1,000 metric tons)	772	2,840	74,407
Forests			
Forest area (1,000 sq. km)	1	168	20,316
Forest area share of total land area (%)	0.1	1.5	36.2
Annual deforestation (% change, 1990–2000)	−3.3	−0.1	0.1
Biodiversity			
Mammal species, total known	98		
Mammal species, threatened	13		
Bird species, total breeding	123		
Bird species, threatened	7		
Nationally protected area (% of land area)	9.7	11.3	7.7
Energy			
GDP per unit of energy use (2000 PPP$/kg oil equiv)	4.6	3.5	4.1
Energy use per capita (kg oil equiv)	789	1,504	1,227
Energy from biomass products and waste (% of total)	2.6	1.0	12.3
Energy imports, net (% of energy use)	−14	−168	−22
Electric power consumption per capita (kWh)	1,073	1,412	1,289
Electricity generated by coal (% of total)	..	2.3	42.8
Emissions and pollution			
CO_2 emissions per unit of GDP (kg/2000 PPP$ GDP)	0.6	0.8	0.6
CO_2 emissions per capita (metric tons)	2.2	4.2	2.9
Particulate matter (pop. weighted average, µg/cu. m)	152	87	49
Passenger cars (per 1,000 people)	..	..	28
Water and sanitation			
Internal freshwater resources per capita (cu. m)	30	761	8,397
Freshwater withdrawal			
Total (% of internal resources)	3,300.0	101.7	5.9
Agriculture (% of total freshwater withdrawal)	82	88	74
Access to improved water source (% of total population)	98	88	82
Rural (% of rural population)	97	78	71
Urban (% of urban population)	100	96	94
Access to sanitation (% of total population)	68	75	60
Rural (% of rural population)	56	56	41
Urban (% of urban population)	84	90	80
Under-five mortality rate (per 1,000)	39	53	39
National accounting aggregates, 2003			
Gross national savings (% of GNI)	20.1	31.2	30.6
Consumption of fixed capital (% of GNI)	9.3	10.0	9.8
Education expenditure (% of GNI)	4.4	5.5	3.2
Energy depletion (% of GNI)	7.7	30.7	8.1
Mineral depletion (% of GNI)	0.1	0.1	0.4
Net forest depletion (% of GNI)	0.2	0.0	0.1
CO_2 damage (% of GNI)	1.1	1.2	1.6
Particulate emission damage (% of GNI)	1.4	0.8	0.7
Adjusted net savings (% of GNI)	4.8	−6.2	13.2

El Salvador

Environmental strategy/action plan prepared in **1994**

	Country data	Latin America & Caribbean	Lower middle income
		Group data	
Population (millions)	6.5	533	2,655
Urban population (% of total)	63.5	76.6	49.8
GDP ($ billions)	14.9	1,741	4,168
GNI per capita, *Atlas* method ($)	2,340	3,280	1,490
Agriculture and fisheries			
Land area (1,000 sq. km)	21	20,057	56,103
Agricultural land (% of land area)	82	39	35
Irrigated land (% of crop land)	4.9	12.5	20.8
Fertilizer consumption (100 grams/ha arable land)	838	892	1,170
Population density, rural (people/sq. km arable land)	365	210	497
Fish catch, total (1,000 metric tons)	18	17,804	74,407
Forests			
Forest area (1,000 sq. km)	1	9,552	20,316
Forest area share of total land area (%)	5.8	47.6	36.2
Annual deforestation (% change, 1990–2000)	4.6	0.5	0.1
Biodiversity			
Mammal species, total known	135		
Mammal species, threatened	2		
Bird species, total breeding	141		
Bird species, threatened	0		
Nationally protected area (% of land area)	0.4	11.2	7.7
Energy			
GDP per unit of energy use (2000 PPP$/kg oil equiv)	7.1	6.1	4.1
Energy use per capita (kg oil equiv)	670	1,156	1,227
Energy from biomass products and waste (% of total)	33.1	14.6	12.3
Energy imports, net (% of energy use)	45	–42	–22
Electric power consumption per capita (kWh)	595	1,506	1,289
Electricity generated by coal (% of total)	..	5.0	42.8
Emissions and pollution			
CO_2 emissions per unit of GDP (kg/2000 PPP$ GDP)	0.2	0.4	0.6
CO_2 emissions per capita (metric tons)	1.1	2.7	2.9
Particulate matter (pop. weighted average, µg/cu. m)	43	40	49
Passenger cars (per 1,000 people)	30	..	28
Water and sanitation			
Internal freshwater resources per capita (cu. m)	2,755	25,245	8,397
Freshwater withdrawal			
Total (% of internal resources)	3.9	2.0	5.9
Agriculture (% of total freshwater withdrawal)	46	74	74
Access to improved water source (% of total population)	82	89	82
Rural (% of rural population)	68	69	71
Urban (% of urban population)	91	96	94
Access to sanitation (% of total population)	63	74	60
Rural (% of rural population)	40	44	41
Urban (% of urban population)	78	84	80
Under-five mortality rate (per 1,000)	36	33	39
National accounting aggregates, 2003			
Gross national savings (% of GNI)	16.4	19.5	30.6
Consumption of fixed capital (% of GNI)	9.8	10.3	9.8
Education expenditure (% of GNI)	2.4	4.2	3.2
Energy depletion (% of GNI)	0.0	6.4	8.1
Mineral depletion (% of GNI)	0.0	0.7	0.4
Net forest depletion (% of GNI)	0.5	0.0	0.1
CO_2 damage (% of GNI)	0.3	0.5	1.6
Particulate emission damage (% of GNI)	0.2	0.5	0.7
Adjusted net savings (% of GNI)	8.0	5.3	13.2

Equatorial Guinea

Environmental strategy/action plan prepared in ..

	Country data	Group data — Sub-Saharan Africa	Group data — Low income
Population (millions)	0.5	705	2,312
Urban population (% of total)	51.4	36.5	30.4
GDP ($ billions)	2.9	439	1,103
GNI per capita, *Atlas* method ($)	..	500	440
Agriculture and fisheries			
Land area (1,000 sq. km)	28	23,596	30,456
Agricultural land (% of land area)	12	43	43
Irrigated land (% of crop land)	..	4.2	26.7
Fertilizer consumption (100 grams/ha arable land)	..	145	654
Population density, rural (people/sq. km arable land)	184	352	509
Fish catch, total (1,000 metric tons)	4	5,191	16,410
Forests			
Forest area (1,000 sq. km)	18	6,435	7,939
Forest area share of total land area (%)	62.5	27.3	26.1
Annual deforestation (% change, 1990–2000)	0.6	0.8	0.7
Biodiversity			
Mammal species, total known	184		
Mammal species, threatened	16		
Bird species, total breeding	172		
Bird species, threatened	5		
Nationally protected area (% of land area)	..	8.7	7.7
Energy			
GDP per unit of energy use (2000 PPP$/kg oil equiv)	..	2.8	4.1
Energy use per capita (kg oil equiv)	..	667	493
Energy from biomass products and waste (% of total)	..	57.5	49.4
Energy imports, net (% of energy use)	..	−56	−6
Electric power consumption per capita (kWh)	..	457	312
Electricity generated by coal (% of total)	..	68.2	47.4
Emissions and pollution			
CO_2 emissions per unit of GDP (kg/2000 PPP$ GDP)	0.0	0.4	0.4
CO_2 emissions per capita (metric tons)	0.4	0.7	0.8
Particulate matter (pop. weighted average, µg/cu. m)	..	54	63
Passenger cars (per 1,000 people)	..	..	..
Water and sanitation			
Internal freshwater resources per capita (cu. m)	52,632	5,546	3,583
Freshwater withdrawal			
Total (% of internal resources)	0.0	1.8	11.5
Agriculture (% of total freshwater withdrawal)	6	85	92
Access to improved water source (% of total population)	44	58	75
Rural (% of rural population)	42	46	70
Urban (% of urban population)	45	82	89
Access to sanitation (% of total population)	53	36	36
Rural (% of rural population)	46	26	24
Urban (% of urban population)	60	55	61
Under-five mortality rate (per 1,000)	146	171	123
National accounting aggregates, 2003			
Gross national savings (% of GNI)	..	16.9	23.1
Consumption of fixed capital (% of GNI)	..	10.6	8.9
Education expenditure (% of GNI)	..	4.7	3.4
Energy depletion (% of GNI)	..	8.0	5.8
Mineral depletion (% of GNI)	..	0.5	0.3
Net forest depletion (% of GNI)	..	0.7	0.8
CO_2 damage (% of GNI)	..	0.9	1.2
Particulate emission damage (% of GNI)	..	0.4	0.6
Adjusted net savings (% of GNI)	..	0.6	8.9

Eritrea

Environmental strategy/action plan prepared in **1995**

	Country data	Group data Sub-Saharan Africa	Low income
Population (millions)	4.4	705	2,312
Urban population (% of total)	20.0	36.5	30.4
GDP ($ billions)	0.8	439	1,103
GNI per capita, *Atlas* method ($)	190	500	440
Agriculture and fisheries			
Land area (1,000 sq. km)	101	23,596	30,456
Agricultural land (% of land area)	74	43	43
Irrigated land (% of crop land)	4.2	4.2	26.7
Fertilizer consumption (100 grams/ha arable land)	74	145	654
Population density, rural (people/sq. km arable land)	691	352	509
Fish catch, total (1,000 metric tons)	9	5,191	16,410
Forests			
Forest area (1,000 sq. km)	16	6,435	7,939
Forest area share of total land area (%)	15.7	27.3	26.1
Annual deforestation (% change, 1990–2000)	0.3	0.8	0.7
Biodiversity			
Mammal species, total known	112		
Mammal species, threatened	12		
Bird species, total breeding	138		
Bird species, threatened	7		
Nationally protected area (% of land area)	4.3	8.7	7.7
Energy			
GDP per unit of energy use (2000 PPP$/kg oil equiv)	..	2.8	4.1
Energy use per capita (kg oil equiv)	..	667	493
Energy from biomass products and waste (% of total)	..	57.5	49.4
Energy imports, net (% of energy use)	..	−56	−6
Electric power consumption per capita (kWh)	..	457	312
Electricity generated by coal (% of total)	..	68.2	47.4
Emissions and pollution			
CO_2 emissions per unit of GDP (kg/2000 PPP$ GDP)	0.2	0.4	0.4
CO_2 emissions per capita (metric tons)	0.1	0.7	0.8
Particulate matter (pop. weighted average, μg/cu. m)	80	54	63
Passenger cars (per 1,000 people)	..	..	..
Water and sanitation			
Internal freshwater resources per capita (cu. m)	683	5,546	3,583
Freshwater withdrawal			
Total (% of internal resources)	..	1.8	11.5
Agriculture (% of total freshwater withdrawal)	..	85	92
Access to improved water source (% of total population)	57	58	75
Rural (% of rural population)	54	46	70
Urban (% of urban population)	72	82	89
Access to sanitation (% of total population)	9	36	36
Rural (% of rural population)	3	26	24
Urban (% of urban population)	34	55	61
Under-five mortality rate (per 1,000)	85	171	123
National accounting aggregates, 2003			
Gross national savings (% of GNI)	3.0	16.9	23.1
Consumption of fixed capital (% of GNI)	5.5	10.6	8.9
Education expenditure (% of GNI)	1.4	4.7	3.4
Energy depletion (% of GNI)	0.0	8.0	5.8
Mineral depletion (% of GNI)	0.0	0.5	0.3
Net forest depletion (% of GNI)	0.0	0.7	0.8
CO_2 damage (% of GNI)	0.4	0.9	1.2
Particulate emission damage (% of GNI)	0.5	0.4	0.6
Adjusted net savings (% of GNI)	−2.0	0.6	8.9

Estonia

Environmental strategy/action plan prepared in **1998**

	Country data	Europe & Central Asia	Upper middle income
		Group data	
Population (millions)	1.4	472	333
Urban population (% of total)	69.5	63.8	75.4
GDP ($ billions)	9.1	1,403	1,856
GNI per capita, *Atlas* method ($)	5,380	2,580	5,440
Agriculture and fisheries			
Land area (1,000 sq. km)	42	23,868	12,741
Agricultural land (% of land area)	21	28	48
Irrigated land (% of crop land)	0.6	10.9	13.5
Fertilizer consumption (100 grams/ha arable land)	440	344	796
Population density, rural (people/sq. km arable land)	68	122	193
Fish catch, total (1,000 metric tons)	106	5,527	10,082
Forests			
Forest area (1,000 sq. km)	21	9,463	2,427
Forest area share of total land area (%)	48.6	39.6	19.1
Annual deforestation (% change, 1990–2000)	–0.6	–0.1	0.6
Biodiversity			
Mammal species, total known	65		
Mammal species, threatened	4		
Bird species, total breeding	204		
Bird species, threatened	3		
Nationally protected area (% of land area)	11.8	6.8	17.3
Energy			
GDP per unit of energy use (2000 PPP$/kg oil equiv)	3.6	2.5	4.3
Energy use per capita (kg oil equiv)	3,324	2,697	2,232
Energy from biomass products and waste (% of total)	11.6	2.3	4.1
Energy imports, net (% of energy use)	30	–23	–91
Electric power consumption per capita (kWh)	3,882	2,808	2,496
Electricity generated by coal (% of total)	90.9	29.4	23.9
Emissions and pollution			
CO_2 emissions per unit of GDP (kg/2000 PPP$ GDP)	1.1	1.1	0.6
CO_2 emissions per capita (metric tons)	11.7	6.7	6.3
Particulate matter (pop. weighted average, µg/cu. m)	20	33	29
Passenger cars (per 1,000 people)	296	138	153
Water and sanitation			
Internal freshwater resources per capita (cu. m)	9,608	11,128	10,741
Freshwater withdrawal			
Total (% of internal resources)	1.5	7.4	5.7
Agriculture (% of total freshwater withdrawal)	5	57	71
Access to improved water source (% of total population)	..	91	..
Rural (% of rural population)	..	80	..
Urban (% of urban population)	..	98	96
Access to sanitation (% of total population)	..	82	..
Rural (% of rural population)	..	64	..
Urban (% of urban population)	93	93	..
Under-five mortality rate (per 1,000)	9	36	22
National accounting aggregates, 2003			
Gross national savings (% of GNI)	19.2	21.9	22.1
Consumption of fixed capital (% of GNI)	14.6	10.7	10.7
Education expenditure (% of GNI)	6.3	4.1	5.0
Energy depletion (% of GNI)	0.6	11.6	11.4
Mineral depletion (% of GNI)	0.0	0.1	0.3
Net forest depletion (% of GNI)	0.0	0.0	0.0
CO_2 damage (% of GNI)	1.8	1.9	0.8
Particulate emission damage (% of GNI)	0.2	0.6	0.6
Adjusted net savings (% of GNI)	8.3	1.1	3.3

Ethiopia

Environmental strategy/action plan prepared in **1994**

	Country data	Sub-Saharan Africa	Low income
		Group data	
Population (millions)	68.6	705	2,312
Urban population (% of total)	16.6	36.5	30.4
GDP ($ billions)	6.7	439	1,103
GNI per capita, *Atlas* method ($)	90	500	440
Agriculture and fisheries			
Land area (1,000 sq. km)	1,000	23,596	30,456
Agricultural land (% of land area)	31	43	43
Irrigated land (% of crop land)	1.8	4.2	26.7
Fertilizer consumption (100 grams/ha arable land)	151	145	654
Population density, rural (people/sq. km arable land)	567	352	509
Fish catch, total (1,000 metric tons)	15	5,191	16,410
Forests			
Forest area (1,000 sq. km)	46	6,435	7,939
Forest area share of total land area (%)	4.6	27.3	26.1
Annual deforestation (% change, 1990–2000)	0.8	0.8	0.7
Biodiversity			
Mammal species, total known	277		
Mammal species, threatened	35		
Bird species, total breeding	262		
Bird species, threatened	16		
Nationally protected area (% of land area)	16.9	8.7	7.7
Energy			
GDP per unit of energy use (2000 PPP$/kg oil equiv)	2.4	2.8	4.1
Energy use per capita (kg oil equiv)	297	667	493
Energy from biomass products and waste (% of total)	91.7	57.5	49.4
Energy imports, net (% of energy use)	7	–56	–6
Electric power consumption per capita (kWh)	25	457	312
Electricity generated by coal (% of total)	..	68.2	47.4
Emissions and pollution			
CO_2 emissions per unit of GDP (kg/2000 PPP$ GDP)	0.1	0.4	0.4
CO_2 emissions per capita (metric tons)	0.1	0.7	0.8
Particulate matter (pop. weighted average, μg/cu. m)	88	54	63
Passenger cars (per 1,000 people)	1	..	..
Water and sanitation			
Internal freshwater resources per capita (cu. m)	1,603	5,546	3,583
Freshwater withdrawal			
Total (% of internal resources)	2.0	1.8	11.5
Agriculture (% of total freshwater withdrawal)	86	85	92
Access to improved water source (% of total population)	22	58	75
Rural (% of rural population)	11	46	70
Urban (% of urban population)	81	82	89
Access to sanitation (% of total population)	6	36	36
Rural (% of rural population)	4	26	24
Urban (% of urban population)	19	55	61
Under-five mortality rate (per 1,000)	169	171	123
National accounting aggregates, 2003			
Gross national savings (% of GNI)	18.4	16.9	23.1
Consumption of fixed capital (% of GNI)	5.9	10.6	8.9
Education expenditure (% of GNI)	4.0	4.7	3.4
Energy depletion (% of GNI)	0.0	8.0	5.8
Mineral depletion (% of GNI)	0.1	0.5	0.3
Net forest depletion (% of GNI)	13.4	0.7	0.8
CO_2 damage (% of GNI)	0.5	0.9	1.2
Particulate emission damage (% of GNI)	0.3	0.4	0.6
Adjusted net savings (% of GNI)	2.1	0.6	8.9

Faeroe Islands

Environmental strategy/action plan prepared in ..

	Country data	Group data — High income
Population (millions)	0.0	972
Urban population (% of total)	39.5	79.9
GDP ($ billions)	..	29,341
GNI per capita, *Atlas* method ($)	..	28,600

Agriculture and fisheries
Land area (1,000 sq. km)	1	31,030
Agricultural land (% of land area)	2	36
Irrigated land (% of crop land)	..	12.3
Fertilizer consumption (100 grams/ha arable land)	..	1,198
Population density, rural (people/sq. km arable land)	..	202
Fish catch, total (1,000 metric tons)	398	28,712

Forests
Forest area (1,000 sq. km)	..	7,929
Forest area share of total land area (%)	..	25.9
Annual deforestation (% change, 1990–2000)	..	–0.1

Biodiversity
Mammal species, total known	..	
Mammal species, threatened	3	
Bird species, total breeding	..	
Bird species, threatened	0	
Nationally protected area (% of land area)	..	19.5

Energy
GDP per unit of energy use (2000 PPP$/kg oil equiv)	..	5.2
Energy use per capita (kg oil equiv)	..	5,395
Energy from biomass products and waste (% of total)	..	3.1
Energy imports, net (% of energy use)	..	26
Electric power consumption per capita (kWh)	..	8,693
Electricity generated by coal (% of total)	..	38.2

Emissions and pollution
CO_2 emissions per unit of GDP (kg/2000 PPP$ GDP)	..	0.5
CO_2 emissions per capita (metric tons)	..	12.4
Particulate matter (pop. weighted average, μg/cu. m)	20	33
Passenger cars (per 1,000 people)	..	436

Water and sanitation
Internal freshwater resources per capita (cu. m)	..	9,479
Freshwater withdrawal		
Total (% of internal resources)	..	9.7
Agriculture (% of total freshwater withdrawal)	..	42
Access to improved water source (% of total population)	..	99
Rural (% of rural population)	..	98
Urban (% of urban population)	..	100
Access to sanitation (% of total population)	..	..
Rural (% of rural population)	..	..
Urban (% of urban population)	..	..
Under-five mortality rate (per 1,000)	..	7

National accounting aggregates, 2003
Gross national savings (% of GNI)	..	19.1
Consumption of fixed capital (% of GNI)	..	13.2
Education expenditure (% of GNI)	..	4.6
Energy depletion (% of GNI)	..	0.8
Mineral depletion (% of GNI)	..	0.0
Net forest depletion (% of GNI)	..	0.0
CO_2 damage (% of GNI)	..	0.3
Particulate emission damage (% of GNI)	..	0.3
Adjusted net savings (% of GNI)	..	9.2

Fiji

Environmental strategy/action plan prepared in **1994**

	Country data	Group data East Asia & Pacific	Group data Lower middle income
Population (millions)	0.8	1,855	2,655
Urban population (% of total)	51.7	39.1	49.8
GDP ($ billions)	2.0	2,033	4,168
GNI per capita, *Atlas* method ($)	2,240	1,070	1,490
Agriculture and fisheries			
Land area (1,000 sq. km)	18	15,886	56,103
Agricultural land (% of land area)	25	50	35
Irrigated land (% of crop land)	1.1	..	20.8
Fertilizer consumption (100 grams/ha arable land)	615	2,297	1,170
Population density, rural (people/sq. km arable land)	202	565	497
Fish catch, total (1,000 metric tons)	45	60,812	74,407
Forests			
Forest area (1,000 sq. km)	8	4,284	20,316
Forest area share of total land area (%)	44.6	27.0	36.2
Annual deforestation (% change, 1990–2000)	0.2	0.2	0.1
Biodiversity			
Mammal species, total known	4		
Mammal species, threatened	5		
Bird species, total breeding	47		
Bird species, threatened	12		
Nationally protected area (% of land area)	..	9.2	7.7
Energy			
GDP per unit of energy use (2000 PPP$/kg oil equiv)	..	4.6	4.1
Energy use per capita (kg oil equiv)	..	904	1,227
Energy from biomass products and waste (% of total)	..	19.6	12.3
Energy imports, net (% of energy use)	..	–4	–22
Electric power consumption per capita (kWh)	..	891	1,289
Electricity generated by coal (% of total)	..	66.8	42.8
Emissions and pollution			
CO_2 emissions per unit of GDP (kg/2000 PPP$ GDP)	0.2	0.5	0.6
CO_2 emissions per capita (metric tons)	0.9	2.1	2.9
Particulate matter (pop. weighted average, µg/cu. m)	34	69	49
Passenger cars (per 1,000 people)	..	10	28
Water and sanitation			
Internal freshwater resources per capita (cu. m)	34,731	5,103	8,397
Freshwater withdrawal			
Total (% of internal resources)	0.0	8.2	5.9
Agriculture (% of total freshwater withdrawal)	60	81	74
Access to improved water source (% of total population)	..	78	82
Rural (% of rural population)	..	69	71
Urban (% of urban population)	..	92	94
Access to sanitation (% of total population)	98	49	60
Rural (% of rural population)	98	35	41
Urban (% of urban population)	99	71	80
Under-five mortality rate (per 1,000)	20	41	39
National accounting aggregates, 2003			
Gross national savings (% of GNI)	..	41.7	30.6
Consumption of fixed capital (% of GNI)	10.6	9.2	9.8
Education expenditure (% of GNI)	4.6	2.3	3.2
Energy depletion (% of GNI)	0.0	3.9	8.1
Mineral depletion (% of GNI)	0.6	0.3	0.4
Net forest depletion (% of GNI)	0.0	0.1	0.1
CO_2 damage (% of GNI)	0.3	1.8	1.6
Particulate emission damage (% of GNI)	..	0.8	0.7
Adjusted net savings (% of GNI)	..	27.9	13.2

Finland

Environmental strategy/action plan prepared in **1995**

	Country data	High income
		Group data
Population (millions)	5.2	972
Urban population (% of total)	59.0	79.9
GDP ($ billions)	162	29,341
GNI per capita, *Atlas* method ($)	27,060	28,600
Agriculture and fisheries		
Land area (1,000 sq. km)	305	31,030
Agricultural land (% of land area)	7	36
Irrigated land (% of crop land)	2.9	12.3
Fertilizer consumption (100 grams/ha arable land)	1,332	1,198
Population density, rural (people/sq. km arable land)	97	202
Fish catch, total (1,000 metric tons)	166	28,712
Forests		
Forest area (1,000 sq. km)	219	7,929
Forest area share of total land area (%)	72.0	25.9
Annual deforestation (% change, 1990–2000)	0.0	–0.1
Biodiversity		
Mammal species, total known	60	
Mammal species, threatened	5	
Bird species, total breeding	243	
Bird species, threatened	3	
Nationally protected area (% of land area)	9.3	19.5
Energy		
GDP per unit of energy use (2000 PPP$/kg oil equiv)	3.7	5.2
Energy use per capita (kg oil equiv)	6,852	5,395
Energy from biomass products and waste (% of total)	19.9	3.1
Energy imports, net (% of energy use)	55	26
Electric power consumption per capita (kWh)	15,326	8,693
Electricity generated by coal (% of total)	26.3	38.2
Emissions and pollution		
CO_2 emissions per unit of GDP (kg/2000 PPP$ GDP)	0.4	0.5
CO_2 emissions per capita (metric tons)	10.3	12.4
Particulate matter (pop. weighted average, µg/cu. m)	21	33
Passenger cars (per 1,000 people)	419	436
Water and sanitation		
Internal freshwater resources per capita (cu. m)	20,530	9,479
Freshwater withdrawal		
Total (% of internal resources)	2.1	9.7
Agriculture (% of total freshwater withdrawal)	3	42
Access to improved water source (% of total population)	100	99
Rural (% of rural population)	100	98
Urban (% of urban population)	100	100
Access to sanitation (% of total population)	100	..
Rural (% of rural population)	100	..
Urban (% of urban population)	100	..
Under-five mortality rate (per 1,000)	4	7
National accounting aggregates, 2003		
Gross national savings (% of GNI)	24.5	19.1
Consumption of fixed capital (% of GNI)	16.2	13.2
Education expenditure (% of GNI)	7.0	4.6
Energy depletion (% of GNI)	0.0	0.8
Mineral depletion (% of GNI)	0.0	0.0
Net forest depletion (% of GNI)	0.0	0.0
CO_2 damage (% of GNI)	0.3	0.3
Particulate emission damage (% of GNI)	0.1	0.3
Adjusted net savings (% of GNI)	14.8	9.2

France

Environmental strategy/action plan prepared in **1990**

	Country data	Group data High income
Population (millions)	59.8	972
Urban population (% of total)	75.9	79.9
GDP ($ billions)	1,758	29,341
GNI per capita, *Atlas* method ($)	24,730	28,600
Agriculture and fisheries		
Land area (1,000 sq. km)	550	31,030
Agricultural land (% of land area)	54	36
Irrigated land (% of crop land)	13.3	12.3
Fertilizer consumption (100 grams/ha arable land)	2,151	1,198
Population density, rural (people/sq. km arable land)	78	202
Fish catch, total (1,000 metric tons)	858	28,712
Forests		
Forest area (1,000 sq. km)	153	7,929
Forest area share of total land area (%)	27.9	25.9
Annual deforestation (% change, 1990–2000)	–0.4	–0.1
Biodiversity		
Mammal species, total known	93	
Mammal species, threatened	18	
Bird species, total breeding	283	
Bird species, threatened	5	
Nationally protected area (% of land area)	13.3	19.5
Energy		
GDP per unit of energy use (2000 PPP$/kg oil equiv)	5.8	5.2
Energy use per capita (kg oil equiv)	4,470	5,395
Energy from biomass products and waste (% of total)	4.2	3.1
Energy imports, net (% of energy use)	49	26
Electric power consumption per capita (kWh)	6,606	8,693
Electricity generated by coal (% of total)	4.5	38.2
Emissions and pollution		
CO_2 emissions per unit of GDP (kg/2000 PPP$ GDP)	0.2	0.5
CO_2 emissions per capita (metric tons)	6.2	12.4
Particulate matter (pop. weighted average, µg/cu. m)	17	33
Passenger cars (per 1,000 people)	491	436
Water and sanitation		
Internal freshwater resources per capita (cu. m)	2,995	9,479
Freshwater withdrawal		
Total (% of internal resources)	18.0	9.7
Agriculture (% of total freshwater withdrawal)	10	42
Access to improved water source (% of total population)	..	99
Rural (% of rural population)	..	98
Urban (% of urban population)	100	100
Access to sanitation (% of total population)	..	..
Rural (% of rural population)	..	..
Urban (% of urban population)	..	..
Under-five mortality rate (per 1,000)	6	7
National accounting aggregates, 2003		
Gross national savings (% of GNI)	20.0	19.1
Consumption of fixed capital (% of GNI)	12.7	13.2
Education expenditure (% of GNI)	5.1	4.6
Energy depletion (% of GNI)	0.0	0.8
Mineral depletion (% of GNI)	0.0	0.0
Net forest depletion (% of GNI)	0.0	0.0
CO_2 damage (% of GNI)	0.1	0.3
Particulate emission damage (% of GNI)	0.0	0.3
Adjusted net savings (% of GNI)	12.3	9.2

French Polynesia

Environmental strategy/action plan prepared in ..

	Country data	Group data — High income
Population (millions)	0.2	972
Urban population (% of total)	52.7	79.9
GDP ($ billions)	..	29,341
GNI per capita, *Atlas* method ($)	..	28,600
Agriculture and fisheries		
Land area (1,000 sq. km)	4	31,030
Agricultural land (% of land area)	12	36
Irrigated land (% of crop land)	4.0	12.3
Fertilizer consumption (100 grams/ha arable land)	4,347	1,198
Population density, rural (people/sq. km arable land)	3,781	202
Fish catch, total (1,000 metric tons)	15	28,712
Forests		
Forest area (1,000 sq. km)	1	7,929
Forest area share of total land area (%)	28.7	25.9
Annual deforestation (% change, 1990–2000)	0.0	–0.1
Biodiversity		
Mammal species, total known	..	
Mammal species, threatened	3	
Bird species, total breeding	..	
Bird species, threatened	23	
Nationally protected area (% of land area)	..	19.5
Energy		
GDP per unit of energy use (2000 PPP$/kg oil equiv)	..	5.2
Energy use per capita (kg oil equiv)	..	5,395
Energy from biomass products and waste (% of total)	..	3.1
Energy imports, net (% of energy use)	..	26
Electric power consumption per capita (kWh)	..	8,693
Electricity generated by coal (% of total)	..	38.2
Emissions and pollution		
CO_2 emissions per unit of GDP (kg/2000 PPP$ GDP)	0.1	0.5
CO_2 emissions per capita (metric tons)	2.3	12.4
Particulate matter (pop. weighted average, µg/cu. m)	..	33
Passenger cars (per 1,000 people)	..	436
Water and sanitation		
Internal freshwater resources per capita (cu. m)	..	9,479
Freshwater withdrawal		
Total (% of internal resources)	..	9.7
Agriculture (% of total freshwater withdrawal)	..	42
Access to improved water source (% of total population)	100	99
Rural (% of rural population)	100	98
Urban (% of urban population)	100	100
Access to sanitation (% of total population)	98	..
Rural (% of rural population)	97	..
Urban (% of urban population)	99	..
Under-five mortality rate (per 1,000)	..	7
National accounting aggregates, 2003		
Gross national savings (% of GNI)	..	19.1
Consumption of fixed capital (% of GNI)	..	13.2
Education expenditure (% of GNI)	..	4.6
Energy depletion (% of GNI)	..	0.8
Mineral depletion (% of GNI)	..	0.0
Net forest depletion (% of GNI)	..	0.0
CO_2 damage (% of GNI)	..	0.3
Particulate emission damage (% of GNI)	..	0.3
Adjusted net savings (% of GNI)	..	9.2

Gabon

Environmental strategy/action plan prepared in ..

	Country data	Sub-Saharan Africa	Upper middle income
		Group data	
Population (millions)	1.3	705	333
Urban population (% of total)	83.6	36.5	75.4
GDP ($ billions)	6.1	439	1,856
GNI per capita, *Atlas* method ($)	3,340	500	5,440

Agriculture and fisheries

Land area (1,000 sq. km)	258	23,596	12,741
Agricultural land (% of land area)	20	43	48
Irrigated land (% of crop land)	3.0	4.2	13.5
Fertilizer consumption (100 grams/ha arable land)	9	145	796
Population density, rural (people/sq. km arable land)	69	352	193
Fish catch, total (1,000 metric tons)	41	5,191	10,082

Forests

Forest area (1,000 sq. km)	218	6,435	2,427
Forest area share of total land area (%)	84.7	27.3	19.1
Annual deforestation (% change, 1990–2000)	0.0	0.8	0.6

Biodiversity

Mammal species, total known	190		
Mammal species, threatened	15		
Bird species, total breeding	156		
Bird species, threatened	5		
Nationally protected area (% of land area)	0.7	8.7	17.3

Energy

GDP per unit of energy use (2000 PPP$/kg oil equiv)	5.1	2.8	4.3
Energy use per capita (kg oil equiv)	1,209	667	2,232
Energy from biomass products and waste (% of total)	61.9	57.5	4.1
Energy imports, net (% of energy use)	–698	–56	–91
Electric power consumption per capita (kWh)	804	457	2,496
Electricity generated by coal (% of total)	..	68.2	23.9

Emissions and pollution

CO_2 emissions per unit of GDP (kg/2000 PPP$ GDP)	0.5	0.4	0.6
CO_2 emissions per capita (metric tons)	2.8	0.7	6.3
Particulate matter (pop. weighted average, µg/cu. m)	21	54	29
Passenger cars (per 1,000 people)	..	..	153

Water and sanitation

Internal freshwater resources per capita (cu. m)	121,984	5,546	10,741
Freshwater withdrawal			
Total (% of internal resources)	0.1	1.8	5.7
Agriculture (% of total freshwater withdrawal)	6	85	71
Access to improved water source (% of total population)	87	58	..
Rural (% of rural population)	47	46	..
Urban (% of urban population)	95	82	96
Access to sanitation (% of total population)	36	36	..
Rural (% of rural population)	30	26	..
Urban (% of urban population)	37	55	..
Under-five mortality rate (per 1,000)	91	171	22

National accounting aggregates, 2003

Gross national savings (% of GNI)	36.4	16.9	22.1
Consumption of fixed capital (% of GNI)	12.8	10.6	10.7
Education expenditure (% of GNI)	2.7	4.7	5.0
Energy depletion (% of GNI)	24.6	8.0	11.4
Mineral depletion (% of GNI)	0.0	0.5	0.3
Net forest depletion (% of GNI)	0.0	0.7	0.0
CO_2 damage (% of GNI)	0.5	0.9	0.8
Particulate emission damage (% of GNI)	0.1	0.4	0.6
Adjusted net savings (% of GNI)	1.1	0.6	3.3

Gambia, The

Environmental strategy/action plan prepared in **1992**

	Country data	Group data	
		Sub-Saharan Africa	Low Income
Population (millions)	1.4	705	2,312
Urban population (% of total)	32.6	36.5	30.4
GDP ($ billions)	0.4	439	1,103
GNI per capita, *Atlas* method ($)	270	500	440
Agriculture and fisheries			
Land area (1,000 sq. km)	10	23,596	30,456
Agricultural land (% of land area)	71	43	43
Irrigated land (% of crop land)	0.8	4.2	26.7
Fertilizer consumption (100 grams/ha arable land)	32	145	654
Population density, rural (people/sq. km arable land)	378	352	509
Fish catch, total (1,000 metric tons)	35	5,191	16,410
Forests			
Forest area (1,000 sq. km)	5	6,435	7,939
Forest area share of total land area (%)	48.1	27.3	26.1
Annual deforestation (% change, 1990–2000)	–1.0	0.8	0.7
Biodiversity			
Mammal species, total known	117		
Mammal species, threatened	3		
Bird species, total breeding	154		
Bird species, threatened	2		
Nationally protected area (% of land area)	2.3	8.7	7.7
Energy			
GDP per unit of energy use (2000 PPP$/kg oil equiv)	..	2.8	4.1
Energy use per capita (kg oil equiv)	..	667	493
Energy from biomass products and waste (% of total)	..	57.5	49.4
Energy imports, net (% of energy use)	..	–56	–6
Electric power consumption per capita (kWh)	..	457	312
Electricity generated by coal (% of total)	..	68.2	47.4
Emissions and pollution			
CO_2 emissions per unit of GDP (kg/2000 PPP$ GDP)	0.1	0.4	0.4
CO_2 emissions per capita (metric tons)	0.2	0.7	0.8
Particulate matter (pop. weighted average, µg/cu. m)	93	54	63
Passenger cars (per 1,000 people)	..	..	..
Water and sanitation			
Internal freshwater resources per capita (cu. m)	2,111	5,546	3,583
Freshwater withdrawal			
Total (% of internal resources)	0.0	1.8	11.5
Agriculture (% of total freshwater withdrawal)	91	85	92
Access to improved water source (% of total population)	82	58	75
Rural (% of rural population)	77	46	70
Urban (% of urban population)	95	82	89
Access to sanitation (% of total population)	53	36	36
Rural (% of rural population)	46	26	24
Urban (% of urban population)	72	55	61
Under-five mortality rate (per 1,000)	123	171	123
National accounting aggregates, 2003			
Gross national savings (% of GNI)	8.8	16.9	23.1
Consumption of fixed capital (% of GNI)	7.8	10.6	8.9
Education expenditure (% of GNI)	3.4	4.7	3.4
Energy depletion (% of GNI)	0.0	8.0	5.8
Mineral depletion (% of GNI)	0.0	0.5	0.3
Net forest depletion (% of GNI)	0.6	0.7	0.8
CO_2 damage (% of GNI)	0.5	0.9	1.2
Particulate emission damage (% of GNI)	0.7	0.4	0.6
Adjusted net savings (% of GNI)	2.5	0.6	8.9

Georgia

Environmental strategy/action plan prepared in **1998**

	Country data	Group data Europe & Central Asia	Group data Lower middle income
Population (millions)	5.1	472	2,655
Urban population (% of total)	57.0	63.8	49.8
GDP ($ billions)	4.0	1,403	4,168
GNI per capita, *Atlas* method ($)	770	2,580	1,490
Agriculture and fisheries			
Land area (1,000 sq. km)	69	23,868	56,103
Agricultural land (% of land area)	43	28	35
Irrigated land (% of crop land)	44.1	10.9	20.8
Fertilizer consumption (100 grams/ha arable land)	355	344	1,170
Population density, rural (people/sq. km arable land)	280	122	497
Fish catch, total (1,000 metric tons)	2	5,527	74,407
Forests			
Forest area (1,000 sq. km)	30	9,463	20,316
Forest area share of total land area (%)	43.0	39.6	36.2
Annual deforestation (% change, 1990–2000)	0.0	–0.1	0.1
Biodiversity			
Mammal species, total known	107		
Mammal species, threatened	13		
Bird species, total breeding	208		
Bird species, threatened	3		
Nationally protected area (% of land area)	2.3	6.8	7.7
Energy			
GDP per unit of energy use (2000 PPP$/kg oil equiv)	4.4	2.5	4.1
Energy use per capita (kg oil equiv)	494	2,697	1,227
Energy from biomass products and waste (% of total)	25.2	2.3	12.3
Energy imports, net (% of energy use)	48	–23	–22
Electric power consumption per capita (kWh)	1,032	2,808	1,289
Electricity generated by coal (% of total)	..	29.4	42.8
Emissions and pollution			
CO_2 emissions per unit of GDP (kg/2000 PPP$ GDP)	0.6	1.1	0.6
CO_2 emissions per capita (metric tons)	1.2	6.7	2.9
Particulate matter (pop. weighted average, μg/cu. m)	98	33	49
Passenger cars (per 1,000 people)	56	138	28
Water and sanitation			
Internal freshwater resources per capita (cu. m)	11,315	11,128	8,397
Freshwater withdrawal			
Total (% of internal resources)	6.0	7.4	5.9
Agriculture (% of total freshwater withdrawal)	59	57	74
Access to improved water source (% of total population)	76	91	82
Rural (% of rural population)	61	80	71
Urban (% of urban population)	90	98	94
Access to sanitation (% of total population)	83	82	60
Rural (% of rural population)	69	64	41
Urban (% of urban population)	96	93	80
Under-five mortality rate (per 1,000)	45	36	39
National accounting aggregates, 2003			
Gross national savings (% of GNI)	14.8	21.9	30.6
Consumption of fixed capital (% of GNI)	16.1	10.7	9.8
Education expenditure (% of GNI)	4.3	4.1	3.2
Energy depletion (% of GNI)	0.5	11.6	8.1
Mineral depletion (% of GNI)	0.0	0.1	0.4
Net forest depletion (% of GNI)	0.0	0.0	0.1
CO_2 damage (% of GNI)	1.0	1.9	1.6
Particulate emission damage (% of GNI)	2.5	0.6	0.7
Adjusted net savings (% of GNI)	–1.0	1.1	13.2

Germany

Environmental strategy/action plan prepared in ..

	Country data	Group data High income
Population (millions)	82.5	972
Urban population (% of total)	88.1	79.9
GDP ($ billions)	2,403	29,341
GNI per capita, *Atlas* method ($)	25,270	28,600

Agriculture and fisheries

Land area (1,000 sq. km)	349	31,030
Agricultural land (% of land area)	49	36
Irrigated land (% of crop land)	4.0	12.3
Fertilizer consumption (100 grams/ha arable land)	2,200	1,198
Population density, rural (people/sq. km arable land)	85	202
Fish catch, total (1,000 metric tons)	265	28,712

Forests

Forest area (1,000 sq. km)	107	7,929
Forest area share of total land area (%)	30.8	25.9
Annual deforestation (% change, 1990–2000)	0.0	–0.1

Biodiversity

Mammal species, total known	76	
Mammal species, threatened	11	
Bird species, total breeding	247	
Bird species, threatened	5	
Nationally protected area (% of land area)	32.6	19.5

Energy

GDP per unit of energy use (2000 PPP$/kg oil equiv)	6.2	5.2
Energy use per capita (kg oil equiv)	4,198	5,395
Energy from biomass products and waste (% of total)	2.6	3.1
Energy imports, net (% of energy use)	61	26
Electric power consumption per capita (kWh)	6,046	8,693
Electricity generated by coal (% of total)	51.4	38.2

Emissions and pollution

CO_2 emissions per unit of GDP (kg/2000 PPP$ GDP)	0.4	0.5
CO_2 emissions per capita (metric tons)	9.6	12.4
Particulate matter (pop. weighted average, μg/cu. m)	22	33
Passenger cars (per 1,000 people)	516	436

Water and sanitation

Internal freshwater resources per capita (cu. m)	1,296	9,479
Freshwater withdrawal		
Total (% of internal resources)	43.3	9.7
Agriculture (% of total freshwater withdrawal)	20	42
Access to improved water source (% of total population)	100	99
Rural (% of rural population)	100	98
Urban (% of urban population)	100	100
Access to sanitation (% of total population)	..	..
Rural (% of rural population)	..	..
Urban (% of urban population)	..	..
Under-five mortality rate (per 1,000)	5	7

National accounting aggregates, 2003

Gross national savings (% of GNI)	20.3	19.1
Consumption of fixed capital (% of GNI)	14.9	13.2
Education expenditure (% of GNI)	4.2	4.6
Energy depletion (% of GNI)	0.1	0.8
Mineral depletion (% of GNI)	0.0	0.0
Net forest depletion (% of GNI)	0.0	0.0
CO_2 damage (% of GNI)	0.2	0.3
Particulate emission damage (% of GNI)	0.1	0.3
Adjusted net savings (% of GNI)	9.3	9.2

Ghana

Environmental strategy/action plan prepared in **1992**

	Country data	Sub-Saharan Africa	Low income
		Group data	
Population (millions)	20.7	705	2,312
Urban population (% of total)	37.1	36.5	30.4
GDP ($ billions)	7.6	439	1,103
GNI per capita, *Atlas* method ($)	320	500	440
Agriculture and fisheries			
Land area (1,000 sq. km)	228	23,596	30,456
Agricultural land (% of land area)	63	43	43
Irrigated land (% of crop land)	0.2	4.2	26.7
Fertilizer consumption (100 grams/ha arable land)	74	145	654
Population density, rural (people/sq. km arable land)	307	352	509
Fish catch, total (1,000 metric tons)	451	5,191	16,410
Forests			
Forest area (1,000 sq. km)	63	6,435	7,939
Forest area share of total land area (%)	27.8	27.3	26.1
Annual deforestation (% change, 1990–2000)	1.7	0.8	0.7
Biodiversity			
Mammal species, total known	222		
Mammal species, threatened	14		
Bird species, total breeding	206		
Bird species, threatened	8		
Nationally protected area (% of land area)	5.6	8.7	7.7
Energy			
GDP per unit of energy use (2000 PPP$/kg oil equiv)	5.0	2.8	4.1
Energy use per capita (kg oil equiv)	411	667	493
Energy from biomass products and waste (% of total)	66.4	57.5	49.4
Energy imports, net (% of energy use)	28	–56	–6
Electric power consumption per capita (kWh)	297	457	312
Electricity generated by coal (% of total)	..	68.2	47.4
Emissions and pollution			
CO_2 emissions per unit of GDP (kg/2000 PPP$ GDP)	0.2	0.4	0.4
CO_2 emissions per capita (metric tons)	0.3	0.7	0.8
Particulate matter (pop. weighted average, µg/cu. m)	33	54	63
Passenger cars (per 1,000 people)	..	..	..
Water and sanitation			
Internal freshwater resources per capita (cu. m)	1,451	5,546	3,583
Freshwater withdrawal			
Total (% of internal resources)	1.0	1.8	11.5
Agriculture (% of total freshwater withdrawal)	52	85	92
Access to improved water source (% of total population)	79	58	75
Rural (% of rural population)	68	46	70
Urban (% of urban population)	93	82	89
Access to sanitation (% of total population)	58	36	36
Rural (% of rural population)	46	26	24
Urban (% of urban population)	74	55	61
Under-five mortality rate (per 1,000)	95	171	123
National accounting aggregates, 2003			
Gross national savings (% of GNI)	28.1	16.9	23.1
Consumption of fixed capital (% of GNI)	7.2	10.6	8.9
Education expenditure (% of GNI)	2.8	4.7	3.4
Energy depletion (% of GNI)	0.0	8.0	5.8
Mineral depletion (% of GNI)	1.1	0.5	0.3
Net forest depletion (% of GNI)	2.5	0.7	0.8
CO_2 damage (% of GNI)	0.7	0.9	1.2
Particulate emission damage (% of GNI)	0.2	0.4	0.6
Adjusted net savings (% of GNI)	19.3	0.6	8.9

Greece

Environmental strategy/action plan prepared in ..

	Country data	Group data High income
Population (millions)	11.0	972
Urban population (% of total)	60.9	79.9
GDP ($ billions)	172	29,341
GNI per capita, *Atlas* method ($)	13,230	28,600

Agriculture and fisheries

Land area (1,000 sq. km)	129	31,030
Agricultural land (% of land area)	66	36
Irrigated land (% of crop land)	37.2	12.3
Fertilizer consumption (100 grams/ha arable land)	1,491	1,198
Population density, rural (people/sq. km arable land)	160	202
Fish catch, total (1,000 metric tons)	192	28,712

Forests

Forest area (1,000 sq. km)	36	7,929
Forest area share of total land area (%)	27.9	25.9
Annual deforestation (% change, 1990–2000)	–0.9	–0.1

Biodiversity

Mammal species, total known	95	
Mammal species, threatened	13	
Bird species, total breeding	255	
Bird species, threatened	7	
Nationally protected area (% of land area)	3.6	19.5

Energy

GDP per unit of energy use (2000 PPP$/kg oil equiv)	6.8	5.2
Energy use per capita (kg oil equiv)	2,637	5,395
Energy from biomass products and waste (% of total)	3.6	3.1
Energy imports, net (% of energy use)	65	26
Electric power consumption per capita (kWh)	4,231	8,693
Electricity generated by coal (% of total)	64.1	38.2

Emissions and pollution

CO_2 emissions per unit of GDP (kg/2000 PPP$ GDP)	0.5	0.5
CO_2 emissions per capita (metric tons)	8.2	12.4
Particulate matter (pop. weighted average, µg/cu. m)	47	33
Passenger cars (per 1,000 people)	254	436

Water and sanitation

Internal freshwater resources per capita (cu. m)	5,257	9,479
Freshwater withdrawal		
Total (% of internal resources)	15.0	9.7
Agriculture (% of total freshwater withdrawal)	87	42
Access to improved water source (% of total population)	..	99
Rural (% of rural population)	..	98
Urban (% of urban population)	..	100
Access to sanitation (% of total population)	..	..
Rural (% of rural population)	..	..
Urban (% of urban population)	..	..
Under-five mortality rate (per 1,000)	5	7

National accounting aggregates, 2003

Gross national savings (% of GNI)	20.3	19.1
Consumption of fixed capital (% of GNI)	8.7	13.2
Education expenditure (% of GNI)	3.1	4.6
Energy depletion (% of GNI)	0.0	0.8
Mineral depletion (% of GNI)	0.0	0.0
Net forest depletion (% of GNI)	0.0	0.0
CO_2 damage (% of GNI)	0.4	0.3
Particulate emission damage (% of GNI)	0.7	0.3
Adjusted net savings (% of GNI)	13.5	9.2

Greenland

Environmental strategy/action plan prepared in ..

	Country data	Group data High income
Population (millions)	0.1	972
Urban population (% of total)	82.7	79.9
GDP ($ billions)	..	29,341
GNI per capita, *Atlas* method ($)	..	28,600
Agriculture and fisheries		
Land area (1,000 sq. km)	410	31,030
Agricultural land (% of land area)	1	36
Irrigated land (% of crop land)	..	12.3
Fertilizer consumption (100 grams/ha arable land)	..	1,198
Population density, rural (people/sq. km arable land)	..	202
Fish catch, total (1,000 metric tons)	158	28,712
Forests		
Forest area (1,000 sq. km)	..	7,929
Forest area share of total land area (%)	..	25.9
Annual deforestation (% change, 1990–2000)	..	–0.1
Biodiversity		
Mammal species, total known	..	
Mammal species, threatened	7	
Bird species, total breeding	..	
Bird species, threatened	0	
Nationally protected area (% of land area)	..	19.5
Energy		
GDP per unit of energy use (2000 PPP$/kg oil equiv)	..	5.2
Energy use per capita (kg oil equiv)	..	5,395
Energy from biomass products and waste (% of total)	..	3.1
Energy imports, net (% of energy use)	..	26
Electric power consumption per capita (kWh)	..	8,693
Electricity generated by coal (% of total)	..	38.2
Emissions and pollution		
CO_2 emissions per unit of GDP (kg/2000 PPP$ GDP)	..	0.5
CO_2 emissions per capita (metric tons)	9.9	12.4
Particulate matter (pop. weighted average, µg/cu. m)	..	33
Passenger cars (per 1,000 people)	..	436
Water and sanitation		
Internal freshwater resources per capita (cu. m)	..	9,479
Freshwater withdrawal		
Total (% of internal resources)	..	9.7
Agriculture (% of total freshwater withdrawal)	..	42
Access to improved water source (% of total population)	..	99
Rural (% of rural population)	..	98
Urban (% of urban population)	..	100
Access to sanitation (% of total population)	..	..
Rural (% of rural population)	..	..
Urban (% of urban population)	..	..
Under-five mortality rate (per 1,000)	..	7
National accounting aggregates, 2003		
Gross national savings (% of GNI)	..	19.1
Consumption of fixed capital (% of GNI)	..	13.2
Education expenditure (% of GNI)	..	4.6
Energy depletion (% of GNI)	..	0.8
Mineral depletion (% of GNI)	..	0.0
Net forest depletion (% of GNI)	..	0.0
CO_2 damage (% of GNI)	..	0.3
Particulate emission damage (% of GNI)	..	0.3
Adjusted net savings (% of GNI)	..	9.2

Grenada

Environmental strategy/action plan prepared in ..

	Country data	Latin America & Caribbean	Upper middle income
		Group data	
Population (millions)	0.1	533	333
Urban population (% of total)	39.6	76.6	75.4
GDP ($ billions)	0.4	1,741	1,856
GNI per capita, *Atlas* method ($)	3,710	3,280	5,440
Agriculture and fisheries			
Land area (1,000 sq. km)	0	20,057	12,741
Agricultural land (% of land area)	38	39	48
Irrigated land (% of crop land)	..	12.5	13.5
Fertilizer consumption (100 grams/ha arable land)	..	892	796
Population density, rural (people/sq. km arable land)	3,157	210	193
Fish catch, total (1,000 metric tons)	2	17,804	10,082
Forests			
Forest area (1,000 sq. km)	0	9,552	2,427
Forest area share of total land area (%)	14.7	47.6	19.1
Annual deforestation (% change, 1990–2000)	0.0	0.5	0.6
Biodiversity			
Mammal species, total known	..		
Mammal species, threatened	0		
Bird species, total breeding	..		
Bird species, threatened	1		
Nationally protected area (% of land area)	..	11.2	17.3
Energy			
GDP per unit of energy use (2000 PPP$/kg oil equiv)	..	6.1	4.3
Energy use per capita (kg oil equiv)	..	1,156	2,232
Energy from biomass products and waste (% of total)	..	14.6	4.1
Energy imports, net (% of energy use)	..	−42	−91
Electric power consumption per capita (kWh)	..	1,506	2,496
Electricity generated by coal (% of total)	..	5.0	23.9
Emissions and pollution			
CO_2 emissions per unit of GDP (kg/2000 PPP$ GDP)	0.3	0.4	0.6
CO_2 emissions per capita (metric tons)	2.1	2.7	6.3
Particulate matter (pop. weighted average, µg/cu. m)	25	40	29
Passenger cars (per 1,000 people)	..	..	153
Water and sanitation			
Internal freshwater resources per capita (cu. m)	..	25,245	10,741
Freshwater withdrawal			
Total (% of internal resources)	..	2.0	5.7
Agriculture (% of total freshwater withdrawal)	..	74	71
Access to improved water source (% of total population)	95	89	..
Rural (% of rural population)	93	69	..
Urban (% of urban population)	97	96	96
Access to sanitation (% of total population)	97	74	..
Rural (% of rural population)	97	44	..
Urban (% of urban population)	96	84	..
Under-five mortality rate (per 1,000)	23	33	22
National accounting aggregates, 2003			
Gross national savings (% of GNI)	7.1	19.5	22.1
Consumption of fixed capital (% of GNI)	12.4	10.3	10.7
Education expenditure (% of GNI)	5.4	4.2	5.0
Energy depletion (% of GNI)	0.0	6.4	11.4
Mineral depletion (% of GNI)	0.0	0.7	0.3
Net forest depletion (% of GNI)	0.0	0.0	0.0
CO_2 damage (% of GNI)	0.4	0.5	0.8
Particulate emission damage (% of GNI)	..	0.5	0.6
Adjusted net savings (% of GNI)	..	5.3	3.3

Guam

Environmental strategy/action plan prepared in ..

	Country data	Group data High income
Population (millions)	0.2	972
Urban population (% of total)	40.3	79.9
GDP ($ billions)	..	29,341
GNI per capita, *Atlas* method ($)	..	28,600

Agriculture and fisheries

Land area (1,000 sq. km)	1	31,030
Agricultural land (% of land area)	40	36
Irrigated land (% of crop land)	..	12.3
Fertilizer consumption (100 grams/ha arable land)	..	1,198
Population density, rural (people/sq. km arable land)	1,915	202
Fish catch, total (1,000 metric tons)	1	28,712

Forests

Forest area (1,000 sq. km)	0	7,929
Forest area share of total land area (%)	38.2	25.9
Annual deforestation (% change, 1990–2000)	0.0	–0.1

Biodiversity

Mammal species, total known	..	
Mammal species, threatened	2	
Bird species, total breeding	..	
Bird species, threatened	2	
Nationally protected area (% of land area)	..	19.5

Energy

GDP per unit of energy use (2000 PPP$/kg oil equiv)	..	5.2
Energy use per capita (kg oil equiv)	..	5,395
Energy from biomass products and waste (% of total)	..	3.1
Energy imports, net (% of energy use)	..	26
Electric power consumption per capita (kWh)	..	8,693
Electricity generated by coal (% of total)	..	38.2

Emissions and pollution

CO_2 emissions per unit of GDP (kg/2000 PPP$ GDP)	..	0.5
CO_2 emissions per capita (metric tons)	26.3	12.4
Particulate matter (pop. weighted average, µg/cu. m)	..	33
Passenger cars (per 1,000 people)	..	436

Water and sanitation

Internal freshwater resources per capita (cu. m)	..	9,479
Freshwater withdrawal		
Total (% of internal resources)	..	9.7
Agriculture (% of total freshwater withdrawal)	..	42
Access to improved water source (% of total population)	100	99
Rural (% of rural population)	100	98
Urban (% of urban population)	100	100
Access to sanitation (% of total population)	99	..
Rural (% of rural population)	98	..
Urban (% of urban population)	99	..
Under-five mortality rate (per 1,000)	..	7

National accounting aggregates, 2003

Gross national savings (% of GNI)	..	19.1
Consumption of fixed capital (% of GNI)	..	13.2
Education expenditure (% of GNI)	..	4.6
Energy depletion (% of GNI)	..	0.8
Mineral depletion (% of GNI)	..	0.0
Net forest depletion (% of GNI)	..	0.0
CO_2 damage (% of GNI)	..	0.3
Particulate emission damage (% of GNI)	..	0.3
Adjusted net savings (% of GNI)	..	9.2

Guatemala

Environmental strategy/action plan prepared in **1994**

	Country data	Group data Latin America & Caribbean	Group data Lower middle income
Population (millions)	12.3	533	2,655
Urban population (% of total)	40.6	76.6	49.8
GDP ($ billions)	24.7	1,741	4,168
GNI per capita, *Atlas* method ($)	1,910	3,280	1,490
Agriculture and fisheries			
Land area (1,000 sq. km)	108	20,057	56,103
Agricultural land (% of land area)	42	39	35
Irrigated land (% of crop land)	6.8	12.5	20.8
Fertilizer consumption (100 grams/ha arable land)	1,369	892	1,170
Population density, rural (people/sq. km arable land)	526	210	497
Fish catch, total (1,000 metric tons)	14	17,804	74,407
Forests			
Forest area (1,000 sq. km)	29	9,552	20,316
Forest area share of total land area (%)	26.3	47.6	36.2
Annual deforestation (% change, 1990–2000)	1.7	0.5	0.1
Biodiversity			
Mammal species, total known	250		
Mammal species, threatened	6		
Bird species, total breeding	221		
Bird species, threatened	6		
Nationally protected area (% of land area)	20.0	11.2	7.7
Energy			
GDP per unit of energy use (2000 PPP$/kg oil equiv)	6.4	6.1	4.1
Energy use per capita (kg oil equiv)	616	1,156	1,227
Energy from biomass products and waste (% of total)	52.8	14.6	12.3
Energy imports, net (% of energy use)	27	–42	–22
Electric power consumption per capita (kWh)	361	1,506	1,289
Electricity generated by coal (% of total)	15.7	5.0	42.8
Emissions and pollution			
CO_2 emissions per unit of GDP (kg/2000 PPP$ GDP)	0.2	0.4	0.6
CO_2 emissions per capita (metric tons)	0.9	2.7	2.9
Particulate matter (pop. weighted average, μg/cu. m)	59	40	49
Passenger cars (per 1,000 people)	1	..	28
Water and sanitation			
Internal freshwater resources per capita (cu. m)	8,857	25,245	8,397
Freshwater withdrawal			
Total (% of internal resources)	1.1	2.0	5.9
Agriculture (% of total freshwater withdrawal)	74	74	74
Access to improved water source (% of total population)	95	89	82
Rural (% of rural population)	92	69	71
Urban (% of urban population)	99	96	94
Access to sanitation (% of total population)	61	74	60
Rural (% of rural population)	52	44	41
Urban (% of urban population)	72	84	80
Under-five mortality rate (per 1,000)	47	33	39
National accounting aggregates, 2003			
Gross national savings (% of GNI)	13.9	19.5	30.6
Consumption of fixed capital (% of GNI)	10.1	10.3	9.8
Education expenditure (% of GNI)	1.6	4.2	3.2
Energy depletion (% of GNI)	0.9	6.4	8.1
Mineral depletion (% of GNI)	0.0	0.7	0.4
Net forest depletion (% of GNI)	0.9	0.0	0.1
CO_2 damage (% of GNI)	0.3	0.5	1.6
Particulate emission damage (% of GNI)	0.2	0.5	0.7
Adjusted net savings (% of GNI)	3.1	5.3	13.2

Guinea

Environmental strategy/action plan prepared in **1994**

	Country data	Sub-Saharan Africa	Low income
		Group data	
Population (millions)	7.9	705	2,312
Urban population (% of total)	28.9	36.5	30.4
GDP ($ billions)	3.6	439	1,103
GNI per capita, *Atlas* method ($)	430	500	440
Agriculture and fisheries			
Land area (1,000 sq. km)	246	23,596	30,456
Agricultural land (% of land area)	50	43	43
Irrigated land (% of crop land)	6.2	4.2	26.7
Fertilizer consumption (100 grams/ha arable land)	36	145	654
Population density, rural (people/sq. km arable land)	616	352	509
Fish catch, total (1,000 metric tons)	90	5,191	16,410
Forests			
Forest area (1,000 sq. km)	69	6,435	7,939
Forest area share of total land area (%)	28.2	27.3	26.1
Annual deforestation (% change, 1990–2000)	0.5	0.8	0.7
Biodiversity			
Mammal species, total known	190		
Mammal species, threatened	12		
Bird species, total breeding	109		
Bird species, threatened	10		
Nationally protected area (% of land area)	0.7	8.7	7.7
Energy			
GDP per unit of energy use (2000 PPP$/kg oil equiv)	..	2.8	4.1
Energy use per capita (kg oil equiv)	..	667	493
Energy from biomass products and waste (% of total)	..	57.5	49.4
Energy imports, net (% of energy use)	..	−56	−6
Electric power consumption per capita (kWh)	..	457	312
Electricity generated by coal (% of total)	..	68.2	47.4
Emissions and pollution			
CO_2 emissions per unit of GDP (kg/2000 PPP$ GDP)	0.1	0.4	0.4
CO_2 emissions per capita (metric tons)	0.2	0.7	0.8
Particulate matter (pop. weighted average, μg/cu. m)	69	54	63
Passenger cars (per 1,000 people)	..	..	..
Water and sanitation			
Internal freshwater resources per capita (cu. m)	28,575	5,546	3,583
Freshwater withdrawal			
Total (% of internal resources)	0.3	1.8	11.5
Agriculture (% of total freshwater withdrawal)	87	85	92
Access to improved water source (% of total population)	51	58	75
Rural (% of rural population)	38	46	70
Urban (% of urban population)	78	82	89
Access to sanitation (% of total population)	13	36	36
Rural (% of rural population)	6	26	24
Urban (% of urban population)	25	55	61
Under-five mortality rate (per 1,000)	160	171	123
National accounting aggregates, 2003			
Gross national savings (% of GNI)	10.3	16.9	23.1
Consumption of fixed capital (% of GNI)	8.0	10.6	8.9
Education expenditure (% of GNI)	2.0	4.7	3.4
Energy depletion (% of GNI)	0.0	8.0	5.8
Mineral depletion (% of GNI)	1.4	0.5	0.3
Net forest depletion (% of GNI)	1.7	0.7	0.8
CO_2 damage (% of GNI)	0.3	0.9	1.2
Particulate emission damage (% of GNI)	0.6	0.4	0.6
Adjusted net savings (% of GNI)	0.2	0.6	8.9

Guinea-Bissau

Environmental strategy/action plan prepared in **1993**

	Country data	Group data Sub-Saharan Africa	Group data Low income
Population (millions)	1.5	705	2,312
Urban population (% of total)	33.9	36.5	30.4
GDP ($ billions)	0.2	439	1,103
GNI per capita, *Atlas* method ($)	140	500	440
Agriculture and fisheries			
Land area (1,000 sq. km)	28	23,596	30,456
Agricultural land (% of land area)	58	43	43
Irrigated land (% of crop land)	3.1	4.2	26.7
Fertilizer consumption (100 grams/ha arable land)	80	145	654
Population density, rural (people/sq. km arable land)	322	352	509
Fish catch, total (1,000 metric tons)	5	5,191	16,410
Forests			
Forest area (1,000 sq. km)	22	6,435	7,939
Forest area share of total land area (%)	77.8	27.3	26.1
Annual deforestation (% change, 1990–2000)	0.9	0.8	0.7
Biodiversity			
Mammal species, total known	108		
Mammal species, threatened	3		
Bird species, total breeding	235		
Bird species, threatened	0		
Nationally protected area (% of land area)	..	8.7	7.7
Energy			
GDP per unit of energy use (2000 PPP$/kg oil equiv)	..	2.8	4.1
Energy use per capita (kg oil equiv)	..	667	493
Energy from biomass products and waste (% of total)	..	57.5	49.4
Energy imports, net (% of energy use)	..	–56	–6
Electric power consumption per capita (kWh)	..	457	312
Electricity generated by coal (% of total)	..	68.2	47.4
Emissions and pollution			
CO_2 emissions per unit of GDP (kg/2000 PPP$ GDP)	0.2	0.4	0.4
CO_2 emissions per capita (metric tons)	0.2	0.7	0.8
Particulate matter (pop. weighted average, µg/cu. m)	86	54	63
Passenger cars (per 1,000 people)	..	..	..
Water and sanitation			
Internal freshwater resources per capita (cu. m)	10,744	5,546	3,583
Freshwater withdrawal			
Total (% of internal resources)	0.0	1.8	11.5
Agriculture (% of total freshwater withdrawal)	36	85	92
Access to improved water source (% of total population)	59	58	75
Rural (% of rural population)	49	46	70
Urban (% of urban population)	79	82	89
Access to sanitation (% of total population)	34	36	36
Rural (% of rural population)	23	26	24
Urban (% of urban population)	57	55	61
Under-five mortality rate (per 1,000)	204	171	123
National accounting aggregates, 2003			
Gross national savings (% of GNI)	–5.7	16.9	23.1
Consumption of fixed capital (% of GNI)	6.9	10.6	8.9
Education expenditure (% of GNI)	..	4.7	3.4
Energy depletion (% of GNI)	0.0	8.0	5.8
Mineral depletion (% of GNI)	0.0	0.5	0.3
Net forest depletion (% of GNI)	0.0	0.7	0.8
CO_2 damage (% of GNI)	0.6	0.9	1.2
Particulate emission damage (% of GNI)	..	0.4	0.6
Adjusted net savings (% of GNI)	..	0.6	8.9

Guyana

Environmental strategy/action plan prepared in ..

	Country data	Latin America & Caribbean	Lower middle income
		Group data	
Population (millions)	0.8	533	2,655
Urban population (% of total)	37.6	76.6	49.8
GDP ($ billions)	0.7	1,741	4,168
GNI per capita, *Atlas* method ($)	900	3,280	1,490
Agriculture and fisheries			
Land area (1,000 sq. km)	197	20,057	56,103
Agricultural land (% of land area)	9	39	35
Irrigated land (% of crop land)	29.4	12.5	20.8
Fertilizer consumption (100 grams/ha arable land)	372	892	1,170
Population density, rural (people/sq. km arable land)	100	210	497
Fish catch, total (1,000 metric tons)	54	17,804	74,407
Forests			
Forest area (1,000 sq. km)	169	9,552	20,316
Forest area share of total land area (%)	85.7	47.6	36.2
Annual deforestation (% change, 1990–2000)	0.3	0.5	0.1
Biodiversity			
Mammal species, total known	193		
Mammal species, threatened	11		
Bird species, total breeding	242		
Bird species, threatened	2		
Nationally protected area (% of land area)	0.3	11.2	7.7
Energy			
GDP per unit of energy use (2000 PPP$/kg oil equiv)	..	6.1	4.1
Energy use per capita (kg oil equiv)	..	1,156	1,227
Energy from biomass products and waste (% of total)	..	14.6	12.3
Energy imports, net (% of energy use)	..	−42	−22
Electric power consumption per capita (kWh)	..	1,506	1,289
Electricity generated by coal (% of total)	..	5.0	42.8
Emissions and pollution			
CO_2 emissions per unit of GDP (kg/2000 PPP$ GDP)	0.5	0.4	0.6
CO_2 emissions per capita (metric tons)	2.1	2.7	2.9
Particulate matter (pop. weighted average, µg/cu. m)	34	40	49
Passenger cars (per 1,000 people)	..	..	28
Water and sanitation			
Internal freshwater resources per capita (cu. m)	313,440	25,245	8,397
Freshwater withdrawal			
Total (% of internal resources)	0.6	2.0	5.9
Agriculture (% of total freshwater withdrawal)	99	74	74
Access to improved water source (% of total population)	83	89	82
Rural (% of rural population)	83	69	71
Urban (% of urban population)	83	96	94
Access to sanitation (% of total population)	70	74	60
Rural (% of rural population)	60	44	41
Urban (% of urban population)	86	84	80
Under-five mortality rate (per 1,000)	69	33	39
National accounting aggregates, 2003			
Gross national savings (% of GNI)	..	19.5	30.6
Consumption of fixed capital (% of GNI)	9.5	10.3	9.8
Education expenditure (% of GNI)	3.3	4.2	3.2
Energy depletion (% of GNI)	0.0	6.4	8.1
Mineral depletion (% of GNI)	5.4	0.7	0.4
Net forest depletion (% of GNI)	0.0	0.0	0.1
CO_2 damage (% of GNI)	1.5	0.5	1.6
Particulate emission damage (% of GNI)	..	0.5	0.7
Adjusted net savings (% of GNI)	..	5.3	13.2

Haiti

Environmental strategy/action plan prepared in **1999**

	Country data	Group data Latin America & Caribbean	Low income
Population (millions)	8.4	533	2,312
Urban population (% of total)	37.6	76.6	30.4
GDP ($ billions)	2.9	1,741	1,103
GNI per capita, *Atlas* method ($)	400	3,280	440
Agriculture and fisheries			
Land area (1,000 sq. km)	28	20,057	30,456
Agricultural land (% of land area)	58	39	43
Irrigated land (% of crop land)	6.8	12.5	26.7
Fertilizer consumption (100 grams/ha arable land)	179	892	654
Population density, rural (people/sq. km arable land)	669	210	509
Fish catch, total (1,000 metric tons)	5	17,804	16,410
Forests			
Forest area (1,000 sq. km)	1	9,552	7,939
Forest area share of total land area (%)	3.2	47.6	26.1
Annual deforestation (% change, 1990–2000)	5.7	0.5	0.7
Biodiversity			
Mammal species, total known	20		
Mammal species, threatened	4		
Bird species, total breeding	62		
Bird species, threatened	14		
Nationally protected area (% of land area)	0.4	11.2	7.7
Energy			
GDP per unit of energy use (2000 PPP$/kg oil equiv)	6.6	6.1	4.1
Energy use per capita (kg oil equiv)	251	1,156	493
Energy from biomass products and waste (% of total)	71.6	14.6	49.4
Energy imports, net (% of energy use)	27	–42	–6
Electric power consumption per capita (kWh)	36	1,506	312
Electricity generated by coal (% of total)	..	5.0	47.4
Emissions and pollution			
CO_2 emissions per unit of GDP (kg/2000 PPP$ GDP)	0.1	0.4	0.4
CO_2 emissions per capita (metric tons)	0.2	2.7	0.8
Particulate matter (pop. weighted average, μg/cu. m)	50	40	63
Passenger cars (per 1,000 people)	..	..	..
Water and sanitation			
Internal freshwater resources per capita (cu. m)	1,540	25,245	3,583
Freshwater withdrawal			
Total (% of internal resources)	7.7	2.0	11.5
Agriculture (% of total freshwater withdrawal)	94	74	92
Access to improved water source (% of total population)	71	89	75
Rural (% of rural population)	59	69	70
Urban (% of urban population)	91	96	89
Access to sanitation (% of total population)	34	74	36
Rural (% of rural population)	23	44	24
Urban (% of urban population)	52	84	61
Under-five mortality rate (per 1,000)	118	33	123
National accounting aggregates, 2003			
Gross national savings (% of GNI)	32.4	19.5	23.1
Consumption of fixed capital (% of GNI)	1.8	10.3	8.9
Education expenditure (% of GNI)	1.5	4.2	3.4
Energy depletion (% of GNI)	0.0	6.4	5.8
Mineral depletion (% of GNI)	0.0	0.7	0.3
Net forest depletion (% of GNI)	1.2	0.0	0.8
CO_2 damage (% of GNI)	0.3	0.5	1.2
Particulate emission damage (% of GNI)	0.2	0.5	0.6
Adjusted net savings (% of GNI)	30.3	5.3	8.9

Honduras

Environmental strategy/action plan prepared in **1993**

	Country data	Latin America & Caribbean	Lower middle income
Population (millions)	7.0	533	2,655
Urban population (% of total)	55.5	76.6	49.8
GDP ($ billions)	7.0	1,741	4,168
GNI per capita, *Atlas* method ($)	970	3,280	1,490
Agriculture and fisheries			
Land area (1,000 sq. km)	112	20,057	56,103
Agricultural land (% of land area)	26	39	35
Irrigated land (% of crop land)	5.6	12.5	20.8
Fertilizer consumption (100 grams/ha arable land)	470	892	1,170
Population density, rural (people/sq. km arable land)	289	210	497
Fish catch, total (1,000 metric tons)	16	17,804	74,407
Forests			
Forest area (1,000 sq. km)	54	9,552	20,316
Forest area share of total land area (%)	48.1	47.6	36.2
Annual deforestation (% change, 1990–2000)	1.0	0.5	0.1
Biodiversity			
Mammal species, total known	173		
Mammal species, threatened	10		
Bird species, total breeding	232		
Bird species, threatened	5		
Nationally protected area (% of land area)	6.4	11.2	7.7
Energy			
GDP per unit of energy use (2000 PPP$/kg oil equiv)	5.0	6.1	4.1
Energy use per capita (kg oil equiv)	504	1,156	1,227
Energy from biomass products and waste (% of total)	41.1	14.6	12.3
Energy imports, net (% of energy use)	53	–42	–22
Electric power consumption per capita (kWh)	537	1,506	1,289
Electricity generated by coal (% of total)	..	5.0	42.8
Emissions and pollution			
CO_2 emissions per unit of GDP (kg/2000 PPP$ GDP)	0.3	0.4	0.6
CO_2 emissions per capita (metric tons)	0.7	2.7	2.9
Particulate matter (pop. weighted average, µg/cu. m)	49	40	49
Passenger cars (per 1,000 people)	51	..	28
Water and sanitation			
Internal freshwater resources per capita (cu. m)	13,776	25,245	8,397
Freshwater withdrawal			
Total (% of internal resources)	1.6	2.0	5.9
Agriculture (% of total freshwater withdrawal)	91	74	74
Access to improved water source (% of total population)	90	89	82
Rural (% of rural population)	82	69	71
Urban (% of urban population)	99	96	94
Access to sanitation (% of total population)	68	74	60
Rural (% of rural population)	52	44	41
Urban (% of urban population)	89	84	80
Under-five mortality rate (per 1,000)	41	33	39
National accounting aggregates, 2003			
Gross national savings (% of GNI)	23.6	19.5	30.6
Consumption of fixed capital (% of GNI)	5.6	10.3	9.8
Education expenditure (% of GNI)	3.5	4.2	3.2
Energy depletion (% of GNI)	0.0	6.4	8.1
Mineral depletion (% of GNI)	0.1	0.7	0.4
Net forest depletion (% of GNI)	0.0	0.0	0.1
CO_2 damage (% of GNI)	0.5	0.5	1.6
Particulate emission damage (% of GNI)	0.2	0.5	0.7
Adjusted net savings (% of GNI)	20.8	5.3	13.2

Hong Kong, China

Environmental strategy/action plan prepared in ..

	Country data	Group data — High income
Population (millions)	6.8	972
Urban population (% of total)	100.0	79.9
GDP ($ billions)	157	29,341
GNI per capita, *Atlas* method ($)	25,860	28,600

Agriculture and fisheries
Land area (1,000 sq. km)	1	31,030
Agricultural land (% of land area)	7	36
Irrigated land (% of crop land)	..	12.3
Fertilizer consumption (100 grams/ha arable land)	..	1,198
Population density, rural (people/sq. km arable land)	..	202
Fish catch, total (1,000 metric tons)	..	28,712

Forests
Forest area (1,000 sq. km)	..	7,929
Forest area share of total land area (%)	..	25.9
Annual deforestation (% change, 1990–2000)	..	−0.1

Biodiversity
Mammal species, total known		
Mammal species, threatened	1	
Bird species, total breeding	..	
Bird species, threatened	11	
Nationally protected area (% of land area)	..	19.5

Energy
GDP per unit of energy use (2000 PPP$/kg oil equiv)	10.6	5.2
Energy use per capita (kg oil equiv)	2,413	5,395
Energy from biomass products and waste (% of total)	0.3	3.1
Energy imports, net (% of energy use)	100	26
Electric power consumption per capita (kWh)	5,612	8,693
Electricity generated by coal (% of total)	63.8	38.2

Emissions and pollution
CO_2 emissions per unit of GDP (kg/2000 PPP$ GDP)	0.2	0.5
CO_2 emissions per capita (metric tons)	5.0	12.4
Particulate matter (pop. weighted average, µg/cu. m)	38	33
Passenger cars (per 1,000 people)	57	436

Water and sanitation
Internal freshwater resources per capita (cu. m)	..	9,479
Freshwater withdrawal		
Total (% of internal resources)	..	9.7
Agriculture (% of total freshwater withdrawal)	..	42
Access to improved water source (% of total population)	..	99
Rural (% of rural population)	..	98
Urban (% of urban population)	..	100
Access to sanitation (% of total population)	..	..
Rural (% of rural population)	..	..
Urban (% of urban population)	..	..
Under-five mortality rate (per 1,000)	..	7

National accounting aggregates, 2003
Gross national savings (% of GNI)	34.3	19.1
Consumption of fixed capital (% of GNI)	12.5	13.2
Education expenditure (% of GNI)	2.8	4.6
Energy depletion (% of GNI)	0.0	0.8
Mineral depletion (% of GNI)	0.0	0.0
Net forest depletion (% of GNI)	0.0	0.0
CO_2 damage (% of GNI)	0.2	0.3
Particulate emission damage (% of GNI)	0.0	0.3
Adjusted net savings (% of GNI)	24.5	9.2

Hungary

Environmental strategy/action plan prepared in **1995**

	Country data	Europe & Central Asia	Upper middle income
		Group data	
Population (millions)	10.1	472	333
Urban population (% of total)	65.4	63.8	75.4
GDP ($ billions)	82.7	1,403	1,856
GNI per capita, *Atlas* method ($)	6,350	2,580	5,440
Agriculture and fisheries			
Land area (1,000 sq. km)	92	23,868	12,741
Agricultural land (% of land area)	64	28	48
Irrigated land (% of crop land)	4.8	10.9	13.5
Fertilizer consumption (100 grams/ha arable land)	1,087	344	796
Population density, rural (people/sq. km arable land)	77	122	193
Fish catch, total (1,000 metric tons)	20	5,527	10,082
Forests			
Forest area (1,000 sq. km)	18	9,463	2,427
Forest area share of total land area (%)	20.0	39.6	19.1
Annual deforestation (% change, 1990–2000)	–0.4	–0.1	0.6
Biodiversity			
Mammal species, total known	83		
Mammal species, threatened	9		
Bird species, total breeding	208		
Bird species, threatened	8		
Nationally protected area (% of land area)	7.0	6.8	17.3
Energy			
GDP per unit of energy use (2000 PPP$/kg oil equiv)	5.3	2.5	4.3
Energy use per capita (kg oil equiv)	2,505	2,697	2,232
Energy from biomass products and waste (% of total)	1.6	2.3	4.1
Energy imports, net (% of energy use)	57	–23	–91
Electric power consumption per capita (kWh)	3,099	2,808	2,496
Electricity generated by coal (% of total)	25.1	29.4	23.9
Emissions and pollution			
CO_2 emissions per unit of GDP (kg/2000 PPP$ GDP)	0.4	1.1	0.6
CO_2 emissions per capita (metric tons)	5.4	6.7	6.3
Particulate matter (pop. weighted average, μg/cu. m)	25	33	29
Passenger cars (per 1,000 people)	259	138	153
Water and sanitation			
Internal freshwater resources per capita (cu. m)	592	11,128	10,741
Freshwater withdrawal			
Total (% of internal resources)	113.3	7.4	5.7
Agriculture (% of total freshwater withdrawal)	36	57	71
Access to improved water source (% of total population)	99	91	..
Rural (% of rural population)	98	80	..
Urban (% of urban population)	100	98	96
Access to sanitation (% of total population)	95	82	..
Rural (% of rural population)	85	64	..
Urban (% of urban population)	100	93	..
Under-five mortality rate (per 1,000)	7	36	22
National accounting aggregates, 2003			
Gross national savings (% of GNI)	17.7	21.9	22.1
Consumption of fixed capital (% of GNI)	12.4	10.7	10.7
Education expenditure (% of GNI)	5.0	4.1	5.0
Energy depletion (% of GNI)	0.5	11.6	11.4
Mineral depletion (% of GNI)	0.0	0.1	0.3
Net forest depletion (% of GNI)	0.0	0.0	0.0
CO_2 damage (% of GNI)	0.6	1.9	0.8
Particulate emission damage (% of GNI)	0.4	0.6	0.6
Adjusted net savings (% of GNI)	8.9	1.1	3.3

Iceland

Environmental strategy/action plan prepared in ..

	Country data	High income
		Group data
	Country data	**High income**
Population (millions)	0.3	972
Urban population (% of total)	92.9	79.9
GDP ($ billions)	11	29,341
GNI per capita, *Atlas* method ($)	30,910	28,600
Agriculture and fisheries		
Land area (1,000 sq. km)	100	31,030
Agricultural land (% of land area)	23	36
Irrigated land (% of crop land)	..	12.3
Fertilizer consumption (100 grams/ha arable land)	25,554	1,198
Population density, rural (people/sq. km arable land)	297	202
Fish catch, total (1,000 metric tons)	1,985	28,712
Forests		
Forest area (1,000 sq. km)	0	7,929
Forest area share of total land area (%)	0.3	25.9
Annual deforestation (% change, 1990–2000)	–2.2	–0.1
Biodiversity		
Mammal species, total known	11	
Mammal species, threatened	6	
Bird species, total breeding	93	
Bird species, threatened	0	
Nationally protected area (% of land area)	9.8	19.5
Energy		
GDP per unit of energy use (2000 PPP$/kg oil equiv)	2.4	5.2
Energy use per capita (kg oil equiv)	11,819	5,395
Energy from biomass products and waste (% of total)	0.1	3.1
Energy imports, net (% of energy use)	28	26
Electric power consumption per capita (kWh)	26,247	8,693
Electricity generated by coal (% of total)	..	38.2
Emissions and pollution		
CO_2 emissions per unit of GDP (kg/2000 PPP$ GDP)	0.3	0.5
CO_2 emissions per capita (metric tons)	7.7	12.4
Particulate matter (pop. weighted average, µg/cu. m)	21	33
Passenger cars (per 1,000 people)	561	436
Water and sanitation		
Internal freshwater resources per capita (cu. m)	588,235	9,479
Freshwater withdrawal		
Total (% of internal resources)	0.1	9.7
Agriculture (% of total freshwater withdrawal)	6	42
Access to improved water source (% of total population)	100	99
Rural (% of rural population)	100	98
Urban (% of urban population)	100	100
Access to sanitation (% of total population)	..	..
Rural (% of rural population)	..	..
Urban (% of urban population)	..	..
Under-five mortality rate (per 1,000)	4	7
National accounting aggregates, 2003		
Gross national savings (% of GNI)	16.1	19.1
Consumption of fixed capital (% of GNI)	13.4	13.2
Education expenditure (% of GNI)	5.2	4.6
Energy depletion (% of GNI)	0.0	0.8
Mineral depletion (% of GNI)	0.0	0.0
Net forest depletion (% of GNI)	0.0	0.0
CO_2 damage (% of GNI)	0.2	0.3
Particulate emission damage (% of GNI)	..	0.3
Adjusted net savings (% of GNI)	7.7	9.2

India

Environmental strategy/action plan prepared in **1993**

	Country data	Group data South Asia	Low income
Population (millions)	1,064.4	1,425	2,312
Urban population (% of total)	28.3	28.3	30.4
GDP ($ billions)	600.6	765	1,103
GNI per capita, *Atlas* method ($)	540	510	440
Agriculture and fisheries			
Land area (1,000 sq. km)	2,973	4,781	30,456
Agricultural land (% of land area)	..	55	43
Irrigated land (% of crop land)	33.6	41.2	26.7
Fertilizer consumption (100 grams/ha arable land)	996	1,027	654
Population density, rural (people/sq. km arable land)	466	559	509
Fish catch, total (1,000 metric tons)	5,965	8,724	16,410
Forests			
Forest area (1,000 sq. km)	641	780	7,939
Forest area share of total land area (%)	21.6	16.3	26.1
Annual deforestation (% change, 1990–2000)	–0.1	0.1	0.7
Biodiversity			
Mammal species, total known	390		
Mammal species, threatened	88		
Bird species, total breeding	458		
Bird species, threatened	72		
Nationally protected area (% of land area)	5.2	4.8	7.7
Energy			
GDP per unit of energy use (2000 PPP$/kg oil equiv)	5.0	5.1	4.1
Energy use per capita (kg oil equiv)	513	468	493
Energy from biomass products and waste (% of total)	38.7	39.3	49.4
Energy imports, net (% of energy use)	18	19	-6
Electric power consumption per capita (kWh)	380	344	312
Electricity generated by coal (% of total)	70.1	59.8	47.4
Emissions and pollution			
CO_2 emissions per unit of GDP (kg/2000 PPP$ GDP)	0.4	0.4	0.4
CO_2 emissions per capita (metric tons)	1.1	0.9	0.8
Particulate matter (pop. weighted average, µg/cu. m)	..	69	63
Passenger cars (per 1,000 people)	6	6	..
Water and sanitation			
Internal freshwater resources per capita (cu. m)	1,185	1,275	3,583
Freshwater withdrawal			
Total (% of internal resources)	39.7	40.5	11.5
Agriculture (% of total freshwater withdrawal)	92	94	92
Access to improved water source (% of total population)	86	84	75
Rural (% of rural population)	82	80	70
Urban (% of urban population)	96	93	89
Access to sanitation (% of total population)	30	35	36
Rural (% of rural population)	18	23	24
Urban (% of urban population)	58	64	61
Under-five mortality rate (per 1,000)	87	92	123
National accounting aggregates, 2003			
Gross national savings (% of GNI)	24.8	24.9	23.1
Consumption of fixed capital (% of GNI)	9.6	9.0	8.9
Education expenditure (% of GNI)	3.9	3.5	3.4
Energy depletion (% of GNI)	2.4	2.4	5.8
Mineral depletion (% of GNI)	0.3	0.3	0.3
Net forest depletion (% of GNI)	0.7	0.7	0.8
CO_2 damage (% of GNI)	1.5	1.3	1.2
Particulate emission damage (% of GNI)	0.7	0.7	0.6
Adjusted net savings (% of GNI)	13.5	14.0	8.9

Indonesia

Environmental strategy/action plan prepared in **1993**

	Country data	East Asia & Pacific	Lower middle income
		Group data	
Population (millions)	214.7	1,855	2,655
Urban population (% of total)	44.1	39.1	49.8
GDP ($ billions)	208.3	2,033	4,168
GNI per capita, *Atlas* method ($)	810	1,070	1,490
Agriculture and fisheries			
Land area (1,000 sq. km)	1,812	15,886	56,103
Agricultural land (% of land area)	25	50	35
Irrigated land (% of crop land)	14.3	..	20.8
Fertilizer consumption (100 grams/ha arable land)	1,460	2,297	1,170
Population density, rural (people/sq. km arable land)	588	565	497
Fish catch, total (1,000 metric tons)	5,068	60,812	74,407
Forests			
Forest area (1,000 sq. km)	1,050	4,284	20,316
Forest area share of total land area (%)	58.0	27.0	36.2
Annual deforestation (% change, 1990–2000)	1.2	0.2	0.1
Biodiversity			
Mammal species, total known	515		
Mammal species, threatened	147		
Bird species, total breeding	929		
Bird species, threatened	114		
Nationally protected area (% of land area)	20.6	9.2	7.7
Energy			
GDP per unit of energy use (2000 PPP$/kg oil equiv)	4.1	4.6	4.1
Energy use per capita (kg oil equiv)	737	904	1,227
Energy from biomass products and waste (% of total)	27.4	19.6	12.3
Energy imports, net (% of energy use)	−54	−4	−22
Electric power consumption per capita (kWh)	411	891	1,289
Electricity generated by coal (% of total)	39.7	66.8	42.8
Emissions and pollution			
CO_2 emissions per unit of GDP (kg/2000 PPP$ GDP)	0.4	0.5	0.6
CO_2 emissions per capita (metric tons)	1.3	2.1	2.9
Particulate matter (pop. weighted average, µg/cu. m)	102	69	49
Passenger cars (per 1,000 people)	..	10	28
Water and sanitation			
Internal freshwater resources per capita (cu. m)	13,220	5,103	8,397
Freshwater withdrawal			
Total (% of internal resources)	2.6	8.2	5.9
Agriculture (% of total freshwater withdrawal)	93	81	74
Access to improved water source (% of total population)	78	78	82
Rural (% of rural population)	69	69	71
Urban (% of urban population)	89	92	94
Access to sanitation (% of total population)	52	49	60
Rural (% of rural population)	38	35	41
Urban (% of urban population)	71	71	80
Under-five mortality rate (per 1,000)	41	41	39
National accounting aggregates, 2003			
Gross national savings (% of GNI)	18.8	41.7	30.6
Consumption of fixed capital (% of GNI)	5.4	9.2	9.8
Education expenditure (% of GNI)	1.3	2.3	3.2
Energy depletion (% of GNI)	8.8	3.9	8.1
Mineral depletion (% of GNI)	1.3	0.3	0.4
Net forest depletion (% of GNI)	0.0	0.1	0.1
CO_2 damage (% of GNI)	0.7	1.8	1.6
Particulate emission damage (% of GNI)	0.5	0.8	0.7
Adjusted net savings (% of GNI)	3.3	27.9	13.2

Iran, Islamic Rep.

Environmental strategy/action plan prepared in ..

	Country data	Middle East & North Africa	Lower middle income
		Group data	
Population (millions)	66.4	312	2,655
Urban population (% of total)	66.1	59.0	49.8
GDP ($ billions)	137.1	745	4,168
GNI per capita, *Atlas* method ($)	2,010	2,390	1,490
Agriculture and fisheries			
Land area (1,000 sq. km)	1,636	11,111	56,103
Agricultural land (% of land area)	37	34	35
Irrigated land (% of crop land)	43.9	38.3	20.8
Fertilizer consumption (100 grams/ha arable land)	860	854	1,170
Population density, rural (people/sq. km arable land)	151	603	497
Fish catch, total (1,000 metric tons)	399	2,840	74,407
Forests			
Forest area (1,000 sq. km)	73	168	20,316
Forest area share of total land area (%)	4.5	1.5	36.2
Annual deforestation (% change, 1990–2000)	0.0	–0.1	0.1
Biodiversity			
Mammal species, total known	140		
Mammal species, threatened	22		
Bird species, total breeding	293		
Bird species, threatened	13		
Nationally protected area (% of land area)	4.8	11.3	7.7
Energy			
GDP per unit of energy use (2000 PPP$/kg oil equiv)	3.1	3.5	4.1
Energy use per capita (kg oil equiv)	2,044	1,504	1,227
Energy from biomass products and waste (% of total)	0.6	1.0	12.3
Energy imports, net (% of energy use)	–80	–168	–22
Electric power consumption per capita (kWh)	1,677	1,412	1,289
Electricity generated by coal (% of total)	..	2.3	42.8
Emissions and pollution			
CO_2 emissions per unit of GDP (kg/2000 PPP$ GDP)	0.9	0.8	0.6
CO_2 emissions per capita (metric tons)	4.9	4.2	2.9
Particulate matter (pop. weighted average, µg/cu. m)	71	87	49
Passenger cars (per 1,000 people)	..	..	28
Water and sanitation			
Internal freshwater resources per capita (cu. m)	1,943	761	8,397
Freshwater withdrawal			
Total (% of internal resources)	54.3	101.7	5.9
Agriculture (% of total freshwater withdrawal)	92	88	74
Access to improved water source (% of total population)	93	88	82
Rural (% of rural population)	83	78	71
Urban (% of urban population)	98	96	94
Access to sanitation (% of total population)	84	75	60
Rural (% of rural population)	78	56	41
Urban (% of urban population)	86	90	80
Under-five mortality rate (per 1,000)	39	53	39
National accounting aggregates, 2003			
Gross national savings (% of GNI)	42.7	31.2	30.6
Consumption of fixed capital (% of GNI)	10.0	10.0	9.8
Education expenditure (% of GNI)	4.6	5.5	3.2
Energy depletion (% of GNI)	33.2	30.7	8.1
Mineral depletion (% of GNI)	0.1	0.1	0.4
Net forest depletion (% of GNI)	0.0	0.0	0.1
CO_2 damage (% of GNI)	1.7	1.2	1.6
Particulate emission damage (% of GNI)	0.7	0.8	0.7
Adjusted net savings (% of GNI)	1.7	–6.2	13.2

Iraq

Environmental strategy/action plan prepared in ..

	Country data	Middle East & North Africa	Lower middle income
Population (millions)	24.7	312	2,655
Urban population (% of total)	67.5	59.0	49.8
GDP ($ billions)	..	745	4,168
GNI per capita, *Atlas* method ($)	..	2,390	1,490
Agriculture and fisheries			
Land area (1,000 sq. km)	437	11,111	56,103
Agricultural land (% of land area)	23	34	35
Irrigated land (% of crop land)	57.9	38.3	20.8
Fertilizer consumption (100 grams/ha arable land)	1,111	854	1,170
Population density, rural (people/sq. km arable land)	137	603	497
Fish catch, total (1,000 metric tons)	23	2,840	74,407
Forests			
Forest area (1,000 sq. km)	8	168	20,316
Forest area share of total land area (%)	1.8	1.5	36.2
Annual deforestation (% change, 1990–2000)	0.0	–0.1	0.1
Biodiversity			
Mammal species, total known	81		
Mammal species, threatened	11		
Bird species, total breeding	140		
Bird species, threatened	11		
Nationally protected area (% of land area)	0.0	11.3	7.7
Energy			
GDP per unit of energy use (2000 PPP$/kg oil equiv)	..	3.5	4.1
Energy use per capita (kg oil equiv)	1,199	1,504	1,227
Energy from biomass products and waste (% of total)	0.1	1.0	12.3
Energy imports, net (% of energy use)	–264	–168	–22
Electric power consumption per capita (kWh)	1,213	1,412	1,289
Electricity generated by coal (% of total)	..	2.3	42.8
Emissions and pollution			
CO_2 emissions per unit of GDP (kg/2000 PPP$ GDP)	..	0.8	0.6
CO_2 emissions per capita (metric tons)	3.3	4.2	2.9
Particulate matter (pop. weighted average, µg/cu. m)	178	87	49
Passenger cars (per 1,000 people)	..	..	28
Water and sanitation			
Internal freshwater resources per capita (cu. m)	1,417	761	8,397
Freshwater withdrawal			
Total (% of internal resources)	122.3	101.7	5.9
Agriculture (% of total freshwater withdrawal)	92	88	74
Access to improved water source (% of total population)	81	88	82
Rural (% of rural population)	50	78	71
Urban (% of urban population)	97	96	94
Access to sanitation (% of total population)	80	75	60
Rural (% of rural population)	48	56	41
Urban (% of urban population)	95	90	80
Under-five mortality rate (per 1,000)	125	53	39
National accounting aggregates, 2003			
Gross national savings (% of GNI)	..	31.2	30.6
Consumption of fixed capital (% of GNI)	..	10.0	9.8
Education expenditure (% of GNI)	..	5.5	3.2
Energy depletion (% of GNI)	..	30.7	8.1
Mineral depletion (% of GNI)	..	0.1	0.4
Net forest depletion (% of GNI)	..	0.0	0.1
CO_2 damage (% of GNI)	..	1.2	1.6
Particulate emission damage (% of GNI)	..	0.8	0.7
Adjusted net savings (% of GNI)	..	–6.2	13.2

Ireland

Environmental strategy/action plan prepared in ..

	Country data	Group data — High income
Population (millions)	4.0	972
Urban population (% of total)	59.8	79.9
GDP ($ billions)	154	29,341
GNI per capita, *Atlas* method ($)	27,010	28,600
Agriculture and fisheries		
Land area (1,000 sq. km)	69	31,030
Agricultural land (% of land area)	64	36
Irrigated land (% of crop land)	..	12.3
Fertilizer consumption (100 grams/ha arable land)	5,236	1,198
Population density, rural (people/sq. km arable land)	142	202
Fish catch, total (1,000 metric tons)	417	28,712
Forests		
Forest area (1,000 sq. km)	7	7,929
Forest area share of total land area (%)	9.6	25.9
Annual deforestation (% change, 1990–2000)	–3.0	–0.1
Biodiversity		
Mammal species, total known	25	
Mammal species, threatened	5	
Bird species, total breeding	143	
Bird species, threatened	1	
Nationally protected area (% of land area)	1.7	19.5
Energy		
GDP per unit of energy use (2000 PPP$/kg oil equiv)	9.1	5.2
Energy use per capita (kg oil equiv)	3,894	5,395
Energy from biomass products and waste (% of total)	1.2	3.1
Energy imports, net (% of energy use)	90	26
Electric power consumption per capita (kWh)	5,555	8,693
Electricity generated by coal (% of total)	35.8	38.2
Emissions and pollution		
CO_2 emissions per unit of GDP (kg/2000 PPP$ GDP)	0.4	0.5
CO_2 emissions per capita (metric tons)	11.1	12.4
Particulate matter (pop. weighted average, µg/cu. m)	23	33
Passenger cars (per 1,000 people)	349	436
Water and sanitation		
Internal freshwater resources per capita (cu. m)	12,268	9,479
Freshwater withdrawal		
Total (% of internal resources)	1.6	9.7
Agriculture (% of total freshwater withdrawal)	10	42
Access to improved water source (% of total population)	..	99
Rural (% of rural population)	..	98
Urban (% of urban population)	100	100
Access to sanitation (% of total population)	..	..
Rural (% of rural population)	..	..
Urban (% of urban population)	..	..
Under-five mortality rate (per 1,000)	7	7
National accounting aggregates, 2003		
Gross national savings (% of GNI)	26.4	19.1
Consumption of fixed capital (% of GNI)	12.6	13.2
Education expenditure (% of GNI)	5.7	4.6
Energy depletion (% of GNI)	0.0	0.8
Mineral depletion (% of GNI)	0.0	0.0
Net forest depletion (% of GNI)	0.0	0.0
CO_2 damage (% of GNI)	0.3	0.3
Particulate emission damage (% of GNI)	0.1	0.3
Adjusted net savings (% of GNI)	19.1	9.2

Isle of Man

Environmental strategy/action plan prepared in ..

	Country data	Group data High income
Population (millions)	0.1	972
Urban population (% of total)	77.4	79.9
GDP ($ billions)	..	29,341
GNI per capita, *Atlas* method ($)	..	28,600

Agriculture and fisheries
Land area (1,000 sq. km)	1	31,030
Agricultural land (% of land area)	..	36
Irrigated land (% of crop land)	..	12.3
Fertilizer consumption (100 grams/ha arable land)	..	1,198
Population density, rural (people/sq. km arable land)	..	202
Fish catch, total (1,000 metric tons)	..	28,712

Forests
Forest area (1,000 sq. km)	..	7,929
Forest area share of total land area (%)	..	25.9
Annual deforestation (% change, 1990–2000)	..	−0.1

Biodiversity
Mammal species, total known	..	
Mammal species, threatened	..	
Bird species, total breeding	..	
Bird species, threatened	..	
Nationally protected area (% of land area)	..	19.5

Energy
GDP per unit of energy use (2000 PPP$/kg oil equiv)	..	5.2
Energy use per capita (kg oil equiv)	..	5,395
Energy from biomass products and waste (% of total)	..	3.1
Energy imports, net (% of energy use)	..	26
Electric power consumption per capita (kWh)	..	8,693
Electricity generated by coal (% of total)	..	38.2

Emissions and pollution
CO_2 emissions per unit of GDP (kg/2000 PPP$ GDP)	..	0.5
CO_2 emissions per capita (metric tons)	..	12.4
Particulate matter (pop. weighted average, µg/cu. m)	..	33
Passenger cars (per 1,000 people)	..	436

Water and sanitation
Internal freshwater resources per capita (cu. m)	..	9,479
Freshwater withdrawal		
Total (% of internal resources)	..	9.7
Agriculture (% of total freshwater withdrawal)	..	42
Access to improved water source (% of total population)	..	99
Rural (% of rural population)	..	98
Urban (% of urban population)	..	100
Access to sanitation (% of total population)	..	..
Rural (% of rural population)	..	..
Urban (% of urban population)	..	..
Under-five mortality rate (per 1,000)	..	7

National accounting aggregates, 2003
Gross national savings (% of GNI)	..	19.1
Consumption of fixed capital (% of GNI)	..	13.2
Education expenditure (% of GNI)	..	4.6
Energy depletion (% of GNI)	..	0.8
Mineral depletion (% of GNI)	..	0.0
Net forest depletion (% of GNI)	..	0.0
CO_2 damage (% of GNI)	..	0.3
Particulate emission damage (% of GNI)	..	0.3
Adjusted net savings (% of GNI)	..	9.2

Israel

Environmental strategy/action plan prepared in ..

	Country data	Group data — High income
Population (millions)	6.7	972
Urban population (% of total)	92.1	79.9
GDP ($ billions)	110	29,341
GNI per capita, *Atlas* method ($)	16,240	28,600
Agriculture and fisheries		
Land area (1,000 sq. km)	22	31,030
Agricultural land (% of land area)	27	36
Irrigated land (% of crop land)	45.8	12.3
Fertilizer consumption (100 grams/ha arable land)	2,405	1,198
Population density, rural (people/sq. km arable land)	157	202
Fish catch, total (1,000 metric tons)	25	28,712
Forests		
Forest area (1,000 sq. km)	1	7,929
Forest area share of total land area (%)	6.1	25.9
Annual deforestation (% change, 1990–2000)	–4.9	–0.1
Biodiversity		
Mammal species, total known	116	
Mammal species, threatened	14	
Bird species, total breeding	162	
Bird species, threatened	12	
Nationally protected area (% of land area)	15.8	19.5
Energy		
GDP per unit of energy use (2000 PPP$/kg oil equiv)	6.0	5.2
Energy use per capita (kg oil equiv)	3,191	5,395
Energy from biomass products and waste (% of total)	0.0	3.1
Energy imports, net (% of energy use)	97	26
Electric power consumption per capita (kWh)	5,857	8,693
Electricity generated by coal (% of total)	77.4	38.2
Emissions and pollution		
CO_2 emissions per unit of GDP (kg/2000 PPP$ GDP)	0.5	0.5
CO_2 emissions per capita (metric tons)	10.0	12.4
Particulate matter (pop. weighted average, µg/cu. m)	52	33
Passenger cars (per 1,000 people)	230	436
Water and sanitation		
Internal freshwater resources per capita (cu. m)	150	9,479
Freshwater withdrawal		
Total (% of internal resources)	160.0	9.7
Agriculture (% of total freshwater withdrawal)	54	42
Access to improved water source (% of total population)	100	99
Rural (% of rural population)	100	98
Urban (% of urban population)	100	100
Access to sanitation (% of total population)	..	..
Rural (% of rural population)	..	..
Urban (% of urban population)	100	..
Under-five mortality rate (per 1,000)	6	7
National accounting aggregates, 2003		
Gross national savings (% of GNI)	14.2	19.1
Consumption of fixed capital (% of GNI)	14.7	13.2
Education expenditure (% of GNI)	6.8	4.6
Energy depletion (% of GNI)	0.0	0.8
Mineral depletion (% of GNI)	0.1	0.0
Net forest depletion (% of GNI)	0.0	0.0
CO_2 damage (% of GNI)	0.4	0.3
Particulate emission damage (% of GNI)	0.0	0.3
Adjusted net savings (% of GNI)	5.8	9.2

Italy

Environmental strategy/action plan prepared in ..

	Country data	Group data High Income
Population (millions)	57.6	972
Urban population (% of total)	67.4	79.9
GDP ($ billions)	1,468	29,341
GNI per capita, *Atlas* method ($)	21,570	28,600
Agriculture and fisheries		
Land area (1,000 sq. km)	294	31,030
Agricultural land (% of land area)	52	36
Irrigated land (% of crop land)	24.9	12.3
Fertilizer consumption (100 grams/ha arable land)	1,729	1,198
Population density, rural (people/sq. km arable land)	228	202
Fish catch, total (1,000 metric tons)	529	28,712
Forests		
Forest area (1,000 sq. km)	100	7,929
Forest area share of total land area (%)	34.0	25.9
Annual deforestation (% change, 1990–2000)	−0.3	−0.1
Biodiversity		
Mammal species, total known	90	
Mammal species, threatened	14	
Bird species, total breeding	250	
Bird species, threatened	5	
Nationally protected area (% of land area)	7.9	19.5
Energy		
GDP per unit of energy use (2000 PPP$/kg oil equiv)	8.5	5.2
Energy use per capita (kg oil equiv)	2,994	5,395
Energy from biomass products and waste (% of total)	1.5	3.1
Energy imports, net (% of energy use)	85	26
Electric power consumption per capita (kWh)	4,901	8,693
Electricity generated by coal (% of total)	14.6	38.2
Emissions and pollution		
CO_2 emissions per unit of GDP (kg/2000 PPP$ GDP)	0.3	0.5
CO_2 emissions per capita (metric tons)	7.4	12.4
Particulate matter (pop. weighted average, µg/cu. m)	33	33
Passenger cars (per 1,000 people)	542	436
Water and sanitation		
Internal freshwater resources per capita (cu. m)	3,175	9,479
Freshwater withdrawal		
Total (% of internal resources)	23.0	9.7
Agriculture (% of total freshwater withdrawal)	48	42
Access to improved water source (% of total population)	..	99
Rural (% of rural population)	..	98
Urban (% of urban population)	100	100
Access to sanitation (% of total population)	..	..
Rural (% of rural population)	..	..
Urban (% of urban population)	..	..
Under-five mortality rate (per 1,000)	6	7
National accounting aggregates, 2003		
Gross national savings (% of GNI)	18.7	19.1
Consumption of fixed capital (% of GNI)	13.7	13.2
Education expenditure (% of GNI)	4.4	4.6
Energy depletion (% of GNI)	0.1	0.8
Mineral depletion (% of GNI)	0.0	0.0
Net forest depletion (% of GNI)	0.0	0.0
CO_2 damage (% of GNI)	0.2	0.3
Particulate emission damage (% of GNI)	0.2	0.3
Adjusted net savings (% of GNI)	8.9	9.2

Jamaica

Environmental strategy/action plan prepared in **1994**

	Country data	Latin America & Caribbean	Lower middle income
		Group data	
Population (millions)	2.6	533	2,655
Urban population (% of total)	57.6	76.6	49.8
GDP ($ billions)	8.1	1,741	4,168
GNI per capita, *Atlas* method ($)	2,980	3,280	1,490
Agriculture and fisheries			
Land area (1,000 sq. km)	11	20,057	56,103
Agricultural land (% of land area)	47	39	35
Irrigated land (% of crop land)	8.8	12.5	20.8
Fertilizer consumption (100 grams/ha arable land)	1,287	892	1,170
Population density, rural (people/sq. km arable land)	647	210	497
Fish catch, total (1,000 metric tons)	10	17,804	74,407
Forests			
Forest area (1,000 sq. km)	3	9,552	20,316
Forest area share of total land area (%)	30.0	47.6	36.2
Annual deforestation (% change, 1990–2000)	1.5	0.5	0.1
Biodiversity			
Mammal species, total known	24		
Mammal species, threatened	5		
Bird species, total breeding	75		
Bird species, threatened	12		
Nationally protected area (% of land area)	84.6	11.2	7.7
Energy			
GDP per unit of energy use (2000 PPP$/kg oil equiv)	2.5	6.1	4.1
Energy use per capita (kg oil equiv)	1,493	1,156	1,227
Energy from biomass products and waste (% of total)	11.6	14.6	12.3
Energy imports, net (% of energy use)	88	–42	–22
Electric power consumption per capita (kWh)	2,406	1,506	1,289
Electricity generated by coal (% of total)	..	5.0	42.8
Emissions and pollution			
CO_2 emissions per unit of GDP (kg/2000 PPP$ GDP)	1.1	0.4	0.6
CO_2 emissions per capita (metric tons)	4.2	2.7	2.9
Particulate matter (pop. weighted average, μg/cu. m)	54	40	49
Passenger cars (per 1,000 people)	..	..	28
Water and sanitation			
Internal freshwater resources per capita (cu. m)	3,406	25,245	8,397
Freshwater withdrawal			
Total (% of internal resources)	10.0	2.0	5.9
Agriculture (% of total freshwater withdrawal)	77	74	74
Access to improved water source (% of total population)	93	89	82
Rural (% of rural population)	87	69	71
Urban (% of urban population)	98	96	94
Access to sanitation (% of total population)	80	74	60
Rural (% of rural population)	68	44	41
Urban (% of urban population)	90	84	80
Under-five mortality rate (per 1,000)	20	33	39
National accounting aggregates, 2003			
Gross national savings (% of GNI)	20.0	19.5	30.6
Consumption of fixed capital (% of GNI)	11.4	10.3	9.8
Education expenditure (% of GNI)	6.0	4.2	3.2
Energy depletion (% of GNI)	0.0	6.4	8.1
Mineral depletion (% of GNI)	1.1	0.7	0.4
Net forest depletion (% of GNI)	0.0	0.0	0.1
CO_2 damage (% of GNI)	1.0	0.5	1.6
Particulate emission damage (% of GNI)	0.3	0.5	0.7
Adjusted net savings (% of GNI)	12.2	5.3	13.2

Japan

Environmental strategy/action plan prepared in ..

	Group data	
	Country data	High Income
Population (millions)	127.6	972
Urban population (% of total)	79.2	79.9
GDP ($ billions)	4,301	29,341
GNI per capita, *Atlas* method ($)	34,180	28,600
Agriculture and fisheries		
Land area (1,000 sq. km)	365	31,030
Agricultural land (% of land area)	14	36
Irrigated land (% of crop land)	54.7	12.3
Fertilizer consumption (100 grams/ha arable land)	2,906	1,198
Population density, rural (people/sq. km arable land)	603	202
Fish catch, total (1,000 metric tons)	5,521	28,712
Forests		
Forest area (1,000 sq. km)	241	7,929
Forest area share of total land area (%)	66.1	25.9
Annual deforestation (% change, 1990–2000)	0.0	–0.1
Biodiversity		
Mammal species, total known	188	
Mammal species, threatened	37	
Bird species, total breeding	210	
Bird species, threatened	34	
Nationally protected area (% of land area)	6.8	19.5
Energy		
GDP per unit of energy use (2000 PPP$/kg oil equiv)	6.4	5.2
Energy use per capita (kg oil equiv)	4,058	5,395
Energy from biomass products and waste (% of total)	1.4	3.1
Energy imports, net (% of energy use)	81	26
Electric power consumption per capita (kWh)	7,718	8,693
Electricity generated by coal (% of total)	26.8	38.2
Emissions and pollution		
CO_2 emissions per unit of GDP (kg/2000 PPP$ GDP)	0.4	0.5
CO_2 emissions per capita (metric tons)	9.3	12.4
Particulate matter (pop. weighted average, µg/cu. m)	33	33
Passenger cars (per 1,000 people)	428	436
Water and sanitation		
Internal freshwater resources per capita (cu. m)	3,371	9,479
Freshwater withdrawal		
Total (% of internal resources)	21.3	9.7
Agriculture (% of total freshwater withdrawal)	64	42
Access to improved water source (% of total population)	100	99
Rural (% of rural population)	100	98
Urban (% of urban population)	100	100
Access to sanitation (% of total population)	100	..
Rural (% of rural population)	100	..
Urban (% of urban population)	100	..
Under-five mortality rate (per 1,000)	5	7
National accounting aggregates, 2003		
Gross national savings (% of GNI)	26.7	19.1
Consumption of fixed capital (% of GNI)	15.9	13.2
Education expenditure (% of GNI)	3.2	4.6
Energy depletion (% of GNI)	0.0	0.8
Mineral depletion (% of GNI)	0.0	0.0
Net forest depletion (% of GNI)	0.0	0.0
CO_2 damage (% of GNI)	0.2	0.3
Particulate emission damage (% of GNI)	0.4	0.3
Adjusted net savings (% of GNI)	13.5	9.2

Jordan

Environmental strategy/action plan prepared in **1991**

	Country data	Group data Middle East & North Africa	Group data Lower middle income
Population (millions)	5.3	312	2,655
Urban population (% of total)	79.1	59.0	49.8
GDP ($ billions)	9.9	745	4,168
GNI per capita, *Atlas* method ($)	1,850	2,390	1,490
Agriculture and fisheries			
Land area (1,000 sq. km)	89	11,111	56,103
Agricultural land (% of land area)	13	34	35
Irrigated land (% of crop land)	18.8	38.3	20.8
Fertilizer consumption (100 grams/ha arable land)	1,136	854	1,170
Population density, rural (people/sq. km arable land)	369	603	497
Fish catch, total (1,000 metric tons)	1	2,840	74,407
Forests			
Forest area (1,000 sq. km)	1	168	20,316
Forest area share of total land area (%)	1.0	1.5	36.2
Annual deforestation (% change, 1990–2000)	0.0	−0.1	0.1
Biodiversity			
Mammal species, total known	71		
Mammal species, threatened	10		
Bird species, total breeding	117		
Bird species, threatened	8		
Nationally protected area (% of land area)	3.4	11.3	7.7
Energy			
GDP per unit of energy use (2000 PPP$/kg oil equiv)	3.9	3.5	4.1
Energy use per capita (kg oil equiv)	1,036	1,504	1,227
Energy from biomass products and waste (% of total)	0.1	1.0	12.3
Energy imports, net (% of energy use)	95	−168	−22
Electric power consumption per capita (kWh)	1,317	1,412	1,289
Electricity generated by coal (% of total)	..	2.3	42.8
Emissions and pollution			
CO_2 emissions per unit of GDP (kg/2000 PPP$ GDP)	0.8	0.8	0.6
CO_2 emissions per capita (metric tons)	3.2	4.2	2.9
Particulate matter (pop. weighted average, μg/cu. m)	77	87	49
Passenger cars (per 1,000 people)	..	..	28
Water and sanitation			
Internal freshwater resources per capita (cu. m)	188	761	8,397
Freshwater withdrawal			
Total (% of internal resources)	100.0	101.7	5.9
Agriculture (% of total freshwater withdrawal)	75	88	74
Access to improved water source (% of total population)	91	88	82
Rural (% of rural population)	91	78	71
Urban (% of urban population)	91	96	94
Access to sanitation (% of total population)	93	75	60
Rural (% of rural population)	85	56	41
Urban (% of urban population)	94	90	80
Under-five mortality rate (per 1,000)	28	53	39
National accounting aggregates, 2003			
Gross national savings (% of GNI)	28.1	31.2	30.6
Consumption of fixed capital (% of GNI)	10.6	10.0	9.8
Education expenditure (% of GNI)	4.4	5.5	3.2
Energy depletion (% of GNI)	0.4	30.7	8.1
Mineral depletion (% of GNI)	1.0	0.1	0.4
Net forest depletion (% of GNI)	0.0	0.0	0.1
CO_2 damage (% of GNI)	1.2	1.2	1.6
Particulate emission damage (% of GNI)	0.7	0.8	0.7
Adjusted net savings (% of GNI)	18.6	−6.2	13.2

Kazakhstan

Environmental strategy/action plan prepared in ..

		Group data	
	Country data	Europe & Central Asia	Lower middle income
Population (millions)	14.9	472	2,655
Urban population (% of total)	55.9	63.8	49.8
GDP ($ billions)	29.7	1,403	4,168
GNI per capita, *Atlas* method ($)	1,780	2,580	1,490
Agriculture and fisheries			
Land area (1,000 sq. km)	2,700	23,868	56,103
Agricultural land (% of land area)	77	28	35
Irrigated land (% of crop land)	10.8	10.9	20.8
Fertilizer consumption (100 grams/ha arable land)	30	344	1,170
Population density, rural (people/sq. km arable land)	30	122	497
Fish catch, total (1,000 metric tons)	31	5,527	74,407
Forests			
Forest area (1,000 sq. km)	121	9,463	20,316
Forest area share of total land area (%)	4.5	39.6	36.2
Annual deforestation (% change, 1990–2000)	−2.2	−0.1	0.1
Biodiversity			
Mammal species, total known	178		
Mammal species, threatened	16		
Bird species, total breeding	379		
Bird species, threatened	15		
Nationally protected area (% of land area)	2.7	6.8	7.7
Energy			
GDP per unit of energy use (2000 PPP$/kg oil equiv)	1.8	2.5	4.1
Energy use per capita (kg oil equiv)	3,123	2,697	1,227
Energy from biomass products and waste (% of total)	0.2	2.3	12.3
Energy imports, net (% of energy use)	−106	−23	−22
Electric power consumption per capita (kWh)	2,911	2,808	1,289
Electricity generated by coal (% of total)	69.9	29.4	42.8
Emissions and pollution			
CO_2 emissions per unit of GDP (kg/2000 PPP$ GDP)	1.8	1.1	0.6
CO_2 emissions per capita (metric tons)	8.1	6.7	2.9
Particulate matter (pop. weighted average, µg/cu. m)	27	33	49
Passenger cars (per 1,000 people)	72	138	28
Water and sanitation			
Internal freshwater resources per capita (cu. m)	5,041	11,128	8,397
Freshwater withdrawal			
Total (% of internal resources)	44.9	7.4	5.9
Agriculture (% of total freshwater withdrawal)	81	57	74
Access to improved water source (% of total population)	86	91	82
Rural (% of rural population)	72	80	71
Urban (% of urban population)	96	98	94
Access to sanitation (% of total population)	72	82	60
Rural (% of rural population)	52	64	41
Urban (% of urban population)	87	93	80
Under-five mortality rate (per 1,000)	73	36	39
National accounting aggregates, 2003			
Gross national savings (% of GNI)	28.1	21.9	30.6
Consumption of fixed capital (% of GNI)	10.5	10.7	9.8
Education expenditure (% of GNI)	4.4	4.1	3.2
Energy depletion (% of GNI)	38.9	11.6	8.1
Mineral depletion (% of GNI)	0.6	0.1	0.4
Net forest depletion (% of GNI)	0.0	0.0	0.1
CO_2 damage (% of GNI)	4.1	1.9	1.6
Particulate emission damage (% of GNI)	0.4	0.6	0.7
Adjusted net savings (% of GNI)	−22.1	1.1	13.2

Kenya

Environmental strategy/action plan prepared in **1994**

	Country data	Sub-Saharan Africa	Low income
		Group data	
Population (millions)	31.9	705	2,312
Urban population (% of total)	36.3	36.5	30.4
GDP ($ billions)	14.4	439	1,103
GNI per capita, *Atlas* method ($)	400	500	440
Agriculture and fisheries			
Land area (1,000 sq. km)	569	23,596	30,456
Agricultural land (% of land area)	46	43	43
Irrigated land (% of crop land)	1.7	4.2	26.7
Fertilizer consumption (100 grams/ha arable land)	310	145	654
Population density, rural (people/sq. km arable land)	441	352	509
Fish catch, total (1,000 metric tons)	165	5,191	16,410
Forests			
Forest area (1,000 sq. km)	171	6,435	7,939
Forest area share of total land area (%)	30.0	27.3	26.1
Annual deforestation (% change, 1990–2000)	0.5	0.8	0.7
Biodiversity			
Mammal species, total known	359		
Mammal species, threatened	51		
Bird species, total breeding	344		
Bird species, threatened	24		
Nationally protected area (% of land area)	8.0	8.7	7.7
Energy			
GDP per unit of energy use (2000 PPP$/kg oil equiv)	2.0	2.8	4.1
Energy use per capita (kg oil equiv)	489	667	493
Energy from biomass products and waste (% of total)	80.1	57.5	49.4
Energy imports, net (% of energy use)	16	–56	–6
Electric power consumption per capita (kWh)	120	457	312
Electricity generated by coal (% of total)	..	68.2	47.4
Emissions and pollution			
CO_2 emissions per unit of GDP (kg/2000 PPP$ GDP)	0.3	0.4	0.4
CO_2 emissions per capita (metric tons)	0.3	0.7	0.8
Particulate matter (pop. weighted average, μg/cu. m)	44	54	63
Passenger cars (per 1,000 people)	8	..	..
Water and sanitation			
Internal freshwater resources per capita (cu. m)	627	5,546	3,583
Freshwater withdrawal			
Total (% of internal resources)	10.0	1.8	11.5
Agriculture (% of total freshwater withdrawal)	76	85	92
Access to improved water source (% of total population)	62	58	75
Rural (% of rural population)	46	46	70
Urban (% of urban population)	89	82	89
Access to sanitation (% of total population)	48	36	36
Rural (% of rural population)	43	26	24
Urban (% of urban population)	56	55	61
Under-five mortality rate (per 1,000)	123	171	123
National accounting aggregates, 2003			
Gross national savings (% of GNI)	13.1	16.9	23.1
Consumption of fixed capital (% of GNI)	8.0	10.6	8.9
Education expenditure (% of GNI)	6.0	4.7	3.4
Energy depletion (% of GNI)	0.0	8.0	5.8
Mineral depletion (% of GNI)	0.0	0.5	0.3
Net forest depletion (% of GNI)	0.7	0.7	0.8
CO_2 damage (% of GNI)	0.4	0.9	1.2
Particulate emission damage (% of GNI)	0.2	0.4	0.6
Adjusted net savings (% of GNI)	9.8	0.6	8.9

Kiribati

Environmental strategy/action plan prepared in ..

		Group data	
	Country data	East Asia & Pacific	Lower middle income
Population (millions)	0.1	1,855	2,655
Urban population (% of total)	39.5	39.1	49.8
GDP ($ billions)	0.1	2,033	4,168
GNI per capita, *Atlas* method ($)	860	1,070	1,490
Agriculture and fisheries			
Land area (1,000 sq. km)	1	15,886	56,103
Agricultural land (% of land area)	53	50	35
Irrigated land (% of crop land)	..	..	20.8
Fertilizer consumption (100 grams/ha arable land)	..	2,297	1,170
Population density, rural (people/sq. km arable land)	2,885	565	497
Fish catch, total (1,000 metric tons)	32	60,812	74,407
Forests			
Forest area (1,000 sq. km)	0	4,284	20,316
Forest area share of total land area (%)	38.4	27.0	36.2
Annual deforestation (% change, 1990–2000)	0.0	0.2	0.1
Biodiversity			
Mammal species, total known	..		
Mammal species, threatened	0		
Bird species, total breeding	..		
Bird species, threatened	4		
Nationally protected area (% of land area)	..	9.2	7.7
Energy			
GDP per unit of energy use (2000 PPP$/kg oil equiv)	..	4.6	4.1
Energy use per capita (kg oil equiv)	..	904	1,227
Energy from biomass products and waste (% of total)	..	19.6	12.3
Energy imports, net (% of energy use)	..	–4	–22
Electric power consumption per capita (kWh)	..	891	1,289
Electricity generated by coal (% of total)	..	66.8	42.8
Emissions and pollution			
CO_2 emissions per unit of GDP (kg/2000 PPP$ GDP)	..	0.5	0.6
CO_2 emissions per capita (metric tons)	0.3	2.1	2.9
Particulate matter (pop. weighted average, µg/cu. m)	..	69	49
Passenger cars (per 1,000 people)	..	10	28
Water and sanitation			
Internal freshwater resources per capita (cu. m)	..	5,103	8,397
Freshwater withdrawal			
Total (% of internal resources)	..	8.2	5.9
Agriculture (% of total freshwater withdrawal)	..	81	74
Access to improved water source (% of total population)	64	78	82
Rural (% of rural population)	53	69	71
Urban (% of urban population)	77	92	94
Access to sanitation (% of total population)	39	49	60
Rural (% of rural population)	22	35	41
Urban (% of urban population)	59	71	80
Under-five mortality rate (per 1,000)	66	41	39
National accounting aggregates, 2003			
Gross national savings (% of GNI)	..	41.7	30.6
Consumption of fixed capital (% of GNI)	5.3	9.2	9.8
Education expenditure (% of GNI)	..	2.3	3.2
Energy depletion (% of GNI)	0.0	3.9	8.1
Mineral depletion (% of GNI)	0.0	0.3	0.4
Net forest depletion (% of GNI)	0.0	0.1	0.1
CO_2 damage (% of GNI)	0.2	1.8	1.6
Particulate emission damage (% of GNI)	..	0.8	0.7
Adjusted net savings (% of GNI)	..	27.9	13.2

Korea, Dem. Rep.

Environmental strategy/action plan prepared in ..

	Country data	East Asia & Pacific	Low income
		Group data	
Population (millions)	22.6	1,855	2,312
Urban population (% of total)	61.1	39.1	30.4
GDP ($ billions)	..	2,033	1,103
GNI per capita, *Atlas* method ($)	..	1,070	440
Agriculture and fisheries			
Land area (1,000 sq. km)	120	15,886	30,456
Agricultural land (% of land area)	24	50	43
Irrigated land (% of crop land)	54.1	..	26.7
Fertilizer consumption (100 grams/ha arable land)	1,065	2,297	654
Population density, rural (people/sq. km arable land)	352	565	509
Fish catch, total (1,000 metric tons)	264	60,812	16,410
Forests			
Forest area (1,000 sq. km)	82	4,284	7,939
Forest area share of total land area (%)	68.2	27.0	26.1
Annual deforestation (% change, 1990–2000)	0.0	0.2	0.7
Biodiversity			
Mammal species, total known	..		
Mammal species, threatened	13		
Bird species, total breeding	150		
Bird species, threatened	19		
Nationally protected area (% of land area)	2.6	9.2	7.7
Energy			
GDP per unit of energy use (2000 PPP$/kg oil equiv)	..	4.6	4.1
Energy use per capita (kg oil equiv)	869	904	493
Energy from biomass products and waste (% of total)	5.2	19.6	49.4
Energy imports, net (% of energy use)	6	–4	–6
Electric power consumption per capita (kWh)	..	891	312
Electricity generated by coal (% of total)	41.2	66.8	47.4
Emissions and pollution			
CO_2 emissions per unit of GDP (kg/2000 PPP$ GDP)	..	0.5	0.4
CO_2 emissions per capita (metric tons)	8.5	2.1	0.8
Particulate matter (pop. weighted average, µg/cu. m)	93	69	63
Passenger cars (per 1,000 people)	..	10	..
Water and sanitation			
Internal freshwater resources per capita (cu. m)	2,963	5,103	3,583
Freshwater withdrawal			
Total (% of internal resources)	21.2	8.2	11.5
Agriculture (% of total freshwater withdrawal)	73	81	92
Access to improved water source (% of total population)	100	78	75
Rural (% of rural population)	100	69	70
Urban (% of urban population)	100	92	89
Access to sanitation (% of total population)	59	49	36
Rural (% of rural population)	60	35	24
Urban (% of urban population)	58	71	61
Under-five mortality rate (per 1,000)	55	41	123
National accounting aggregates, 2003			
Gross national savings (% of GNI)	..	41.7	23.1
Consumption of fixed capital (% of GNI)	..	9.2	8.9
Education expenditure (% of GNI)	..	2.3	3.4
Energy depletion (% of GNI)	..	3.9	5.8
Mineral depletion (% of GNI)	..	0.3	0.3
Net forest depletion (% of GNI)	..	0.1	0.8
CO_2 damage (% of GNI)	..	1.8	1.2
Particulate emission damage (% of GNI)	..	0.8	0.6
Adjusted net savings (% of GNI)	..	27.9	8.9

Korea, Rep.

Environmental strategy/action plan prepared in ..

	Country data	Group data High Income
Population (millions)	47.9	972
Urban population (% of total)	83.5	79.9
GDP ($ billions)	605	29,341
GNI per capita, *Atlas* method ($)	12,030	28,600
Agriculture and fisheries		
Land area (1,000 sq. km)	99	31,030
Agricultural land (% of land area)	20	36
Irrigated land (% of crop land)	60.6	12.3
Fertilizer consumption (100 grams/ha arable land)	4,097	1,198
Population density, rural (people/sq. km arable land)	481	202
Fish catch, total (1,000 metric tons)	2,282	28,712
Forests		
Forest area (1,000 sq. km)	62	7,929
Forest area share of total land area (%)	63.3	25.9
Annual deforestation (% change, 1990–2000)	0.1	–0.1
Biodiversity		
Mammal species, total known	49	
Mammal species, threatened	13	
Bird species, total breeding	138	
Bird species, threatened	25	
Nationally protected area (% of land area)	6.9	19.5
Energy		
GDP per unit of energy use (2000 PPP$/kg oil equiv)	3.9	5.2
Energy use per capita (kg oil equiv)	4,272	5,395
Energy from biomass products and waste (% of total)	1.4	3.1
Energy imports, net (% of energy use)	82	26
Electric power consumption per capita (kWh)	6,171	8,693
Electricity generated by coal (% of total)	39.9	38.2
Emissions and pollution		
CO_2 emissions per unit of GDP (kg/2000 PPP$ GDP)	0.6	0.5
CO_2 emissions per capita (metric tons)	9.1	12.4
Particulate matter (pop. weighted average, µg/cu. m)	43	33
Passenger cars (per 1,000 people)	205	436
Water and sanitation		
Internal freshwater resources per capita (cu. m)	1,357	9,479
Freshwater withdrawal		
Total (% of internal resources)	36.5	9.7
Agriculture (% of total freshwater withdrawal)	63	42
Access to improved water source (% of total population)	92	99
Rural (% of rural population)	71	98
Urban (% of urban population)	97	100
Access to sanitation (% of total population)	..	..
Rural (% of rural population)	..	..
Urban (% of urban population)	..	..
Under-five mortality rate (per 1,000)	5	7
National accounting aggregates, 2003		
Gross national savings (% of GNI)	31.5	19.1
Consumption of fixed capital (% of GNI)	12.4	13.2
Education expenditure (% of GNI)	3.0	4.6
Energy depletion (% of GNI)	0.0	0.8
Mineral depletion (% of GNI)	0.0	0.0
Net forest depletion (% of GNI)	0.0	0.0
CO_2 damage (% of GNI)	0.5	0.3
Particulate emission damage (% of GNI)	0.8	0.3
Adjusted net savings (% of GNI)	20.9	9.2

Kuwait

Environmental strategy/action plan prepared in ..

	Country data	Group data — High income
Population (millions)	2.4	972
Urban population (% of total)	96.2	79.9
GDP ($ billions)	42	29,341
GNI per capita, *Atlas* method ($)	17,960	28,600
Agriculture and fisheries		
Land area (1,000 sq. km)	18	31,030
Agricultural land (% of land area)	8	36
Irrigated land (% of crop land)	86.7	12.3
Fertilizer consumption (100 grams/ha arable land)	808	1,198
Population density, rural (people/sq. km arable land)	689	202
Fish catch, total (1,000 metric tons)	6	28,712
Forests		
Forest area (1,000 sq. km)	0	7,929
Forest area share of total land area (%)	0.3	25.9
Annual deforestation (% change, 1990–2000)	−5.2	−0.1
Biodiversity		
Mammal species, total known	21	
Mammal species, threatened	1	
Bird species, total breeding	35	
Bird species, threatened	7	
Nationally protected area (% of land area)	1.5	19.5
Energy		
GDP per unit of energy use (2000 PPP$/kg oil equiv)	1.7	5.2
Energy use per capita (kg oil equiv)	9,503	5,395
Energy from biomass products and waste (% of total)	..	3.1
Energy imports, net (% of energy use)	−378	26
Electric power consumption per capita (kWh)	10,888	8,693
Electricity generated by coal (% of total)	..	38.2
Emissions and pollution		
CO_2 emissions per unit of GDP (kg/2000 PPP$ GDP)	1.4	0.5
CO_2 emissions per capita (metric tons)	21.9	12.4
Particulate matter (pop. weighted average, μg/cu. m)	134	33
Passenger cars (per 1,000 people)	..	436
Water and sanitation		
Internal freshwater resources per capita (cu. m)	0	9,479
Freshwater withdrawal		
Total (% of internal resources)	..	9.7
Agriculture (% of total freshwater withdrawal)	60	42
Access to improved water source (% of total population)	..	99
Rural (% of rural population)	..	98
Urban (% of urban population)	..	100
Access to sanitation (% of total population)	..	..
Rural (% of rural population)	..	..
Urban (% of urban population)	..	..
Under-five mortality rate (per 1,000)	9	7
National accounting aggregates, 2003		
Gross national savings (% of GNI)	24.8	19.1
Consumption of fixed capital (% of GNI)	7.2	13.2
Education expenditure (% of GNI)	5.0	4.6
Energy depletion (% of GNI)	50.8	0.8
Mineral depletion (% of GNI)	0.0	0.0
Net forest depletion (% of GNI)	0.0	0.0
CO_2 damage (% of GNI)	0.7	0.3
Particulate emission damage (% of GNI)	2.0	0.3
Adjusted net savings (% of GNI)	−30.9	9.2

Kyrgyz Republic

Environmental strategy/action plan prepared in **1995**

	Country data	Europe & Central Asia	Low income
		Group data	
Population (millions)	5.1	472	2,312
Urban population (% of total)	34.4	63.8	30.4
GDP ($ billions)	1.9	1,403	1,103
GNI per capita, *Atlas* method ($)	340	2,580	440
Agriculture and fisheries			
Land area (1,000 sq. km)	192	23,868	30,456
Agricultural land (% of land area)	56	28	43
Irrigated land (% of crop land)	76.0	10.9	26.7
Fertilizer consumption (100 grams/ha arable land)	205	344	654
Population density, rural (people/sq. km arable land)	244	122	509
Fish catch, total (1,000 metric tons)	0	5,527	16,410
Forests			
Forest area (1,000 sq. km)	10	9,463	7,939
Forest area share of total land area (%)	5.2	39.6	26.1
Annual deforestation (% change, 1990–2000)	–2.6	–0.1	0.7
Biodiversity			
Mammal species, total known	83		
Mammal species, threatened	7		
Bird species, total breeding	168		
Bird species, threatened	4		
Nationally protected area (% of land area)	15.0	6.8	7.7
Energy			
GDP per unit of energy use (2000 PPP$/kg oil equiv)	3.1	2.5	4.1
Energy use per capita (kg oil equiv)	507	2,697	493
Energy from biomass products and waste (% of total)	0.2	2.3	49.4
Energy imports, net (% of energy use)	53	–23	–6
Electric power consumption per capita (kWh)	1,269	2,808	312
Electricity generated by coal (% of total)	4.8	29.4	47.4
Emissions and pollution			
CO_2 emissions per unit of GDP (kg/2000 PPP$ GDP)	0.6	1.1	0.4
CO_2 emissions per capita (metric tons)	0.9	6.7	0.8
Particulate matter (pop. weighted average, µg/cu. m)	41	33	63
Passenger cars (per 1,000 people)	38	138	..
Water and sanitation			
Internal freshwater resources per capita (cu. m)	9,105	11,128	3,583
Freshwater withdrawal			
Total (% of internal resources)	22.0	7.4	11.5
Agriculture (% of total freshwater withdrawal)	94	57	92
Access to improved water source (% of total population)	76	91	75
Rural (% of rural population)	66	80	70
Urban (% of urban population)	98	98	89
Access to sanitation (% of total population)	60	82	36
Rural (% of rural population)	51	64	24
Urban (% of urban population)	75	93	61
Under-five mortality rate (per 1,000)	68	36	123
National accounting aggregates, 2003			
Gross national savings (% of GNI)	15.1	21.9	23.1
Consumption of fixed capital (% of GNI)	8.0	10.7	8.9
Education expenditure (% of GNI)	3.1	4.1	3.4
Energy depletion (% of GNI)	1.2	11.6	5.8
Mineral depletion (% of GNI)	0.0	0.1	0.3
Net forest depletion (% of GNI)	0.0	0.0	0.8
CO_2 damage (% of GNI)	2.4	1.9	1.2
Particulate emission damage (% of GNI)	0.2	0.6	0.6
Adjusted net savings (% of GNI)	6.5	1.1	8.9

Lao PDR

Environmental strategy/action plan prepared in **1995**

	Country data	Group data East Asia & Pacific	Low income
Population (millions)	5.7	1,855	2,312
Urban population (% of total)	20.7	39.1	30.4
GDP ($ billions)	2.1	2,033	1,103
GNI per capita, *Atlas* method ($)	340	1,070	440
Agriculture and fisheries			
Land area (1,000 sq. km)	231	15,886	30,456
Agricultural land (% of land area)	8	50	43
Irrigated land (% of crop land)	17.5	..	26.7
Fertilizer consumption (100 grams/ha arable land)	76	2,297	654
Population density, rural (people/sq. km arable land)	480	565	509
Fish catch, total (1,000 metric tons)	80	60,812	16,410
Forests			
Forest area (1,000 sq. km)	126	4,284	7,939
Forest area share of total land area (%)	54.4	27.0	26.1
Annual deforestation (% change, 1990–2000)	0.4	0.2	0.7
Biodiversity			
Mammal species, total known	172		
Mammal species, threatened	31		
Bird species, total breeding	212		
Bird species, threatened	20		
Nationally protected area (% of land area)	3.0	9.2	7.7
Energy			
GDP per unit of energy use (2000 PPP$/kg oil equiv)	..	4.6	4.1
Energy use per capita (kg oil equiv)	..	904	493
Energy from biomass products and waste (% of total)	..	19.6	49.4
Energy imports, net (% of energy use)	..	–4	–6
Electric power consumption per capita (kWh)	..	891	312
Electricity generated by coal (% of total)	..	66.8	47.4
Emissions and pollution			
CO_2 emissions per unit of GDP (kg/2000 PPP$ GDP)	0.1	0.5	0.4
CO_2 emissions per capita (metric tons)	0.1	2.1	0.8
Particulate matter (pop. weighted average, µg/cu. m)	47	69	63
Passenger cars per 1,000 people)	..	10	..
Water and sanitation			
Internal freshwater resources per capita (cu. m)	33,570	5,103	3,583
Freshwater withdrawal			
Total (% of internal resources)	0.5	8.2	11.5
Agriculture (% of total freshwater withdrawal)	82	81	92
Access to improved water source (% of total population)	43	78	75
Rural (% of rural population)	38	69	70
Urban (% of urban population)	66	92	89
Access to sanitation (% of total population)	24	49	36
Rural (% of rural population)	14	35	24
Urban (% of urban population)	61	71	61
Under-five mortality rate (per 1,000)	91	41	123
National accounting aggregates, 2003			
Gross national savings (% of GNI)	19.1	41.7	23.1
Consumption of fixed capital (% of GNI)	7.8	9.2	8.9
Education expenditure (% of GNI)	1.8	2.3	3.4
Energy depletion (% of GNI)	0.0	3.9	5.8
Mineral depletion (% of GNI)	0.0	0.3	0.3
Net forest depletion (% of GNI)	0.0	0.1	0.8
CO_2 damage (% of GNI)	0.2	1.8	1.2
Particulate emission damage (% of GNI)	0.2	0.8	0.6
Adjusted net savings (% of GNI)	12.8	27.9	8.9

Latvia

Environmental strategy/action plan prepared in ..

	Country data	Europe & Central Asia	Upper middle income
		Group data	
Population (millions)	2.3	472	333
Urban population (% of total)	60.4	63.8	75.4
GDP ($ billions)	11.1	1,403	1,856
GNI per capita, *Atlas* method ($)	4,400	2,580	5,440
Agriculture and fisheries			
Land area (1,000 sq. km)	62	23,868	12,741
Agricultural land (% of land area)	40	28	48
Irrigated land (% of crop land)	1.1	10.9	13.5
Fertilizer consumption (100 grams/ha arable land)	273	344	796
Population density, rural (people/sq. km arable land)	50	122	193
Fish catch, total (1,000 metric tons)	126	5,527	10,082
Forests			
Forest area (1,000 sq. km)	29	9,463	2,427
Forest area share of total land area (%)	47.1	39.6	19.1
Annual deforestation (% change, 1990–2000)	–0.4	–0.1	0.6
Biodiversity			
Mammal species, total known	83		
Mammal species, threatened	4		
Bird species, total breeding	216		
Bird species, threatened	3		
Nationally protected area (% of land area)	13.4	6.8	17.3
Energy			
GDP per unit of energy use (2000 PPP$/kg oil equiv)	4.9	2.5	4.3
Energy use per capita (kg oil equiv)	1,825	2,697	2,232
Energy from biomass products and waste (% of total)	30.1	2.3	4.1
Energy imports, net (% of energy use)	56	–23	–91
Electric power consumption per capita (kWh)	2,088	2,808	2,496
Electricity generated by coal (% of total)	1.0	29.4	23.9
Emissions and pollution			
CO_2 emissions per unit of GDP (kg/2000 PPP$ GDP)	0.3	1.1	0.6
CO_2 emissions per capita (metric tons)	2.5	6.7	6.3
Particulate matter (pop. weighted average, µg/cu. m)	22	33	29
Passenger cars (per 1,000 people)	266	138	153
Water and sanitation			
Internal freshwater resources per capita (cu. m)	7,324	11,128	10,741
Freshwater withdrawal			
Total (% of internal resources)	1.8	7.4	5.7
Agriculture (% of total freshwater withdrawal)	13	57	71
Access to improved water source (% of total population)	..	91	..
Rural (% of rural population)	..	80	..
Urban (% of urban population)	..	98	96
Access to sanitation (% of total population)	..	82	..
Rural (% of rural population)	..	64	..
Urban (% of urban population)	..	93	..
Under-five mortality rate (per 1,000)	12	36	22
National accounting aggregates, 2003			
Gross national savings (% of GDP)	20.5	21.9	22.1
Consumption of fixed capital (% of GNI)	10.8	10.7	10.7
Education expenditure (% of GNI)	5.1	4.1	5.0
Energy depletion (% of GNI)	0.0	11.6	11.4
Mineral depletion (% of GNI)	0.0	0.1	0.3
Net forest depletion (% of GNI)	0.0	0.0	0.0
CO_2 damage (% of GNI)	0.6	1.9	0.8
Particulate emission damage (% of GNI)	0.3	0.6	0.6
Adjusted net savings (% of GNI)	13.8	1.1	3.3

Lebanon

Environmental strategy/action plan prepared in ..

	Country data	Middle East & North Africa	Upper middle income
		Group data	
Population (millions)	4.5	312	333
Urban population (% of total)	90.6	59.0	75.4
GDP ($ billions)	19.0	745	1,856
GNI per capita, *Atlas* method ($)	4,040	2,390	5,440
Agriculture and fisheries			
Land area (1,000 sq. km)	10	11,111	12,741
Agricultural land (% of land area)	32	34	48
Irrigated land (% of crop land)	33.2	38.3	13.5
Fertilizer consumption (100 grams/ha arable land)	2,319	854	796
Population density, rural (people/sq. km arable land)	253	603	193
Fish catch, total (1,000 metric tons)	4	2,840	10,082
Forests			
Forest area (1,000 sq. km)	0	168	2,427
Forest area share of total land area (%)	3.5	1.5	19.1
Annual deforestation (% change, 1990–2000)	0.3	–0.1	0.6
Biodiversity			
Mammal species, total known	57		
Mammal species, threatened	5		
Bird species, total breeding	116		
Bird species, threatened	7		
Nationally protected area (% of land area)	0.5	11.3	17.3
Energy			
GDP per unit of energy use (2000 PPP$/kg oil equiv)	3.8	3.5	4.3
Energy use per capita (kg oil equiv)	1,209	1,504	2,232
Energy from biomass products and waste (% of total)	2.4	1.0	4.1
Energy imports, net (% of energy use)	96	–168	–91
Electric power consumption per capita (kWh)	1,951	1,412	2,496
Electricity generated by coal (% of total)	..	2.3	23.9
Emissions and pollution			
CO_2 emissions per unit of GDP (kg/2000 PPP$ GDP)	0.8	0.8	0.6
CO_2 emissions per capita (metric tons)	3.5	4.2	6.3
Particulate matter (pop. weighted average, µg/cu. m)	45	87	29
Passenger cars (per 1,000 people)	..	..	153
Water and sanitation			
Internal freshwater resources per capita (cu. m)	1,112	761	10,741
Freshwater withdrawal			
Total (% of internal resources)	26.0	101.7	5.7
Agriculture (% of total freshwater withdrawal)	68	88	71
Access to improved water source (% of total population)	100	88	..
Rural (% of rural population)	100	78	..
Urban (% of urban population)	100	96	96
Access to sanitation (% of total population)	98	75	..
Rural (% of rural population)	87	56	..
Urban (% of urban population)	100	90	..
Under-five mortality rate (per 1,000)	31	53	22
National accounting aggregates, 2003			
Gross national savings (% of GNI)	–7.9	31.2	22.1
Consumption of fixed capital (% of GNI)	11.5	10.0	10.7
Education expenditure (% of GNI)	2.5	5.5	5.0
Energy depletion (% of GNI)	0.0	30.7	11.4
Mineral depletion (% of GNI)	0.0	0.1	0.3
Net forest depletion (% of GNI)	0.0	0.0	0.0
CO_2 damage (% of GNI)	0.6	1.2	0.8
Particulate emission damage (% of GNI)	0.6	0.8	0.6
Adjusted net savings (% of GNI)	–18.1	–6.2	3.3

Lesotho

Environmental strategy/action plan prepared in **1989**

	Country data	Group data Sub-Saharan Africa	Group data Low Income
Population (millions)	1.8	705	2,312
Urban population (% of total)	30.3	36.5	30.4
GDP ($ billions)	1.1	439	1,103
GNI per capita, *Atlas* method ($)	610	500	440
Agriculture and fisheries			
Land area (1,000 sq. km)	30	23,596	30,456
Agricultural land (% of land area)	77	43	43
Irrigated land (% of crop land)	0.3	4.2	26.7
Fertilizer consumption (100 grams/ha arable land)	342	145	654
Population density, rural (people/sq. km arable land)	379	352	509
Fish catch, total (1,000 metric tons)	0	5,191	16,410
Forests			
Forest area (1,000 sq. km)	0	6,435	7,939
Forest area share of total land area (%)	0.5	27.3	26.1
Annual deforestation (% change, 1990–2000)	0.0	0.8	0.7
Biodiversity			
Mammal species, total known	33		
Mammal species, threatened	3		
Bird species, total breeding	123		
Bird species, threatened	7		
Nationally protected area (% of land area)	0.2	8.7	7.7
Energy			
GDP per unit of energy use (2000 PPP$/kg oil equiv)	..	2.8	4.1
Energy use per capita (kg oil equiv)	..	667	493
Energy from biomass products and waste (% of total)	..	57.5	49.4
Energy imports, net (% of energy use)	..	−56	−6
Electric power consumption per capita (kWh)	..	457	312
Electricity generated by coal (% of total)	..	68.2	47.4
Emissions and pollution			
CO_2 emissions per unit of GDP (kg/2000 PPP$ GDP)	..	0.4	0.4
CO_2 emissions per capita (metric tons)	..	0.7	0.8
Particulate matter (pop. weighted average, μg/cu. m)	54	54	63
Passenger cars (per 1,000 people)	..	..	..
Water and sanitation			
Internal freshwater resources per capita (cu. m)	2,789	5,546	3,583
Freshwater withdrawal			
Total (% of internal resources)	2.0	1.8	11.5
Agriculture (% of total freshwater withdrawal)	56	85	92
Access to improved water source (% of total population)	76	58	75
Rural (% of rural population)	74	46	70
Urban (% of urban population)	88	82	89
Access to sanitation (% of total population)	37	36	36
Rural (% of rural population)	32	26	24
Urban (% of urban population)	61	55	61
Under-five mortality rate (per 1,000)	110	171	123
National accounting aggregates, 2003			
Gross national savings (% of GNI)	−2.4	16.9	23.1
Consumption of fixed capital (% of GNI)	6.9	10.6	8.9
Education expenditure (% of GNI)	7.3	4.7	3.4
Energy depletion (% of GNI)	0.0	8.0	5.8
Mineral depletion (% of GNI)	0.0	0.5	0.3
Net forest depletion (% of GNI)	1.7	0.7	0.8
CO_2 damage (% of GNI)	..	0.9	1.2
Particulate emission damage (% of GNI)	0.4	0.4	0.6
Adjusted net savings (% of GNI)	−4.1	0.6	8.9

Liberia

Environmental strategy/action plan prepared in ..

	Country data	Sub-Saharan Africa	Low income
		Group data	
Population (millions)	3.4	705	2,312
Urban population (% of total)	46.7	36.5	30.4
GDP ($ billions)	0.4	439	1,103
GNI per capita, *Atlas* method ($)	110	500	440
Agriculture and fisheries			
Land area (1,000 sq. km)	96	23,596	30,456
Agricultural land (% of land area)	27	43	43
Irrigated land (% of crop land)	0.5	4.2	26.7
Fertilizer consumption (100 grams/ha arable land)	..	145	654
Population density, rural (people/sq. km arable land)	467	352	509
Fish catch, total (1,000 metric tons)	11	5,191	16,410
Forests			
Forest area (1,000 sq. km)	35	6,435	7,939
Forest area share of total land area (%)	36.1	27.3	26.1
Annual deforestation (% change, 1990–2000)	2.0	0.8	0.7
Biodiversity			
Mammal species, total known	193		
Mammal species, threatened	17		
Bird species, total breeding	146		
Bird species, threatened	11		
Nationally protected area (% of land area)	1.7	8.7	7.7
Energy			
GDP per unit of energy use (2000 PPP$/kg oil equiv)	..	2.8	4.1
Energy use per capita (kg oil equiv)	..	667	493
Energy from biomass products and waste (% of total)	..	57.5	49.4
Energy imports, net (% of energy use)	..	–56	–6
Electric power consumption per capita (kWh)	..	457	312
Electricity generated by coal (% of total)	..	68.2	47.4
Emissions and pollution			
CO_2 emissions per unit of GDP (kg/2000 PPP$ GDP)	..	0.4	0.4
CO_2 emissions per capita (metric tons)	0.1	0.7	0.8
Particulate matter (pop. weighted average, μg/cu. m)	41	54	63
Passenger cars (per 1,000 people)	..	..	..
Water and sanitation			
Internal freshwater resources per capita (cu. m)	59,285	5,546	3,583
Freshwater withdrawal			
Total (% of internal resources)	0.1	1.8	11.5
Agriculture (% of total freshwater withdrawal)	60	85	92
Access to improved water source (% of total population)	62	58	75
Rural (% of rural population)	52	46	70
Urban (% of urban population)	72	82	89
Access to sanitation (% of total population)	26	36	36
Rural (% of rural population)	7	26	24
Urban (% of urban population)	49	55	61
Under-five mortality rate (per 1,000)	235	171	123
National accounting aggregates, 2003			
Gross national savings (% of GNI)	0.6	16.9	23.1
Consumption of fixed capital (% of GNI)	7.4	10.6	8.9
Education expenditure (% of GNI)	..	4.7	3.4
Energy depletion (% of GNI)	0.0	8.0	5.8
Mineral depletion (% of GNI)	0.3	0.5	0.3
Net forest depletion (% of GNI)	5.4	0.7	0.8
CO_2 damage (% of GNI)	1.0	0.9	1.2
Particulate emission damage (% of GNI)	0.0	0.4	0.6
Adjusted net savings (% of GNI)	..	0.6	8.9

Libya

Environmental strategy/action plan prepared in ..

| | | Group data | |
	Country data	Middle East & North Africa	Upper middle income
Population (millions)	5.6	312	333
Urban population (% of total)	88.5	59.0	75.4
GDP ($ billions)	19.1	745	1,856
GNI per capita, *Atlas* method ($)	..	2,390	5,440
Agriculture and fisheries			
Land area (1,000 sq. km)	1,760	11,111	12,741
Agricultural land (% of land area)	9	34	48
Irrigated land (% of crop land)	21.9	38.3	13.5
Fertilizer consumption (100 grams/ha arable land)	341	854	796
Population density, rural (people/sq. km arable land)	35	603	193
Fish catch, total (1,000 metric tons)	33	2,840	10,082
Forests			
Forest area (1,000 sq. km)	4	168	2,427
Forest area share of total land area (%)	0.2	1.5	19.1
Annual deforestation (% change, 1990–2000)	−1.4	−0.1	0.6
Biodiversity			
Mammal species, total known	76		
Mammal species, threatened	8		
Bird species, total breeding	76		
Bird species, threatened	1		
Nationally protected area (% of land area)	0.1	11.3	17.3
Energy			
GDP per unit of energy use (2000 PPP$/kg oil equiv)	..	3.5	4.3
Energy use per capita (kg oil equiv)	3,433	1,504	2,232
Energy from biomass products and waste (% of total)	0.8	1.0	4.1
Energy imports, net (% of energy use)	−272	−168	−91
Electric power consumption per capita (kWh)	2,250	1,412	2,496
Electricity generated by coal (% of total)	..	2.3	23.9
Emissions and pollution			
CO_2 emissions per unit of GDP (kg/2000 PPP$ GDP)	..	0.8	0.6
CO_2 emissions per capita (metric tons)	10.9	4.2	6.3
Particulate matter (pop. weighted average, µg/cu. m)	..	87	29
Passenger cars (per 1,000 people)	..	..	153
Water and sanitation			
Internal freshwater resources per capita (cu. m)	180	761	10,741
Freshwater withdrawal			
Total (% of internal resources)	450.0	101.7	5.7
Agriculture (% of total freshwater withdrawal)	84	88	71
Access to improved water source (% of total population)	72	88	..
Rural (% of rural population)	68	78	..
Urban (% of urban population)	72	96	96
Access to sanitation (% of total population)	97	75	..
Rural (% of rural population)	96	56	..
Urban (% of urban population)	97	90	..
Under-five mortality rate (per 1,000)	16	53	22
National accounting aggregates, 2003			
Gross national savings (% of GNI)	..	31.2	22.1
Consumption of fixed capital (% of GNI)	..	10.0	10.7
Education expenditure (% of GNI)	..	5.5	5.0
Energy depletion (% of GNI)	..	30.7	11.4
Mineral depletion (% of GNI)	..	0.1	0.3
Net forest depletion (% of GNI)	..	0.0	0.0
CO_2 damage (% of GNI)	..	1.2	0.8
Particulate emission damage (% of GNI)	..	0.8	0.6
Adjusted net savings (% of GNI)	..	−6.2	3.3

Liechtenstein

Environmental strategy/action plan prepared in ..

	Country data	Group data
		High income
Population (millions)	0.0	972
Urban population (% of total)	21.9	79.9
GDP ($ billions)	..	29,341
GNI per capita, *Atlas* method ($)	..	28,600

Agriculture and fisheries
Land area (1,000 sq. km)	0	31,030
Agricultural land (% of land area)	56	36
Irrigated land (% of crop land)	..	12.3
Fertilizer consumption (100 grams/ha arable land)	..	1,198
Population density, rural (people/sq. km arable land)	..	202
Fish catch, total (1,000 metric tons)	..	28,712

Forests
Forest area (1,000 sq. km)	0	7,929
Forest area share of total land area (%)	43.8	25.9
Annual deforestation (% change, 1990–2000)	–1.6	–0.1

Biodiversity
Mammal species, total known	..	
Mammal species, threatened	2	
Bird species, total breeding	..	
Bird species, threatened	1	
Nationally protected area (% of land area)	..	19.5

Energy
GDP per unit of energy use (2000 PPP$/kg oil equiv)	..	5.2
Energy use per capita (kg oil equiv)	..	5,395
Energy from biomass products and waste (% of total)	..	3.1
Energy imports, net (% of energy use)	..	26
Electric power consumption per capita (kWh)	..	8,693
Electricity generated by coal (% of total)	..	38.2

Emissions and pollution
CO_2 emissions per unit of GDP (kg/2000 PPP$ GDP)	..	0.5
CO_2 emissions per capita (metric tons)	..	12.4
Particulate matter (pop. weighted average, μg/cu. m)	42	33
Passenger cars (per 1,000 people)	..	436

Water and sanitation
Internal freshwater resources per capita (cu. m)	..	9,479
Freshwater withdrawal		
Total (% of internal resources)	..	9.7
Agriculture (% of total freshwater withdrawal)	..	42
Access to improved water source (% of total population)	..	99
Rural (% of rural population)	..	98
Urban (% of urban population)	..	100
Access to sanitation (% of total population)	..	..
Rural (% of rural population)	..	..
Urban (% of urban population)	..	..
Under-five mortality rate (per 1,000)	11	7

National accounting aggregates, 2003
Gross national savings (% of GNI)	..	19.1
Consumption of fixed capital (% of GNI)	..	13.2
Education expenditure (% of GNI)	..	4.6
Energy depletion (% of GNI)	..	0.8
Mineral depletion (% of GNI)	..	0.0
Net forest depletion (% of GNI)	..	0.0
CO_2 damage (% of GNI)	..	0.3
Particulate emission damage (% of GNI)	..	0.3
Adjusted net savings (% of GNI)	..	9.2

Lithuania

Environmental strategy/action plan prepared in ..

	Country data	Group data Europe & Central Asia	Group data Upper middle income
Population (millions)	3.5	472	333
Urban population (% of total)	68.9	63.8	75.4
GDP ($ billions)	18.2	1,403	1,856
GNI per capita, *Atlas* method ($)	4,500	2,580	5,440
Agriculture and fisheries			
Land area (1,000 sq. km)	63	23,868	12,741
Agricultural land (% of land area)	54	28	48
Irrigated land (% of crop land)	0.2	10.9	13.5
Fertilizer consumption (100 grams/ha arable land)	662	344	796
Population density, rural (people/sq. km arable land)	37	122	193
Fish catch, total (1,000 metric tons)	154	5,527	10,082
Forests			
Forest area (1,000 sq. km)	20	9,463	2,427
Forest area share of total land area (%)	31.8	39.6	19.1
Annual deforestation (% change, 1990–2000)	–0.2	–0.1	0.6
Biodiversity			
Mammal species, total known	68		
Mammal species, threatened	5		
Bird species, total breeding	201		
Bird species, threatened	4		
Nationally protected area (% of land area)	10.3	6.8	17.3
Energy			
GDP per unit of energy use (2000 PPP$/kg oil equiv)	4.0	2.5	4.3
Energy use per capita (kg oil equiv)	2,476	2,697	2,232
Energy from biomass products and waste (% of total)	7.7	2.3	4.1
Energy imports, net (% of energy use)	43	–23	–91
Electric power consumption per capita (kWh)	1,938	2,808	2,496
Electricity generated by coal (% of total)	..	29.4	23.9
Emissions and pollution			
CO_2 emissions per unit of GDP (kg/2000 PPP$ GDP)	0.4	1.1	0.6
CO_2 emissions per capita (metric tons)	3.4	6.7	6.3
Particulate matter (pop. weighted average, µg/cu. m)	29	33	29
Passenger cars (per 1,000 people)	346	138	153
Water and sanitation			
Internal freshwater resources per capita (cu. m)	4,632	11,128	10,741
Freshwater withdrawal			
Total (% of internal resources)	1.9	7.4	5.7
Agriculture (% of total freshwater withdrawal)	3	57	71
Access to improved water source (% of total population)	..	91	..
Rural (% of rural population)	..	80	..
Urban (% of urban population)	..	98	96
Access to sanitation (% of total population)	..	82	..
Rural (% of rural population)	..	64	..
Urban (% of urban population)	..	93	..
Under-five mortality rate (per 1,000)	11	36	22
National accounting aggregates, 2003			
Gross national savings (% of GNI)	15.8	21.9	22.1
Consumption of fixed capital (% of GNI)	10.3	10.7	10.7
Education expenditure (% of GNI)	5.2	4.1	5.0
Energy depletion (% of GNI)	0.0	11.6	11.4
Mineral depletion (% of GNI)	0.0	0.1	0.3
Net forest depletion (% of GNI)	0.0	0.0	0.0
CO_2 damage (% of GNI)	0.7	1.9	0.8
Particulate emission damage (% of GNI)	0.7	0.6	0.6
Adjusted net savings (% of GNI)	9.3	1.1	3.3

Luxembourg

Environmental strategy/action plan prepared in ..

	Country data	Group data High income
Population (millions)	0.4	972
Urban population (% of total)	92.5	79.9
GDP ($ billions)	26	29,341
GNI per capita, *Atlas* method ($)	45,740	28,600

Agriculture and fisheries

Land area (1,000 sq. km)	3	31,030
Agricultural land (% of land area)	..	36
Irrigated land (% of crop land)	..	12.3
Fertilizer consumption (100 grams/ha arable land)	..	1,198
Population density, rural (people/sq. km arable land)	..	202
Fish catch, total (1,000 metric tons)	..	28,712

Forests

Forest area (1,000 sq. km)	..	7,929
Forest area share of total land area (%)	..	25.9
Annual deforestation (% change, 1990–2000)	..	−0.1

Biodiversity

Mammal species, total known	..	
Mammal species, threatened	3	
Bird species, total breeding	..	
Bird species, threatened	1	
Nationally protected area (% of land area)	..	19.5

Energy

GDP per unit of energy use (2000 PPP$/kg oil equiv)	6.3	5.2
Energy use per capita (kg oil equiv)	9,112	5,395
Energy from biomass products and waste (% of total)	1.1	3.1
Energy imports, net (% of energy use)	99	26
Electric power consumption per capita (kWh)	12,791	8,693
Electricity generated by coal (% of total)	20.7	38.2

Emissions and pollution

CO_2 emissions per unit of GDP (kg/2000 PPP$ GDP)	0.3	0.5
CO_2 emissions per capita (metric tons)	19.4	12.4
Particulate matter (pop. weighted average, μg/cu. m)	18	33
Passenger cars (per 1,000 people)	576	436

Water and sanitation

Internal freshwater resources per capita (cu. m)	2,029	9,479
Freshwater withdrawal		
Total (% of internal resources)	..	9.7
Agriculture (% of total freshwater withdrawal)	0	42
Access to improved water source (% of total population)	100	99
Rural (% of rural population)	100	98
Urban (% of urban population)	100	100
Access to sanitation (% of total population)	..	..
Rural (% of rural population)	..	..
Urban (% of urban population)	..	..
Under-five mortality rate (per 1,000)	6	7

National accounting aggregates, 2003

Gross national savings (% of GNI)	29.1	19.1
Consumption of fixed capital (% of GNI)	13.6	13.2
Education expenditure (% of GNI)	3.7	4.6
Energy depletion (% of GNI)	0.0	0.8
Mineral depletion (% of GNI)	0.0	0.0
Net forest depletion (% of GNI)	0.0	0.0
CO_2 damage (% of GNI)	0.3	0.3
Particulate emission damage (% of GNI)	..	0.3
Adjusted net savings (% of GNI)	18.9	9.2

Macao, China

Environmental strategy/action plan prepared in ..

	Country data	Group data High income
Population (millions)	0.4	972
Urban population (% of total)	98.9	79.9
GDP ($ billions)	7	29,341
GNI per capita, *Atlas* method ($)	..	28,600
Agriculture and fisheries		
Land area (1,000 sq. km)	0	31,030
Agricultural land (% of land area)	..	36
Irrigated land (% of crop land)	..	12.3
Fertilizer consumption (100 grams/ha arable land)	..	1,198
Population density, rural (people/sq. km arable land)	..	202
Fish catch, total (1,000 metric tons)	..	28,712
Forests		
Forest area (1,000 sq. km)	..	7,929
Forest area share of total land area (%)	..	25.9
Annual deforestation (% change, 1990–2000)	..	–0.1
Biodiversity		
Mammal species, total known	..	
Mammal species, threatened	0	
Bird species, total breeding	..	
Bird species, threatened	1	
Nationally protected area (% of land area)	..	19.5
Energy		
GDP per unit of energy use (2000 PPP$/kg oil equiv)	..	5.2
Energy use per capita (kg oil equiv)	..	5,395
Energy from biomass products and waste (% of total)	..	3.1
Energy imports, net (% of energy use)	..	26
Electric power consumption per capita (kWh)	..	8,693
Electricity generated by coal (% of total)	..	38.2
Emissions and pollution		
CO_2 emissions per unit of GDP (kg/2000 PPP$ GDP)	0.2	0.5
CO_2 emissions per capita (metric tons)	3.8	12.4
Particulate matter (pop. weighted average, µg/cu. m)	102	33
Passenger cars (per 1,000 people)	121	436
Water and sanitation		
Internal freshwater resources per capita (cu. m)	..	9,479
Freshwater withdrawal		
Total (% of internal resources)	..	9.7
Agriculture (% of total freshwater withdrawal)	..	42
Access to improved water source (% of total population)	..	99
Rural (% of rural population)	..	98
Urban (% of urban population)	..	100
Access to sanitation (% of total population)	..	..
Rural (% of rural population)	..	..
Urban (% of urban population)	..	..
Under-five mortality rate (per 1,000)	..	7
National accounting aggregates, 2003		
Gross national savings (% of GNI)	..	19.1
Consumption of fixed capital (% of GNI)	..	13.2
Education expenditure (% of GNI)	3.6	4.6
Energy depletion (% of GNI)	..	0.8
Mineral depletion (% of GNI)	..	0.0
Net forest depletion (% of GNI)	..	0.0
CO_2 damage (% of GNI)	..	0.3
Particulate emission damage (% of GNI)	..	0.3
Adjusted net savings (% of GNI)	..	9.2

Macedonia, FYR

Environmental strategy/action plan prepared in ..

	Country data	Group data Europe & Central Asia	Group data Lower middle income
Population (millions)	2.0	472	2,655
Urban population (% of total)	59.6	63.8	49.8
GDP ($ billions)	4.7	1,403	4,168
GNI per capita, *Atlas* method ($)	1,980	2,580	1,490
Agriculture and fisheries			
Land area (1,000 sq. km)	25	23,868	56,103
Agricultural land (% of land area)	49	28	35
Irrigated land (% of crop land)	9.0	10.9	20.8
Fertilizer consumption (100 grams/ha arable land)	394	344	1,170
Population density, rural (people/sq. km arable land)	146	122	497
Fish catch, total (1,000 metric tons)	1	5,527	74,407
Forests			
Forest area (1,000 sq. km)	9	9,463	20,316
Forest area share of total land area (%)	35.6	39.6	36.2
Annual deforestation (% change, 1990–2000)	0.0	–0.1	0.1
Biodiversity			
Mammal species, total known	78		
Mammal species, threatened	11		
Bird species, total breeding	199		
Bird species, threatened	3		
Nationally protected area (% of land area)	7.1	6.8	7.7
Energy			
GDP per unit of energy use (2000 PPP$/kg oil equiv)	..	2.5	4.1
Energy use per capita (kg oil equiv)	..	2,697	1,227
Energy from biomass products and waste (% of total)	..	2.3	12.3
Energy imports, net (% of energy use)	..	–23	–22
Electric power consumption per capita (kWh)	..	2,808	1,289
Electricity generated by coal (% of total)	..	29.4	42.8
Emissions and pollution			
CO_2 emissions per unit of GDP (kg/2000 PPP$ GDP)	0.8	1.1	0.6
CO_2 emissions per capita (metric tons)	5.5	6.7	2.9
Particulate matter (pop. weighted average, µg/cu. m)	33	33	49
Passenger cars (per 1,000 people)	..	138	28
Water and sanitation			
Internal freshwater resources per capita (cu. m)	2,440	11,128	8,397
Freshwater withdrawal			
Total (% of internal resources)	38.0	7.4	5.9
Agriculture (% of total freshwater withdrawal)	74	57	74
Access to improved water source (% of total population)	..	91	82
Rural (% of rural population)	..	80	71
Urban (% of urban population)	..	98	94
Access to sanitation (% of total population)	..	82	60
Rural (% of rural population)	..	64	41
Urban (% of urban population)	..	93	80
Under-five mortality rate (per 1,000)	11	36	39
National accounting aggregates, 2003			
Gross national savings (% of GNI)	17.6	21.9	30.6
Consumption of fixed capital (% of GNI)	10.2	10.7	9.8
Education expenditure (% of GNI)	4.9	4.1	3.2
Energy depletion (% of GNI)	0.0	11.6	8.1
Mineral depletion (% of GNI)	0.0	0.1	0.4
Net forest depletion (% of GNI)	0.0	0.0	0.1
CO_2 damage (% of GNI)	1.7	1.9	1.6
Particulate emission damage (% of GNI)	0.3	0.6	0.7
Adjusted net savings (% of GNI)	10.3	1.1	13.2

Madagascar

Environmental strategy/action plan prepared in **1988**

	Country data	Sub-Saharan Africa	Low income
		Group data	
Population (millions)	16.9	705	2,312
Urban population (% of total)	31.4	36.5	30.4
GDP ($ billions)	5.5	439	1,103
GNI per capita, *Atlas* method ($)	290	500	440
Agriculture and fisheries			
Land area (1,000 sq. km)	582	23,596	30,456
Agricultural land (% of land area)	47	43	43
Irrigated land (% of crop land)	30.7	4.2	26.7
Fertilizer consumption (100 grams/ha arable land)	31	145	654
Population density, rural (people/sq. km arable land)	386	352	509
Fish catch, total (1,000 metric tons)	143	5,191	16,410
Forests			
Forest area (1,000 sq. km)	117	6,435	7,939
Forest area share of total land area (%)	20.2	27.3	26.1
Annual deforestation (% change, 1990–2000)	0.9	0.8	0.7
Biodiversity			
Mammal species, total known	141		
Mammal species, threatened	50		
Bird species, total breeding	172		
Bird species, threatened	27		
Nationally protected area (% of land area)	4.3	8.7	7.7
Energy			
GDP per unit of energy use (2000 PPP$/kg oil equiv)	..	2.8	4.1
Energy use per capita (kg oil equiv)	..	667	493
Energy from biomass products and waste (% of total)	..	57.5	49.4
Energy imports, net (% of energy use)	..	−56	−6
Electric power consumption per capita (kWh)	..	457	312
Electricity generated by coal (% of total)	..	68.2	47.4
Emissions and pollution			
CO_2 emissions per unit of GDP (kg/2000 PPP$ GDP)	0.2	0.4	0.4
CO_2 emissions per capita (metric tons)	0.1	0.7	0.8
Particulate matter (pop. weighted average, µg/cu. m)	47	54	63
Passenger cars (per 1,000 people)	..	..	..
Water and sanitation			
Internal freshwater resources per capita (cu. m)	19,948	5,546	3,583
Freshwater withdrawal			
Total (% of internal resources)	4.8	1.8	11.5
Agriculture (% of total freshwater withdrawal)	99	85	92
Access to improved water source (% of total population)	45	58	75
Rural (% of rural population)	34	46	70
Urban (% of urban population)	75	82	89
Access to sanitation (% of total population)	33	36	36
Rural (% of rural population)	27	26	24
Urban (% of urban population)	49	55	61
Under-five mortality rate (per 1,000)	126	171	123
National accounting aggregates, 2003			
Gross national savings (% of GNI)	12.0	16.9	23.1
Consumption of fixed capital (% of GNI)	7.6	10.6	8.9
Education expenditure (% of GNI)	1.7	4.7	3.4
Energy depletion (% of GNI)	0.0	8.0	5.8
Mineral depletion (% of GNI)	0.0	0.5	0.3
Net forest depletion (% of GNI)	0.0	0.7	0.8
CO_2 damage (% of GNI)	0.2	0.9	1.2
Particulate emission damage (% of GNI)	0.2	0.4	0.6
Adjusted net savings (% of GNI)	5.6	0.6	8.9

Malawi

Environmental strategy/action plan prepared in **1994**

	Country data	Sub-Saharan Africa	Low income
		Group data	
Population (millions)	11.0	705	2,312
Urban population (% of total)	15.9	36.5	30.4
GDP ($ billions)	1.7	439	1,103
GNI per capita, *Atlas* method ($)	160	500	440
Agriculture and fisheries			
Land area (1,000 sq. km)	94	23,596	30,456
Agricultural land (% of land area)	45	43	43
Irrigated land (% of crop land)	1.2	4.2	26.7
Fertilizer consumption (100 grams/ha arable land)	839	145	654
Population density, rural (people/sq. km arable land)	395	352	509
Fish catch, total (1,000 metric tons)	41	5,191	16,410
Forests			
Forest area (1,000 sq. km)	26	6,435	7,939
Forest area share of total land area (%)	27.2	27.3	26.1
Annual deforestation (% change, 1990–2000)	2.4	0.8	0.7
Biodiversity			
Mammal species, total known	195		
Mammal species, threatened	8		
Bird species, total breeding	219		
Bird species, threatened	11		
Nationally protected area (% of land area)	11.2	8.7	7.7
Energy			
GDP per unit of energy use (2000 PPP$/kg oil equiv)	..	2.8	4.1
Energy use per capita (kg oil equiv)	..	667	493
Energy from biomass products and waste (% of total)	..	57.5	49.4
Energy imports, net (% of energy use)	..	−56	−6
Electric power consumption per capita (kWh)	..	457	312
Electricity generated by coal (% of total)	..	68.2	47.4
Emissions and pollution			
CO_2 emissions per unit of GDP (kg/2000 PPP$ GDP)	0.1	0.4	0.4
CO_2 emissions per capita (metric tons)	0.1	0.7	0.8
Particulate matter (pop. weighted average, µg/cu. m)	46	54	63
Passenger cars (per 1,000 people)	..	..	..
Water and sanitation			
Internal freshwater resources per capita (cu. m)	1,460	5,546	3,583
Freshwater withdrawal			
Total (% of internal resources)	5.6	1.8	11.5
Agriculture (% of total freshwater withdrawal)	86	85	92
Access to improved water source (% of total population)	67	58	75
Rural (% of rural population)	62	46	70
Urban (% of urban population)	96	82	89
Access to sanitation (% of total population)	46	36	36
Rural (% of rural population)	42	26	24
Urban (% of urban population)	66	55	61
Under-five mortality rate (per 1,000)	178	171	123
National accounting aggregates, 2003			
Gross national savings (% of GNI)	−6.5	16.9	23.1
Consumption of fixed capital (% of GNI)	6.7	10.6	8.9
Education expenditure (% of GNI)	4.4	4.7	3.4
Energy depletion (% of GNI)	0.0	8.0	5.8
Mineral depletion (% of GNI)	0.0	0.5	0.3
Net forest depletion (% of GNI)	2.8	0.7	0.8
CO_2 damage (% of GNI)	0.3	0.9	1.2
Particulate emission damage (% of GNI)	0.2	0.4	0.6
Adjusted net savings (% of GNI)	−12.0	0.6	8.9

Malaysia

Environmental strategy/action plan prepared in **1991**

	Country data	East Asia & Pacific	Upper middle income
		Group data	
Population (millions)	24.8	1,855	333
Urban population (% of total)	59.4	39.1	75.4
GDP ($ billions)	103.7	2,033	1,856
GNI per capita, *Atlas* method ($)	3,880	1,070	5,440
Agriculture and fisheries			
Land area (1,000 sq. km)	329	15,886	12,741
Agricultural land (% of land area)	24	50	48
Irrigated land (% of crop land)	4.8	..	13.5
Fertilizer consumption (100 grams/ha arable land)	6,833	2,297	796
Population density, rural (people/sq. km arable land)	557	565	193
Fish catch, total (1,000 metric tons)	1,393	60,812	10,082
Forests			
Forest area (1,000 sq. km)	193	4,284	2,427
Forest area share of total land area (%)	58.7	27.0	19.1
Annual deforestation (% change, 1990–2000)	1.2	0.2	0.6
Biodiversity			
Mammal species, total known	300		
Mammal species, threatened	50		
Bird species, total breeding	254		
Bird species, threatened	37		
Nationally protected area (% of land area)	5.7	9.2	17.3
Energy			
GDP per unit of energy use (2000 PPP$/kg oil equiv)	4.1	4.6	4.3
Energy use per capita (kg oil equiv)	2,129	904	2,232
Energy from biomass products and waste (% of total)	4.8	19.6	4.1
Energy imports, net (% of energy use)	-55	-4	-91
Electric power consumption per capita (kWh)	2,832	891	2,496
Electricity generated by coal (% of total)	6.0	66.8	23.9
Emissions and pollution			
CO_2 emissions per unit of GDP (kg/2000 PPP$ GDP)	0.7	0.5	0.6
CO_2 emissions per capita (metric tons)	6.2	2.1	6.3
Particulate matter (pop. weighted average, µg/cu. m)	24	69	29
Passenger cars (per 1,000 people)	..	10	153
Water and sanitation			
Internal freshwater resources per capita (cu. m)	23,411	5,103	10,741
Freshwater withdrawal			
Total (% of internal resources)	2.2	8.2	5.7
Agriculture (% of total freshwater withdrawal)	77	81	71
Access to improved water source (% of total population)	95	78	..
Rural (% of rural population)	94	69	..
Urban (% of urban population)	96	92	96
Access to sanitation (% of total population)	..	49	..
Rural (% of rural population)	98	35	..
Urban (% of urban population)	..	71	..
Under-five mortality rate (per 1,000)	7	41	22
National accounting aggregates, 2003			
Gross national savings (% of GNI)	36.3	41.7	22.1
Consumption of fixed capital (% of GNI)	11.6	9.2	10.7
Education expenditure (% of GNI)	5.3	2.3	5.0
Energy depletion (% of GNI)	12.1	3.9	11.4
Mineral depletion (% of GNI)	0.0	0.3	0.3
Net forest depletion (% of GNI)	0.0	0.1	0.0
CO_2 damage (% of GNI)	1.0	1.8	0.8
Particulate emission damage (% of GNI)	0.1	0.8	0.6
Adjusted net savings (% of GNI)	17.0	27.9	3.3

Maldives

Environmental strategy/action plan prepared in **1994**

| | | Group data | |
	Country data	South Asia	Lower middle income
Population (millions)	0.3	1,425	2,655
Urban population (% of total)	28.9	28.3	49.8
GDP ($ billions)	0.7	765	4,168
GNI per capita, *Atlas* method ($)	2,350	510	1,490
Agriculture and fisheries			
Land area (1,000 sq. km)	0	4,781	56,103
Agricultural land (% of land area)	33	55	35
Irrigated land (% of crop land)	..	41.2	20.8
Fertilizer consumption (100 grams/ha arable land)	..	1,027	1,170
Population density, rural (people/sq. km arable land)	5,126	559	497
Fish catch, total (1,000 metric tons)	126	8,724	74,407
Forests			
Forest area (1,000 sq. km)	0	780	20,316
Forest area share of total land area (%)	3.3	16.3	36.2
Annual deforestation (% change, 1990–2000)	0.0	0.1	0.1
Biodiversity			
Mammal species, total known	..		
Mammal species, threatened	0		
Bird species, total breeding	..		
Bird species, threatened	1		
Nationally protected area (% of land area)	..	4.8	7.7
Energy			
GDP per unit of energy use (2000 PPP$/kg oil equiv)	..	5.1	4.1
Energy use per capita (kg oil equiv)	..	468	1,227
Energy from biomass products and waste (% of total)	..	39.3	12.3
Energy imports, net (% of energy use)	..	19	-22
Electric power consumption per capita (kWh)	..	344	1,289
Electricity generated by coal (% of total)	..	59.8	42.8
Emissions and pollution			
CO_2 emissions per unit of GDP (kg/2000 PPP$ GDP)	..	0.4	0.6
CO_2 emissions per capita (metric tons)	1.8	0.9	2.9
Particulate matter (pop. weighted average, µg/cu. m)	49	69	49
Passenger cars (per 1,000 people)	..	6	28
Water and sanitation			
Internal freshwater resources per capita (cu. m)	0	1,275	8,397
Freshwater withdrawal			
Total (% of internal resources)	..	40.5	5.9
Agriculture (% of total freshwater withdrawal)	0	94	74
Access to improved water source (% of total population)	84	84	82
Rural (% of rural population)	78	80	71
Urban (% of urban population)	99	93	94
Access to sanitation (% of total population)	58	35	60
Rural (% of rural population)	42	23	41
Urban (% of urban population)	100	64	80
Under-five mortality rate (per 1,000)	72	92	39
National accounting aggregates, 2003			
Gross national savings (% of GNI)	42.7	24.9	30.6
Consumption of fixed capital (% of GNI)	10.7	9.0	9.8
Education expenditure (% of GNI)	6.1	3.5	3.2
Energy depletion (% of GNI)	0.0	2.4	8.1
Mineral depletion (% of GNI)	0.0	0.3	0.4
Net forest depletion (% of GNI)	0.0	0.7	0.1
CO_2 damage (% of GNI)	0.5	1.3	1.6
Particulate emission damage (% of GNI)	..	0.7	0.7
Adjusted net savings (% of GNI)	37.5	14.0	13.2

Mali

Environmental strategy/action plan prepared in ..

	Country data	Group data	
		Sub-Saharan Africa	Low income
Population (millions)	11.7	705	2,312
Urban population (% of total)	32.3	36.5	30.4
GDP ($ billions)	4.3	439	1,103
GNI per capita, *Atlas* method ($)	290	500	440
Agriculture and fisheries			
Land area (1,000 sq. km)	1,220	23,596	30,456
Agricultural land (% of land area)	28	43	43
Irrigated land (% of crop land)	2.9	4.2	26.7
Fertilizer consumption (100 grams/ha arable land)	90	145	654
Population density, rural (people/sq. km arable land)	167	352	509
Fish catch, total (1,000 metric tons)	100	5,191	16,410
Forests			
Forest area (1,000 sq. km)	132	6,435	7,939
Forest area share of total land area (%)	10.8	27.3	26.1
Annual deforestation (% change, 1990–2000)	0.7	0.8	0.7
Biodiversity			
Mammal species, total known	137		
Mammal species, threatened	13		
Bird species, total breeding	191		
Bird species, threatened	4		
Nationally protected area (% of land area)	3.7	8.7	7.7
Energy			
GDP per unit of energy use (2000 PPP$/kg oil equiv)	..	2.8	4.1
Energy use per capita (kg oil equiv)	..	667	493
Energy from biomass products and waste (% of total)	..	57.5	49.4
Energy imports, net (% of energy use)	..	−56	−6
Electric power consumption per capita (kWh)	..	457	312
Electricity generated by coal (% of total)	..	68.2	47.4
Emissions and pollution			
CO_2 emissions per unit of GDP (kg/2000 PPP$ GDP)	0.1	0.4	0.4
CO_2 emissions per capita (metric tons)	0.1	0.7	0.8
Particulate matter (pop. weighted average, μg/cu. m)	194	54	63
Passenger cars (per 1,000 people)	..	..	..
Water and sanitation			
Internal freshwater resources per capita (cu. m)	5,150	5,546	3,583
Freshwater withdrawal			
Total (% of internal resources)	2.3	1.8	11.5
Agriculture (% of total freshwater withdrawal)	97	85	92
Access to improved water source (% of total population)	48	58	75
Rural (% of rural population)	35	46	70
Urban (% of urban population)	76	82	89
Access to sanitation (% of total population)	45	36	36
Rural (% of rural population)	38	26	24
Urban (% of urban population)	59	55	61
Under-five mortality rate (per 1,000)	220	171	123
National accounting aggregates, 2003			
Gross national savings (% of GNI)	15.6	16.9	23.1
Consumption of fixed capital (% of GNI)	8.0	10.6	8.9
Education expenditure (% of GNI)	2.1	4.7	3.4
Energy depletion (% of GNI)	0.0	8.0	5.8
Mineral depletion (% of GNI)	0.0	0.5	0.3
Net forest depletion (% of GNI)	0.0	0.7	0.8
CO_2 damage (% of GNI)	0.1	0.9	1.2
Particulate emission damage (% of GNI)	0.5	0.4	0.6
Adjusted net savings (% of GNI)	9.2	0.6	8.9

Malta

Environmental strategy/action plan prepared in ..

	Country data	Group data High income
Population (millions)	0.4	972
Urban population (% of total)	91.6	79.9
GDP ($ billions)	5	29,341
GNI per capita, *Atlas* method ($)	10,780	28,600

Agriculture and fisheries

Land area (1,000 sq. km)	0	31,030
Agricultural land (% of land area)	31	36
Irrigated land (% of crop land)	20.0	12.3
Fertilizer consumption (100 grams/ha arable land)	778	1,198
Population density, rural (people/sq. km arable land)	379	202
Fish catch, total (1,000 metric tons)	2	28,712

Forests

Forest area (1,000 sq. km)	0	7,929
Forest area share of total land area (%)	0.0	25.9
Annual deforestation (% change, 1990–2000)	..	−0.1

Biodiversity

Mammal species, total known	..	
Mammal species, threatened	2	
Bird species, total breeding	..	
Bird species, threatened	1	
Nationally protected area (% of land area)	..	19.5

Energy

GDP per unit of energy use (2000 PPP$/kg oil equiv)	7.6	5.2
Energy use per capita (kg oil equiv)	2,247	5,395
Energy from biomass products and waste (% of total)	..	3.1
Energy imports, net (% of energy use)	..	26
Electric power consumption per capita (kWh)	4,174	8,693
Electricity generated by coal (% of total)	..	38.2

Emissions and pollution

CO_2 emissions per unit of GDP (kg/2000 PPP$ GDP)	0.4	0.5
CO_2 emissions per capita (metric tons)	7.2	12.4
Particulate matter (pop. weighted average, µg/cu. m)	..	33
Passenger cars (per 1,000 people)	505	436

Water and sanitation

Internal freshwater resources per capita (cu. m)	252	9,479
Freshwater withdrawal		
Total (% of internal resources)	..	9.7
Agriculture (% of total freshwater withdrawal)	26	42
Access to improved water source (% of total population)	100	99
Rural (% of rural population)	100	98
Urban (% of urban population)	100	100
Access to sanitation (% of total population)	..	..
Rural (% of rural population)	..	..
Urban (% of urban population)	100	..
Under-five mortality rate (per 1,000)	6	7

National accounting aggregates, 2003

Gross national savings (% of GNI)	16.9	19.1
Consumption of fixed capital (% of GNI)	7.2	13.2
Education expenditure (% of GNI)	4.9	4.6
Energy depletion (% of GNI)	0.0	0.8
Mineral depletion (% of GNI)	0.0	0.0
Net forest depletion (% of GNI)	0.0	0.0
CO_2 damage (% of GNI)	0.5	0.3
Particulate emission damage (% of GNI)	..	0.3
Adjusted net savings (% of GNI)	14.1	9.2

Marshall Islands

Environmental strategy/action plan prepared in ..

	Country data	Group data	
		East Asia & Pacific	Lower middle income
Population (millions)	0.1	1,855	2,655
Urban population (% of total)	66.4	39.1	49.8
GDP ($ billions)	0.1	2,033	4,168
GNI per capita, *Atlas* method ($)	2,710	1,070	1,490
Agriculture and fisheries			
Land area (1,000 sq. km)	0	15,886	56,103
Agricultural land (% of land area)	..	50	35
Irrigated land (% of crop land)	..	..	20.8
Fertilizer consumption (100 grams/ha arable land)	..	2,297	1,170
Population density, rural (people/sq. km arable land)	..	565	497
Fish catch, total (1,000 metric tons)	..	60,812	74,407
Forests			
Forest area (1,000 sq. km)	..	4,284	20,316
Forest area share of total land area (%)	..	27.0	36.2
Annual deforestation (% change, 1990–2000)	..	0.2	0.1
Biodiversity			
Mammal species, total known	..		
Mammal species, threatened	1		
Bird species, total breeding	..		
Bird species, threatened	1		
Nationally protected area (% of land area)	..	9.2	7.7
Energy			
GDP per unit of energy use (2000 PPP$/kg oil equiv)	..	4.6	4.1
Energy use per capita (kg oil equiv)	..	904	1,227
Energy from biomass products and waste (% of total)	..	19.6	12.3
Energy imports, net (% of energy use)	..	−4	−22
Electric power consumption per capita (kWh)	..	891	1,289
Electricity generated by coal (% of total)	..	66.8	42.8
Emissions and pollution			
CO_2 emissions per unit of GDP (kg/2000 PPP$ GDP)	..	0.5	0.6
CO_2 emissions per capita (metric tons)	..	2.1	2.9
Particulate matter (pop. weighted average, µg/cu. m)	..	69	49
Passenger cars (per 1,000 people)	..	10	28
Water and sanitation			
Internal freshwater resources per capita (cu. m)	..	5,103	8,397
Freshwater withdrawal			
Total (% of internal resources)	..	8.2	5.9
Agriculture (% of total freshwater withdrawal)	..	81	74
Access to improved water source (% of total population)	85	78	82
Rural (% of rural population)	95	69	71
Urban (% of urban population)	80	92	94
Access to sanitation (% of total population)	82	49	60
Rural (% of rural population)	59	35	41
Urban (% of urban population)	93	71	80
Under-five mortality rate (per 1,000)	61	41	39
National accounting aggregates, 2003			
Gross national savings (% of GNI)	..	41.7	30.6
Consumption of fixed capital (% of GNI)	7.6	9.2	9.8
Education expenditure (% of GNI)	..	2.3	3.2
Energy depletion (% of GNI)	0.0	3.9	8.1
Mineral depletion (% of GNI)	0.0	0.3	0.4
Net forest depletion (% of GNI)	0.0	0.1	0.1
CO_2 damage (% of GNI)	..	1.8	1.6
Particulate emission damage (% of GNI)	..	0.8	0.7
Adjusted net savings (% of GNI)	..	27.9	13.2

Mauritania

Environmental strategy/action plan prepared in **1988**

	Country data	Group data Sub-Saharan Africa	Low income
Population (millions)	2.8	705	2,312
Urban population (% of total)	61.7	36.5	30.4
GDP ($ billions)	1.1	439	1,103
GNI per capita, *Atlas* method ($)	400	500	440
Agriculture and fisheries			
Land area (1,000 sq. km)	1,025	23,596	30,456
Agricultural land (% of land area)	39	43	43
Irrigated land (% of crop land)	9.8	4.2	26.7
Fertilizer consumption (100 grams/ha arable land)	59	145	654
Population density, rural (people/sq. km arable land)	226	352	509
Fish catch, total (1,000 metric tons)	84	5,191	16,410
Forests			
Forest area (1,000 sq. km)	3	6,435	7,939
Forest area share of total land area (%)	0.3	27.3	26.1
Annual deforestation (% change, 1990–2000)	2.7	0.8	0.7
Biodiversity			
Mammal species, total known	61		
Mammal species, threatened	10		
Bird species, total breeding	172		
Bird species, threatened	2		
Nationally protected area (% of land area)	1.7	8.7	7.7
Energy			
GDP per unit of energy use (2000 PPP$/kg oil equiv)	..	2.8	4.1
Energy use per capita (kg oil equiv)	..	667	493
Energy from biomass products and waste (% of total)	..	57.5	49.4
Energy imports, net (% of energy use)	..	−56	−6
Electric power consumption per capita (kWh)	..	457	312
Electricity generated by coal (% of total)	..	68.2	47.4
Emissions and pollution			
CO_2 emissions per unit of GDP (kg/2000 PPP$ GDP)	0.7	0.4	0.4
CO_2 emissions per capita (metric tons)	1.2	0.7	0.8
Particulate matter (pop. weighted average, µg/cu. m)	113	54	63
Passenger cars (per 1,000 people)	..	..	..
Water and sanitation			
Internal freshwater resources per capita (cu. m)	0	5,546	3,583
Freshwater withdrawal			
Total (% of internal resources)	400.0	1.8	11.5
Agriculture (% of total freshwater withdrawal)	92	85	92
Access to improved water source (% of total population)	56	58	75
Rural (% of rural population)	45	46	70
Urban (% of urban population)	63	82	89
Access to sanitation (% of total population)	42	36	36
Rural (% of rural population)	9	26	24
Urban (% of urban population)	64	55	61
Under-five mortality rate (per 1,000)	107	171	123
National accounting aggregates, 2003			
Gross national savings (% of GNI)	8.7	16.9	23.1
Consumption of fixed capital (% of GNI)	7.4	10.6	8.9
Education expenditure (% of GNI)	3.7	4.7	3.4
Energy depletion (% of GNI)	0.0	8.0	5.8
Mineral depletion (% of GNI)	18.8	0.5	0.3
Net forest depletion (% of GNI)	0.8	0.7	0.8
CO_2 damage (% of GNI)	2.1	0.9	1.2
Particulate emission damage (% of GNI)	..	0.4	0.6
Adjusted net savings (% of GNI)	..	0.6	8.9

Mauritius

Environmental strategy/action plan prepared in **1990**

		Group data	
	Country data	Sub-Saharan Africa	Upper middle income
Population (millions)	1.2	705	333
Urban population (% of total)	42.3	36.5	75.4
GDP ($ billions)	5.2	439	1,856
GNI per capita, *Atlas* method ($)	4,100	500	5,440

Agriculture and fisheries

Land area (1,000 sq. km)	2	23,596	12,741
Agricultural land (% of land area)	56	43	48
Irrigated land (% of crop land)	20.8	4.2	13.5
Fertilizer consumption (100 grams/ha arable land)	2,500	145	796
Population density, rural (people/sq. km arable land)	702	352	193
Fish catch, total (1,000 metric tons)	11	5,191	10,082

Forests

Forest area (1,000 sq. km)	0	6,435	2,427
Forest area share of total land area (%)	7.9	27.3	19.1
Annual deforestation (% change, 1990–2000)	0.6	0.8	0.6

Biodiversity

Mammal species, total known	..		
Mammal species, threatened	3		
Bird species, total breeding	..		
Bird species, threatened	9		
Nationally protected area (% of land area)	..	8.7	17.3

Energy

GDP per unit of energy use (2000 PPP$/kg oil equiv)	..	2.8	4.3
Energy use per capita (kg oil equiv)	..	667	2,232
Energy from biomass products and waste (% of total)	..	57.5	4.1
Energy imports, net (% of energy use)	..	–56	–91
Electric power consumption per capita (kWh)	..	457	2,496
Electricity generated by coal (% of total)	..	68.2	23.9

Emissions and pollution

CO_2 emissions per unit of GDP (kg/2000 PPP$ GDP)	0.3	0.4	0.6
CO_2 emissions per capita (metric tons)	2.4	0.7	6.3
Particulate matter (pop. weighted average, μg/cu. m)	..	54	29
Passenger cars (per 1,000 people)	86	..	153

Water and sanitation

Internal freshwater resources per capita (cu. m)	1,818	5,546	10,741
Freshwater withdrawal			
Total (% of internal resources)	..	1.8	5.7
Agriculture (% of total freshwater withdrawal)	77	85	71
Access to improved water source (% of total population)	100	58	..
Rural (% of rural population)	100	46	..
Urban (% of urban population)	100	82	96
Access to sanitation (% of total population)	99	36	..
Rural (% of rural population)	99	26	..
Urban (% of urban population)	100	55	..
Under-five mortality rate (per 1,000)	18	171	22

National accounting aggregates, 2003

Gross national savings (% of GNI)	26.3	16.9	22.1
Consumption of fixed capital (% of GNI)	10.9	10.6	10.7
Education expenditure (% of GNI)	3.3	4.7	5.0
Energy depletion (% of GNI)	0.0	8.0	11.4
Mineral depletion (% of GNI)	0.0	0.5	0.3
Net forest depletion (% of GNI)	0.0	0.7	0.0
CO_2 damage (% of GNI)	0.4	0.9	0.8
Particulate emission damage (% of GNI)	..	0.4	0.6
Adjusted net savings (% of GNI)	18.3	0.6	3.3

Mayotte

Environmental strategy/action plan prepared in **1988**

	Country data	Group data Sub-Saharan Africa	Group data Upper middle income
Population (millions)	0.2	705	333
Urban population (% of total)	..	36.5	75.4
GDP ($ billions)	..	439	1,856
GNI per capita, *Atlas* method ($)	..	500	5,440
Agriculture and fisheries			
Land area (1,000 sq. km)	0	23,596	12,741
Agricultural land (% of land area)	..	43	48
Irrigated land (% of crop land)	..	4.2	13.5
Fertilizer consumption (100 grams/ha arable land)	..	145	796
Population density, rural (people/sq. km arable land)	..	352	193
Fish catch, total (1,000 metric tons)	..	5,191	10,082
Forests			
Forest area (1,000 sq. km)	..	6,435	2,427
Forest area share of total land area (%)	..	27.3	19.1
Annual deforestation (% change, 1990–2000)	..	0.8	0.6
Biodiversity			
Mammal species, total known	..		
Mammal species, threatened	0		
Bird species, total breeding	..		
Bird species, threatened	3		
Nationally protected area (% of land area)	..	8.7	17.3
Energy			
GDP per unit of energy use (2000 PPP$/kg oil equiv)	..	2.8	4.3
Energy use per capita (kg oil equiv)	..	667	2,232
Energy from biomass products and waste (% of total)	..	57.5	4.1
Energy imports, net (% of energy use)	..	−56	−91
Electric power consumption per capita (kWh)	..	457	2,496
Electricity generated by coal (% of total)	..	68.2	23.9
Emissions and pollution			
CO_2 emissions per unit of GDP (kg/2000 PPP$ GDP)	..	0.4	0.6
CO_2 emissions per capita (metric tons)	..	0.7	6.3
Particulate matter (pop. weighted average, µg/cu. m)	..	54	29
Passenger cars (per 1,000 people)	..	..	153
Water and sanitation			
Internal freshwater resources per capita (cu. m)	..	5,546	10,741
Freshwater withdrawal			
Total (% of internal resources)	..	1.8	5.7
Agriculture (% of total freshwater withdrawal)	..	85	71
Access to improved water source (% of total population)	..	58	..
Rural (% of rural population)	..	46	..
Urban (% of urban population)	..	82	96
Access to sanitation (% of total population)	..	36	..
Rural (% of rural population)	..	26	..
Urban (% of urban population)	..	55	..
Under-five mortality rate (per 1,000)	..	171	22
National accounting aggregates, 2003			
Gross national savings (% of GNI)	..	16.9	22.1
Consumption of fixed capital (% of GNI)	..	10.6	10.7
Education expenditure (% of GNI)	..	4.7	5.0
Energy depletion (% of GNI)	..	8.0	11.4
Mineral depletion (% of GNI)	..	0.5	0.3
Net forest depletion (% of GNI)	..	0.7	0.0
CO_2 damage (% of GNI)	..	0.9	0.8
Particulate emission damage (% of GNI)	..	0.4	0.6
Adjusted net savings (% of GNI)	..	0.6	3.3

Mexico

Environmental strategy/action plan prepared in ..

	Country data	Latin America & Caribbean	Upper middle income
		Group data	
Population (millions)	102.3	533	333
Urban population (% of total)	75.0	76.6	75.4
GDP ($ billions)	626.1	1,741	1,856
GNI per capita, *Atlas* method ($)	6,230	3,280	5,440
Agriculture and fisheries			
Land area (1,000 sq. km)	1,909	20,057	12,741
Agricultural land (% of land area)	56	39	48
Irrigated land (% of crop land)	23.2	12.5	13.5
Fertilizer consumption (100 grams/ha arable land)	690	892	796
Population density, rural (people/sq. km arable land)	102	210	193
Fish catch, total (1,000 metric tons)	1,475	17,804	10,082
Forests			
Forest area (1,000 sq. km)	552	9,552	2,427
Forest area share of total land area (%)	28.9	47.6	19.1
Annual deforestation (% change, 1990–2000)	1.1	0.5	0.6
Biodiversity			
Mammal species, total known	491		
Mammal species, threatened	70		
Bird species, total breeding	440		
Bird species, threatened	39		
Nationally protected area (% of land area)	10.2	11.2	17.3
Energy			
GDP per unit of energy use (2000 PPP$/kg oil equiv)	5.6	6.1	4.3
Energy use per capita (kg oil equiv)	1,560	1,156	2,232
Energy from biomass products and waste (% of total)	5.2	14.6	4.1
Energy imports, net (% of energy use)	–46	–42	–91
Electric power consumption per capita (kWh)	1,660	1,506	2,496
Electricity generated by coal (% of total)	12.1	5.0	23.9
Emissions and pollution			
CO_2 emissions per unit of GDP (kg/2000 PPP$ GDP)	0.5	0.4	0.6
CO_2 emissions per capita (metric tons)	4.3	2.7	6.3
Particulate matter (pop. weighted average, µg/cu. m)	53	40	29
Passenger cars (per 1,000 people)	107	..	153
Water and sanitation			
Internal freshwater resources per capita (cu. m)	3,998	25,245	10,741
Freshwater withdrawal			
Total (% of internal resources)	19.0	2.0	5.7
Agriculture (% of total freshwater withdrawal)	78	74	71
Access to improved water source (% of total population)	91	89	..
Rural (% of rural population)	72	69	..
Urban (% of urban population)	97	96	96
Access to sanitation (% of total population)	77	74	..
Rural (% of rural population)	39	44	..
Urban (% of urban population)	90	84	..
Under-five mortality rate (per 1,000)	28	33	22
National accounting aggregates, 2003			
Gross national savings (% of GNI)	18.7	19.5	22.1
Consumption of fixed capital (% of GNI)	10.5	10.3	10.7
Education expenditure (% of GNI)	5.1	4.2	5.0
Energy depletion (% of GNI)	6.1	6.4	11.4
Mineral depletion (% of GNI)	0.1	0.7	0.3
Net forest depletion (% of GNI)	0.0	0.0	0.0
CO_2 damage (% of GNI)	0.5	0.5	0.8
Particulate emission damage (% of GNI)	0.5	0.5	0.6
Adjusted net savings (% of GNI)	6.0	5.3	3.3

Micronesia, Fed. Sts.

Environmental strategy/action plan prepared in ..

		Group data	
	Country data	East Asia & Pacific	Lower middle income
Population (millions)	0.1	1,855	2,655
Urban population (% of total)	29.3	39.1	49.8
GDP ($ billions)	0.2	2,033	4,168
GNI per capita, *Atlas* method ($)	2,070	1,070	1,490
Agriculture and fisheries			
Land area (1,000 sq. km)	1	15,886	56,103
Agricultural land (% of land area)	..	50	35
Irrigated land (% of crop land)	..	..	20.8
Fertilizer consumption (100 grams/ha arable land)	..	2,297	1,170
Population density, rural (people/sq. km arable land)	..	565	497
Fish catch, total (1,000 metric tons)	..	60,812	74,407
Forests			
Forest area (1,000 sq. km)	..	4,284	20,316
Forest area share of total land area (%)	..	27.0	36.2
Annual deforestation (% change, 1990–2000)	..	0.2	0.1
Biodiversity			
Mammal species, total known	..		
Mammal species, threatened	6		
Bird species, total breeding	..		
Bird species, threatened	5		
Nationally protected area (% of land area)	..	9.2	7.7
Energy			
GDP per unit of energy use (2000 PPP$/kg oil equiv)	..	4.6	4.1
Energy use per capita (kg oil equiv)	..	904	1,227
Energy from biomass products and waste (% of total)	..	19.6	12.3
Energy imports, net (% of energy use)	..	-4	-22
Electric power consumption per capita (kWh)	..	891	1,289
Electricity generated by coal (% of total)	..	66.8	42.8
Emissions and pollution			
CO_2 emissions per unit of GDP (kg/2000 PPP$ GDP)	..	0.5	0.6
CO_2 emissions per capita (metric tons)	..	2.1	2.9
Particulate matter (pop. weighted average, µg/cu. m)	..	69	49
Passenger cars (per 1,000 people)	..	10	28
Water and sanitation			
Internal freshwater resources per capita (cu. m)	..	5,103	8,397
Freshwater withdrawal			
Total (% of internal resources)	..	8.2	5.9
Agriculture (% of total freshwater withdrawal)	..	81	74
Access to improved water source (% of total population)	94	78	82
Rural (% of rural population)	94	69	71
Urban (% of urban population)	95	92	94
Access to sanitation (% of total population)	28	49	60
Rural (% of rural population)	14	35	41
Urban (% of urban population)	61	71	80
Under-five mortality rate (per 1,000)	23	41	39
National accounting aggregates, 2003			
Gross national savings (% of GNI)	..	41.7	30.6
Consumption of fixed capital (% of GNI)	9.2	9.2	9.8
Education expenditure (% of GNI)	..	2.3	3.2
Energy depletion (% of GNI)	0.0	3.9	8.1
Mineral depletion (% of GNI)	0.0	0.3	0.4
Net forest depletion (% of GNI)	0.0	0.1	0.1
CO_2 damage (% of GNI)	..	1.8	1.6
Particulate emission damage (% of GNI)	..	0.8	0.7
Adjusted net savings (% of GNI)	..	27.9	13.2

Moldova

Environmental strategy/action plan prepared in ..

	Country data	Europe & Central Asia	Low income
		Group data	
Population (millions)	4.2	472	2,312
Urban population (% of total)	41.9	63.8	30.4
GDP ($ billions)	2.0	1,403	1,103
GNI per capita, *Atlas* method ($)	590	2,580	440
Agriculture and fisheries			
Land area (1,000 sq. km)	33	23,868	30,456
Agricultural land (% of land area)	78	28	43
Irrigated land (% of crop land)	14.0	10.9	26.7
Fertilizer consumption (100 grams/ha arable land)	55	344	654
Population density, rural (people/sq. km arable land)	134	122	509
Fish catch, total (1,000 metric tons)	2	5,527	16,410
Forests			
Forest area (1,000 sq. km)	3	9,463	7,939
Forest area share of total land area (%)	9.9	39.6	26.1
Annual deforestation (% change, 1990–2000)	–0.2	–0.1	0.7
Biodiversity			
Mammal species, total known	68		
Mammal species, threatened	6		
Bird species, total breeding	175		
Bird species, threatened	5		
Nationally protected area (% of land area)	1.4	6.8	7.7
Energy			
GDP per unit of energy use (2000 PPP$/kg oil equiv)	2.0	2.5	4.1
Energy use per capita (kg oil equiv)	703	2,697	493
Energy from biomass products and waste (% of total)	2.0	2.3	49.4
Energy imports, net (% of energy use)	98	–23	–6
Electric power consumption per capita (kWh)	909	2,808	312
Electricity generated by coal (% of total)	3.8	29.4	47.4
Emissions and pollution			
CO_2 emissions per unit of GDP (kg/2000 PPP$ GDP)	1.2	1.1	0.4
CO_2 emissions per capita (metric tons)	1.5	6.7	0.8
Particulate matter (pop. weighted average, µg/cu. m)	35	33	63
Passenger cars (per 1,000 people)	74	138	..
Water and sanitation			
Internal freshwater resources per capita (cu. m)	236	11,128	3,583
Freshwater withdrawal			
Total (% of internal resources)	300.0	7.4	11.5
Agriculture (% of total freshwater withdrawal)	26	57	92
Access to improved water source (% of total population)	92	91	75
Rural (% of rural population)	88	80	70
Urban (% of urban population)	97	98	89
Access to sanitation (% of total population)	68	82	36
Rural (% of rural population)	52	64	24
Urban (% of urban population)	86	93	61
Under-five mortality rate (per 1,000)	32	36	123
National accounting aggregates, 2003			
Gross national savings (% of GNI)	17.0	21.9	23.1
Consumption of fixed capital (% of GNI)	6.8	10.7	8.9
Education expenditure (% of GNI)	3.5	4.1	3.4
Energy depletion (% of GNI)	0.0	11.6	5.8
Mineral depletion (% of GNI)	0.0	0.1	0.3
Net forest depletion (% of GNI)	0.0	0.0	0.8
CO_2 damage (% of GNI)	2.8	1.9	1.2
Particulate emission damage (% of GNI)	0.5	0.6	0.6
Adjusted net savings (% of GNI)	10.3	1.1	8.9

Monaco

Environmental strategy/action plan prepared in ..

	Country data	Group data High income
Population (millions)	0.0	972
Urban population (% of total)	100.0	79.9
GDP ($ billions)	..	29,341
GNI per capita, *Atlas* method ($)	..	28,600

Agriculture and fisheries		
Land area (1,000 sq. km)	0	31,030
Agricultural land (% of land area)	..	36
Irrigated land (% of crop land)	..	12.3
Fertilizer consumption (100 grams/ha arable land)	..	1,198
Population density, rural (people/sq. km arable land)	..	202
Fish catch, total (1,000 metric tons)	..	28,712

Forests		
Forest area (1,000 sq. km)	..	7,929
Forest area share of total land area (%)	..	25.9
Annual deforestation (% change, 1990–2000)	..	–0.1

Biodiversity		
Mammal species, total known	..	
Mammal species, threatened	..	
Bird species, total breeding	..	
Bird species, threatened	..	
Nationally protected area (% of land area)	..	19.5

Energy		
GDP per unit of energy use (2000 PPP$/kg oil equiv)	..	5.2
Energy use per capita (kg oil equiv)	..	5,395
Energy from biomass products and waste (% of total)	..	3.1
Energy imports, net (% of energy use)	..	26
Electric power consumption per capita (kWh)	..	8,693
Electricity generated by coal (% of total)	..	38.2

Emissions and pollution		
CO_2 emissions per unit of GDP (kg/2000 PPP$ GDP)	..	0.5
CO_2 emissions per capita (metric tons)	..	12.4
Particulate matter (pop. weighted average, µg/cu. m)	..	33
Passenger cars (per 1,000 people)	..	436

Water and sanitation		
Internal freshwater resources per capita (cu. m)	..	9,479
Freshwater withdrawal		
Total (% of internal resources)	..	9.7
Agriculture (% of total freshwater withdrawal)	..	42
Access to improved water source (% of total population)	..	99
Rural (% of rural population)	..	98
Urban (% of urban population)	100	100
Access to sanitation (% of total population)	..	..
Rural (% of rural population)	..	..
Urban (% of urban population)	100	..
Under-five mortality rate (per 1,000)	4	7

National accounting aggregates, 2003		
Gross national savings (% of GNI)	..	19.1
Consumption of fixed capital (% of GNI)	..	13.2
Education expenditure (% of GNI)	..	4.6
Energy depletion (% of GNI)	..	0.8
Mineral depletion (% of GNI)	..	0.0
Net forest depletion (% of GNI)	..	0.0
CO_2 damage (% of GNI)	..	0.3
Particulate emission damage (% of GNI)	..	0.3
Adjusted net savings (% of GNI)	..	9.2

Mongolia

Environmental strategy/action plan prepared in **1995**

	Country data	East Asia & Pacific	Low income
		Group data	
Population (millions)	2.5	1,855	2,312
Urban population (% of total)	56.8	39.1	30.4
GDP ($ billions)	1.3	2,033	1,103
GNI per capita, *Atlas* method ($)	480	1,070	440
Agriculture and fisheries			
Land area (1,000 sq. km)	1,567	15,886	30,456
Agricultural land (% of land area)	83	50	43
Irrigated land (% of crop land)	7.0	..	26.7
Fertilizer consumption (100 grams/ha arable land)	37	2,297	654
Population density, rural (people/sq. km arable land)	88	565	509
Fish catch, total (1,000 metric tons)	0	60,812	16,410
Forests			
Forest area (1,000 sq. km)	106	4,284	7,939
Forest area share of total land area (%)	6.8	27.0	26.1
Annual deforestation (% change, 1990–2000)	0.5	0.2	0.7
Biodiversity			
Mammal species, total known	133		
Mammal species, threatened	14		
Bird species, total breeding	274		
Bird species, threatened	16		
Nationally protected area (% of land area)	11.5	9.2	7.7
Energy			
GDP per unit of energy use (2000 PPP$/kg oil equiv)	..	4.6	4.1
Energy use per capita (kg oil equiv)	..	904	493
Energy from biomass products and waste (% of total)	..	19.6	49.4
Energy imports, net (% of energy use)	..	–4	–6
Electric power consumption per capita (kWh)	..	891	312
Electricity generated by coal (% of total)	..	66.8	47.4
Emissions and pollution			
CO_2 emissions per unit of GDP (kg/2000 PPP$ GDP)	1.9	0.5	0.4
CO_2 emissions per capita (metric tons)	3.1	2.1	0.8
Particulate matter (pop. weighted average, µg/cu. m)	71	69	63
Passenger cars (per 1,000 people)	26	10	..
Water and sanitation			
Internal freshwater resources per capita (cu. m)	14,115	5,103	3,583
Freshwater withdrawal			
Total (% of internal resources)	1.1	8.2	11.5
Agriculture (% of total freshwater withdrawal)	53	81	92
Access to improved water source (% of total population)	62	78	75
Rural (% of rural population)	30	69	70
Urban (% of urban population)	87	92	89
Access to sanitation (% of total population)	59	49	36
Rural (% of rural population)	37	35	24
Urban (% of urban population)	75	71	61
Under-five mortality rate (per 1,000)	68	41	123
National accounting aggregates, 2003			
Gross national savings (% of GNI)	18.1	41.7	23.1
Consumption of fixed capital (% of GNI)	10.9	9.2	8.9
Education expenditure (% of GNI)	5.7	2.3	3.4
Energy depletion (% of GNI)	0.0	3.9	5.8
Mineral depletion (% of GNI)	2.4	0.3	0.3
Net forest depletion (% of GNI)	0.0	0.1	0.8
CO_2 damage (% of GNI)	4.6	1.8	1.2
Particulate emission damage (% of GNI)	0.5	0.8	0.6
Adjusted net savings (% of GNI)	5.3	27.9	8.9

Morocco

Environmental strategy/action plan prepared in ..

	Country data	Middle East & North Africa	Lower middle income
		Group data	
Population (millions)	30.1	312	2,655
Urban population (% of total)	57.4	59.0	49.8
GDP ($ billions)	43.7	745	4,168
GNI per capita, *Atlas* method ($)	1,310	2,390	1,490
Agriculture and fisheries			
Land area (1,000 sq. km)	446	11,111	56,103
Agricultural land (% of land area)	69	34	35
Irrigated land (% of crop land)	14.5	38.3	20.8
Fertilizer consumption (100 grams/ha arable land)	475	854	1,170
Population density, rural (people/sq. km arable land)	153	603	497
Fish catch, total (1,000 metric tons)	1,085	2,840	74,407
Forests			
Forest area (1,000 sq. km)	30	168	20,316
Forest area share of total land area (%)	6.8	1.5	36.2
Annual deforestation (% change, 1990–2000)	0.0	–0.1	0.1
Biodiversity			
Mammal species, total known	105		
Mammal species, threatened	16		
Bird species, total breeding	206		
Bird species, threatened	9		
Nationally protected area (% of land area)	0.7	11.3	7.7
Energy			
GDP per unit of energy use (2000 PPP$/kg oil equiv)	10.1	3.5	4.1
Energy use per capita (kg oil equiv)	363	1,504	1,227
Energy from biomass products and waste (% of total)	4.2	1.0	12.3
Energy imports, net (% of energy use)	95	–168	–22
Electric power consumption per capita (kWh)	475	1,412	1,289
Electricity generated by coal (% of total)	70.1	2.3	42.8
Emissions and pollution			
CO_2 emissions per unit of GDP (kg/2000 PPP$ GDP)	0.4	0.8	0.6
CO_2 emissions per capita (metric tons)	1.3	4.2	2.9
Particulate matter (pop. weighted average, µg/cu. m)	29	87	49
Passenger cars (per 1,000 people)	44	..	28
Water and sanitation			
Internal freshwater resources per capita (cu. m)	963	761	8,397
Freshwater withdrawal			
Total (% of internal resources)	39.7	101.7	5.9
Agriculture (% of total freshwater withdrawal)	89	88	74
Access to improved water source (% of total population)	80	88	82
Rural (% of rural population)	56	78	71
Urban (% of urban population)	99	96	94
Access to sanitation (% of total population)	61	75	60
Rural (% of rural population)	31	56	41
Urban (% of urban population)	83	90	80
Under-five mortality rate (per 1,000)	39	53	39
National accounting aggregates, 2003			
Gross national savings (% of GNI)	27.9	31.2	30.6
Consumption of fixed capital (% of GNI)	9.7	10.0	9.8
Education expenditure (% of GNI)	4.8	5.5	3.2
Energy depletion (% of GNI)	0.0	30.7	8.1
Mineral depletion (% of GNI)	0.3	0.1	0.4
Net forest depletion (% of GNI)	0.0	0.0	0.1
CO_2 damage (% of GNI)	0.6	1.2	1.6
Particulate emission damage (% of GNI)	0.2	0.8	0.7
Adjusted net savings (% of GNI)	21.9	–6.2	13.2

Mozambique

Environmental strategy/action plan prepared in **1994**

	Country data	Group data Sub-Saharan Africa	Low income
Population (millions)	18.8	705	2,312
Urban population (% of total)	35.6	36.5	30.4
GDP ($ billions)	4.3	439	1,103
GNI per capita, *Atlas* method ($)	210	500	440
Agriculture and fisheries			
Land area (1,000 sq. km)	784	23,596	30,456
Agricultural land (% of land area)	62	43	43
Irrigated land (% of crop land)	2.4	4.2	26.7
Fertilizer consumption (100 grams/ha arable land)	59	145	654
Population density, rural (people/sq. km arable land)	288	352	509
Fish catch, total (1,000 metric tons)	33	5,191	16,410
Forests			
Forest area (1,000 sq. km)	306	6,435	7,939
Forest area share of total land area (%)	39.0	27.3	26.1
Annual deforestation (% change, 1990–2000)	0.2	0.8	0.7
Biodiversity			
Mammal species, total known	179		
Mammal species, threatened	14		
Bird species, total breeding	144		
Bird species, threatened	16		
Nationally protected area (% of land area)	8.4	8.7	7.7
Energy			
GDP per unit of energy use (2000 PPP$/kg oil equiv)	2.3	2.8	4.1
Energy use per capita (kg oil equiv)	436	667	493
Energy from biomass products and waste (% of total)	86.1	57.5	49.4
Energy imports, net (% of energy use)	0	–56	–6
Electric power consumption per capita (kWh)	341	457	312
Electricity generated by coal (% of total)	..	68.2	47.4
Emissions and pollution			
CO_2 emissions per unit of GDP (kg/2000 PPP$ GDP)	0.1	0.4	0.4
CO_2 emissions per capita (metric tons)	0.1	0.7	0.8
Particulate matter (pop. weighted average, μg/cu. m)	46	54	63
Passenger cars (per 1,000 people)	..	..	..
Water and sanitation			
Internal freshwater resources per capita (cu. m)	5,268	5,546	3,583
Freshwater withdrawal			
Total (% of internal resources)	0.6	1.8	11.5
Agriculture (% of total freshwater withdrawal)	89	85	92
Access to improved water source (% of total population)	42	58	75
Rural (% of rural population)	24	46	70
Urban (% of urban population)	76	82	89
Access to sanitation (% of total population)	27	36	36
Rural (% of rural population)	14	26	24
Urban (% of urban population)	51	55	61
Under-five mortality rate (per 1,000)	147	171	123
National accounting aggregates, 2003			
Gross national savings (% of GNI)	12.6	16.9	23.1
Consumption of fixed capital (% of GNI)	7.4	10.6	8.9
Education expenditure (% of GNI)	3.8	4.7	3.4
Energy depletion (% of GNI)	0.0	8.0	5.8
Mineral depletion (% of GNI)	0.0	0.5	0.3
Net forest depletion (% of GNI)	0.0	0.7	0.8
CO_2 damage (% of GNI)	0.3	0.9	1.2
Particulate emission damage (% of GNI)	0.4	0.4	0.6
Adjusted net savings (% of GNI)	8.3	0.6	8.9

Myanmar

Environmental strategy/action plan prepared in ..

	Country data	East Asia & Pacific	Low income
		Group data	
Population (millions)	49.4	1,855	2,312
Urban population (% of total)	29.2	39.1	30.4
GDP ($ billions)	..	2,033	1,103
GNI per capita, *Atlas* method ($)	..	1,070	440
Agriculture and fisheries			
Land area (1,000 sq. km)	658	15,886	30,456
Agricultural land (% of land area)	17	50	43
Irrigated land (% of crop land)	18.8	..	26.7
Fertilizer consumption (100 grams/ha arable land)	134	2,297	654
Population density, rural (people/sq. km arable land)	353	565	509
Fish catch, total (1,000 metric tons)	1,288	60,812	16,410
Forests			
Forest area (1,000 sq. km)	344	4,284	7,939
Forest area share of total land area (%)	52.3	27.0	26.1
Annual deforestation (% change, 1990–2000)	1.4	0.2	0.7
Biodiversity			
Mammal species, total known	300		
Mammal species, threatened	39		
Bird species, total breeding	310		
Bird species, threatened	35		
Nationally protected area (% of land area)	0.3	9.2	7.7
Energy			
GDP per unit of energy use (2000 PPP$/kg oil equiv)	..	4.6	4.1
Energy use per capita (kg oil equiv)	258	904	493
Energy from biomass products and waste (% of total)	76.7	19.6	49.4
Energy imports, net (% of energy use)	−26	−4	−6
Electric power consumption per capita (kWh)	108	891	312
Electricity generated by coal (% of total)	..	66.8	47.4
Emissions and pollution			
CO_2 emissions per unit of GDP (kg/2000 PPP$ GDP)	..	0.5	0.4
CO_2 emissions per capita (metric tons)	0.2	2.1	0.8
Particulate matter (pop. weighted average, μg/cu. m)	89	69	63
Passenger cars (per 1,000 people)	..	10	..
Water and sanitation			
Internal freshwater resources per capita (cu. m)	17,848	5,103	3,583
Freshwater withdrawal			
Total (% of internal resources)	0.5	8.2	11.5
Agriculture (% of total freshwater withdrawal)	90	81	92
Access to improved water source (% of total population)	80	78	75
Rural (% of rural population)	74	69	70
Urban (% of urban population)	95	92	89
Access to sanitation (% of total population)	73	49	36
Rural (% of rural population)	63	35	24
Urban (% of urban population)	96	71	61
Under-five mortality rate (per 1,000)	107	41	123
National accounting aggregates, 2003			
Gross national savings (% of GNI)	..	41.7	23.1
Consumption of fixed capital (% of GNI)	..	9.2	8.9
Education expenditure (% of GNI)	0.9	2.3	3.4
Energy depletion (% of GNI)	..	3.9	5.8
Mineral depletion (% of GNI)	..	0.3	0.3
Net forest depletion (% of GNI)	..	0.1	0.8
CO_2 damage (% of GNI)	..	1.8	1.2
Particulate emission damage (% of GNI)	..	0.8	0.6
Adjusted net savings (% of GNI)	..	27.9	8.9

Namibia

Environmental strategy/action plan prepared in **1992**

	Country data	Sub-Saharan Africa	Lower middle income
		Group data	
Population (millions)	2.0	705	2,655
Urban population (% of total)	32.4	36.5	49.8
GDP ($ billions)	4.3	439	4,168
GNI per capita, *Atlas* method ($)	1,930	500	1,490
Agriculture and fisheries			
Land area (1,000 sq. km)	823	23,596	56,103
Agricultural land (% of land area)	47	43	35
Irrigated land (% of crop land)	0.9	4.2	20.8
Fertilizer consumption (100 grams/ha arable land)	4	145	1,170
Population density, rural (people/sq. km arable land)	166	352	497
Fish catch, total (1,000 metric tons)	548	5,191	74,407
Forests			
Forest area (1,000 sq. km)	80	6,435	20,316
Forest area share of total land area (%)	9.8	27.3	36.2
Annual deforestation (% change, 1990–2000)	0.9	0.8	0.1
Biodiversity			
Mammal species, total known	250		
Mammal species, threatened	15		
Bird species, total breeding	201		
Bird species, threatened	11		
Nationally protected area (% of land area)	13.6	8.7	7.7
Energy			
GDP per unit of energy use (2000 PPP$/kg oil equiv)	10.2	2.8	4.1
Energy use per capita (kg oil equiv)	599	667	1,227
Energy from biomass products and waste (% of total)	15.2	57.5	12.3
Energy imports, net (% of energy use)	75	–56	–22
Electric power consumption per capita (kWh)	..	457	1,289
Electricity generated by coal (% of total)	0.4	68.2	42.8
Emissions and pollution			
CO_2 emissions per unit of GDP (kg/2000 PPP$ GDP)	0.2	0.4	0.6
CO_2 emissions per capita (metric tons)	1.0	0.7	2.9
Particulate matter (pop. weighted average, μg/cu. m)	53	54	49
Passenger cars (per 1,000 people)	38	..	28
Water and sanitation			
Internal freshwater resources per capita (cu. m)	2,978	5,546	8,397
Freshwater withdrawal			
Total (% of internal resources)	3.3	1.8	5.9
Agriculture (% of total freshwater withdrawal)	68	85	74
Access to improved water source (% of total population)	80	58	82
Rural (% of rural population)	72	46	71
Urban (% of urban population)	98	82	94
Access to sanitation (% of total population)	30	36	60
Rural (% of rural population)	14	26	41
Urban (% of urban population)	66	55	80
Under-five mortality rate (per 1,000)	65	171	39
National accounting aggregates, 2003			
Gross national savings (% of GNI)	31.5	16.9	30.6
Consumption of fixed capital (% of GNI)	12.3	10.6	9.8
Education expenditure (% of GNI)	7.4	4.7	3.2
Energy depletion (% of GNI)	0.0	8.0	8.1
Mineral depletion (% of GNI)	0.3	0.5	0.4
Net forest depletion (% of GNI)	0.0	0.7	0.1
CO_2 damage (% of GNI)	0.3	0.9	1.6
Particulate emission damage (% of GNI)	0.2	0.4	0.7
Adjusted net savings (% of GNI)	25.9	0.6	13.2

Nepal

Environmental strategy/action plan prepared in **1993**

	Country data	South Asia	Low income
		Group data	
Population (millions)	24.7	1,425	2,312
Urban population (% of total)	12.9	28.3	30.4
GDP ($ billions)	5.9	765	1,103
GNI per capita, *Atlas* method ($)	240	510	440
Agriculture and fisheries			
Land area (1,000 sq. km)	143	4,781	30,456
Agricultural land (% of land area)	35	55	43
Irrigated land (% of crop land)	34.5	41.2	26.7
Fertilizer consumption (100 grams/ha arable land)	278	1,027	654
Population density, rural (people/sq. km arable land)	659	559	509
Fish catch, total (1,000 metric tons)	33	8,724	16,410
Forests			
Forest area (1,000 sq. km)	39	780	7,939
Forest area share of total land area (%)	27.3	16.3	26.1
Annual deforestation (% change, 1990–2000)	1.8	0.1	0.7
Biodiversity			
Mammal species, total known	181		
Mammal species, threatened	31		
Bird species, total breeding	274		
Bird species, threatened	25		
Nationally protected area (% of land area)	8.9	4.8	7.7
Energy			
GDP per unit of energy use (2000 PPP$/kg oil equiv)	3.8	5.1	4.1
Energy use per capita (kg oil equiv)	353	468	493
Energy from biomass products and waste (% of total)	87.2	39.3	49.4
Energy imports, net (% of energy use)	11	19	-6
Electric power consumption per capita (kWh)	64	344	312
Electricity generated by coal (% of total)	..	59.8	47.4
Emissions and pollution			
CO_2 emissions per unit of GDP (kg/2000 PPP$ GDP)	0.1	0.4	0.4
CO_2 emissions per capita (metric tons)	0.1	0.9	0.8
Particulate matter (pop. weighted average, µg/cu. m)	50	69	63
Passenger cars (per 1,000 people)	..	6	..
Water and sanitation			
Internal freshwater resources per capita (cu. m)	8,029	1,275	3,583
Freshwater withdrawal			
Total (% of internal resources)	14.6	40.5	11.5
Agriculture (% of total freshwater withdrawal)	99	94	92
Access to improved water source (% of total population)	84	84	75
Rural (% of rural population)	82	80	70
Urban (% of urban population)	93	93	89
Access to sanitation (% of total population)	27	35	36
Rural (% of rural population)	20	23	24
Urban (% of urban population)	68	64	61
Under-five mortality rate (per 1,000)	82	92	123
National accounting aggregates, 2003			
Gross national savings (% of GNI)	31.6	24.9	23.1
Consumption of fixed capital (% of GNI)	2.4	9.0	8.9
Education expenditure (% of GNI)	3.2	3.5	3.4
Energy depletion (% of GNI)	0.0	2.4	5.8
Mineral depletion (% of GNI)	0.0	0.3	0.3
Net forest depletion (% of GNI)	3.0	0.7	0.8
CO_2 damage (% of GNI)	0.4	1.3	1.2
Particulate emission damage (% of GNI)	0.1	0.7	0.6
Adjusted net savings (% of GNI)	28.8	14.0	8.9

Netherlands

Environmental strategy/action plan prepared in **1994**

	Country data	Group data — High income
Population (millions)	16.2	972
Urban population (% of total)	89.8	79.9
GDP ($ billions)	512	29,341
GNI per capita, *Atlas* method ($)	26,230	28,600
Agriculture and fisheries		
Land area (1,000 sq. km)	34	31,030
Agricultural land (% of land area)	57	36
Irrigated land (% of crop land)	59.5	12.3
Fertilizer consumption (100 grams/ha arable land)	3,668	1,198
Population density, rural (people/sq. km arable land)	182	202
Fish catch, total (1,000 metric tons)	570	28,712
Forests		
Forest area (1,000 sq. km)	4	7,929
Forest area share of total land area (%)	11.1	25.9
Annual deforestation (% change, 1990–2000)	–0.3	–0.1
Biodiversity		
Mammal species, total known	55	
Mammal species, threatened	10	
Bird species, total breeding	192	
Bird species, threatened	4	
Nationally protected area (% of land area)	14.2	19.5
Energy		
GDP per unit of energy use (2000 PPP$/kg oil equiv)	5.8	5.2
Energy use per capita (kg oil equiv)	4,827	5,395
Energy from biomass products and waste (% of total)	1.7	3.1
Energy imports, net (% of energy use)	23	26
Electric power consumption per capita (kWh)	6,179	8,693
Electricity generated by coal (% of total)	28.0	38.2
Emissions and pollution		
CO_2 emissions per unit of GDP (kg/2000 PPP$ GDP)	0.3	0.5
CO_2 emissions per capita (metric tons)	8.7	12.4
Particulate matter (pop. weighted average, µg/cu. m)	37	33
Passenger cars (per 1,000 people)	384	436
Water and sanitation		
Internal freshwater resources per capita (cu. m)	678	9,479
Freshwater withdrawal		
Total (% of internal resources)	70.9	9.7
Agriculture (% of total freshwater withdrawal)	34	42
Access to improved water source (% of total population)	100	99
Rural (% of rural population)	99	98
Urban (% of urban population)	100	100
Access to sanitation (% of total population)	100	..
Rural (% of rural population)	100	..
Urban (% of urban population)	100	..
Under-five mortality rate (per 1,000)	6	7
National accounting aggregates, 2003		
Gross national savings (% of GNI)	23.3	19.1
Consumption of fixed capital (% of GNI)	15.2	13.2
Education expenditure (% of GNI)	4.9	4.6
Energy depletion (% of GNI)	0.7	0.8
Mineral depletion (% of GNI)	0.0	0.0
Net forest depletion (% of GNI)	0.0	0.0
CO_2 damage (% of GNI)	0.2	0.3
Particulate emission damage (% of GNI)	0.4	0.3
Adjusted net savings (% of GNI)	11.7	9.2

Netherlands Antilles

Environmental strategy/action plan prepared in ..

	Country data	Group data High income
Population (millions)	0.2	972
Urban population (% of total)	69.7	79.9
GDP ($ billions)	..	29,341
GNI per capita, *Atlas* method ($)	..	28,600

Agriculture and fisheries
Land area (1,000 sq. km)	1	31,030
Agricultural land (% of land area)	10	36
Irrigated land (% of crop land)	..	12.3
Fertilizer consumption (100 grams/ha arable land)	..	1,198
Population density, rural (people/sq. km arable land)	832	202
Fish catch, total (1,000 metric tons)	1	28,712

Forests
Forest area (1,000 sq. km)	0	7,929
Forest area share of total land area (%)	1.3	25.9
Annual deforestation (% change, 1990–2000)	0.0	–0.1

Biodiversity
Mammal species, total known	..	
Mammal species, threatened	3	
Bird species, total breeding	..	
Bird species, threatened	1	
Nationally protected area (% of land area)	..	19.5

Energy
GDP per unit of energy use (2000 PPP$/kg oil equiv)	..	5.2
Energy use per capita (kg oil equiv)	6,782	5,395
Energy from biomass products and waste (% of total)	..	3.1
Energy imports, net (% of energy use)	..	26
Electric power consumption per capita (kWh)	3,817	8,693
Electricity generated by coal (% of total)	..	38.2

Emissions and pollution
CO_2 emissions per unit of GDP (kg/2000 PPP$ GDP)	..	0.5
CO_2 emissions per capita (metric tons)	46.2	12.4
Particulate matter (pop. weighted average, µg/cu. m)	32	33
Passenger cars (per 1,000 people)	..	436

Water and sanitation
Internal freshwater resources per capita (cu. m)	..	9,479
Freshwater withdrawal		
Total (% of internal resources)	..	9.7
Agriculture (% of total freshwater withdrawal)	..	42
Access to improved water source (% of total population)	..	99
Rural (% of rural population)	..	98
Urban (% of urban population)	..	100
Access to sanitation (% of total population)	..	..
Rural (% of rural population)	..	..
Urban (% of urban population)	..	..
Under-five mortality rate (per 1,000)	..	7

National accounting aggregates, 2003
Gross national savings (% of GNI)	..	19.1
Consumption of fixed capital (% of GNI)	..	13.2
Education expenditure (% of GNI)	..	4.6
Energy depletion (% of GNI)	..	0.8
Mineral depletion (% of GNI)	..	0.0
Net forest depletion (% of GNI)	..	0.0
CO_2 damage (% of GNI)	..	0.3
Particulate emission damage (% of GNI)	..	0.3
Adjusted net savings (% of GNI)	..	9.2

New Caledonia

Environmental strategy/action plan prepared in ..

	Country data	High income
		Group data
Population (millions)	0.2	972
Urban population (% of total)	79.9	79.9
GDP ($ billions)	..	29,341
GNI per capita, *Atlas* method ($)	..	28,600
Agriculture and fisheries		
Land area (1,000 sq. km)	18	31,030
Agricultural land (% of land area)	13	36
Irrigated land (% of crop land)	100.0	12.3
Fertilizer consumption (100 grams/ha arable land)	1,800	1,198
Population density, rural (people/sq. km arable land)	929	202
Fish catch, total (1,000 metric tons)	5	28,712
Forests		
Forest area (1,000 sq. km)	4	7,929
Forest area share of total land area (%)	20.4	25.9
Annual deforestation (% change, 1990–2000)	0.0	–0.1
Biodiversity		
Mammal species, total known	..	
Mammal species, threatened	6	
Bird species, total breeding	..	
Bird species, threatened	10	
Nationally protected area (% of land area)	..	19.5
Energy		
GDP per unit of energy use (2000 PPP$/kg oil equiv)	..	5.2
Energy use per capita (kg oil equiv)	..	5,395
Energy from biomass products and waste (% of total)	..	3.1
Energy imports, net (% of energy use)	..	26
Electric power consumption per capita (kWh)	..	8,693
Electricity generated by coal (% of total)	..	38.2
Emissions and pollution		
CO_2 emissions per unit of GDP (kg/2000 PPP$ GDP)	0.4	0.5
CO_2 emissions per capita (metric tons)	7.8	12.4
Particulate matter (pop. weighted average, μg/cu. m)	74	33
Passenger cars (per 1,000 people)	..	436
Water and sanitation		
Internal freshwater resources per capita (cu. m)	..	9,479
Freshwater withdrawal		
Total (% of internal resources)	..	9.7
Agriculture (% of total freshwater withdrawal)	..	42
Access to improved water source (% of total population)	..	99
Rural (% of rural population)	..	98
Urban (% of urban population)	..	100
Access to sanitation (% of total population)	..	..
Rural (% of rural population)	..	..
Urban (% of urban population)	..	..
Under-five mortality rate (per 1,000)	..	7
National accounting aggregates, 2003		
Gross national savings (% of GNI)	..	19.1
Consumption of fixed capital (% of GNI)	..	13.2
Education expenditure (% of GNI)	..	4.6
Energy depletion (% of GNI)	..	0.8
Mineral depletion (% of GNI)	..	0.0
Net forest depletion (% of GNI)	..	0.0
CO_2 damage (% of GNI)	..	0.3
Particulate emission damage (% of GNI)	..	0.3
Adjusted net savings (% of GNI)	..	9.2

New Zealand

Environmental strategy/action plan prepared in **1994**

	Country data	Group data — High Income
Population (millions)	4.0	972
Urban population (% of total)	86.1	79.9
GDP ($ billions)	80	29,341
GNI per capita, *Atlas* method ($)	15,530	28,600
Agriculture and fisheries		
Land area (1,000 sq. km)	268	31,030
Agricultural land (% of land area)	64	36
Irrigated land (% of crop land)	8.5	12.3
Fertilizer consumption (100 grams/ha arable land)	5,686	1,198
Population density, rural (people/sq. km arable land)	37	202
Fish catch, total (1,000 metric tons)	637	28,712
Forests		
Forest area (1,000 sq. km)	79	7,929
Forest area share of total land area (%)	29.7	25.9
Annual deforestation (% change, 1990–2000)	–0.5	–0.1
Biodiversity		
Mammal species, total known	..	
Mammal species, threatened	8	
Bird species, total breeding	..	
Bird species, threatened	63	
Nationally protected area (% of land area)	29.6	19.5
Energy		
GDP per unit of energy use (2000 PPP$/kg oil equiv)	4.6	5.2
Energy use per capita (kg oil equiv)	4,573	5,395
Energy from biomass products and waste (% of total)	6.9	3.1
Energy imports, net (% of energy use)	17	26
Electric power consumption per capita (kWh)	8,832	8,693
Electricity generated by coal (% of total)	4.0	38.2
Emissions and pollution		
CO_2 emissions per unit of GDP (kg/2000 PPP$ GDP)	0.4	0.5
CO_2 emissions per capita (metric tons)	8.3	12.4
Particulate matter (pop. weighted average, µg/cu. m)	17	33
Passenger cars (per 1,000 people)	613	436
Water and sanitation		
Internal freshwater resources per capita (cu. m)	81,562	9,479
Freshwater withdrawal		
Total (% of internal resources)	0.6	9.7
Agriculture (% of total freshwater withdrawal)	44	42
Access to improved water source (% of total population)	..	99
Rural (% of rural population)	..	98
Urban (% of urban population)	100	100
Access to sanitation (% of total population)	..	..
Rural (% of rural population)	..	..
Urban (% of urban population)	..	..
Under-five mortality rate (per 1,000)	6	7
National accounting aggregates, 2003		
Gross national savings (% of GNI)	21.9	19.1
Consumption of fixed capital (% of GNI)	10.8	13.2
Education expenditure (% of GNI)	6.9	4.6
Energy depletion (% of GNI)	0.9	0.8
Mineral depletion (% of GNI)	0.1	0.0
Net forest depletion (% of GNI)	0.0	0.0
CO_2 damage (% of GNI)	0.3	0.3
Particulate emission damage (% of GNI)	0.0	0.3
Adjusted net savings (% of GNI)	16.6	9.2

Nicaragua

Environmental strategy/action plan prepared in **1994**

	Country data	Group data Latin America & Caribbean	Low income
Population (millions)	5.5	533	2,312
Urban population (% of total)	57.3	76.6	30.4
GDP ($ billions)	4.1	1,741	1,103
GNI per capita, *Atlas* method ($)	740	3,280	440
Agriculture and fisheries			
Land area (1,000 sq. km)	121	20,057	30,456
Agricultural land (% of land area)	58	39	43
Irrigated land (% of crop land)	4.3	12.5	26.7
Fertilizer consumption (100 grams/ha arable land)	279	892	654
Population density, rural (people/sq. km arable land)	120	210	509
Fish catch, total (1,000 metric tons)	29	17,804	16,410
Forests			
Forest area (1,000 sq. km)	33	9,552	7,939
Forest area share of total land area (%)	27.0	47.6	26.1
Annual deforestation (% change, 1990–2000)	3.0	0.5	0.7
Biodiversity			
Mammal species, total known	200		
Mammal species, threatened	6		
Bird species, total breeding	215		
Bird species, threatened	5		
Nationally protected area (% of land area)	17.8	11.2	7.7
Energy			
GDP per unit of energy use (2000 PPP$/kg oil equiv)	5.7	6.1	4.1
Energy use per capita (kg oil equiv)	544	1,156	493
Energy from biomass products and waste (% of total)	49.9	14.6	49.4
Energy imports, net (% of energy use)	43	−42	−6
Electric power consumption per capita (kWh)	279	1,506	312
Electricity generated by coal (% of total)	..	5.0	47.4
Emissions and pollution			
CO_2 emissions per unit of GDP (kg/2000 PPP$ GDP)	0.2	0.4	0.4
CO_2 emissions per capita (metric tons)	0.7	2.7	0.8
Particulate matter (pop. weighted average, μg/cu. m)	42	40	63
Passenger cars (per 1,000 people)	16	..	..
Water and sanitation			
Internal freshwater resources per capita (cu. m)	34,672	25,245	3,583
Freshwater withdrawal			
Total (% of internal resources)	0.7	2.0	11.5
Agriculture (% of total freshwater withdrawal)	84	74	92
Access to improved water source (% of total population)	81	89	75
Rural (% of rural population)	65	69	70
Urban (% of urban population)	93	96	89
Access to sanitation (% of total population)	66	74	36
Rural (% of rural population)	51	44	24
Urban (% of urban population)	78	84	61
Under-five mortality rate (per 1,000)	38	33	123
National accounting aggregates, 2003			
Gross national savings (% of GNI)	21.6	19.5	23.1
Consumption of fixed capital (% of GNI)	8.8	10.3	8.9
Education expenditure (% of GNI)	3.7	4.2	3.4
Energy depletion (% of GNI)	0.0	6.4	5.8
Mineral depletion (% of GNI)	0.1	0.7	0.3
Net forest depletion (% of GNI)	1.0	0.0	0.8
CO_2 damage (% of GNI)	0.6	0.5	1.2
Particulate emission damage (% of GNI)	0.0	0.5	0.6
Adjusted net savings (% of GNI)	14.7	5.3	8.9

Niger

Environmental strategy/action plan prepared in ..

	Country data	Group data	
		Sub-Saharan Africa	Low income
Population (millions)	11.8	705	2,312
Urban population (% of total)	22.1	36.5	30.4
GDP ($ billions)	2.7	439	1,103
GNI per capita, *Atlas* method ($)	200	500	440
Agriculture and fisheries			
Land area (1,000 sq. km)	1,267	23,596	30,456
Agricultural land (% of land area)	13	43	43
Irrigated land (% of crop land)	1.5	4.2	26.7
Fertilizer consumption (100 grams/ha arable land)	11	145	654
Population density, rural (people/sq. km arable land)	200	352	509
Fish catch, total (1,000 metric tons)	21	5,191	16,410
Forests			
Forest area (1,000 sq. km)	13	6,435	7,939
Forest area share of total land area (%)	1.0	27.3	26.1
Annual deforestation (% change, 1990–2000)	3.7	0.8	0.7
Biodiversity			
Mammal species, total known	131		
Mammal species, threatened	11		
Bird species, total breeding	125		
Bird species, threatened	3		
Nationally protected area (% of land area)	7.7	8.7	7.7
Energy			
GDP per unit of energy use (2000 PPP$/kg oil equiv)	..	2.8	4.1
Energy use per capita (kg oil equiv)	..	667	493
Energy from biomass products and waste (% of total)	..	57.5	49.4
Energy imports, net (% of energy use)	..	–56	–6
Electric power consumption per capita (kWh)	..	457	312
Electricity generated by coal (% of total)	..	68.2	47.4
Emissions and pollution			
CO_2 emissions per unit of GDP (kg/2000 PPP$ GDP)	0.1	0.4	0.4
CO_2 emissions per capita (metric tons)	0.1	0.7	0.8
Particulate matter (pop. weighted average, µg/cu. m)	164	54	63
Passenger cars (per 1,000 people)	..	..	..
Water and sanitation			
Internal freshwater resources per capita (cu. m)	340	5,546	3,583
Freshwater withdrawal			
Total (% of internal resources)	12.5	1.8	11.5
Agriculture (% of total freshwater withdrawal)	82	85	92
Access to improved water source (% of total population)	46	58	75
Rural (% of rural population)	36	46	70
Urban (% of urban population)	80	82	89
Access to sanitation (% of total population)	12	36	36
Rural (% of rural population)	4	26	24
Urban (% of urban population)	43	55	61
Under-five mortality rate (per 1,000)	262	171	123
National accounting aggregates, 2003			
Gross national savings (% of GNI)	4.6	16.9	23.1
Consumption of fixed capital (% of GNI)	7.1	10.6	8.9
Education expenditure (% of GNI)	2.3	4.7	3.4
Energy depletion (% of GNI)	0.0	8.0	5.8
Mineral depletion (% of GNI)	0.0	0.5	0.3
Net forest depletion (% of GNI)	3.1	0.7	0.8
CO_2 damage (% of GNI)	0.3	0.9	1.2
Particulate emission damage (% of GNI)	0.4	0.4	0.6
Adjusted net savings (% of GNI)	–4.1	0.6	8.9

Nigeria

Environmental strategy/action plan prepared in **1990**

	Country data	Sub-Saharan Africa	Low Income
		Group data	
Population (millions)	136.5	705	2,312
Urban population (% of total)	46.6	36.5	30.4
GDP ($ billions)	58.4	439	1,103
GNI per capita, *Atlas* method ($)	350	500	440
Agriculture and fisheries			
Land area (1,000 sq. km)	911	23,596	30,456
Agricultural land (% of land area)	77	43	43
Irrigated land (% of crop land)	0.7	4.2	26.7
Fertilizer consumption (100 grams/ha arable land)	55	145	654
Population density, rural (people/sq. km arable land)	239	352	509
Fish catch, total (1,000 metric tons)	477	5,191	16,410
Forests			
Forest area (1,000 sq. km)	135	6,435	7,939
Forest area share of total land area (%)	14.8	27.3	26.1
Annual deforestation (% change, 1990–2000)	2.6	0.8	0.7
Biodiversity			
Mammal species, total known	274		
Mammal species, threatened	27		
Bird species, total breeding	286		
Bird species, threatened	9		
Nationally protected area (% of land area)	3.3	8.7	7.7
Energy			
GDP per unit of energy use (2000 PPP$/kg oil equiv)	1.3	2.8	4.1
Energy use per capita (kg oil equiv)	718	667	493
Energy from biomass products and waste (% of total)	79.1	57.5	49.4
Energy imports, net (% of energy use)	–101	–56	–6
Electric power consumption per capita (kWh)	68	457	312
Electricity generated by coal (% of total)	..	68.2	47.4
Emissions and pollution			
CO_2 emissions per unit of GDP (kg/2000 PPP$ GDP)	0.3	0.4	0.4
CO_2 emissions per capita (metric tons)	0.3	0.7	0.8
Particulate matter (pop. weighted average, µg/cu. m)	104	54	63
Passenger cars (per 1,000 people)	..	..	..
Water and sanitation			
Internal freshwater resources per capita (cu. m)	1,620	5,546	3,583
Freshwater withdrawal			
Total (% of internal resources)	1.6	1.8	11.5
Agriculture (% of total freshwater withdrawal)	54	85	92
Access to improved water source (% of total population)	60	58	75
Rural (% of rural population)	49	46	70
Urban (% of urban population)	72	82	89
Access to sanitation (% of total population)	38	36	36
Rural (% of rural population)	30	26	24
Urban (% of urban population)	48	55	61
Under-five mortality rate (per 1,000)	198	171	123
National accounting aggregates, 2003			
Gross national savings (% of GNI)	20.3	16.9	23.1
Consumption of fixed capital (% of GNI)	9.2	10.6	8.9
Education expenditure (% of GNI)	0.9	4.7	3.4
Energy depletion (% of GNI)	42.1	8.0	5.8
Mineral depletion (% of GNI)	0.0	0.5	0.3
Net forest depletion (% of GNI)	0.0	0.7	0.8
CO_2 damage (% of GNI)	0.5	0.9	1.2
Particulate emission damage (% of GNI)	0.8	0.4	0.6
Adjusted net savings (% of GNI)	–31.4	0.6	8.9

Northern Mariana Islands

Environmental strategy/action plan prepared in ..

	Country data	East Asia & Pacific	Upper middle income
		Group data	
Population (millions)	0.1	1,855	333
Urban population (% of total)	53.1	39.1	75.4
GDP ($ billions)	..	2,033	1,856
GNI per capita, *Atlas* method ($)	..	1,070	5,440
Agriculture and fisheries			
Land area (1,000 sq. km)	0	15,886	12,741
Agricultural land (% of land area)	..	50	48
Irrigated land (% of crop land)	..	..	13.5
Fertilizer consumption (100 grams/ha arable land)	..	2,297	796
Population density, rural (people/sq. km arable land)	..	565	193
Fish catch, total (1,000 metric tons)	..	60,812	10,082
Forests			
Forest area (1,000 sq. km)	0	4,284	2,427
Forest area share of total land area (%)	..	27.0	19.1
Annual deforestation (% change, 1990–2000)	0.0	0.2	0.6
Biodiversity			
Mammal species, total known	..		
Mammal species, threatened	2		
Bird species, total breeding	..		
Bird species, threatened	8		
Nationally protected area (% of land area)	..	9.2	17.3
Energy			
GDP per unit of energy use (2000 PPP$/kg oil equiv)	..	4.6	4.3
Energy use per capita (kg oil equiv)	..	904	2,232
Energy from biomass products and waste (% of total)	..	19.6	4.1
Energy imports, net (% of energy use)	..	–4	–91
Electric power consumption per capita (kWh)	..	891	2,496
Electricity generated by coal (% of total)	..	66.8	23.9
Emissions and pollution			
CO_2 emissions per unit of GDP (kg/2000 PPP$ GDP)	..	0.5	0.6
CO_2 emissions per capita (metric tons)	..	2.1	6.3
Particulate matter (pop. weighted average, µg/cu. m)	..	69	29
Passenger cars (per 1,000 people)	..	10	153
Water and sanitation			
Internal freshwater resources per capita (cu. m)	..	5,103	10,741
Freshwater withdrawal			
Total (% of internal resources)	..	8.2	5.7
Agriculture (% of total freshwater withdrawal)	..	81	71
Access to improved water source (% of total population)	98	78	..
Rural (% of rural population)	97	69	..
Urban (% of urban population)	98	92	96
Access to sanitation (% of total population)	94	49	..
Rural (% of rural population)	96	35	..
Urban (% of urban population)	94	71	..
Under-five mortality rate (per 1,000)	..	41	22
National accounting aggregates, 2003			
Gross national savings (% of GNI)	..	41.7	22.1
Consumption of fixed capital (% of GNI)	..	9.2	10.7
Education expenditure (% of GNI)	..	2.3	5.0
Energy depletion (% of GNI)	..	3.9	11.4
Mineral depletion (% of GNI)	..	0.3	0.3
Net forest depletion (% of GNI)	..	0.1	0.0
CO_2 damage (% of GNI)	..	1.8	0.8
Particulate emission damage (% of GNI)	..	0.8	0.6
Adjusted net savings (% of GNI)	..	27.9	3.3

Norway

Environmental strategy/action plan prepared in ..

	Country data	Group data — High Income
Population (millions)	4.6	972
Urban population (% of total)	75.5	79.9
GDP ($ billions)	221	29,341
GNI per capita, *Atlas* method ($)	43,400	28,600

Agriculture and fisheries

Land area (1,000 sq. km)	306	31,030
Agricultural land (% of land area)	3	36
Irrigated land (% of crop land)	..	12.3
Fertilizer consumption (100 grams/ha arable land)	2,113	1,198
Population density, rural (people/sq. km arable land)	129	202
Fish catch, total (1,000 metric tons)	3,199	28,712

Forests

Forest area (1,000 sq. km)	89	7,929
Forest area share of total land area (%)	29.0	25.9
Annual deforestation (% change, 1990–2000)	−0.4	−0.1

Biodiversity

Mammal species, total known	54	
Mammal species, threatened	10	
Bird species, total breeding	241	
Bird species, threatened	2	
Nationally protected area (% of land area)	6.8	19.5

Energy

GDP per unit of energy use (2000 PPP$/kg oil equiv)	6.1	5.2
Energy use per capita (kg oil equiv)	5,843	5,395
Energy from biomass products and waste (% of total)	5.5	3.1
Energy imports, net (% of energy use)	−776	26
Electric power consumption per capita (kWh)	23,855	8,693
Electricity generated by coal (% of total)	0.2	38.2

Emissions and pollution

CO_2 emissions per unit of GDP (kg/2000 PPP$ GDP)	0.3	0.5
CO_2 emissions per capita (metric tons)	11.1	12.4
Particulate matter (pop. weighted average, μg/cu. m)	21	33
Passenger cars (per 1,000 people)	417	436

Water and sanitation

Internal freshwater resources per capita (cu. m)	83,735	9,479
Freshwater withdrawal		
Total (% of internal resources)	0.5	9.7
Agriculture (% of total freshwater withdrawal)	8	42
Access to improved water source (% of total population)	100	99
Rural (% of rural population)	100	98
Urban (% of urban population)	100	100
Access to sanitation (% of total population)	..	..
Rural (% of rural population)	..	..
Urban (% of urban population)	..	..
Under-five mortality rate (per 1,000)	5	7

National accounting aggregates, 2003

Gross national savings (% of GNI)	30.3	19.1
Consumption of fixed capital (% of GNI)	15.9	13.2
Education expenditure (% of GNI)	6.1	4.6
Energy depletion (% of GNI)	6.9	0.8
Mineral depletion (% of GNI)	0.0	0.0
Net forest depletion (% of GNI)	0.0	0.0
CO_2 damage (% of GNI)	0.2	0.3
Particulate emission damage (% of GNI)	0.1	0.3
Adjusted net savings (% of GNI)	13.3	9.2

Oman

Environmental strategy/action plan prepared in ..

	Country data	Middle East & North Africa	Upper middle income
		Group data	
Population (millions)	2.6	312	333
Urban population (% of total)	77.6	59.0	75.4
GDP ($ billions)	20.3	745	1,856
GNI per capita, *Atlas* method ($)	7,830	2,390	5,440
Agriculture and fisheries			
Land area (1,000 sq. km)	310	11,111	12,741
Agricultural land (% of land area)	3	34	48
Irrigated land (% of crop land)	76.5	38.3	13.5
Fertilizer consumption (100 grams/ha arable land)	3,219	854	796
Population density, rural (people/sq. km arable land)	1,534	603	193
Fish catch, total (1,000 metric tons)	109	2,840	10,082
Forests			
Forest area (1,000 sq. km)	0	168	2,427
Forest area share of total land area (%)	0.0	1.5	19.1
Annual deforestation (% change, 1990–2000)	0.0	–0.1	0.6
Biodiversity			
Mammal species, total known	56		
Mammal species, threatened	9		
Bird species, total breeding	109		
Bird species, threatened	10		
Nationally protected area (% of land area)	14.0	11.3	17.3
Energy			
GDP per unit of energy use (2000 PPP$/kg oil equiv)	3.0	3.5	4.3
Energy use per capita (kg oil equiv)	4,265	1,504	2,232
Energy from biomass products and waste (% of total)	..	1.0	4.1
Energy imports, net (% of energy use)	–478	–168	–91
Electric power consumption per capita (kWh)	3,177	1,412	2,496
Electricity generated by coal (% of total)	..	2.3	23.9
Emissions and pollution			
CO_2 emissions per unit of GDP (kg/2000 PPP$ GDP)	0.7	0.8	0.6
CO_2 emissions per capita (metric tons)	8.2	4.2	6.3
Particulate matter (pop. weighted average, µg/cu. m)	105	87	29
Passenger cars (per 1,000 people)	..	..	153
Water and sanitation			
Internal freshwater resources per capita (cu. m)	385	761	10,741
Freshwater withdrawal			
Total (% of internal resources)	120.0	101.7	5.7
Agriculture (% of total freshwater withdrawal)	94	88	71
Access to improved water source (% of total population)	79	88	..
Rural (% of rural population)	72	78	..
Urban (% of urban population)	81	96	96
Access to sanitation (% of total population)	89	75	..
Rural (% of rural population)	61	56	..
Urban (% of urban population)	97	90	..
Under-five mortality rate (per 1,000)	12	53	22
National accounting aggregates, 2003			
Gross national savings (% of GNI)	..	31.2	22.1
Consumption of fixed capital (% of GNI)	..	10.0	10.7
Education expenditure (% of GNI)	3.7	5.5	5.0
Energy depletion (% of GNI)	..	30.7	11.4
Mineral depletion (% of GNI)	..	0.1	0.3
Net forest depletion (% of GNI)	..	0.0	0.0
CO_2 damage (% of GNI)	..	1.2	0.8
Particulate emission damage (% of GNI)	..	0.8	0.6
Adjusted net savings (% of GNI)	..	–6.2	3.3

Pakistan

Environmental strategy/action plan prepared in **1994**

	Country data	South Asia	Low Income
		Group data	
Population (millions)	148.4	1,425	2,312
Urban population (% of total)	34.1	28.3	30.4
GDP ($ billions)	82.3	765	1,103
GNI per capita, *Atlas* method ($)	520	510	440
Agriculture and fisheries			
Land area (1,000 sq. km)	771	4,781	30,456
Agricultural land (% of land area)	35	55	43
Irrigated land (% of crop land)	80.5	41.2	26.7
Fertilizer consumption (100 grams/ha arable land)	1,381	1,027	654
Population density, rural (people/sq. km arable land)	447	559	509
Fish catch, total (1,000 metric tons)	623	8,724	16,410
Forests			
Forest area (1,000 sq. km)	24	780	7,939
Forest area share of total land area (%)	3.1	16.3	26.1
Annual deforestation (% change, 1990–2000)	1.5	0.1	0.7
Biodiversity			
Mammal species, total known	188		
Mammal species, threatened	19		
Bird species, total breeding	237		
Bird species, threatened	17		
Nationally protected area (% of land area)	4.9	4.8	7.7
Energy			
GDP per unit of energy use (2000 PPP$/kg oil equiv)	4.3	5.1	4.1
Energy use per capita (kg oil equiv)	454	468	493
Energy from biomass products and waste (% of total)	37.4	39.3	49.4
Energy imports, net (% of energy use)	25	19	-6
Electric power consumption per capita (kWh)	363	344	312
Electricity generated by coal (% of total)	0.3	59.8	47.4
Emissions and pollution			
CO_2 emissions per unit of GDP (kg/2000 PPP$ GDP)	0.4	0.4	0.4
CO_2 emissions per capita (metric tons)	0.8	0.9	0.8
Particulate matter (pop. weighted average, µg/cu. m)	180	69	63
Passenger cars (per 1,000 people)	7	6	..
Water and sanitation			
Internal freshwater resources per capita (cu. m)	350	1,275	3,583
Freshwater withdrawal			
Total (% of internal resources)	299.2	40.5	11.5
Agriculture (% of total freshwater withdrawal)	97	94	92
Access to improved water source (% of total population)	90	84	75
Rural (% of rural population)	87	80	70
Urban (% of urban population)	95	93	89
Access to sanitation (% of total population)	54	35	36
Rural (% of rural population)	35	23	24
Urban (% of urban population)	92	64	61
Under-five mortality rate (per 1,000)	98	92	123
National accounting aggregates, 2003			
Gross national savings (% of GNI)	22.7	24.9	23.1
Consumption of fixed capital (% of GNI)	7.8	9.0	8.9
Education expenditure (% of GNI)	2.3	3.5	3.4
Energy depletion (% of GNI)	3.7	2.4	5.8
Mineral depletion (% of GNI)	0.0	0.3	0.3
Net forest depletion (% of GNI)	0.6	0.7	0.8
CO_2 damage (% of GNI)	0.9	1.3	1.2
Particulate emission damage (% of GNI)	1.0	0.7	0.6
Adjusted net savings (% of GNI)	11.0	14.0	8.9

Palau

Environmental strategy/action plan prepared in ..

	Country data	Group data	
		East Asia & Pacific	Upper middle income
Population (millions)	0.0	1,855	333
Urban population (% of total)	69.5	39.1	75.4
GDP ($ billions)	0.1	2,033	1,856
GNI per capita, *Atlas* method ($)	6,500	1,070	5,440
Agriculture and fisheries			
Land area (1,000 sq. km)	0	15,886	12,741
Agricultural land (% of land area)	20	50	48
Irrigated land (% of crop land)	..	..	13.5
Fertilizer consumption (100 grams/ha arable land)	..	2,297	796
Population density, rural (people/sq. km arable land)	..	565	193
Fish catch, total (1,000 metric tons)	2	60,812	10,082
Forests			
Forest area (1,000 sq. km)	0	4,284	2,427
Forest area share of total land area (%)	76.1	27.0	19.1
Annual deforestation (% change, 1990–2000)	0.0	0.2	0.6
Biodiversity			
Mammal species, total known	..		
Mammal species, threatened	3		
Bird species, total breeding	..		
Bird species, threatened	2		
Nationally protected area (% of land area)	..	9.2	17.3
Energy			
GDP per unit of energy use (2000 PPP$/kg oil equiv)	..	4.6	4.3
Energy use per capita (kg oil equiv)	..	904	2,232
Energy from biomass products and waste (% of total)	..	19.6	4.1
Energy imports, net (% of energy use)	..	–4	–91
Electric power consumption per capita (kWh)	..	891	2,496
Electricity generated by coal (% of total)	..	66.8	23.9
Emissions and pollution			
CO_2 emissions per unit of GDP (kg/2000 PPP$ GDP)	..	0.5	0.6
CO_2 emissions per capita (metric tons)	..	2.1	6.3
Particulate matter (pop. weighted average, µg/cu. m)	..	69	29
Passenger cars (per 1,000 people)	..	10	153
Water and sanitation			
Internal freshwater resources per capita (cu. m)	..	5,103	10,741
Freshwater withdrawal			
Total (% of internal resources)	..	8.2	5.7
Agriculture (% of total freshwater withdrawal)	..	81	71
Access to improved water source (% of total population)	84	78	..
Rural (% of rural population)	94	69	..
Urban (% of urban population)	79	92	96
Access to sanitation (% of total population)	83	49	..
Rural (% of rural population)	52	35	..
Urban (% of urban population)	96	71	..
Under-five mortality rate (per 1,000)	28	41	22
National accounting aggregates, 2003			
Gross national savings (% of GNI)	..	41.7	22.1
Consumption of fixed capital (% of GNI)	11.1	9.2	10.7
Education expenditure (% of GNI)	..	2.3	5.0
Energy depletion (% of GNI)	0.0	3.9	11.4
Mineral depletion (% of GNI)	0.0	0.3	0.3
Net forest depletion (% of GNI)	0.0	0.1	0.0
CO_2 damage (% of GNI)	1.2	1.8	0.8
Particulate emission damage (% of GNI)	..	0.8	0.6
Adjusted net savings (% of GNI)	..	27.9	3.3

Panama

Environmental strategy/action plan prepared in **1990**

	Country data	Group data Latin America & Caribbean	Upper middle income
Population (millions)	3.0	533	333
Urban population (% of total)	57.2	76.6	75.4
GDP ($ billions)	12.9	1,741	1,856
GNI per capita, *Atlas* method ($)	4,060	3,280	5,440
Agriculture and fisheries			
Land area (1,000 sq. km)	74	20,057	12,741
Agricultural land (% of land area)	30	39	48
Irrigated land (% of crop land)	5.0	12.5	13.5
Fertilizer consumption (100 grams/ha arable land)	524	892	796
Population density, rural (people/sq. km arable land)	231	210	193
Fish catch, total (1,000 metric tons)	237	17,804	10,082
Forests			
Forest area (1,000 sq. km)	29	9,552	2,427
Forest area share of total land area (%)	38.6	47.6	19.1
Annual deforestation (% change, 1990–2000)	1.6	0.5	0.6
Biodiversity			
Mammal species, total known	218		
Mammal species, threatened	20		
Bird species, total breeding	302		
Bird species, threatened	16		
Nationally protected area (% of land area)	21.7	11.2	17.3
Energy			
GDP per unit of energy use (2000 PPP$/kg oil equiv)	5.9	6.1	4.3
Energy use per capita (kg oil equiv)	1,028	1,156	2,232
Energy from biomass products and waste (% of total)	14.7	14.6	4.1
Energy imports, net (% of energy use)	76	–42	–91
Electric power consumption per capita (kWh)	1,375	1,506	2,496
Electricity generated by coal (% of total)	..	5.0	23.9
Emissions and pollution			
CO_2 emissions per unit of GDP (kg/2000 PPP$ GDP)	0.4	0.4	0.6
CO_2 emissions per capita (metric tons)	2.2	2.7	6.3
Particulate matter (pop. weighted average, μg/cu. m)	53	40	29
Passenger cars (per 1,000 people)	..	..	153
Water and sanitation			
Internal freshwater resources per capita (cu. m)	49,262	25,245	10,741
Freshwater withdrawal			
Total (% of internal resources)	1.1	2.0	5.7
Agriculture (% of total freshwater withdrawal)	70	74	71
Access to improved water source (% of total population)	91	89	..
Rural (% of rural population)	79	69	..
Urban (% of urban population)	99	96	96
Access to sanitation (% of total population)	72	74	..
Rural (% of rural population)	51	44	..
Urban (% of urban population)	89	84	..
Under-five mortality rate (per 1,000)	24	33	22
National accounting aggregates, 2003			
Gross national savings (% of GNI)	24.0	19.5	22.1
Consumption of fixed capital (% of GNI)	8.0	10.3	10.7
Education expenditure (% of GNI)	4.2	4.2	5.0
Energy depletion (% of GNI)	0.0	6.4	11.4
Mineral depletion (% of GNI)	0.0	0.7	0.3
Net forest depletion (% of GNI)	0.0	0.0	0.0
CO_2 damage (% of GNI)	0.4	0.5	0.8
Particulate emission damage (% of GNI)	0.3	0.5	0.6
Adjusted net savings (% of GNI)	19.5	5.3	3.3

Papua New Guinea

Environmental strategy/action plan prepared in **1992**

	Country data	Group data	
		East Asia & Pacific	Low income
Population (millions)	5.5	1,855	2,312
Urban population (% of total)	18.2	39.1	30.4
GDP ($ billions)	3.2	2,033	1,103
GNI per capita, *Atlas* method ($)	500	1,070	440

Agriculture and fisheries

Land area (1,000 sq. km)	453	15,886	30,456
Agricultural land (% of land area)	2	50	43
Irrigated land (% of crop land)	..	..	26.7
Fertilizer consumption (100 grams/ha arable land)	536	2,297	654
Population density, rural (people/sq. km arable land)	2,007	565	509
Fish catch, total (1,000 metric tons)	54	60,812	16,410

Forests

Forest area (1,000 sq. km)	306	4,284	7,939
Forest area share of total land area (%)	67.6	27.0	26.1
Annual deforestation (% change, 1990–2000)	0.4	0.2	0.7

Biodiversity

Mammal species, total known	214		
Mammal species, threatened	58		
Bird species, total breeding	414		
Bird species, threatened	32		
Nationally protected area (% of land area)	2.3	9.2	7.7

Energy

GDP per unit of energy use (2000 PPP$/kg oil equiv)	..	4.6	4.1
Energy use per capita (kg oil equiv)	..	904	493
Energy from biomass products and waste (% of total)	..	19.6	49.4
Energy imports, net (% of energy use)	..	–4	–6
Electric power consumption per capita (kWh)	..	891	312
Electricity generated by coal (% of total)	..	66.8	47.4

Emissions and pollution

CO_2 emissions per unit of GDP (kg/2000 PPP$ GDP)	0.2	0.5	0.4
CO_2 emissions per capita (metric tons)	0.5	2.1	0.8
Particulate matter (pop. weighted average, µg/cu. m)	31	69	63
Passenger cars (per 1,000 people)	..	10	..

Water and sanitation

Internal freshwater resources per capita (cu. m)	145,587	5,103	3,583
Freshwater withdrawal			
Total (% of internal resources)	0.0	8.2	11.5
Agriculture (% of total freshwater withdrawal)	49	81	92
Access to improved water source (% of total population)	39	78	75
Rural (% of rural population)	32	69	70
Urban (% of urban population)	88	92	89
Access to sanitation (% of total population)	45	49	36
Rural (% of rural population)	41	35	24
Urban (% of urban population)	67	71	61
Under-five mortality rate (per 1,000)	93	41	123

National accounting aggregates, 2003

Gross national savings (% of GNI)	..	41.7	23.1
Consumption of fixed capital (% of GNI)	9.6	9.2	8.9
Education expenditure (% of GNI)	..	2.3	3.4
Energy depletion (% of GNI)	13.5	3.9	5.8
Mineral depletion (% of GNI)	8.2	0.3	0.3
Net forest depletion (% of GNI)	0.0	0.1	0.8
CO_2 damage (% of GNI)	0.6	1.8	1.2
Particulate emission damage (% of GNI)	0.0	0.8	0.6
Adjusted net savings (% of GNI)	..	27.9	8.9

Paraguay

Environmental strategy/action plan prepared in ..

	Country data	Group data Latin America & Caribbean	Lower middle income
Population (millions)	5.6	533	2,655
Urban population (% of total)	58.0	76.6	49.8
GDP ($ billions)	6.0	1,741	4,168
GNI per capita, *Atlas* method ($)	1,110	3,280	1,490
Agriculture and fisheries			
Land area (1,000 sq. km)	397	20,057	56,103
Agricultural land (% of land area)	62	39	35
Irrigated land (% of crop land)	2.2	12.5	20.8
Fertilizer consumption (100 grams/ha arable land)	507	892	1,170
Population density, rural (people/sq. km arable land)	78	210	497
Fish catch, total (1,000 metric tons)	25	17,804	74,407
Forests			
Forest area (1,000 sq. km)	234	9,552	20,316
Forest area share of total land area (%)	58.8	47.6	36.2
Annual deforestation (% change, 1990–2000)	0.5	0.5	0.1
Biodiversity			
Mammal species, total known	305		
Mammal species, threatened	10		
Bird species, total breeding	233		
Bird species, threatened	26		
Nationally protected area (% of land area)	3.5	11.2	7.7
Energy			
GDP per unit of energy use (2000 PPP$/kg oil equiv)	6.3	6.1	4.1
Energy use per capita (kg oil equiv)	709	1,156	1,227
Energy from biomass products and waste (% of total)	55.0	14.6	12.3
Energy imports, net (% of energy use)	–61	–42	–22
Electric power consumption per capita (kWh)	842	1,506	1,289
Electricity generated by coal (% of total)	..	5.0	42.8
Emissions and pollution			
CO_2 emissions per unit of GDP (kg/2000 PPP$ GDP)	0.2	0.4	0.6
CO_2 emissions per capita (metric tons)	0.7	2.7	2.9
Particulate matter (pop. weighted average, µg/cu. m)	97	40	49
Passenger cars (per 1,000 people)	..	..	28
Water and sanitation			
Internal freshwater resources per capita (cu. m)	16,658	25,245	8,397
Freshwater withdrawal			
Total (% of internal resources)	0.4	2.0	5.9
Agriculture (% of total freshwater withdrawal)	78	74	74
Access to improved water source (% of total population)	83	89	82
Rural (% of rural population)	62	69	71
Urban (% of urban population)	100	96	94
Access to sanitation (% of total population)	78	74	60
Rural (% of rural population)	58	44	41
Urban (% of urban population)	94	84	80
Under-five mortality rate (per 1,000)	29	33	39
National accounting aggregates, 2003			
Gross national savings (% of GNI)	8.2	19.5	30.6
Consumption of fixed capital (% of GNI)	9.1	10.3	9.8
Education expenditure (% of GNI)	3.9	4.2	3.2
Energy depletion (% of GNI)	0.0	6.4	8.1
Mineral depletion (% of GNI)	0.0	0.7	0.4
Net forest depletion (% of GNI)	0.0	0.0	0.1
CO_2 damage (% of GNI)	0.5	0.5	1.6
Particulate emission damage (% of GNI)	0.4	0.5	0.7
Adjusted net savings (% of GNI)	2.2	5.3	13.2

Peru

Environmental strategy/action plan prepared in ..

	Country data	Group data Latin America & Caribbean	Group data Lower middle income
Population (millions)	27.1	533	2,655
Urban population (% of total)	73.9	76.6	49.8
GDP ($ billions)	60.6	1,741	4,168
GNI per capita, *Atlas* method ($)	2,140	3,280	1,490
Agriculture and fisheries			
Land area (1,000 sq. km)	1,280	20,057	56,103
Agricultural land (% of land area)	24	39	35
Irrigated land (% of crop land)	27.7	12.5	20.8
Fertilizer consumption (100 grams/ha arable land)	741	892	1,170
Population density, rural (people/sq. km arable land)	192	210	497
Fish catch, total (1,000 metric tons)	7,996	17,804	74,407
Forests			
Forest area (1,000 sq. km)	652	9,552	20,316
Forest area share of total land area (%)	50.9	47.6	36.2
Annual deforestation (% change, 1990–2000)	0.4	0.5	0.1
Biodiversity			
Mammal species, total known	460		
Mammal species, threatened	49		
Bird species, total breeding	695		
Bird species, threatened	76		
Nationally protected area (% of land area)	6.1	11.2	7.7
Energy			
GDP per unit of energy use (2000 PPP$/kg oil equiv)	10.7	6.1	4.1
Energy use per capita (kg oil equiv)	450	1,156	1,227
Energy from biomass products and waste (% of total)	18.8	14.6	12.3
Energy imports, net (% of energy use)	23	–42	–22
Electric power consumption per capita (kWh)	723	1,506	1,289
Electricity generated by coal (% of total)	2.3	5.0	42.8
Emissions and pollution			
CO_2 emissions per unit of GDP (kg/2000 PPP$ GDP)	0.2	0.4	0.6
CO_2 emissions per capita (metric tons)	1.1	2.7	2.9
Particulate matter (pop. weighted average, μg/cu. m)	62	40	49
Passenger cars (per 1,000 people)	30	..	28
Water and sanitation			
Internal freshwater resources per capita (cu. m)	59,526	25,245	8,397
Freshwater withdrawal			
Total (% of internal resources)	1.2	2.0	5.9
Agriculture (% of total freshwater withdrawal)	86	74	74
Access to improved water source (% of total population)	81	89	82
Rural (% of rural population)	66	69	71
Urban (% of urban population)	87	96	94
Access to sanitation (% of total population)	62	74	60
Rural (% of rural population)	33	44	41
Urban (% of urban population)	72	84	80
Under-five mortality rate (per 1,000)	34	33	39
National accounting aggregates, 2003			
Gross national savings (% of GNI)	18.1	19.5	30.6
Consumption of fixed capital (% of GNI)	10.4	10.3	9.8
Education expenditure (% of GNI)	2.6	4.2	3.2
Energy depletion (% of GNI)	1.1	6.4	8.1
Mineral depletion (% of GNI)	1.5	0.7	0.4
Net forest depletion (% of GNI)	0.0	0.0	0.1
CO_2 damage (% of GNI)	0.3	0.5	1.6
Particulate emission damage (% of GNI)	0.6	0.5	0.7
Adjusted net savings (% of GNI)	6.6	5.3	13.2

Philippines

Environmental strategy/action plan prepared in **1989**

	Country data	Group data — East Asia & Pacific	Group data — Lower middle income
Population (millions)	81.5	1,855	2,655
Urban population (% of total)	61.0	39.1	49.8
GDP ($ billions)	80.6	2,033	4,168
GNI per capita, *Atlas* method ($)	1,080	1,070	1,490
Agriculture and fisheries			
Land area (1,000 sq. km)	298	15,886	56,103
Agricultural land (% of land area)	40	50	35
Irrigated land (% of crop land)	14.5	..	20.8
Fertilizer consumption (100 grams/ha arable land)	1,268	2,297	1,170
Population density, rural (people/sq. km arable land)	559	565	497
Fish catch, total (1,000 metric tons)	2,380	60,812	74,407
Forests			
Forest area (1,000 sq. km)	58	4,284	20,316
Forest area share of total land area (%)	19.4	27.0	36.2
Annual deforestation (% change, 1990–2000)	1.4	0.2	0.1
Biodiversity			
Mammal species, total known	153		
Mammal species, threatened	50		
Bird species, total breeding	404		
Bird species, threatened	67		
Nationally protected area (% of land area)	5.7	9.2	7.7
Energy			
GDP per unit of energy use (2000 PPP$/kg oil equiv)	7.6	4.6	4.1
Energy use per capita (kg oil equiv)	525	904	1,227
Energy from biomass products and waste (% of total)	23.9	19.6	12.3
Energy imports, net (% of energy use)	48	–4	–22
Electric power consumption per capita (kWh)	459	891	1,289
Electricity generated by coal (% of total)	33.3	66.8	42.8
Emissions and pollution			
CO_2 emissions per unit of GDP (kg/2000 PPP$ GDP)	0.3	0.5	0.6
CO_2 emissions per capita (metric tons)	1.0	2.1	2.9
Particulate matter (pop. weighted average, µg/cu. m)	49	69	49
Passenger cars (per 1,000 people)	9	10	28
Water and sanitation			
Internal freshwater resources per capita (cu. m)	5,877	5,103	8,397
Freshwater withdrawal			
Total (% of internal resources)	11.6	8.2	5.9
Agriculture (% of total freshwater withdrawal)	88	81	74
Access to improved water source (% of total population)	85	78	82
Rural (% of rural population)	77	69	71
Urban (% of urban population)	90	92	94
Access to sanitation (% of total population)	73	49	60
Rural (% of rural population)	61	35	41
Urban (% of urban population)	81	71	80
Under-five mortality rate (per 1,000)	36	41	39
National accounting aggregates, 2003			
Gross national savings (% of GNI)	22.8	41.7	30.6
Consumption of fixed capital (% of GNI)	8.0	9.2	9.8
Education expenditure (% of GNI)	2.8	2.3	3.2
Energy depletion (% of GNI)	0.2	3.9	8.1
Mineral depletion (% of GNI)	0.2	0.3	0.4
Net forest depletion (% of GNI)	0.2	0.1	0.1
CO_2 damage (% of GNI)	0.7	1.8	1.6
Particulate emission damage (% of GNI)	0.4	0.8	0.7
Adjusted net savings (% of GNI)	16.0	27.9	13.2

Poland

Environmental strategy/action plan prepared in **1993**

	Country data	Group data	
		Europe & Central Asia	Upper middle income
Population (millions)	38.2	472	333
Urban population (% of total)	63.0	63.8	75.4
GDP ($ billions)	209.6	1,403	1,856
GNI per capita, *Atlas* method ($)	5,280	2,580	5,440
Agriculture and fisheries			
Land area (1,000 sq. km)	306	23,868	12,741
Agricultural land (% of land area)	60	28	48
Irrigated land (% of crop land)	0.7	10.9	13.5
Fertilizer consumption (100 grams/ha arable land)	1,086	344	796
Population density, rural (people/sq. km arable land)	102	122	193
Fish catch, total (1,000 metric tons)	261	5,527	10,082
Forests			
Forest area (1,000 sq. km)	90	9,463	2,427
Forest area share of total land area (%)	29.7	39.6	19.1
Annual deforestation (% change, 1990–2000)	–0.2	–0.1	0.6
Biodiversity			
Mammal species, total known	84		
Mammal species, threatened	15		
Bird species, total breeding	233		
Bird species, threatened	4		
Nationally protected area (% of land area)	12.4	6.8	17.3
Energy			
GDP per unit of energy use (2000 PPP$/kg oil equiv)	4.4	2.5	4.3
Energy use per capita (kg oil equiv)	2,333	2,697	2,232
Energy from biomass products and waste (% of total)	5.0	2.3	4.1
Energy imports, net (% of energy use)	11	–23	–91
Electric power consumption per capita (kWh)	2,514	2,808	2,496
Electricity generated by coal (% of total)	94.5	29.4	23.9
Emissions and pollution			
CO_2 emissions per unit of GDP (kg/2000 PPP$ GDP)	0.8	1.1	0.6
CO_2 emissions per capita (metric tons)	7.8	6.7	6.3
Particulate matter (pop. weighted average, μg/cu. m)	44	33	29
Passenger cars (per 1,000 people)	259	138	153
Water and sanitation			
Internal freshwater resources per capita (cu. m)	1,414	11,128	10,741
Freshwater withdrawal			
Total (% of internal resources)	22.8	7.4	5.7
Agriculture (% of total freshwater withdrawal)	11	57	71
Access to improved water source (% of total population)	..	91	..
Rural (% of rural population)	..	80	..
Urban (% of urban population)	100	98	96
Access to sanitation (% of total population)	..	82	..
Rural (% of rural population)	..	64	..
Urban (% of urban population)	..	93	..
Under-five mortality rate (per 1,000)	7	36	22
National accounting aggregates, 2003			
Gross national savings (% of GNI)	17.1	21.9	22.1
Consumption of fixed capital (% of GNI)	11.4	10.7	10.7
Education expenditure (% of GNI)	5.0	4.1	5.0
Energy depletion (% of GNI)	0.5	11.6	11.4
Mineral depletion (% of GNI)	0.1	0.1	0.3
Net forest depletion (% of GNI)	0.0	0.0	0.0
CO_2 damage (% of GNI)	1.2	1.9	0.8
Particulate emission damage (% of GNI)	0.7	0.6	0.6
Adjusted net savings (% of GNI)	8.3	1.1	3.3

Portugal

Environmental strategy/action plan prepared in **1995**

	Country data	Group data High income
Population (millions)	10.4	972
Urban population (% of total)	68.1	79.9
GDP ($ billions)	148	29,341
GNI per capita, *Atlas* method ($)	11,800	28,600
Agriculture and fisheries		
Land area (1,000 sq. km)	92	31,030
Agricultural land (% of land area)	45	36
Irrigated land (% of crop land)	24.0	12.3
Fertilizer consumption (100 grams/ha arable land)	1,040	1,198
Population density, rural (people/sq. km arable land)	173	202
Fish catch, total (1,000 metric tons)	199	28,712
Forests		
Forest area (1,000 sq. km)	37	7,929
Forest area share of total land area (%)	40.1	25.9
Annual deforestation (% change, 1990–2000)	−1.7	−0.1
Biodiversity		
Mammal species, total known	63	
Mammal species, threatened	17	
Bird species, total breeding	235	
Bird species, threatened	7	
Nationally protected area (% of land area)	6.6	19.5
Energy		
GDP per unit of energy use (2000 PPP$/kg oil equiv)	6.9	5.2
Energy use per capita (kg oil equiv)	2,546	5,395
Energy from biomass products and waste (% of total)	10.7	3.1
Energy imports, net (% of energy use)	86	26
Electric power consumption per capita (kWh)	4,000	8,693
Electricity generated by coal (% of total)	33.3	38.2
Emissions and pollution		
CO_2 emissions per unit of GDP (kg/2000 PPP$ GDP)	0.3	0.5
CO_2 emissions per capita (metric tons)	5.8	12.4
Particulate matter (pop. weighted average, µg/cu. m)	34	33
Passenger cars (per 1,000 people)	426	436
Water and sanitation		
Internal freshwater resources per capita (cu. m)	3,638	9,479
Freshwater withdrawal		
Total (% of internal resources)	19.2	9.7
Agriculture (% of total freshwater withdrawal)	48	42
Access to improved water source (% of total population)	..	99
Rural (% of rural population)	..	98
Urban (% of urban population)	..	100
Access to sanitation (% of total population)	..	..
Rural (% of rural population)	..	..
Urban (% of urban population)	..	..
Under-five mortality rate (per 1,000)	5	7
National accounting aggregates, 2003		
Gross national savings (% of GNI)	..	19.1
Consumption of fixed capital (% of GNI)	15.3	13.2
Education expenditure (% of GNI)	5.7	4.6
Energy depletion (% of GNI)	0.0	0.8
Mineral depletion (% of GNI)	0.0	0.0
Net forest depletion (% of GNI)	0.0	0.0
CO_2 damage (% of GNI)	0.3	0.3
Particulate emission damage (% of GNI)	0.4	0.3
Adjusted net savings (% of GNI)	..	9.2

Puerto Rico

Environmental strategy/action plan prepared in ..

	Country data	Group data — High income
Population (millions)	3.9	972
Urban population (% of total)	76.3	79.9
GDP ($ billions)	..	29,341
GNI per capita, *Atlas* method ($)	..	28,600
Agriculture and fisheries		
Land area (1,000 sq. km)	9	31,030
Agricultural land (% of land area)	33	36
Irrigated land (% of crop land)	47.6	12.3
Fertilizer consumption (100 grams/ha arable land)	..	1,198
Population density, rural (people/sq. km arable land)	2,662	202
Fish catch, total (1,000 metric tons)	4	28,712
Forests		
Forest area (1,000 sq. km)	2	7,929
Forest area share of total land area (%)	25.8	25.9
Annual deforestation (% change, 1990–2000)	0.2	–0.1
Biodiversity		
Mammal species, total known	..	
Mammal species, threatened	2	
Bird species, total breeding	..	
Bird species, threatened	8	
Nationally protected area (% of land area)	..	19.5
Energy		
GDP per unit of energy use (2000 PPP$/kg oil equiv)	..	5.2
Energy use per capita (kg oil equiv)	..	5,395
Energy from biomass products and waste (% of total)	..	3.1
Energy imports, net (% of energy use)	..	26
Electric power consumption per capita (kWh)	..	8,693
Electricity generated by coal (% of total)	..	38.2
Emissions and pollution		
CO_2 emissions per unit of GDP (kg/2000 PPP$ GDP)	0.1	0.5
CO_2 emissions per capita (metric tons)	2.3	12.4
Particulate matter (pop. weighted average, µg/cu. m)	25	33
Passenger cars (per 1,000 people)	..	436
Water and sanitation		
Internal freshwater resources per capita (cu. m)	..	9,479
Freshwater withdrawal		
Total (% of internal resources)	..	9.7
Agriculture (% of total freshwater withdrawal)	..	42
Access to improved water source (% of total population)	..	99
Rural (% of rural population)	..	98
Urban (% of urban population)	..	100
Access to sanitation (% of total population)	..	..
Rural (% of rural population)	..	..
Urban (% of urban population)	..	..
Under-five mortality rate (per 1,000)	..	7
National accounting aggregates, 2003		
Gross national savings (% of GNI)	..	19.1
Consumption of fixed capital (% of GNI)	..	13.2
Education expenditure (% of GNI)	..	4.6
Energy depletion (% of GNI)	..	0.8
Mineral depletion (% of GNI)	..	0.0
Net forest depletion (% of GNI)	..	0.0
CO_2 damage (% of GNI)	..	0.3
Particulate emission damage (% of GNI)	..	0.3
Adjusted net savings (% of GNI)	..	9.2

Qatar

Environmental strategy/action plan prepared in ..

	Country data	Group data High income
Population (millions)	0.6	972
Urban population (% of total)	93.3	79.9
GDP ($ billions)	17	29,341
GNI per capita, *Atlas* method ($)	..	28,600
Agriculture and fisheries		
Land area (1,000 sq. km)	11	31,030
Agricultural land (% of land area)	6	36
Irrigated land (% of crop land)	61.9	12.3
Fertilizer consumption (100 grams/ha arable land)	..	1,198
Population density, rural (people/sq. km arable land)	234	202
Fish catch, total (1,000 metric tons)	9	28,712
Forests		
Forest area (1,000 sq. km)	0	7,929
Forest area share of total land area (%)	0.1	25.9
Annual deforestation (% change, 1990–2000)	..	–0.1
Biodiversity		
Mammal species, total known	..	
Mammal species, threatened	0	
Bird species, total breeding	..	
Bird species, threatened	6	
Nationally protected area (% of land area)	..	19.5
Energy		
GDP per unit of energy use (2000 PPP$/kg oil equiv)	..	5.2
Energy use per capita (kg oil equiv)	19,915	5,395
Energy from biomass products and waste (% of total)	0.0	3.1
Energy imports, net (% of energy use)	–361	26
Electric power consumption per capita (kWh)	15,515	8,693
Electricity generated by coal (% of total)	..	38.2
Emissions and pollution		
CO_2 emissions per unit of GDP (kg/2000 PPP$ GDP)	..	0.5
CO_2 emissions per capita (metric tons)	69.6	12.4
Particulate matter (pop. weighted average, µg/cu. m)	67	33
Passenger cars (per 1,000 people)	..	436
Water and sanitation		
Internal freshwater resources per capita (cu. m)	164	9,479
Freshwater withdrawal		
Total (% of internal resources)	..	9.7
Agriculture (% of total freshwater withdrawal)	74	42
Access to improved water source (% of total population)	100	99
Rural (% of rural population)	100	98
Urban (% of urban population)	100	100
Access to sanitation (% of total population)	100	..
Rural (% of rural population)	100	..
Urban (% of urban population)	100	..
Under-five mortality rate (per 1,000)	15	7
National accounting aggregates, 2003		
Gross national savings (% of GNI)	..	19.1
Consumption of fixed capital (% of GNI)	..	13.2
Education expenditure (% of GNI)	..	4.6
Energy depletion (% of GNI)	..	0.8
Mineral depletion (% of GNI)	..	0.0
Net forest depletion (% of GNI)	..	0.0
CO_2 damage (% of GNI)	..	0.3
Particulate emission damage (% of GNI)	..	0.3
Adjusted net savings (% of GNI)	..	9.2

Romania

Environmental strategy/action plan prepared in **1995**

	Country data	Europe & Central Asia	Lower middle income
		Group data	
Population (millions)	21.7	472	2,655
Urban population (% of total)	55.7	63.8	49.8
GDP ($ billions)	57.0	1,403	4,168
GNI per capita, *Atlas* method ($)	2,260	2,580	1,490
Agriculture and fisheries			
Land area (1,000 sq. km)	230	23,868	56,103
Agricultural land (% of land area)	64	28	35
Irrigated land (% of crop land)	31.1	10.9	20.8
Fertilizer consumption (100 grams/ha arable land)	347	344	1,170
Population density, rural (people/sq. km arable land)	103	122	497
Fish catch, total (1,000 metric tons)	18	5,527	74,407
Forests			
Forest area (1,000 sq. km)	64	9,463	20,316
Forest area share of total land area (%)	28.0	39.6	36.2
Annual deforestation (% change, 1990–2000)	–0.2	–0.1	0.1
Biodiversity			
Mammal species, total known	84		
Mammal species, threatened	17		
Bird species, total breeding	257		
Bird species, threatened	8		
Nationally protected area (% of land area)	4.7	6.8	7.7
Energy			
GDP per unit of energy use (2000 PPP$/kg oil equiv)	3.8	2.5	4.1
Energy use per capita (kg oil equiv)	1,696	2,697	1,227
Energy from biomass products and waste (% of total)	6.7	2.3	12.3
Energy imports, net (% of energy use)	23	–23	–22
Electric power consumption per capita (kWh)	1,632	2,808	1,289
Electricity generated by coal (% of total)	37.6	29.4	42.8
Emissions and pollution			
CO_2 emissions per unit of GDP (kg/2000 PPP$ GDP)	0.7	1.1	0.6
CO_2 emissions per capita (metric tons)	3.8	6.7	2.9
Particulate matter (pop. weighted average, µg/cu. m)	23	33	49
Passenger cars (per 1,000 people)	144	138	28
Water and sanitation			
Internal freshwater resources per capita (cu. m)	1,932	11,128	8,397
Freshwater withdrawal			
Total (% of internal resources)	61.9	7.4	5.9
Agriculture (% of total freshwater withdrawal)	59	57	74
Access to improved water source (% of total population)	57	91	82
Rural (% of rural population)	16	80	71
Urban (% of urban population)	91	98	94
Access to sanitation (% of total population)	51	82	60
Rural (% of rural population)	10	64	41
Urban (% of urban population)	86	93	80
Under-five mortality rate (per 1,000)	20	36	39
National accounting aggregates, 2003			
Gross national savings (% of GNI)	18.5	21.9	30.6
Consumption of fixed capital (% of GNI)	10.5	10.7	9.8
Education expenditure (% of GNI)	3.6	4.1	3.2
Energy depletion (% of GNI)	3.2	11.6	8.1
Mineral depletion (% of GNI)	0.0	0.1	0.4
Net forest depletion (% of GNI)	0.0	0.0	0.1
CO_2 damage (% of GNI)	1.2	1.9	1.6
Particulate emission damage (% of GNI)	0.2	0.6	0.7
Adjusted net savings (% of GNI)	7.1	1.1	13.2

Russian Federation

Environmental strategy/action plan prepared in **1999**

	Country data	Group data	
		Europe & Central Asia	Lower middle income
Population (millions)	143.4	472	2,655
Urban population (% of total)	72.9	63.8	49.8
GDP ($ billions)	432.9	1,403	4,168
GNI per capita, *Atlas* method ($)	2,610	2,580	1,490
Agriculture and fisheries			
Land area (1,000 sq. km)	16,889	23,868	56,103
Agricultural land (% of land area)	13	28	35
Irrigated land (% of crop land)	3.7	10.9	20.8
Fertilizer consumption (100 grams/ha arable land)	119	344	1,170
Population density, rural (people/sq. km arable land)	32	122	497
Fish catch, total (1,000 metric tons)	3,718	5,527	74,407
Forests			
Forest area (1,000 sq. km)	8,514	9,463	20,316
Forest area share of total land area (%)	50.4	39.6	36.2
Annual deforestation (% change, 1990–2000)	0.0	–0.1	0.1
Biodiversity			
Mammal species, total known	269		
Mammal species, threatened	45		
Bird species, total breeding	528		
Bird species, threatened	38		
Nationally protected area (% of land area)	7.8	6.8	7.7
Energy			
GDP per unit of energy use (2000 PPP$/kg oil equiv)	1.9	2.5	4.1
Energy use per capita (kg oil equiv)	4,288	2,697	1,227
Energy from biomass products and waste (% of total)	1.1	2.3	12.3
Energy imports, net (% of energy use)	–67	–23	–22
Electric power consumption per capita (kWh)	4,291	2,808	1,289
Electricity generated by coal (% of total)	19.2	29.4	42.8
Emissions and pollution			
CO_2 emissions per unit of GDP (kg/2000 PPP$ GDP)	1.4	1.1	0.6
CO_2 emissions per capita (metric tons)	9.9	6.7	2.9
Particulate matter (pop. weighted average, μg/cu. m)	26	33	49
Passenger cars (per 1,000 people)	132	138	28
Water and sanitation			
Internal freshwater resources per capita (cu. m)	30,071	11,128	8,397
Freshwater withdrawal			
Total (% of internal resources)	1.8	7.4	5.9
Agriculture (% of total freshwater withdrawal)	20	57	74
Access to improved water source (% of total population)	96	91	82
Rural (% of rural population)	88	80	71
Urban (% of urban population)	99	98	94
Access to sanitation (% of total population)	87	82	60
Rural (% of rural population)	70	64	41
Urban (% of urban population)	93	93	80
Under-five mortality rate (per 1,000)	21	36	39
National accounting aggregates, 2003			
Gross national savings (% of GNI)	29.8	21.9	30.6
Consumption of fixed capital (% of GNI)	10.8	10.7	9.8
Education expenditure (% of GNI)	3.5	4.1	3.2
Energy depletion (% of GNI)	29.6	11.6	8.1
Mineral depletion (% of GNI)	0.3	0.1	0.4
Net forest depletion (% of GNI)	0.0	0.0	0.1
CO_2 damage (% of GNI)	2.8	1.9	1.6
Particulate emission damage (% of GNI)	0.6	0.6	0.7
Adjusted net savings (% of GNI)	–10.7	1.1	13.2

Rwanda

Environmental strategy/action plan prepared in **1991**

	Country data	Sub-Saharan Africa	Low income
		Group data	
Population (millions)	8.4	705	2,312
Urban population (% of total)	6.6	36.5	30.4
GDP ($ billions)	1.6	439	1,103
GNI per capita, *Atlas* method ($)	220	500	440
Agriculture and fisheries			
Land area (1,000 sq. km)	25	23,596	30,456
Agricultural land (% of land area)	75	43	43
Irrigated land (% of crop land)	0.4	4.2	26.7
Fertilizer consumption (100 grams/ha arable land)	137	145	654
Population density, rural (people/sq. km arable land)	684	352	509
Fish catch, total (1,000 metric tons)	7	5,191	16,410
Forests			
Forest area (1,000 sq. km)	3	6,435	7,939
Forest area share of total land area (%)	12.4	27.3	26.1
Annual deforestation (% change, 1990–2000)	3.9	0.8	0.7
Biodiversity			
Mammal species, total known	151		
Mammal species, threatened	9		
Bird species, total breeding	200		
Bird species, threatened	9		
Nationally protected area (% of land area)	6.2	8.7	7.7
Energy			
GDP per unit of energy use (2000 PPP$/kg oil equiv)	..	2.8	4.1
Energy use per capita (kg oil equiv)	..	667	493
Energy from biomass products and waste (% of total)	..	57.5	49.4
Energy imports, net (% of energy use)	..	−56	−6
Electric power consumption per capita (kWh)	..	457	312
Electricity generated by coal (% of total)	..	68.2	47.4
Emissions and pollution			
CO_2 emissions per unit of GDP (kg/2000 PPP$ GDP)	0.1	0.4	0.4
CO_2 emissions per capita (metric tons)	0.1	0.7	0.8
Particulate matter (pop. weighted average, µg/cu. m)	35	54	63
Passenger cars (per 1,000 people)	..	..	..
Water and sanitation			
Internal freshwater resources per capita (cu. m)	596	5,546	3,583
Freshwater withdrawal			
Total (% of internal resources)	16.0	1.8	11.5
Agriculture (% of total freshwater withdrawal)	94	85	92
Access to improved water source (% of total population)	73	58	75
Rural (% of rural population)	69	46	70
Urban (% of urban population)	92	82	89
Access to sanitation (% of total population)	41	36	36
Rural (% of rural population)	38	26	24
Urban (% of urban population)	56	55	61
Under-five mortality rate (per 1,000)	203	171	123
National accounting aggregates, 2003			
Gross national savings (% of GNI)	11.7	16.9	23.1
Consumption of fixed capital (% of GNI)	6.7	10.6	8.9
Education expenditure (% of GNI)	3.5	4.7	3.4
Energy depletion (% of GNI)	0.0	8.0	5.8
Mineral depletion (% of GNI)	0.0	0.5	0.3
Net forest depletion (% of GNI)	3.9	0.7	0.8
CO_2 damage (% of GNI)	0.3	0.9	1.2
Particulate emission damage (% of GNI)	0.0	0.4	0.6
Adjusted net savings (% of GNI)	4.2	0.6	8.9

Samoa

Environmental strategy/action plan prepared in ..

	Country data	Group data East Asia & Pacific	Group data Lower middle income
Population (millions)	0.2	1,855	2,655
Urban population (% of total)	22.8	39.1	49.8
GDP ($ billions)	0.3	2,033	4,168
GNI per capita, *Atlas* method ($)	1,440	1,070	1,490
Agriculture and fisheries			
Land area (1,000 sq. km)	3	15,886	56,103
Agricultural land (% of land area)	46	50	35
Irrigated land (% of crop land)	..	..	20.8
Fertilizer consumption (100 grams/ha arable land)	583	2,297	1,170
Population density, rural (people/sq. km arable land)	227	565	497
Fish catch, total (1,000 metric tons)	13	60,812	74,407
Forests			
Forest area (1,000 sq. km)	1	4,284	20,316
Forest area share of total land area (%)	37.1	27.0	36.2
Annual deforestation (% change, 1990–2000)	2.1	0.2	0.1
Biodiversity			
Mammal species, total known	..		
Mammal species, threatened	3		
Bird species, total breeding	..		
Bird species, threatened	7		
Nationally protected area (% of land area)	..	9.2	7.7
Energy			
GDP per unit of energy use (2000 PPP$/kg oil equiv)	..	4.6	4.1
Energy use per capita (kg oil equiv)	..	904	1,227
Energy from biomass products and waste (% of total)	..	19.6	12.3
Energy imports, net (% of energy use)	..	–4	–22
Electric power consumption per capita (kWh)	..	891	1,289
Electricity generated by coal (% of total)	..	66.8	42.8
Emissions and pollution			
CO_2 emissions per unit of GDP (kg/2000 PPP$ GDP)	0.2	0.5	0.6
CO_2 emissions per capita (metric tons)	0.8	2.1	2.9
Particulate matter (pop. weighted average, µg/cu. m)	..	69	49
Passenger cars (per 1,000 people)	..	10	28
Water and sanitation			
Internal freshwater resources per capita (cu. m)	..	5,103	8,397
Freshwater withdrawal			
Total (% of internal resources)	..	8.2	5.9
Agriculture (% of total freshwater withdrawal)	..	81	74
Access to improved water source (% of total population)	88	78	82
Rural (% of rural population)	88	69	71
Urban (% of urban population)	91	92	94
Access to sanitation (% of total population)	100	49	60
Rural (% of rural population)	100	35	41
Urban (% of urban population)	100	71	80
Under-five mortality rate (per 1,000)	24	41	39
National accounting aggregates, 2003			
Gross national savings (% of GNI)	..	41.7	30.6
Consumption of fixed capital (% of GNI)	9.7	9.2	9.8
Education expenditure (% of GNI)	4.0	2.3	3.2
Energy depletion (% of GNI)	0.0	3.9	8.1
Mineral depletion (% of GNI)	0.0	0.3	0.4
Net forest depletion (% of GNI)	1.4	0.1	0.1
CO_2 damage (% of GNI)	0.4	1.8	1.6
Particulate emission damage (% of GNI)	..	0.8	0.7
Adjusted net savings (% of GNI)	..	27.9	13.2

San Marino

Environmental strategy/action plan prepared in ..

	Country data	Group data — High income
Population (millions)	0.0	972
Urban population (% of total)	90.7	79.9
GDP ($ billions)	1	29,341
GNI per capita, *Atlas* method ($)	..	28,600

Agriculture and fisheries
Land area (1,000 sq. km)	0	31,030
Agricultural land (% of land area)	17	36
Irrigated land (% of crop land)	..	12.3
Fertilizer consumption (100 grams/ha arable land)	..	1,198
Population density, rural (people/sq. km arable land)	..	202
Fish catch, total (1,000 metric tons)	..	28,712

Forests
Forest area (1,000 sq. km)	..	7,929
Forest area share of total land area (%)	..	25.9
Annual deforestation (% change, 1990–2000)	..	−0.1

Biodiversity
Mammal species, total known	..	
Mammal species, threatened	2	
Bird species, total breeding	..	
Bird species, threatened	0	
Nationally protected area (% of land area)	..	19.5

Energy
GDP per unit of energy use (2000 PPP$/kg oil equiv)	..	5.2
Energy use per capita (kg oil equiv)	..	5,395
Energy from biomass products and waste (% of total)	..	3.1
Energy imports, net (% of energy use)	..	26
Electric power consumption per capita (kWh)	..	8,693
Electricity generated by coal (% of total)	..	38.2

Emissions and pollution
CO_2 emissions per unit of GDP (kg/2000 PPP$ GDP)	..	0.5
CO_2 emissions per capita (metric tons)	..	12.4
Particulate matter (pop. weighted average, µg/cu. m)	..	33
Passenger cars (per 1,000 people)	..	436

Water and sanitation
Internal freshwater resources per capita (cu. m)	..	9,479
Freshwater withdrawal		
Total (% of internal resources)	..	9.7
Agriculture (% of total freshwater withdrawal)	..	42
Access to improved water source (% of total population)	..	99
Rural (% of rural population)	..	98
Urban (% of urban population)	..	100
Access to sanitation (% of total population)	..	..
Rural (% of rural population)	..	..
Urban (% of urban population)	..	..
Under-five mortality rate (per 1,000)	5	7

National accounting aggregates, 2003
Gross national savings (% of GNI)	..	19.1
Consumption of fixed capital (% of GNI)	..	13.2
Education expenditure (% of GNI)	..	4.6
Energy depletion (% of GNI)	..	0.8
Mineral depletion (% of GNI)	..	0.0
Net forest depletion (% of GNI)	..	0.0
CO_2 damage (% of GNI)	..	0.3
Particulate emission damage (% of GNI)	..	0.3
Adjusted net savings (% of GNI)	..	9.2

São Tomé and Principe

Environmental strategy/action plan prepared in ..

	Country data	Group data Sub-Saharan Africa	Group data Low income
Population (millions)	0.2	705	2,312
Urban population (% of total)	49.0	36.5	30.4
GDP ($ billions)	0.1	439	1,103
GNI per capita, *Atlas* method ($)	300	500	440
Agriculture and fisheries			
Land area (1,000 sq. km)	1	23,596	30,456
Agricultural land (% of land area)	56	43	43
Irrigated land (% of crop land)	18.5	4.2	26.7
Fertilizer consumption (100 grams/ha arable land)	..	145	654
Population density, rural (people/sq. km arable land)	1,138	352	509
Fish catch, total (1,000 metric tons)	4	5,191	16,410
Forests			
Forest area (1,000 sq. km)	0	6,435	7,939
Forest area share of total land area (%)	28.1	27.3	26.1
Annual deforestation (% change, 1990–2000)	0.0	0.8	0.7
Biodiversity			
Mammal species, total known	..		
Mammal species, threatened	3		
Bird species, total breeding	..		
Bird species, threatened	9		
Nationally protected area (% of land area)	..	8.7	7.7
Energy			
GDP per unit of energy use (2000 PPP$/kg oil equiv)	..	2.8	4.1
Energy use per capita (kg oil equiv)	..	667	493
Energy from biomass products and waste (% of total)	..	57.5	49.4
Energy imports, net (% of energy use)	..	−56	−6
Electric power consumption per capita (kWh)	..	457	312
Electricity generated by coal (% of total)	..	68.2	47.4
Emissions and pollution			
CO_2 emissions per unit of GDP (kg/2000 PPP$ GDP)	..	0.4	0.4
CO_2 emissions per capita (metric tons)	0.6	0.7	0.8
Particulate matter (pop. weighted average, µg/cu. m)	52	54	63
Passenger cars (per 1,000 people)	..	..	..
Water and sanitation			
Internal freshwater resources per capita (cu. m)	14,266	5,546	3,583
Freshwater withdrawal			
Total (% of internal resources)	..	1.8	11.5
Agriculture (% of total freshwater withdrawal)	..	85	92
Access to improved water source (% of total population)	79	58	75
Rural (% of rural population)	73	46	70
Urban (% of urban population)	89	82	89
Access to sanitation (% of total population)	24	36	36
Rural (% of rural population)	20	26	24
Urban (% of urban population)	32	55	61
Under-five mortality rate (per 1,000)	118	171	123
National accounting aggregates, 2003			
Gross national savings (% of GNI)	−35.4	16.9	23.1
Consumption of fixed capital (% of GNI)	9.1	10.6	8.9
Education expenditure (% of GNI)	..	4.7	3.4
Energy depletion (% of GNI)	0.0	8.0	5.8
Mineral depletion (% of GNI)	0.0	0.5	0.3
Net forest depletion (% of GNI)	0.0	0.7	0.8
CO_2 damage (% of GNI)	1.2	0.9	1.2
Particulate emission damage (% of GNI)	..	0.4	0.6
Adjusted net savings (% of GNI)	..	0.6	8.9

Saudi Arabia

Environmental strategy/action plan prepared in ..

	Country data	Group data Middle East & North Africa	Upper middle income
Population (millions)	22.5	312	333
Urban population (% of total)	87.5	59.0	75.4
GDP ($ billions)	214.7	745	1,856
GNI per capita, *Atlas* method ($)	9,240	2,390	5,440

Agriculture and fisheries
Land area (1,000 sq. km)	2,150	11,111	12,741
Agricultural land (% of land area)	81	34	48
Irrigated land (% of crop land)	42.7	38.3	13.5
Fertilizer consumption (100 grams/ha arable land)	1,059	854	796
Population density, rural (people/sq. km arable land)	79	603	193
Fish catch, total (1,000 metric tons)	57	2,840	10,082

Forests
Forest area (1,000 sq. km)	15	168	2,427
Forest area share of total land area (%)	0.7	1.5	19.1
Annual deforestation (% change, 1990–2000)	0.0	–0.1	0.6

Biodiversity
Mammal species, total known	77		
Mammal species, threatened	8		
Bird species, total breeding	125		
Bird species, threatened	15		
Nationally protected area (% of land area)	38.3	11.3	17.3

Energy
GDP per unit of energy use (2000 PPP$/kg oil equiv)	2.1	3.5	4.3
Energy use per capita (kg oil equiv)	5,775	1,504	2,232
Energy from biomass products and waste (% of total)	0.0	1.0	4.1
Energy imports, net (% of energy use)	–266	–168	–91
Electric power consumption per capita (kWh)	5,275	1,412	2,496
Electricity generated by coal (% of total)	..	2.3	23.9

Emissions and pollution
CO_2 emissions per unit of GDP (kg/2000 PPP$ GDP)	1.4	0.8	0.6
CO_2 emissions per capita (metric tons)	18.1	4.2	6.3
Particulate matter (pop. weighted average, µg/cu. m)	106	87	29
Passenger cars (per 1,000 people)	..	..	153

Water and sanitation
Internal freshwater resources per capita (cu. m)	89	761	10,741
Freshwater withdrawal			
Total (% of internal resources)	850.0	101.7	5.7
Agriculture (% of total freshwater withdrawal)	90	88	71
Access to improved water source (% of total population)	..	88	..
Rural (% of rural population)	..	78	..
Urban (% of urban population)	97	96	96
Access to sanitation (% of total population)	..	75	..
Rural (% of rural population)	..	56	..
Urban (% of urban population)	100	90	..
Under-five mortality rate (per 1,000)	26	53	22

National accounting aggregates, 2003
Gross national savings (% of GNI)	35.3	31.2	22.1
Consumption of fixed capital (% of GNI)	10.0	10.0	10.7
Education expenditure (% of GNI)	7.2	5.5	5.0
Energy depletion (% of GNI)	49.2	30.7	11.4
Mineral depletion (% of GNI)	0.0	0.1	0.3
Net forest depletion (% of GNI)	0.0	0.0	0.0
CO_2 damage (% of GNI)	1.1	1.2	0.8
Particulate emission damage (% of GNI)	1.0	0.8	0.6
Adjusted net savings (% of GNI)	–18.8	–6.2	3.3

Senegal

Environmental strategy/action plan prepared in **1984**

	Country data	Group data Sub-Saharan Africa	Group data Low income
Population (millions)	10.2	705	2,312
Urban population (% of total)	49.6	36.5	30.4
GDP ($ billions)	6.5	439	1,103
GNI per capita, *Atlas* method ($)	540	500	440
Agriculture and fisheries			
Land area (1,000 sq. km)	193	23,596	30,456
Agricultural land (% of land area)	42	43	43
Irrigated land (% of crop land)	2.8	4.2	26.7
Fertilizer consumption (100 grams/ha arable land)	136	145	654
Population density, rural (people/sq. km arable land)	208	352	509
Fish catch, total (1,000 metric tons)	406	5,191	16,410
Forests			
Forest area (1,000 sq. km)	62	6,435	7,939
Forest area share of total land area (%)	32.2	27.3	26.1
Annual deforestation (% change, 1990–2000)	0.7	0.8	0.7
Biodiversity			
Mammal species, total known	192		
Mammal species, threatened	12		
Bird species, total breeding	175		
Bird species, threatened	4		
Nationally protected area (% of land area)	11.6	8.7	7.7
Energy			
GDP per unit of energy use (2000 PPP$/kg oil equiv)	4.8	2.8	4.1
Energy use per capita (kg oil equiv)	319	667	493
Energy from biomass products and waste (% of total)	56.6	57.5	49.4
Energy imports, net (% of energy use)	43	−56	−6
Electric power consumption per capita (kWh)	135	457	312
Electricity generated by coal (% of total)	..	68.2	47.4
Emissions and pollution			
CO_2 emissions per unit of GDP (kg/2000 PPP$ GDP)	0.3	0.4	0.4
CO_2 emissions per capita (metric tons)	0.4	0.7	0.8
Particulate matter (pop. weighted average, µg/cu. m)	92	54	63
Passenger cars (per 1,000 people)	11	..	..
Water and sanitation			
Internal freshwater resources per capita (cu. m)	2,539	5,546	3,583
Freshwater withdrawal			
Total (% of internal resources)	5.4	1.8	11.5
Agriculture (% of total freshwater withdrawal)	92	85	92
Access to improved water source (% of total population)	72	58	75
Rural (% of rural population)	54	46	70
Urban (% of urban population)	90	82	89
Access to sanitation (% of total population)	52	36	36
Rural (% of rural population)	34	26	24
Urban (% of urban population)	70	55	61
Under-five mortality rate (per 1,000)	137	171	123
National accounting aggregates, 2003			
Gross national savings (% of GNI)	13.9	16.9	23.1
Consumption of fixed capital (% of GNI)	8.5	10.6	8.9
Education expenditure (% of GNI)	3.7	4.7	3.4
Energy depletion (% of GNI)	0.0	8.0	5.8
Mineral depletion (% of GNI)	0.1	0.5	0.3
Net forest depletion (% of GNI)	0.3	0.7	0.8
CO_2 damage (% of GNI)	0.5	0.9	1.2
Particulate emission damage (% of GNI)	..	0.4	0.6
Adjusted net savings (% of GNI)	8.2	0.6	8.9

Serbia and Montenegro

Environmental strategy/action plan prepared in ..

	Country data	Europe & Central Asia	Lower middle income
Population (millions)	8.1	472	2,655
Urban population (% of total)	52.0	63.8	49.8
GDP ($ billions)	20.7	1,403	4,168
GNI per capita, *Atlas* method ($)	1,910	2,580	1,490
Agriculture and fisheries			
Land area (1,000 sq. km)	102	23,868	56,103
Agricultural land (% of land area)	..	28	35
Irrigated land (% of crop land)	..	10.9	20.8
Fertilizer consumption (100 grams/ha arable land)	..	344	1,170
Population density, rural (people/sq. km arable land)	116	122	497
Fish catch, total (1,000 metric tons)	4	5,527	74,407
Forests			
Forest area (1,000 sq. km)	29	9,463	20,316
Forest area share of total land area (%)	..	39.6	36.2
Annual deforestation (% change, 1990–2000)	0.0	−0.1	0.1
Biodiversity			
Mammal species, total known	96		
Mammal species, threatened	12		
Bird species, total breeding	238		
Bird species, threatened	5		
Nationally protected area (% of land area)	..	6.8	7.7
Energy			
GDP per unit of energy use (2000 PPP$/kg oil equiv)	..	2.5	4.1
Energy use per capita (kg oil equiv)	1,981	2,697	1,227
Energy from biomass products and waste (% of total)	5.0	2.3	12.3
Energy imports, net (% of energy use)	33	−23	−22
Electric power consumption per capita (kWh)	..	2,808	1,289
Electricity generated by coal (% of total)	66.1	29.4	42.8
Emissions and pollution			
CO_2 emissions per unit of GDP (kg/2000 PPP$ GDP)	..	1.1	0.6
CO_2 emissions per capita (metric tons)	3.7	6.7	2.9
Particulate matter (pop. weighted average, μg/cu. m)	26	33	49
Passenger cars (per 1,000 people)	142	138	28
Water and sanitation			
Internal freshwater resources per capita (cu. m)	5,429	11,128	8,397
Freshwater withdrawal			
Total (% of internal resources)	29.5	7.4	5.9
Agriculture (% of total freshwater withdrawal)	8	57	74
Access to improved water source (% of total population)	93	91	82
Rural (% of rural population)	86	80	71
Urban (% of urban population)	99	98	94
Access to sanitation (% of total population)	87	82	60
Rural (% of rural population)	77	64	41
Urban (% of urban population)	97	93	80
Under-five mortality rate (per 1,000)	14	36	39
National accounting aggregates, 2003			
Gross national savings (% of GNI)	−6.5	21.9	30.6
Consumption of fixed capital (% of GNI)	10.4	10.7	9.8
Education expenditure (% of GNI)	..	4.1	3.2
Energy depletion (% of GNI)	1.0	11.6	8.1
Mineral depletion (% of GNI)	0.1	0.1	0.4
Net forest depletion (% of GNI)	0.0	0.0	0.1
CO_2 damage (% of GNI)	1.6	1.9	1.6
Particulate emission damage (% of GNI)	0.2	0.6	0.7
Adjusted net savings (% of GNI)	..	1.1	13.2

Seychelles

Environmental strategy/action plan prepared in ..

	Country data	Group data Sub-Saharan Africa	Group data Upper middle income
Population (millions)	0.1	705	333
Urban population (% of total)	66.0	36.5	75.4
GDP ($ billions)	0.7	439	1,856
GNI per capita, *Atlas* method ($)	7,490	500	5,440
Agriculture and fisheries			
Land area (1,000 sq. km)	0	23,596	12,741
Agricultural land (% of land area)	16	43	48
Irrigated land (% of crop land)	..	4.2	13.5
Fertilizer consumption (100 grams/ha arable land)	170	145	796
Population density, rural (people/sq. km arable land)	2,860	352	193
Fish catch, total (1,000 metric tons)	48	5,191	10,082
Forests			
Forest area (1,000 sq. km)	0	6,435	2,427
Forest area share of total land area (%)	66.7	27.3	19.1
Annual deforestation (% change, 1990–2000)	0.0	0.8	0.6
Biodiversity			
Mammal species, total known	..		
Mammal species, threatened	4		
Bird species, total breeding	..		
Bird species, threatened	10		
Nationally protected area (% of land area)	..	8.7	17.3
Energy			
GDP per unit of energy use (2000 PPP$/kg oil equiv)	..	2.8	4.3
Energy use per capita (kg oil equiv)	..	667	2,232
Energy from biomass products and waste (% of total)	..	57.5	4.1
Energy imports, net (% of energy use)	..	−56	−91
Electric power consumption per capita (kWh)	..	457	2,496
Electricity generated by coal (% of total)	..	68.2	23.9
Emissions and pollution			
CO_2 emissions per unit of GDP (kg/2000 PPP$ GDP)	..	0.4	0.6
CO_2 emissions per capita (metric tons)	2.8	0.7	6.3
Particulate matter (pop. weighted average, µg/cu. m)	..	54	29
Passenger cars (per 1,000 people)	..	..	153
Water and sanitation			
Internal freshwater resources per capita (cu. m)	..	5,546	10,741
Freshwater withdrawal			
Total (% of internal resources)	..	1.8	5.7
Agriculture (% of total freshwater withdrawal)	..	85	71
Access to improved water source (% of total population)	87	58	..
Rural (% of rural population)	75	46	..
Urban (% of urban population)	100	82	96
Access to sanitation (% of total population)	..	36	..
Rural (% of rural population)	100	26	..
Urban (% of urban population)	..	55	..
Under-five mortality rate (per 1,000)	15	171	22
National accounting aggregates, 2003			
Gross national savings (% of GNI)	14.5	16.9	22.1
Consumption of fixed capital (% of GNI)	9.4	10.6	10.7
Education expenditure (% of GNI)	6.3	4.7	5.0
Energy depletion (% of GNI)	0.0	8.0	11.4
Mineral depletion (% of GNI)	0.0	0.5	0.3
Net forest depletion (% of GNI)	0.0	0.7	0.0
CO_2 damage (% of GNI)	0.2	0.9	0.8
Particulate emission damage (% of GNI)	..	0.4	0.6
Adjusted net savings (% of GNI)	11.3	0.6	3.3

Sierra Leone

Environmental strategy/action plan prepared in **1994**

	Country data	Group data Sub-Saharan Africa	Low income
Population (millions)	5.3	705	2,312
Urban population (% of total)	38.7	36.5	30.4
GDP ($ billions)	0.8	439	1,103
GNI per capita, *Atlas* method ($)	150	500	440
Agriculture and fisheries			
Land area (1,000 sq. km)	72	23,596	30,456
Agricultural land (% of land area)	39	43	43
Irrigated land (% of crop land)	5.0	4.2	26.7
Fertilizer consumption (100 grams/ha arable land)	6	145	654
Population density, rural (people/sq. km arable land)	607	352	509
Fish catch, total (1,000 metric tons)	75	5,191	16,410
Forests			
Forest area (1,000 sq. km)	11	6,435	7,939
Forest area share of total land area (%)	14.7	27.3	26.1
Annual deforestation (% change, 1990–2000)	2.9	0.8	0.7
Biodiversity			
Mammal species, total known	147		
Mammal species, threatened	12		
Bird species, total breeding	172		
Bird species, threatened	10		
Nationally protected area (% of land area)	2.1	8.7	7.7
Energy			
GDP per unit of energy use (2000 PPP$/kg oil equiv)	..	2.8	4.1
Energy use per capita (kg oil equiv)	..	667	493
Energy from biomass products and waste (% of total)	..	57.5	49.4
Energy imports, net (% of energy use)	..	−56	−6
Electric power consumption per capita (kWh)	..	457	312
Electricity generated by coal (% of total)	..	68.2	47.4
Emissions and pollution			
CO_2 emissions per unit of GDP (kg/2000 PPP$ GDP)	0.2	0.4	0.4
CO_2 emissions per capita (metric tons)	0.1	0.7	0.8
Particulate matter (pop. weighted average, µg/cu. m)	63	54	63
Passenger cars (per 1,000 people)	..	..	..
Water and sanitation			
Internal freshwater resources per capita (cu. m)	29,982	5,546	3,583
Freshwater withdrawal			
Total (% of internal resources)	0.3	1.8	11.5
Agriculture (% of total freshwater withdrawal)	89	85	92
Access to improved water source (% of total population)	57	58	75
Rural (% of rural population)	46	46	70
Urban (% of urban population)	75	82	89
Access to sanitation (% of total population)	39	36	36
Rural (% of rural population)	30	26	24
Urban (% of urban population)	53	55	61
Under-five mortality rate (per 1,000)	284	171	123
National accounting aggregates, 2003			
Gross national savings (% of GNI)	1.6	16.9	23.1
Consumption of fixed capital (% of GNI)	6.7	10.6	8.9
Education expenditure (% of GNI)	3.9	4.7	3.4
Energy depletion (% of GNI)	0.0	8.0	5.8
Mineral depletion (% of GNI)	0.0	0.5	0.3
Net forest depletion (% of GNI)	5.5	0.7	0.8
CO_2 damage (% of GNI)	0.5	0.9	1.2
Particulate emission damage (% of GNI)	0.4	0.4	0.6
Adjusted net savings (% of GNI)	−7.6	0.6	8.9

Singapore

Environmental strategy/action plan prepared in **1993**

	Country data	High income
		Group data
Population (millions)	4.3	972
Urban population (% of total)	100.0	79.9
GDP ($ billions)	91	29,341
GNI per capita, *Atlas* method ($)	21,230	28,600

Agriculture and fisheries		
Land area (1,000 sq. km)	1	31,030
Agricultural land (% of land area)	2	36
Irrigated land (% of crop land)	..	12.3
Fertilizer consumption (100 grams/ha arable land)	24,180	1,198
Population density, rural (people/sq. km arable land)	..	202
Fish catch, total (1,000 metric tons)	9	28,712

Forests		
Forest area (1,000 sq. km)	0	7,929
Forest area share of total land area (%)	3.0	25.9
Annual deforestation (% change, 1990–2000)	0.0	−0.1

Biodiversity		
Mammal species, total known	85	
Mammal species, threatened	3	
Bird species, total breeding	142	
Bird species, threatened	7	
Nationally protected area (% of land area)	4.9	19.5

Energy		
GDP per unit of energy use (2000 PPP$/kg oil equiv)	3.8	5.2
Energy use per capita (kg oil equiv)	6,078	5,395
Energy from biomass products and waste (% of total)	..	3.1
Energy imports, net (% of energy use)	100	26
Electric power consumption per capita (kWh)	7,039	8,693
Electricity generated by coal (% of total)	..	38.2

Emissions and pollution		
CO_2 emissions per unit of GDP (kg/2000 PPP$ GDP)	0.6	0.5
CO_2 emissions per capita (metric tons)	14.7	12.4
Particulate matter (pop. weighted average, μg/cu. m)	41	33
Passenger cars (per 1,000 people)	122	436

Water and sanitation		
Internal freshwater resources per capita (cu. m)	..	9,479
Freshwater withdrawal		
Total (% of internal resources)	..	9.7
Agriculture (% of total freshwater withdrawal)	4	42
Access to improved water source (% of total population)	..	99
Rural (% of rural population)	..	98
Urban (% of urban population)	100	100
Access to sanitation (% of total population)	..	..
Rural (% of rural population)	..	..
Urban (% of urban population)	100	..
Under-five mortality rate (per 1,000)	5	7

National accounting aggregates, 2003		
Gross national savings (% of GNI)	44.8	19.1
Consumption of fixed capital (% of GNI)	14.3	13.2
Education expenditure (% of GNI)	2.3	4.6
Energy depletion (% of GNI)	0.0	0.8
Mineral depletion (% of GNI)	0.0	0.0
Net forest depletion (% of GNI)	0.0	0.0
CO_2 damage (% of GNI)	0.5	0.3
Particulate emission damage (% of GNI)	0.4	0.3
Adjusted net savings (% of GNI)	31.8	9.2

Slovak Republic

Environmental strategy/action plan prepared in ..

	Country data	Group data Europe & Central Asia	Group data Upper middle income
Population (millions)	5.4	472	333
Urban population (% of total)	58.0	63.8	75.4
GDP ($ billions)	32.5	1,403	1,856
GNI per capita, *Atlas* method ($)	4,940	2,580	5,440
Agriculture and fisheries			
Land area (1,000 sq. km)	49	23,868	12,741
Agricultural land (% of land area)	51	28	48
Irrigated land (% of crop land)	..	10.9	13.5
Fertilizer consumption (100 grams/ha arable land)	..	344	796
Population density, rural (people/sq. km arable land)	..	122	193
Fish catch, total (1,000 metric tons)	..	5,527	10,082
Forests			
Forest area (1,000 sq. km)	22	9,463	2,427
Forest area share of total land area (%)	..	39.6	19.1
Annual deforestation (% change, 1990–2000)	–1.0	–0.1	0.6
Biodiversity			
Mammal species, total known	85		
Mammal species, threatened	9		
Bird species, total breeding	199		
Bird species, threatened	4		
Nationally protected area (% of land area)	..	6.8	17.3
Energy			
GDP per unit of energy use (2000 PPP$/kg oil equiv)	3.6	2.5	4.3
Energy use per capita (kg oil equiv)	3,448	2,697	2,232
Energy from biomass products and waste (% of total)	1.7	2.3	4.1
Energy imports, net (% of energy use)	64	–23	–91
Electric power consumption per capita (kWh)	4,222	2,808	2,496
Electricity generated by coal (% of total)	17.3	29.4	23.9
Emissions and pollution			
CO_2 emissions per unit of GDP (kg/2000 PPP$ GDP)	0.6	1.1	0.6
CO_2 emissions per capita (metric tons)	6.6	6.7	6.3
Particulate matter (pop. weighted average, µg/cu. m)	22	33	29
Passenger cars (per 1,000 people)	247	138	153
Water and sanitation			
Internal freshwater resources per capita (cu. m)	2,412	11,128	10,741
Freshwater withdrawal			
Total (% of internal resources)	13.8	7.4	5.7
Agriculture (% of total freshwater withdrawal)	..	57	71
Access to improved water source (% of total population)	100	91	..
Rural (% of rural population)	100	80	..
Urban (% of urban population)	100	98	96
Access to sanitation (% of total population)	100	82	..
Rural (% of rural population)	100	64	..
Urban (% of urban population)	100	93	..
Under-five mortality rate (per 1,000)	8	36	22
National accounting aggregates, 2003			
Gross national savings (% of GNI)	24.2	21.9	22.1
Consumption of fixed capital (% of GNI)	11.4	10.7	10.7
Education expenditure (% of GNI)	4.0	4.1	5.0
Energy depletion (% of GNI)	0.1	11.6	11.4
Mineral depletion (% of GNI)	0.0	0.1	0.3
Net forest depletion (% of GNI)	0.0	0.0	0.0
CO_2 damage (% of GNI)	0.9	1.9	0.8
Particulate emission damage (% of GNI)	0.1	0.6	0.6
Adjusted net savings (% of GNI)	15.7	1.1	3.3

Slovenia

Environmental strategy/action plan prepared in **1994**

	Country data	Group data High income
Population (millions)	2.0	972
Urban population (% of total)	49.2	79.9
GDP ($ billions)	28	29,341
GNI per capita, *Atlas* method ($)	11,920	28,600
Agriculture and fisheries		
Land area (1,000 sq. km)	20	31,030
Agricultural land (% of land area)	25	36
Irrigated land (% of crop land)	1.5	12.3
Fertilizer consumption (100 grams/ha arable land)	4,160	1,198
Population density, rural (people/sq. km arable land)	603	202
Fish catch, total (1,000 metric tons)	3	28,712
Forests		
Forest area (1,000 sq. km)	11	7,929
Forest area share of total land area (%)	55.0	25.9
Annual deforestation (% change, 1990–2000)	–0.2	–0.1
Biodiversity		
Mammal species, total known	75	
Mammal species, threatened	9	
Bird species, total breeding	201	
Bird species, threatened	1	
Nationally protected area (% of land area)	6.0	19.5
Energy		
GDP per unit of energy use (2000 PPP$/kg oil equiv)	5.1	5.2
Energy use per capita (kg oil equiv)	3,486	5,395
Energy from biomass products and waste (% of total)	6.7	3.1
Energy imports, net (% of energy use)	51	26
Electric power consumption per capita (kWh)	5,907	8,693
Electricity generated by coal (% of total)	36.1	38.2
Emissions and pollution		
CO_2 emissions per unit of GDP (kg/2000 PPP$ GDP)	0.4	0.5
CO_2 emissions per capita (metric tons)	7.3	12.4
Particulate matter (pop. weighted average, µg/cu. m)	36	33
Passenger cars (per 1,000 people)	438	436
Water and sanitation		
Internal freshwater resources per capita (cu. m)	9,524	9,479
Freshwater withdrawal		
Total (% of internal resources)	6.8	9.7
Agriculture (% of total freshwater withdrawal)	1	42
Access to improved water source (% of total population)	..	99
Rural (% of rural population)	..	98
Urban (% of urban population)	..	100
Access to sanitation (% of total population)	..	..
Rural (% of rural population)	..	..
Urban (% of urban population)	..	..
Under-five mortality rate (per 1,000)	4	7
National accounting aggregates, 2003		
Gross national savings (% of GNI)	25.5	19.1
Consumption of fixed capital (% of GNI)	12.6	13.2
Education expenditure (% of GNI)	5.4	4.6
Energy depletion (% of GNI)	0.0	0.8
Mineral depletion (% of GNI)	0.0	0.0
Net forest depletion (% of GNI)	0.0	0.0
CO_2 damage (% of GNI)	0.4	0.3
Particulate emission damage (% of GNI)	0.2	0.3
Adjusted net savings (% of GNI)	17.7	9.2

Solomon Islands

Environmental strategy/action plan prepared in ..

	Country data	East Asia & Pacific	Low income
		Group data	
Population (millions)	0.5	1,855	2,312
Urban population (% of total)	21.4	39.1	30.4
GDP ($ billions)	0.3	2,033	1,103
GNI per capita, *Atlas* method ($)	560	1,070	440
Agriculture and fisheries			
Land area (1,000 sq. km)	28	15,886	30,456
Agricultural land (% of land area)	4	50	43
Irrigated land (% of crop land)	..		26.7
Fertilizer consumption (100 grams/ha arable land)	..	2,297	654
Population density, rural (people/sq. km arable land)	1,950	565	509
Fish catch, total (1,000 metric tons)	30	60,812	16,410
Forests			
Forest area (1,000 sq. km)	25	4,284	7,939
Forest area share of total land area (%)	90.6	27.0	26.1
Annual deforestation (% change, 1990–2000)	0.2	0.2	0.7
Biodiversity			
Mammal species, total known	53		
Mammal species, threatened	20		
Bird species, total breeding	111		
Bird species, threatened	23		
Nationally protected area (% of land area)	0.3	9.2	7.7
Energy			
GDP per unit of energy use (2000 PPP$/kg oil equiv)	..	4.6	4.1
Energy use per capita (kg oil equiv)	..	904	493
Energy from biomass products and waste (% of total)	..	19.6	49.4
Energy imports, net (% of energy use)	..	–4	–6
Electric power consumption per capita (kWh)	..	891	312
Electricity generated by coal (% of total)	..	66.8	47.4
Emissions and pollution			
CO_2 emissions per unit of GDP (kg/2000 PPP$ GDP)	0.2	0.5	0.4
CO_2 emissions per capita (metric tons)	0.4	2.1	0.8
Particulate matter (pop. weighted average, µg/cu. m)	31	69	63
Passenger cars (per 1,000 people)	..	10	..
Water and sanitation			
Internal freshwater resources per capita (cu. m)	98,545	5,103	3,583
Freshwater withdrawal			
Total (% of internal resources)	..	8.2	11.5
Agriculture (% of total freshwater withdrawal)	40	81	92
Access to improved water source (% of total population)	70	78	75
Rural (% of rural population)	65	69	70
Urban (% of urban population)	94	92	89
Access to sanitation (% of total population)	31	49	36
Rural (% of rural population)	18	35	24
Urban (% of urban population)	98	71	61
Under-five mortality rate (per 1,000)	22	41	123
National accounting aggregates, 2003			
Gross national savings (% of GNI)	..	41.7	23.1
Consumption of fixed capital (% of GNI)	8.4	9.2	8.9
Education expenditure (% of GNI)	3.8	2.3	3.4
Energy depletion (% of GNI)	0.0	3.9	5.8
Mineral depletion (% of GNI)	0.0	0.3	0.3
Net forest depletion (% of GNI)	6.8	0.1	0.8
CO_2 damage (% of GNI)	0.3	1.8	1.2
Particulate emission damage (% of GNI)	..	0.8	0.6
Adjusted net savings (% of GNI)	..	27.9	8.9

Somalia

Environmental strategy/action plan prepared in ..

	Country data	Group data Sub-Saharan Africa	Low Income
Population (millions)	9.6	705	2,312
Urban population (% of total)	28.9	36.5	30.4
GDP ($ billions)	..	439	1,103
GNI per capita, *Atlas* method ($)	..	500	440
Agriculture and fisheries			
Land area (1,000 sq. km)	627	23,596	30,456
Agricultural land (% of land area)	70	43	43
Irrigated land (% of crop land)	18.7	4.2	26.7
Fertilizer consumption (100 grams/ha arable land)	5	145	654
Population density, rural (people/sq. km arable land)	638	352	509
Fish catch, total (1,000 metric tons)	20	5,191	16,410
Forests			
Forest area (1,000 sq. km)	75	6,435	7,939
Forest area share of total land area (%)	12.0	27.3	26.1
Annual deforestation (% change, 1990–2000)	1.0	0.8	0.7
Biodiversity			
Mammal species, total known	171		
Mammal species, threatened	19		
Bird species, total breeding	179		
Bird species, threatened	10		
Nationally protected area (% of land area)	0.8	8.7	7.7
Energy			
GDP per unit of energy use (2000 PPP$/kg oil equiv)	..	2.8	4.1
Energy use per capita (kg oil equiv)	..	667	493
Energy from biomass products and waste (% of total)	..	57.5	49.4
Energy imports, net (% of energy use)	..	−56	−6
Electric power consumption per capita (kWh)	..	457	312
Electricity generated by coal (% of total)	..	68.2	47.4
Emissions and pollution			
CO_2 emissions per unit of GDP (kg/2000 PPP$ GDP)	..	0.4	0.4
CO_2 emissions per capita (metric tons)	..	0.7	0.8
Particulate matter (pop. weighted average, µg/cu. m)	39	54	63
Passenger cars (per 1,000 people)	..	..	..
Water and sanitation			
Internal freshwater resources per capita (cu. m)	623	5,546	3,583
Freshwater withdrawal			
Total (% of internal resources)	13.3	1.8	11.5
Agriculture (% of total freshwater withdrawal)	97	85	92
Access to improved water source (% of total population)	29	58	75
Rural (% of rural population)	27	46	70
Urban (% of urban population)	32	82	89
Access to sanitation (% of total population)	25	36	36
Rural (% of rural population)	14	26	24
Urban (% of urban population)	47	55	61
Under-five mortality rate (per 1,000)	225	171	123
National accounting aggregates, 2003			
Gross national savings (% of GNI)	..	16.9	23.1
Consumption of fixed capital (% of GNI)	..	10.6	8.9
Education expenditure (% of GNI)	..	4.7	3.4
Energy depletion (% of GNI)	..	8.0	5.8
Mineral depletion (% of GNI)	..	0.5	0.3
Net forest depletion (% of GNI)	..	0.7	0.8
CO_2 damage (% of GNI)	..	0.9	1.2
Particulate emission damage (% of GNI)	..	0.4	0.6
Adjusted net savings (% of GNI)	..	0.6	8.9

South Africa

Environmental strategy/action plan prepared in **1993**

	Country data	Sub-Saharan Africa	Lower middle income
		Group data	
Population (millions)	45.8	705	2,655
Urban population (% of total)	59.2	36.5	49.8
GDP ($ billions)	159.9	439	4,168
GNI per capita, *Atlas* method ($)	2,750	500	1,490
Agriculture and fisheries			
Land area (1,000 sq. km)	1,214	23,596	56,103
Agricultural land (% of land area)	82	43	35
Irrigated land (% of crop land)	9.5	4.2	20.8
Fertilizer consumption (100 grams/ha arable land)	654	145	1,170
Population density, rural (people/sq. km arable land)	128	352	497
Fish catch, total (1,000 metric tons)	760	5,191	74,407
Forests			
Forest area (1,000 sq. km)	89	6,435	20,316
Forest area share of total land area (%)	7.3	27.3	36.2
Annual deforestation (% change, 1990–2000)	0.1	0.8	0.1
Biodiversity			
Mammal species, total known	247		
Mammal species, threatened	42		
Bird species, total breeding	304		
Bird species, threatened	28		
Nationally protected area (% of land area)	5.5	8.7	7.7
Energy			
GDP per unit of energy use (2000 PPP$/kg oil equiv)	3.9	2.8	4.1
Energy use per capita (kg oil equiv)	2,502	667	1,227
Energy from biomass products and waste (% of total)	11.2	57.5	12.3
Energy imports, net (% of energy use)	–29	–56	–22
Electric power consumption per capita (kWh)	3,860	457	1,289
Electricity generated by coal (% of total)	93.1	68.2	42.8
Emissions and pollution			
CO_2 emissions per unit of GDP (kg/2000 PPP$ GDP)	0.8	0.4	0.6
CO_2 emissions per capita (metric tons)	7.4	0.7	2.9
Particulate matter (pop. weighted average, µg/cu. m)	24	54	49
Passenger cars per 1,000 people	94	..	28
Water and sanitation			
Internal freshwater resources per capita (cu. m)	982	5,546	8,397
Freshwater withdrawal			
Total (% of internal resources)	29.6	1.8	5.9
Agriculture (% of total freshwater withdrawal)	72	85	74
Access to improved water source (% of total population)	87	58	82
Rural (% of rural population)	73	46	71
Urban (% of urban population)	98	82	94
Access to sanitation (% of total population)	67	36	60
Rural (% of rural population)	44	26	41
Urban (% of urban population)	86	55	80
Under-five mortality rate (per 1,000)	66	171	39
National accounting aggregates, 2003			
Gross national savings (% of GNI)	16.3	16.9	30.6
Consumption of fixed capital (% of GNI)	13.3	10.6	9.8
Education expenditure (% of GNI)	7.5	4.7	3.2
Energy depletion (% of GNI)	1.1	8.0	8.1
Mineral depletion (% of GNI)	0.9	0.5	0.4
Net forest depletion (% of GNI)	0.3	0.7	0.1
CO_2 damage (% of GNI)	1.5	0.9	1.6
Particulate emission damage (% of GNI)	0.2	0.4	0.7
Adjusted net savings (% of GNI)	6.5	0.6	13.2

Spain

Environmental strategy/action plan prepared in ..

	Country data	Group data High income
Population (millions)	41.1	972
Urban population (% of total)	78.3	79.9
GDP ($ billions)	839	29,341
GNI per capita, *Atlas* method ($)	17,040	28,600

Agriculture and fisheries

Land area (1,000 sq. km)	499	31,030
Agricultural land (% of land area)	59	36
Irrigated land (% of crop land)	20.2	12.3
Fertilizer consumption (100 grams/ha arable land)	1,572	1,198
Population density, rural (people/sq. km arable land)	65	202
Fish catch, total (1,000 metric tons)	1,397	28,712

Forests

Forest area (1,000 sq. km)	144	7,929
Forest area share of total land area (%)	28.8	25.9
Annual deforestation (% change, 1990–2000)	–0.6	–0.1

Biodiversity

Mammal species, total known	82	
Mammal species, threatened	24	
Bird species, total breeding	281	
Bird species, threatened	7	
Nationally protected area (% of land area)	8.5	19.5

Energy

GDP per unit of energy use (2000 PPP$/kg oil equiv)	6.5	5.2
Energy use per capita (kg oil equiv)	3,215	5,395
Energy from biomass products and waste (% of total)	3.3	3.1
Energy imports, net (% of energy use)	76	26
Electric power consumption per capita (kWh)	5,048	8,693
Electricity generated by coal (% of total)	34.0	38.2

Emissions and pollution

CO_2 emissions per unit of GDP (kg/2000 PPP$ GDP)	0.3	0.5
CO_2 emissions per capita (metric tons)	7.0	12.4
Particulate matter (pop. weighted average, µg/cu. m)	40	33
Passenger cars (per 1,000 people)	441	436

Water and sanitation

Internal freshwater resources per capita (cu. m)	2,701	9,479
Freshwater withdrawal		
Total (% of internal resources)	31.7	9.7
Agriculture (% of total freshwater withdrawal)	68	42
Access to improved water source (% of total population)	..	99
Rural (% of rural population)	..	98
Urban (% of urban population)	..	100
Access to sanitation (% of total population)	..	..
Rural (% of rural population)	..	..
Urban (% of urban population)	..	..
Under-five mortality rate (per 1,000)	4	7

National accounting aggregates, 2003

Gross national savings (% of GNI)	23.3	19.1
Consumption of fixed capital (% of GNI)	12.9	13.2
Education expenditure (% of GNI)	4.3	4.6
Energy depletion (% of GNI)	0.0	0.8
Mineral depletion (% of GNI)	0.0	0.0
Net forest depletion (% of GNI)	0.0	0.0
CO_2 damage (% of GNI)	0.2	0.3
Particulate emission damage (% of GNI)	0.4	0.3
Adjusted net savings (% of GNI)	14.0	9.2

Sri Lanka

Environmental strategy/action plan prepared in **1994**

	Country data	Group data	
		South Asia	Lower middle income
Population (millions)	19.2	1,425	2,655
Urban population (% of total)	23.8	28.3	49.8
GDP ($ billions)	18.2	765	4,168
GNI per capita, *Atlas* method ($)	930	510	1,490
Agriculture and fisheries			
Land area (1,000 sq. km)	65	4,781	56,103
Agricultural land (% of land area)	36	55	35
Irrigated land (% of crop land)	33.3	41.2	20.8
Fertilizer consumption (100 grams/ha arable land)	3,103	1,027	1,170
Population density, rural (people/sq. km arable land)	1,588	559	497
Fish catch, total (1,000 metric tons)	288	8,724	74,407
Forests			
Forest area (1,000 sq. km)	19	780	20,316
Forest area share of total land area (%)	30.0	16.3	36.2
Annual deforestation (% change, 1990–2000)	1.6	0.1	0.1
Biodiversity			
Mammal species, total known	88		
Mammal species, threatened	22		
Bird species, total breeding	126		
Bird species, threatened	14		
Nationally protected area (% of land area)	13.5	4.8	7.7
Energy			
GDP per unit of energy use (2000 PPP$/kg oil equiv)	8.0	5.1	4.1
Energy use per capita (kg oil equiv)	430	468	1,227
Energy from biomass products and waste (% of total)	52.9	39.3	12.3
Energy imports, net (% of energy use)	44	19	−22
Electric power consumption per capita (kWh)	297	344	1,289
Electricity generated by coal (% of total)	..	59.8	42.8
Emissions and pollution			
CO_2 emissions per unit of GDP (kg/2000 PPP$ GDP)	0.2	0.4	0.6
CO_2 emissions per capita (metric tons)	0.6	0.9	2.9
Particulate matter (pop. weighted average, µg/cu. m)	94	69	49
Passenger cars (per 1,000 people)	11	6	28
Water and sanitation			
Internal freshwater resources per capita (cu. m)	2,600	1,275	8,397
Freshwater withdrawal			
Total (% of internal resources)	19.6	40.5	5.9
Agriculture (% of total freshwater withdrawal)	96	94	74
Access to improved water source (% of total population)	78	84	82
Rural (% of rural population)	72	80	71
Urban (% of urban population)	99	93	94
Access to sanitation (% of total population)	91	35	60
Rural (% of rural population)	89	23	41
Urban (% of urban population)	98	64	80
Under-five mortality rate (per 1,000)	15	92	39
National accounting aggregates, 2003			
Gross national savings (% of GNI)	21.7	24.9	30.6
Consumption of fixed capital (% of GNI)	5.2	9.0	9.8
Education expenditure (% of GNI)	2.9	3.5	3.2
Energy depletion (% of GNI)	0.0	2.4	8.1
Mineral depletion (% of GNI)	0.0	0.3	0.4
Net forest depletion (% of GNI)	0.4	0.7	0.1
CO_2 damage (% of GNI)	0.3	1.3	1.6
Particulate emission damage (% of GNI)	0.3	0.7	0.7
Adjusted net savings (% of GNI)	18.3	14.0	13.2

St. Kitts and Nevis

Environmental strategy/action plan prepared in ..

	Country data	Latin America & Caribbean	Upper middle income
Population (millions)	0.0	533	333
Urban population (% of total)	34.7	76.6	75.4
GDP ($ billions)	0.3	1,741	1,856
GNI per capita, *Atlas* method ($)	6,630	3,280	5,440
Agriculture and fisheries			
Land area (1,000 sq. km)	0	20,057	12,741
Agricultural land (% of land area)	28	39	48
Irrigated land (% of crop land)	..	12.5	13.5
Fertilizer consumption (100 grams/ha arable land)	2,429	892	796
Population density, rural (people/sq. km arable land)	437	210	193
Fish catch, total (1,000 metric tons)	1	17,804	10,082
Forests			
Forest area (1,000 sq. km)	0	9,552	2,427
Forest area share of total land area (%)	11.1	47.6	19.1
Annual deforestation (% change, 1990–2000)	0.0	0.5	0.6
Biodiversity			
Mammal species, total known	..		
Mammal species, threatened	0		
Bird species, total breeding	..		
Bird species, threatened	1		
Nationally protected area (% of land area)	..	11.2	17.3
Energy			
GDP per unit of energy use (2000 PPP$/kg oil equiv)	..	6.1	4.3
Energy use per capita (kg oil equiv)	..	1,156	2,232
Energy from biomass products and waste (% of total)	..	14.6	4.1
Energy imports, net (% of energy use)	..	−42	−91
Electric power consumption per capita (kWh)	..	1,506	2,496
Electricity generated by coal (% of total)	..	5.0	23.9
Emissions and pollution			
CO_2 emissions per unit of GDP (kg/2000 PPP$ GDP)	0.2	0.4	0.6
CO_2 emissions per capita (metric tons)	2.4	2.7	6.3
Particulate matter (pop. weighted average, μg/cu. m)	23	40	29
Passenger cars (per 1,000 people)	..	..	153
Water and sanitation			
Internal freshwater resources per capita (cu. m)	..	25,245	10,741
Freshwater withdrawal			
Total (% of internal resources)	..	2.0	5.7
Agriculture (% of total freshwater withdrawal)	..	74	71
Access to improved water source (% of total population)	99	89	..
Rural (% of rural population)	99	69	..
Urban (% of urban population)	99	96	96
Access to sanitation (% of total population)	96	74	..
Rural (% of rural population)	96	44	..
Urban (% of urban population)	96	84	..
Under-five mortality rate (per 1,000)	22	33	22
National accounting aggregates, 2003			
Gross national savings (% of GNI)	25.8	19.5	22.1
Consumption of fixed capital (% of GNI)	13.5	10.3	10.7
Education expenditure (% of GNI)	4.2	4.2	5.0
Energy depletion (% of GNI)	0.0	6.4	11.4
Mineral depletion (% of GNI)	0.0	0.7	0.3
Net forest depletion (% of GNI)	0.0	0.0	0.0
CO_2 damage (% of GNI)	0.3	0.5	0.8
Particulate emission damage (% of GNI)	..	0.5	0.6
Adjusted net savings (% of GNI)	16.3	5.3	3.3

St. Lucia

Environmental strategy/action plan prepared in ..

	Country data	Latin America & Caribbean	Upper middle income
		Group data	
Population (millions)	0.2	533	333
Urban population (% of total)	38.6	76.6	75.4
GDP ($ billions)	0.7	1,741	1,856
GNI per capita, *Atlas* method ($)	4,050	3,280	5,440
Agriculture and fisheries			
Land area (1,000 sq. km)	1	20,057	12,741
Agricultural land (% of land area)	..	39	48
Irrigated land (% of crop land)	16.7	12.5	13.5
Fertilizer consumption (100 grams/ha arable land)	3,358	892	796
Population density, rural (people/sq. km arable land)	2,455	210	193
Fish catch, total (1,000 metric tons)	2	17,804	10,082
Forests			
Forest area (1,000 sq. km)	0	9,552	2,427
Forest area share of total land area (%)	14.8	47.6	19.1
Annual deforestation (% change, 1990–2000)	4.3	0.5	0.6
Biodiversity			
Mammal species, total known	..		
Mammal species, threatened	1		
Bird species, total breeding	..		
Bird species, threatened	5		
Nationally protected area (% of land area)	..	11.2	17.3
Energy			
GDP per unit of energy use (2000 PPP$/kg oil equiv)	..	6.1	4.3
Energy use per capita (kg oil equiv)	..	1,156	2,232
Energy from biomass products and waste (% of total)	..	14.6	4.1
Energy imports, net (% of energy use)	..	–42	–91
Electric power consumption per capita (kWh)	..	1,506	2,496
Electricity generated by coal (% of total)	..	5.0	23.9
Emissions and pollution			
CO_2 emissions per unit of GDP (kg/2000 PPP$ GDP)	0.4	0.4	0.6
CO_2 emissions per capita (metric tons)	2.1	2.7	6.3
Particulate matter (pop. weighted average, µg/cu. m)	..	40	29
Passenger cars (per 1,000 people)	..	..	153
Water and sanitation			
Internal freshwater resources per capita (cu. m)	..	25,245	10,741
Freshwater withdrawal			
Total (% of internal resources)	..	2.0	5.7
Agriculture (% of total freshwater withdrawal)	0	74	71
Access to improved water source (% of total population)	98	89	..
Rural (% of rural population)	98	69	..
Urban (% of urban population)	98	96	96
Access to sanitation (% of total population)	89	74	..
Rural (% of rural population)	89	44	..
Urban (% of urban population)	89	84	..
Under-five mortality rate (per 1,000)	18	33	22
National accounting aggregates, 2003			
Gross national savings (% of GNI)	8.8	19.5	22.1
Consumption of fixed capital (% of GNI)	11.8	10.3	10.7
Education expenditure (% of GNI)	7.7	4.2	5.0
Energy depletion (% of GNI)	0.0	6.4	11.4
Mineral depletion (% of GNI)	0.0	0.7	0.3
Net forest depletion (% of GNI)	0.0	0.0	0.0
CO_2 damage (% of GNI)	0.3	0.5	0.8
Particulate emission damage (% of GNI)	..	0.5	0.6
Adjusted net savings (% of GNI)	4.4	5.3	3.3

St. Vincent & Grenadines

Environmental strategy/action plan prepared in ..

	Country data	Latin America & Caribbean	Upper middle income
		Group data	
Population (millions)	0.1	533	333
Urban population (% of total)	58.1	76.6	75.4
GDP ($ billions)	0.4	1,741	1,856
GNI per capita, *Atlas* method ($)	3,310	3,280	5,440
Agriculture and fisheries			
Land area (1,000 sq. km)	0	20,057	12,741
Agricultural land (% of land area)	41	39	48
Irrigated land (% of crop land)	7.1	12.5	13.5
Fertilizer consumption (100 grams/ha arable land)	3,047	892	796
Population density, rural (people/sq. km arable land)	670	210	193
Fish catch, total (1,000 metric tons)	46	17,804	10,082
Forests			
Forest area (1,000 sq. km)	0	9,552	2,427
Forest area share of total land area (%)	15.4	47.6	19.1
Annual deforestation (% change, 1990–2000)	1.5	0.5	0.6
Biodiversity			
Mammal species, total known	..		
Mammal species, threatened	2		
Bird species, total breeding	..		
Bird species, threatened	2		
Nationally protected area (% of land area)	..	11.2	17.3
Energy			
GDP per unit of energy use (2000 PPP$/kg oil equiv)	..	6.1	4.3
Energy use per capita (kg oil equiv)	..	1,156	2,232
Energy from biomass products and waste (% of total)	..	14.6	4.1
Energy imports, net (% of energy use)	..	–42	–91
Electric power consumption per capita (kWh)	..	1,506	2,496
Electricity generated by coal (% of total)	..	5.0	23.9
Emissions and pollution			
CO_2 emissions per unit of GDP (kg/2000 PPP$ GDP)	0.3	0.4	0.6
CO_2 emissions per capita (metric tons)	1.4	2.7	6.3
Particulate matter (pop. weighted average, μg/cu. m)	33	40	29
Passenger cars (per 1,000 people)	..	..	153
Water and sanitation			
Internal freshwater resources per capita (cu. m)	..	25,245	10,741
Freshwater withdrawal			
Total (% of internal resources)	..	2.0	5.7
Agriculture (% of total freshwater withdrawal)	0	74	71
Access to improved water source (% of total population)	..	89	..
Rural (% of rural population)	93	69	..
Urban (% of urban population)	..	96	96
Access to sanitation (% of total population)	..	74	..
Rural (% of rural population)	96	44	..
Urban (% of urban population)	..	84	..
Under-five mortality rate (per 1,000)	27	33	22
National accounting aggregates, 2003			
Gross national savings (% of GNI)	12.6	19.5	22.1
Consumption of fixed capital (% of GNI)	11.1	10.3	10.7
Education expenditure (% of GNI)	4.7	4.2	5.0
Energy depletion (% of GNI)	0.0	6.4	11.4
Mineral depletion (% of GNI)	0.0	0.7	0.3
Net forest depletion (% of GNI)	0.0	0.0	0.0
CO_2 damage (% of GNI)	0.3	0.5	0.8
Particulate emission damage (% of GNI)	..	0.5	0.6
Adjusted net savings (% of GNI)	5.9	5.3	3.3

Sudan

Environmental strategy/action plan prepared in ..

	Country data	Sub-Saharan Africa	Low income
		Group data	
Population (millions)	33.5	705	2,312
Urban population (% of total)	38.9	36.5	30.4
GDP ($ billions)	17.8	439	1,103
GNI per capita, *Atlas* method ($)	460	500	440
Agriculture and fisheries			
Land area (1,000 sq. km)	2,376	23,596	30,456
Agricultural land (% of land area)	56	43	43
Irrigated land (% of crop land)	11.7	4.2	26.7
Fertilizer consumption (100 grams/ha arable land)	43	145	654
Population density, rural (people/sq. km arable land)	125	352	509
Fish catch, total (1,000 metric tons)	59	5,191	16,410
Forests			
Forest area (1,000 sq. km)	616	6,435	7,939
Forest area share of total land area (%)	25.9	27.3	26.1
Annual deforestation (% change, 1990–2000)	1.4	0.8	0.7
Biodiversity			
Mammal species, total known	267		
Mammal species, threatened	23		
Bird species, total breeding	280		
Bird species, threatened	6		
Nationally protected area (% of land area)	5.2	8.7	7.7
Energy			
GDP per unit of energy use (2000 PPP$/kg oil equiv)	3.6	2.8	4.1
Energy use per capita (kg oil equiv)	483	667	493
Energy from biomass products and waste (% of total)	79.8	57.5	49.4
Energy imports, net (% of energy use)	−58	−56	−6
Electric power consumption per capita (kWh)	74	457	312
Electricity generated by coal (% of total)	..	68.2	47.4
Emissions and pollution			
CO_2 emissions per unit of GDP (kg/2000 PPP$ GDP)	0.1	0.4	0.4
CO_2 emissions per capita (metric tons)	0.2	0.7	0.8
Particulate matter (pop. weighted average, µg/cu. m)	246	54	63
Passenger cars (per 1,000 people)	..	..	..
Water and sanitation			
Internal freshwater resources per capita (cu. m)	894	5,546	3,583
Freshwater withdrawal			
Total (% of internal resources)	59.3	1.8	11.5
Agriculture (% of total freshwater withdrawal)	94	85	92
Access to improved water source (% of total population)	69	58	75
Rural (% of rural population)	64	46	70
Urban (% of urban population)	78	82	89
Access to sanitation (% of total population)	34	36	36
Rural (% of rural population)	24	26	24
Urban (% of urban population)	50	55	61
Under-five mortality rate (per 1,000)	93	171	123
National accounting aggregates, 2003			
Gross national savings (% of GNI)	22.4	16.9	23.1
Consumption of fixed capital (% of GNI)	8.9	10.6	8.9
Education expenditure (% of GNI)	0.9	4.7	3.4
Energy depletion (% of GNI)	0.0	8.0	5.8
Mineral depletion (% of GNI)	0.0	0.5	0.3
Net forest depletion (% of GNI)	0.0	0.7	0.8
CO_2 damage (% of GNI)	0.2	0.9	1.2
Particulate emission damage (% of GNI)	0.6	0.4	0.6
Adjusted net savings (% of GNI)	13.6	0.6	8.9

Suriname

Environmental strategy/action plan prepared in ..

	Country data	Latin America & Caribbean	Lower middle income
		Group data	
Population (millions)	0.4	533	2,655
Urban population (% of total)	76.0	76.6	49.8
GDP ($ billions)	1.2	1,741	4,168
GNI per capita, *Atlas* method ($)	2,280	3,280	1,490
Agriculture and fisheries			
Land area (1,000 sq. km)	156	20,057	56,103
Agricultural land (% of land area)	1	39	35
Irrigated land (% of crop land)	76.1	12.5	20.8
Fertilizer consumption (100 grams/ha arable land)	982	892	1,170
Population density, rural (people/sq. km arable land)	188	210	497
Fish catch, total (1,000 metric tons)	19	17,804	74,407
Forests			
Forest area (1,000 sq. km)	141	9,552	20,316
Forest area share of total land area (%)	90.5	47.6	36.2
Annual deforestation (% change, 1990–2000)	0.0	0.5	0.1
Biodiversity			
Mammal species, total known	180		
Mammal species, threatened	12		
Bird species, total breeding	235		
Bird species, threatened	1		
Nationally protected area (% of land area)	4.9	11.2	7.7
Energy			
GDP per unit of energy use (2000 PPP$/kg oil equiv)	..	6.1	4.1
Energy use per capita (kg oil equiv)	..	1,156	1,227
Energy from biomass products and waste (% of total)	..	14.6	12.3
Energy imports, net (% of energy use)	..	−42	−22
Electric power consumption per capita (kWh)	..	1,506	1,289
Electricity generated by coal (% of total)	..	5.0	42.8
Emissions and pollution			
CO_2 emissions per unit of GDP (kg/2000 PPP$ GDP)	..	0.4	0.6
CO_2 emissions per capita (metric tons)	5.0	2.7	2.9
Particulate matter (pop. weighted average, µg/cu. m)	51	40	49
Passenger cars (per 1,000 people)	43	..	28
Water and sanitation			
Internal freshwater resources per capita (cu. m)	200,866	25,245	8,397
Freshwater withdrawal			
Total (% of internal resources)	0.6	2.0	5.9
Agriculture (% of total freshwater withdrawal)	89	74	74
Access to improved water source (% of total population)	92	89	82
Rural (% of rural population)	73	69	71
Urban (% of urban population)	98	96	94
Access to sanitation (% of total population)	93	74	60
Rural (% of rural population)	76	44	41
Urban (% of urban population)	99	84	80
Under-five mortality rate (per 1,000)	39	33	39
National accounting aggregates, 2003			
Gross national savings (% of GNI)	−1.9	19.5	30.6
Consumption of fixed capital (% of GNI)	9.1	10.3	9.8
Education expenditure (% of GNI)	..	4.2	3.2
Energy depletion (% of GNI)	0.0	6.4	8.1
Mineral depletion (% of GNI)	0.4	0.7	0.4
Net forest depletion (% of GNI)	0.0	0.0	0.1
CO_2 damage (% of GNI)	1.4	0.5	1.6
Particulate emission damage (% of GNI)	..	0.5	0.7
Adjusted net savings (% of GNI)	..	5.3	13.2

Swaziland

Environmental strategy/action plan prepared in ..

	Country data	Group data Sub-Saharan Africa	Group data Lower middle income
Population (millions)	1.1	705	2,655
Urban population (% of total)	27.4	36.5	49.8
GDP ($ billions)	1.8	439	4,168
GNI per capita, *Atlas* method ($)	1,350	500	1,490
Agriculture and fisheries			
Land area (1,000 sq. km)	17	23,596	56,103
Agricultural land (% of land area)	81	43	35
Irrigated land (% of crop land)	36.8	4.2	20.8
Fertilizer consumption (100 grams/ha arable land)	393	145	1,170
Population density, rural (people/sq. km arable land)	446	352	497
Fish catch, total (1,000 metric tons)	0	5,191	74,407
Forests			
Forest area (1,000 sq. km)	5	6,435	20,316
Forest area share of total land area (%)	30.3	27.3	36.2
Annual deforestation (% change, 1990–2000)	−1.2	0.8	0.1
Biodiversity			
Mammal species, total known	..		
Mammal species, threatened	4		
Bird species, total breeding	..		
Bird species, threatened	5		
Nationally protected area (% of land area)	..	8.7	7.7
Energy			
GDP per unit of energy use (2000 PPP$/kg oil equiv)	..	2.8	4.1
Energy use per capita (kg oil equiv)	..	667	1,227
Energy from biomass products and waste (% of total)	..	57.5	12.3
Energy imports, net (% of energy use)	..	−56	−22
Electric power consumption per capita (kWh)	..	457	1,289
Electricity generated by coal (% of total)	..	68.2	42.8
Emissions and pollution			
CO_2 emissions per unit of GDP (kg/2000 PPP$ GDP)	0.1	0.4	0.6
CO_2 emissions per capita (metric tons)	0.4	0.7	2.9
Particulate matter (pop. weighted average, µg/cu. m)	40	54	49
Passenger cars (per 1,000 people)	41	..	28
Water and sanitation			
Internal freshwater resources per capita (cu. m)	2,389	5,546	8,397
Freshwater withdrawal			
Total (% of internal resources)	..	1.8	5.9
Agriculture (% of total freshwater withdrawal)	96	85	74
Access to improved water source (% of total population)	52	58	82
Rural (% of rural population)	42	46	71
Urban (% of urban population)	87	82	94
Access to sanitation (% of total population)	52	36	60
Rural (% of rural population)	44	26	41
Urban (% of urban population)	78	55	80
Under-five mortality rate (per 1,000)	153	171	39
National accounting aggregates, 2003			
Gross national savings (% of GNI)	14.2	16.9	30.6
Consumption of fixed capital (% of GNI)	9.4	10.6	9.8
Education expenditure (% of GNI)	5.1	4.7	3.2
Energy depletion (% of GNI)	0.0	8.0	8.1
Mineral depletion (% of GNI)	0.0	0.5	0.4
Net forest depletion (% of GNI)	0.0	0.7	0.1
CO_2 damage (% of GNI)	0.2	0.9	1.6
Particulate emission damage (% of GNI)	0.1	0.4	0.7
Adjusted net savings (% of GNI)	9.7	0.6	13.2

Sweden

Environmental strategy/action plan prepared in ..

	Country data	Group data High income
Population (millions)	9.0	972
Urban population (% of total)	83.4	79.9
GDP ($ billions)	302	29,341
GNI per capita, *Atlas* method ($)	28,910	28,600
Agriculture and fisheries		
Land area (1,000 sq. km)	412	31,030
Agricultural land (% of land area)	8	36
Irrigated land (% of crop land)	4.3	12.3
Fertilizer consumption (100 grams/ha arable land)	1,000	1,198
Population density, rural (people/sq. km arable land)	56	202
Fish catch, total (1,000 metric tons)	319	28,712
Forests		
Forest area (1,000 sq. km)	271	7,929
Forest area share of total land area (%)	65.9	25.9
Annual deforestation (% change, 1990–2000)	0.0	−0.1
Biodiversity		
Mammal species, total known	60	
Mammal species, threatened	7	
Bird species, total breeding	259	
Bird species, threatened	2	
Nationally protected area (% of land area)	9.1	19.5
Energy		
GDP per unit of energy use (2000 PPP$/kg oil equiv)	4.4	5.2
Energy use per capita (kg oil equiv)	5,718	5,395
Energy from biomass products and waste (% of total)	16.3	3.1
Energy imports, net (% of energy use)	37	26
Electric power consumption per capita (kWh)	14,742	8,693
Electricity generated by coal (% of total)	2.6	38.2
Emissions and pollution		
CO_2 emissions per unit of GDP (kg/2000 PPP$ GDP)	0.2	0.5
CO_2 emissions per capita (metric tons)	5.3	12.4
Particulate matter (pop. weighted average, µg/cu. m)	15	33
Passenger cars (per 1,000 people)	452	436
Water and sanitation		
Internal freshwater resources per capita (cu. m)	19,093	9,479
Freshwater withdrawal		
Total (% of internal resources)	1.7	9.7
Agriculture (% of total freshwater withdrawal)	9	42
Access to improved water source (% of total population)	100	99
Rural (% of rural population)	100	98
Urban (% of urban population)	100	100
Access to sanitation (% of total population)	100	..
Rural (% of rural population)	100	..
Urban (% of urban population)	100	..
Under-five mortality rate (per 1,000)	4	7
National accounting aggregates, 2003		
Gross national savings (% of GNI)	23.1	19.1
Consumption of fixed capital (% of GNI)	13.9	13.2
Education expenditure (% of GNI)	7.7	4.6
Energy depletion (% of GNI)	0.0	0.8
Mineral depletion (% of GNI)	0.1	0.0
Net forest depletion (% of GNI)	0.0	0.0
CO_2 damage (% of GNI)	0.1	0.3
Particulate emission damage (% of GNI)	0.0	0.3
Adjusted net savings (% of GNI)	16.7	9.2

Switzerland

Environmental strategy/action plan prepared in ..

	Country data	Group data: High income
Population (millions)	7.4	972
Urban population (% of total)	67.5	79.9
GDP ($ billions)	320	29,341
GNI per capita, *Atlas* method ($)	40,680	28,600

Agriculture and fisheries

Land area (1,000 sq. km)	40	31,030
Agricultural land (% of land area)	40	36
Irrigated land (% of crop land)	5.8	12.3
Fertilizer consumption (100 grams/ha arable land)	2,275	1,198
Population density, rural (people/sq. km arable land)	579	202
Fish catch, total (1,000 metric tons)	3	28,712

Forests

Forest area (1,000 sq. km)	12	7,929
Forest area share of total land area (%)	30.3	25.9
Annual deforestation (% change, 1990–2000)	–0.4	–0.1

Biodiversity

Mammal species, total known	75	
Mammal species, threatened	5	
Bird species, total breeding	199	
Bird species, threatened	2	
Nationally protected area (% of land area)	30.0	19.5

Energy

GDP per unit of energy use (2000 PPP$/kg oil equiv)	7.8	5.2
Energy use per capita (kg oil equiv)	3,723	5,395
Energy from biomass products and waste (% of total)	6.1	3.1
Energy imports, net (% of energy use)	56	26
Electric power consumption per capita (kWh)	7,381	8,693
Electricity generated by coal (% of total)	..	38.2

Emissions and pollution

CO_2 emissions per unit of GDP (kg/2000 PPP$ GDP)	0.2	0.5
CO_2 emissions per capita (metric tons)	5.4	12.4
Particulate matter (pop. weighted average, µg/cu. m)	26	33
Passenger cars (per 1,000 people)	507	436

Water and sanitation

Internal freshwater resources per capita (cu. m)	5,442	9,479
Freshwater withdrawal		
Total (% of internal resources)	3.0	9.7
Agriculture (% of total freshwater withdrawal)	4	42
Access to improved water source (% of total population)	100	99
Rural (% of rural population)	100	98
Urban (% of urban population)	100	100
Access to sanitation (% of total population)	100	..
Rural (% of rural population)	100	..
Urban (% of urban population)	100	..
Under-five mortality rate (per 1,000)	6	7

National accounting aggregates, 2003

Gross national savings (% of GNI)	..	19.1
Consumption of fixed capital (% of GNI)	14.9	13.2
Education expenditure (% of GNI)	4.9	4.6
Energy depletion (% of GNI)	0.0	0.8
Mineral depletion (% of GNI)	0.0	0.0
Net forest depletion (% of GNI)	0.0	0.0
CO_2 damage (% of GNI)	0.1	0.3
Particulate emission damage (% of GNI)	0.2	0.3
Adjusted net savings (% of GNI)	..	9.2

Syrian Arab Republic

Environmental strategy/action plan prepared in **1999**

	Country data	Middle East & North Africa	Lower middle income
		Group data	
Population (millions)	17.4	312	2,655
Urban population (% of total)	52.5	59.0	49.8
GDP ($ billions)	21.5	745	4,168
GNI per capita, *Atlas* method ($)	1,160	2,390	1,490
Agriculture and fisheries			
Land area (1,000 sq. km)	184	11,111	56,103
Agricultural land (% of land area)	75	34	35
Irrigated land (% of crop land)	24.6	38.3	20.8
Fertilizer consumption (100 grams/ha arable land)	703	854	1,170
Population density, rural (people/sq. km arable land)	177	603	497
Fish catch, total (1,000 metric tons)	14	2,840	74,407
Forests			
Forest area (1,000 sq. km)	5	168	20,316
Forest area share of total land area (%)	2.5	1.5	36.2
Annual deforestation (% change, 1990–2000)	0.0	–0.1	0.1
Biodiversity			
Mammal species, total known	63		
Mammal species, threatened	4		
Bird species, total breeding	145		
Bird species, threatened	8		
Nationally protected area (% of land area)	..	11.3	7.7
Energy			
GDP per unit of energy use (2000 PPP$/kg oil equiv)	3.2	3.5	4.1
Energy use per capita (kg oil equiv)	1,063	1,504	1,227
Energy from biomass products and waste (% of total)	0.0	1.0	12.3
Energy imports, net (% of energy use)	–103	–168	–22
Electric power consumption per capita (kWh)	1,000	1,412	1,289
Electricity generated by coal (% of total)	..	2.3	42.8
Emissions and pollution			
CO_2 emissions per unit of GDP (kg/2000 PPP$ GDP)	1.0	0.8	0.6
CO_2 emissions per capita (metric tons)	3.3	4.2	2.9
Particulate matter (pop. weighted average, µg/cu. m)	102	87	49
Passenger cars (per 1,000 people)	9	..	28
Water and sanitation			
Internal freshwater resources per capita (cu. m)	403	761	8,397
Freshwater withdrawal			
Total (% of internal resources)	171.4	101.7	5.9
Agriculture (% of total freshwater withdrawal)	90	88	74
Access to improved water source (% of total population)	79	88	82
Rural (% of rural population)	64	78	71
Urban (% of urban population)	94	96	94
Access to sanitation (% of total population)	77	75	60
Rural (% of rural population)	56	56	41
Urban (% of urban population)	97	90	80
Under-five mortality rate (per 1,000)	18	53	39
National accounting aggregates, 2003			
Gross national savings (% of GNI)	28.0	31.2	30.6
Consumption of fixed capital (% of GNI)	9.7	10.0	9.8
Education expenditure (% of GNI)	3.5	5.5	3.2
Energy depletion (% of GNI)	33.1	30.7	8.1
Mineral depletion (% of GNI)	0.1	0.1	0.4
Net forest depletion (% of GNI)	0.0	0.0	0.1
CO_2 damage (% of GNI)	1.7	1.2	1.6
Particulate emission damage (% of GNI)	0.8	0.8	0.7
Adjusted net savings (% of GNI)	–13.9	–6.2	13.2

Tajikistan

	Country data	Europe & Central Asia	Low Income
		Group data	
Population (millions)	6.3	472	2,312
Urban population (% of total)	27.6	63.8	30.4
GDP ($ billions)	1.6	1,403	1,103
GNI per capita, *Atlas* method ($)	210	2,580	440
Agriculture and fisheries			
Land area (1,000 sq. km)	141	23,868	30,456
Agricultural land (% of land area)	32	28	43
Irrigated land (% of crop land)	68.0	10.9	26.7
Fertilizer consumption (100 grams/ha arable land)	300	344	654
Population density, rural (people/sq. km arable land)	488	122	509
Fish catch, total (1,000 metric tons)	0	5,527	16,410
Forests			
Forest area (1,000 sq. km)	4	9,463	7,939
Forest area share of total land area (%)	2.8	39.6	26.1
Annual deforestation (% change, 1990–2000)	–0.5	–0.1	0.7
Biodiversity			
Mammal species, total known	84		
Mammal species, threatened	9		
Bird species, total breeding	210		
Bird species, threatened	7		
Nationally protected area (% of land area)	4.2	6.8	7.7
Energy			
GDP per unit of energy use (2000 PPP$/kg oil equiv)	1.8	2.5	4.1
Energy use per capita (kg oil equiv)	518	2,697	493
Energy from biomass products and waste (% of total)	..	2.3	49.4
Energy imports, net (% of energy use)	59	–23	–6
Electric power consumption per capita (kWh)	2,236	2,808	312
Electricity generated by coal (% of total)	..	29.4	47.4
Emissions and pollution			
CO_2 emissions per unit of GDP (kg/2000 PPP$ GDP)	0.8	1.1	0.4
CO_2 emissions per capita (metric tons)	0.6	6.7	0.8
Particulate matter (pop. weighted average, µg/cu. m)	64	33	63
Passenger cars (per 1,000 people)	..	138	..
Water and sanitation			
Internal freshwater resources per capita (cu. m)	10,468	11,128	3,583
Freshwater withdrawal			
Total (% of internal resources)	18.0	7.4	11.5
Agriculture (% of total freshwater withdrawal)	92	57	92
Access to improved water source (% of total population)	58	91	75
Rural (% of rural population)	47	80	70
Urban (% of urban population)	93	98	89
Access to sanitation (% of total population)	53	82	36
Rural (% of rural population)	47	64	24
Urban (% of urban population)	71	93	61
Under-five mortality rate (per 1,000)	95	36	123
National accounting aggregates, 2003			
Gross national savings (% of GNI)	–7.6	21.9	23.1
Consumption of fixed capital (% of GNI)	7.6	10.7	8.9
Education expenditure (% of GNI)	2.0	4.1	3.4
Energy depletion (% of GNI)	0.2	11.6	5.8
Mineral depletion (% of GNI)	0.0	0.1	0.3
Net forest depletion (% of GNI)	0.0	0.0	0.8
CO_2 damage (% of GNI)	3.4	1.9	1.2
Particulate emission damage (% of GNI)	0.2	0.6	0.6
Adjusted net savings (% of GNI)	–16.9	1.1	8.9

Tanzania

Environmental strategy/action plan prepared in **1994**

	Country data	Group data Sub-Saharan Africa	Group data Low income
Population (millions)	35.9	705	2,312
Urban population (% of total)	35.4	36.5	30.4
GDP ($ billions)	10.3	439	1,103
GNI per capita, *Atlas* method ($)	300	500	440
Agriculture and fisheries			
Land area (1,000 sq. km)	884	23,596	30,456
Agricultural land (% of land area)	45	43	43
Irrigated land (% of crop land)	3.3	4.2	26.7
Fertilizer consumption (100 grams/ha arable land)	18	145	654
Population density, rural (people/sq. km arable land)	578	352	509
Fish catch, total (1,000 metric tons)	336	5,191	16,410
Forests			
Forest area (1,000 sq. km)	388	6,435	7,939
Forest area share of total land area (%)	43.9	27.3	26.1
Annual deforestation (% change, 1990–2000)	0.2	0.8	0.7
Biodiversity			
Mammal species, total known	316		
Mammal species, threatened	42		
Bird species, total breeding	229		
Bird species, threatened	33		
Nationally protected area (% of land area)	29.8	8.7	7.7
Energy			
GDP per unit of energy use (2000 PPP$/kg oil equiv)	1.4	2.8	4.1
Energy use per capita (kg oil equiv)	408	667	493
Energy from biomass products and waste (% of total)	90.7	57.5	49.4
Energy imports, net (% of energy use)	7	−56	−6
Electric power consumption per capita (kWh)	62	457	312
Electricity generated by coal (% of total)	3.5	68.2	47.4
Emissions and pollution			
CO_2 emissions per unit of GDP (kg/2000 PPP$ GDP)	0.2	0.4	0.4
CO_2 emissions per capita (metric tons)	0.1	0.7	0.8
Particulate matter (pop. weighted average, µg/cu. m)	37	54	63
Passenger cars (per 1,000 people)	..	..	..
Water and sanitation			
Internal freshwater resources per capita (cu. m)	2,285	5,546	3,583
Freshwater withdrawal			
Total (% of internal resources)	1.5	1.8	11.5
Agriculture (% of total freshwater withdrawal)	89	85	92
Access to improved water source (% of total population)	73	58	75
Rural (% of rural population)	62	46	70
Urban (% of urban population)	92	82	89
Access to sanitation (% of total population)	46	36	36
Rural (% of rural population)	41	26	24
Urban (% of urban population)	54	55	61
Under-five mortality rate (per 1,000)	165	171	123
National accounting aggregates, 2003			
Gross national savings (% of GNI)	9.4	16.9	23.1
Consumption of fixed capital (% of GNI)	7.4	10.6	8.9
Education expenditure (% of GNI)	2.4	4.7	3.4
Energy depletion (% of GNI)	0.0	8.0	5.8
Mineral depletion (% of GNI)	0.5	0.5	0.3
Net forest depletion (% of GNI)	0.0	0.7	0.8
CO_2 damage (% of GNI)	0.2	0.9	1.2
Particulate emission damage (% of GNI)	0.2	0.4	0.6
Adjusted net savings (% of GNI)	3.4	0.6	8.9

Thailand

Environmental strategy/action plan prepared in ..

	Country data	East Asia & Pacific	Lower middle income
		Group data	
Population (millions)	62.0	1,855	2,655
Urban population (% of total)	20.4	39.1	49.8
GDP ($ billions)	143.0	2,033	4,168
GNI per capita, *Atlas* method ($)	2,190	1,070	1,490
Agriculture and fisheries			
Land area (1,000 sq. km)	511	15,886	56,103
Agricultural land (% of land area)	37	50	35
Irrigated land (% of crop land)	25.6	..	20.8
Fertilizer consumption (100 grams/ha arable land)	1,072	2,297	1,170
Population density, rural (people/sq. km arable land)	310	565	497
Fish catch, total (1,000 metric tons)	3,606	60,812	74,407
Forests			
Forest area (1,000 sq. km)	148	4,284	20,316
Forest area share of total land area (%)	28.9	27.0	36.2
Annual deforestation (% change, 1990–2000)	0.7	0.2	0.1
Biodiversity			
Mammal species, total known	265		
Mammal species, threatened	37		
Bird species, total breeding	285		
Bird species, threatened	37		
Nationally protected area (% of land area)	13.9	9.2	7.7
Energy			
GDP per unit of energy use (2000 PPP$/kg oil equiv)	5.0	4.6	4.1
Energy use per capita (kg oil equiv)	1,353	904	1,227
Energy from biomass products and waste (% of total)	16.4	19.6	12.3
Energy imports, net (% of energy use)	46	–4	–22
Electric power consumption per capita (kWh)	1,626	891	1,289
Electricity generated by coal (% of total)	16.5	66.8	42.8
Emissions and pollution			
CO_2 emissions per unit of GDP (kg/2000 PPP$ GDP)	0.5	0.5	0.6
CO_2 emissions per capita (metric tons)	3.3	2.1	2.9
Particulate matter (pop. weighted average, μg/cu. m)	76	69	49
Passenger cars (per 1,000 people)	..	10	28
Water and sanitation			
Internal freshwater resources per capita (cu. m)	3,386	5,103	8,397
Freshwater withdrawal			
Total (% of internal resources)	15.8	8.2	5.9
Agriculture (% of total freshwater withdrawal)	91	81	74
Access to improved water source (% of total population)	85	78	82
Rural (% of rural population)	80	69	71
Urban (% of urban population)	95	92	94
Access to sanitation (% of total population)	99	49	60
Rural (% of rural population)	100	35	41
Urban (% of urban population)	97	71	80
Under-five mortality rate (per 1,000)	26	41	39
National accounting aggregates, 2003			
Gross national savings (% of GNI)	31.1	41.7	30.6
Consumption of fixed capital (% of GNI)	15.0	9.2	9.8
Education expenditure (% of GNI)	3.6	2.3	3.2
Energy depletion (% of GNI)	2.0	3.9	8.1
Mineral depletion (% of GNI)	0.0	0.3	0.4
Net forest depletion (% of GNI)	0.3	0.1	0.1
CO_2 damage (% of GNI)	1.0	1.8	1.6
Particulate emission damage (% of GNI)	0.4	0.8	0.7
Adjusted net savings (% of GNI)	16.1	27.9	13.2

Timor-Leste

Environmental strategy/action plan prepared in ..

	Country data	Group data	
		East Asia & Pacific	Low Income
Population (millions)	0.9	1,855	2,312
Urban population (% of total)	7.7	39.1	30.4
GDP ($ billions)	0.3	2,033	1,103
GNI per capita, *Atlas* method ($)	460	1,070	440
Agriculture and fisheries			
Land area (1,000 sq. km)	15	15,886	30,456
Agricultural land (% of land area)	15	50	43
Irrigated land (% of crop land)	..	..	26.7
Fertilizer consumption (100 grams/ha arable land)	..	2,297	654
Population density, rural (people/sq. km arable land)	1,098	565	509
Fish catch, total (1,000 metric tons)	0	60,812	16,410
Forests			
Forest area (1,000 sq. km)	5	4,284	7,939
Forest area share of total land area (%)	34.1	27.0	26.1
Annual deforestation (% change, 1990–2000)	0.6	0.2	0.7
Biodiversity			
Mammal species, total known	..		
Mammal species, threatened	0		
Bird species, total breeding	..		
Bird species, threatened	6		
Nationally protected area (% of land area)	..	9.2	7.7
Energy			
GDP per unit of energy use (2000 PPP$/kg oil equiv)	..	4.6	4.1
Energy use per capita (kg oil equiv)	..	904	493
Energy from biomass products and waste (% of total)	..	19.6	49.4
Energy imports, net (% of energy use)	..	–4	–6
Electric power consumption per capita (kWh)	..	891	312
Electricity generated by coal (% of total)	..	66.8	47.4
Emissions and pollution			
CO_2 emissions per unit of GDP (kg/2000 PPP$ GDP)	..	0.5	0.4
CO_2 emissions per capita (metric tons)	..	2.1	0.8
Particulate matter (pop. weighted average, µg/cu. m)	..	69	63
Passenger cars (per 1,000 people)	..	10	..
Water and sanitation			
Internal freshwater resources per capita (cu. m)	..	5,103	3,583
Freshwater withdrawal			
Total (% of internal resources)	..	8.2	11.5
Agriculture (% of total freshwater withdrawal)	..	81	92
Access to improved water source (% of total population)	52	78	75
Rural (% of rural population)	51	69	70
Urban (% of urban population)	73	92	89
Access to sanitation (% of total population)	33	49	36
Rural (% of rural population)	30	35	24
Urban (% of urban population)	65	71	61
Under-five mortality rate (per 1,000)	124	41	123
National accounting aggregates, 2003			
Gross national savings (% of GNI)	..	41.7	23.1
Consumption of fixed capital (% of GNI)	..	9.2	8.9
Education expenditure (% of GNI)	..	2.3	3.4
Energy depletion (% of GNI)	..	3.9	5.8
Mineral depletion (% of GNI)	..	0.3	0.3
Net forest depletion (% of GNI)	..	0.1	0.8
CO_2 damage (% of GNI)	..	1.8	1.2
Particulate emission damage (% of GNI)	..	0.8	0.6
Adjusted net savings (% of GNI)	..	27.9	8.9

Togo

Environmental strategy/action plan prepared in **1991**

	Country data	Group data Sub-Saharan Africa	Group data Low income
Population (millions)	4.9	705	2,312
Urban population (% of total)	35.1	36.5	30.4
GDP ($ billions)	1.8	439	1,103
GNI per capita, *Atlas* method ($)	310	500	440
Agriculture and fisheries			
Land area (1,000 sq. km)	54	23,596	30,456
Agricultural land (% of land area)	67	43	43
Irrigated land (% of crop land)	0.7	4.2	26.7
Fertilizer consumption (100 grams/ha arable land)	68	145	654
Population density, rural (people/sq. km arable land)	124	352	509
Fish catch, total (1,000 metric tons)	23	5,191	16,410
Forests			
Forest area (1,000 sq. km)	5	6,435	7,939
Forest area share of total land area (%)	9.4	27.3	26.1
Annual deforestation (% change, 1990–2000)	3.4	0.8	0.7
Biodiversity			
Mammal species, total known	196		
Mammal species, threatened	9		
Bird species, total breeding	117		
Bird species, threatened	0		
Nationally protected area (% of land area)	7.9	8.7	7.7
Energy			
GDP per unit of energy use (2000 PPP$/kg oil equiv)	4.9	2.8	4.1
Energy use per capita (kg oil equiv)	324	667	493
Energy from biomass products and waste (% of total)	70.2	57.5	49.4
Energy imports, net (% of energy use)	30	–56	–6
Electric power consumption per capita (kWh)	..	457	312
Electricity generated by coal (% of total)	..	68.2	47.4
Emissions and pollution			
CO_2 emissions per unit of GDP (kg/2000 PPP$ GDP)	0.2	0.4	0.4
CO_2 emissions per capita (metric tons)	0.4	0.7	0.8
Particulate matter (pop. weighted average, µg/cu. m)	46	54	63
Passenger cars (per 1,000 people)	..	..	..
Water and sanitation			
Internal freshwater resources per capita (cu. m)	2,468	5,546	3,583
Freshwater withdrawal			
Total (% of internal resources)	0.8	1.8	11.5
Agriculture (% of total freshwater withdrawal)	25	85	92
Access to improved water source (% of total population)	51	58	75
Rural (% of rural population)	36	46	70
Urban (% of urban population)	80	82	89
Access to sanitation (% of total population)	34	36	36
Rural (% of rural population)	15	26	24
Urban (% of urban population)	71	55	61
Under-five mortality rate (per 1,000)	140	171	123
National accounting aggregates, 2003			
Gross national savings (% of GNI)	2.0	16.9	23.1
Consumption of fixed capital (% of GNI)	7.9	10.6	8.9
Education expenditure (% of GNI)	4.2	4.7	3.4
Energy depletion (% of GNI)	0.0	8.0	5.8
Mineral depletion (% of GNI)	0.7	0.5	0.3
Net forest depletion (% of GNI)	3.3	0.7	0.8
CO_2 damage (% of GNI)	0.9	0.9	1.2
Particulate emission damage (% of GNI)	0.3	0.4	0.6
Adjusted net savings (% of GNI)	–6.9	0.6	8.9

Tonga

Environmental strategy/action plan prepared in ..

	Country data	Group data East Asia & Pacific	Group data Lower middle Income
Population (millions)	0.1	1,855	2,655
Urban population (% of total)	33.5	39.1	49.8
GDP ($ billions)	0.2	2,033	4,168
GNI per capita, *Atlas* method ($)	1,490	1,070	1,490
Agriculture and fisheries			
Land area (1,000 sq. km)	1	15,886	56,103
Agricultural land (% of land area)	72	50	35
Irrigated land (% of crop land)	..	..	20.8
Fertilizer consumption (100 grams/ha arable land)	..	2,297	1,170
Population density, rural (people/sq. km arable land)	397	565	497
Fish catch, total (1,000 metric tons)	5	60,812	74,407
Forests			
Forest area (1,000 sq. km)	0	4,284	20,316
Forest area share of total land area (%)	5.6	27.0	36.2
Annual deforestation (% change, 1990–2000)	0.0	0.2	0.1
Biodiversity			
Mammal species, total known	..		
Mammal species, threatened	2		
Bird species, total breeding	..		
Bird species, threatened	3		
Nationally protected area (% of land area)	..	9.2	7.7
Energy			
GDP per unit of energy use (2000 PPP$/kg oil equiv)	..	4.6	4.1
Energy use per capita (kg oil equiv)	..	904	1,227
Energy from biomass products and waste (% of total)	..	19.6	12.3
Energy imports, net (% of energy use)	..	-4	-22
Electric power consumption per capita (kWh)	..	891	1,289
Electricity generated by coal (% of total)	..	66.8	42.8
Emissions and pollution			
CO_2 emissions per unit of GDP (kg/2000 PPP$ GDP)	0.2	0.5	0.6
CO_2 emissions per capita (metric tons)	1.2	2.1	2.9
Particulate matter (pop. weighted average, μg/cu. m)	..	69	49
Passenger cars (per 1,000 people)	..	10	28
Water and sanitation			
Internal freshwater resources per capita (cu. m)	..	5,103	8,397
Freshwater withdrawal			
Total (% of internal resources)	..	8.2	5.9
Agriculture (% of total freshwater withdrawal)	..	81	74
Access to improved water source (% of total population)	100	78	82
Rural (% of rural population)	100	69	71
Urban (% of urban population)	100	92	94
Access to sanitation (% of total population)	97	49	60
Rural (% of rural population)	96	35	41
Urban (% of urban population)	98	71	80
Under-five mortality rate (per 1,000)	19	41	39
National accounting aggregates, 2003			
Gross national savings (% of GNI)	..	41.7	30.6
Consumption of fixed capital (% of GNI)	9.7	9.2	9.8
Education expenditure (% of GNI)	4.7	2.3	3.2
Energy depletion (% of GNI)	0.0	3.9	8.1
Mineral depletion (% of GNI)	0.0	0.3	0.4
Net forest depletion (% of GNI)	0.1	0.1	0.1
CO_2 damage (% of GNI)	0.5	1.8	1.6
Particulate emission damage (% of GNI)	..	0.8	0.7
Adjusted net savings (% of GNI)	..	27.9	13.2

Trinidad and Tobago

Environmental strategy/action plan prepared in ..

	Country data	Latin America & Caribbean	Upper middle income
Population (millions)	1.3	533	333
Urban population (% of total)	75.3	76.6	75.4
GDP ($ billions)	10.5	1,741	1,856
GNI per capita, *Atlas* method ($)	7,790	3,280	5,440
Agriculture and fisheries			
Land area (1,000 sq. km)	5	20,057	12,741
Agricultural land (% of land area)	26	39	48
Irrigated land (% of crop land)	3.3	12.5	13.5
Fertilizer consumption (100 grams/ha arable land)	434	892	796
Population density, rural (people/sq. km arable land)	437	210	193
Fish catch, total (1,000 metric tons)	11	17,804	10,082
Forests			
Forest area (1,000 sq. km)	3	9,552	2,427
Forest area share of total land area (%)	50.5	47.6	19.1
Annual deforestation (% change, 1990–2000)	0.8	0.5	0.6
Biodiversity			
Mammal species, total known	100		
Mammal species, threatened	1		
Bird species, total breeding	131		
Bird species, threatened	1		
Nationally protected area (% of land area)	6.0	11.2	17.3
Energy			
GDP per unit of energy use (2000 PPP$/kg oil equiv)	1.3	6.1	4.3
Energy use per capita (kg oil equiv)	7,121	1,156	2,232
Energy from biomass products and waste (% of total)	0.3	14.6	4.1
Energy imports, net (% of energy use)	−130	−42	−91
Electric power consumption per capita (kWh)	4,330	1,506	2,496
Electricity generated by coal (% of total)	..	5.0	23.9
Emissions and pollution			
CO_2 emissions per unit of GDP (kg/2000 PPP$ GDP)	2.3	0.4	0.6
CO_2 emissions per capita (metric tons)	20.5	2.7	6.3
Particulate matter (pop. weighted average, µg/cu. m)	24	40	29
Passenger cars (per 1,000 people)	..	..	153
Water and sanitation			
Internal freshwater resources per capita (cu. m)	3,047	25,245	10,741
Freshwater withdrawal			
Total (% of internal resources)	7.5	2.0	5.7
Agriculture (% of total freshwater withdrawal)	6	74	71
Access to improved water source (% of total population)	91	89	..
Rural (% of rural population)	88	69	..
Urban (% of urban population)	92	96	96
Access to sanitation (% of total population)	100	74	..
Rural (% of rural population)	100	44	..
Urban (% of urban population)	100	84	..
Under-five mortality rate (per 1,000)	20	33	22
National accounting aggregates, 2003			
Gross national savings (% of GNI)	25.9	19.5	22.1
Consumption of fixed capital (% of GNI)	12.2	10.3	10.7
Education expenditure (% of GNI)	3.9	4.2	5.0
Energy depletion (% of GNI)	38.5	6.4	11.4
Mineral depletion (% of GNI)	0.0	0.7	0.3
Net forest depletion (% of GNI)	0.0	0.0	0.0
CO_2 damage (% of GNI)	1.9	0.5	0.8
Particulate emission damage (% of GNI)	0.0	0.5	0.6
Adjusted net savings (% of GNI)	−22.8	5.3	3.3

Tunisia

Environmental strategy/action plan prepared in **1994**

	Country data	Middle East & North Africa	Lower middle income
		Group data	
Population (millions)	9.9	312	2,655
Urban population (% of total)	67.4	59.0	49.8
GDP ($ billions)	25.0	745	4,168
GNI per capita, *Atlas* method ($)	2,240	2,390	1,490
Agriculture and fisheries			
Land area (1,000 sq. km)	155	11,111	56,103
Agricultural land (% of land area)	58	34	35
Irrigated land (% of crop land)	7.8	38.3	20.8
Fertilizer consumption (100 grams/ha arable land)	368	854	1,170
Population density, rural (people/sq. km arable land)	117	603	497
Fish catch, total (1,000 metric tons)	100	2,840	74,407
Forests			
Forest area (1,000 sq. km)	5	168	20,316
Forest area share of total land area (%)	3.3	1.5	36.2
Annual deforestation (% change, 1990–2000)	–0.2	–0.1	0.1
Biodiversity			
Mammal species, total known	78		
Mammal species, threatened	11		
Bird species, total breeding	165		
Bird species, threatened	5		
Nationally protected area (% of land area)	0.3	11.3	7.7
Energy			
GDP per unit of energy use (2000 PPP$/kg oil equiv)	7.7	3.5	4.1
Energy use per capita (kg oil equiv)	846	1,504	1,227
Energy from biomass products and waste (% of total)	15.3	1.0	12.3
Energy imports, net (% of energy use)	16	–168	–22
Electric power consumption per capita (kWh)	1,019	1,412	1,289
Electricity generated by coal (% of total)	..	2.3	42.8
Emissions and pollution			
CO_2 emissions per unit of GDP (kg/2000 PPP$ GDP)	0.3	0.8	0.6
CO_2 emissions per capita (metric tons)	1.9	4.2	2.9
Particulate matter (pop. weighted average, µg/cu. m)	47	87	49
Passenger cars (per 1,000 people)	53	..	28
Water and sanitation			
Internal freshwater resources per capita (cu. m)	404	761	8,397
Freshwater withdrawal			
Total (% of internal resources)	70.0	101.7	5.9
Agriculture (% of total freshwater withdrawal)	86	88	74
Access to improved water source (% of total population)	82	88	82
Rural (% of rural population)	60	78	71
Urban (% of urban population)	94	96	94
Access to sanitation (% of total population)	80	75	60
Rural (% of rural population)	62	56	41
Urban (% of urban population)	90	90	80
Under-five mortality rate (per 1,000)	24	53	39
National accounting aggregates, 2003			
Gross national savings (% of GNI)	22.9	31.2	30.6
Consumption of fixed capital (% of GNI)	10.0	10.0	9.8
Education expenditure (% of GNI)	6.4	5.5	3.2
Energy depletion (% of GNI)	3.7	30.7	8.1
Mineral depletion (% of GNI)	0.4	0.1	0.4
Net forest depletion (% of GNI)	0.1	0.0	0.1
CO_2 damage (% of GNI)	0.6	1.2	1.6
Particulate emission damage (% of GNI)	0.3	0.8	0.7
Adjusted net savings (% of GNI)	14.0	–6.2	13.2

Turkey

Environmental strategy/action plan prepared in **1998**

	Country data	Europe & Central Asia	Lower middle income
		Group data	
Population (millions)	70.7	472	2,655
Urban population (% of total)	67.0	63.8	49.8
GDP ($ billions)	240.4	1,403	4,168
GNI per capita, *Atlas* method ($)	2,800	2,580	1,490
Agriculture and fisheries			
Land area (1,000 sq. km)	770	23,868	56,103
Agricultural land (% of land area)	50	28	35
Irrigated land (% of crop land)	18.3	10.9	20.8
Fertilizer consumption (100 grams/ha arable land)	672	344	1,170
Population density, rural (people/sq. km arable land)	90	122	497
Fish catch, total (1,000 metric tons)	595	5,527	74,407
Forests			
Forest area (1,000 sq. km)	102	9,463	20,316
Forest area share of total land area (%)	13.3	39.6	36.2
Annual deforestation (% change, 1990–2000)	–0.2	–0.1	0.1
Biodiversity			
Mammal species, total known	116		
Mammal species, threatened	17		
Bird species, total breeding	278		
Bird species, threatened	11		
Nationally protected area (% of land area)	1.6	6.8	7.7
Energy			
GDP per unit of energy use (2000 PPP$/kg oil equiv)	5.7	2.5	4.1
Energy use per capita (kg oil equiv)	1,083	2,697	1,227
Energy from biomass products and waste (% of total)	8.0	2.3	12.3
Energy imports, net (% of energy use)	68	–23	–22
Electric power consumption per capita (kWh)	1,458	2,808	1,289
Electricity generated by coal (% of total)	24.8	29.4	42.8
Emissions and pollution			
CO_2 emissions per unit of GDP (kg/2000 PPP$ GDP)	0.5	1.1	0.6
CO_2 emissions per capita (metric tons)	3.3	6.7	2.9
Particulate matter (pop. weighted average, µg/cu. m)	54	33	49
Passenger cars (per 1,000 people)	66	138	28
Water and sanitation			
Internal freshwater resources per capita (cu. m)	3,210	11,128	8,397
Freshwater withdrawal			
Total (% of internal resources)	15.6	7.4	5.9
Agriculture (% of total freshwater withdrawal)	73	57	74
Access to improved water source (% of total population)	93	91	82
Rural (% of rural population)	87	80	71
Urban (% of urban population)	96	98	94
Access to sanitation (% of total population)	83	82	60
Rural (% of rural population)	62	64	41
Urban (% of urban population)	94	93	80
Under-five mortality rate (per 1,000)	39	36	39
National accounting aggregates, 2003			
Gross national savings (% of GNI)	19.2	21.9	30.6
Consumption of fixed capital (% of GNI)	7.0	10.7	9.8
Education expenditure (% of GNI)	3.3	4.1	3.2
Energy depletion (% of GNI)	0.2	11.6	8.1
Mineral depletion (% of GNI)	0.0	0.1	0.4
Net forest depletion (% of GNI)	0.0	0.0	0.1
CO_2 damage (% of GNI)	0.6	1.9	1.6
Particulate emission damage (% of GNI)	1.2	0.6	0.7
Adjusted net savings (% of GNI)	13.5	1.1	13.2

Turkmenistan

Environmental strategy/action plan prepared in ..

	Country data	Europe & Central Asia	Lower middle income
		Group data	
Population (millions)	4.9	472	2,655
Urban population (% of total)	45.4	63.8	49.8
GDP ($ billions)	6.2	1,403	4,168
GNI per capita, *Atlas* method ($)	1,120	2,580	1,490
Agriculture and fisheries			
Land area (1,000 sq. km)	470	23,868	56,103
Agricultural land (% of land area)	69	28	35
Irrigated land (% of crop land)	94.0	10.9	20.8
Fertilizer consumption (100 grams/ha arable land)	529	344	1,170
Population density, rural (people/sq. km arable land)	142	122	497
Fish catch, total (1,000 metric tons)	13	5,527	74,407
Forests			
Forest area (1,000 sq. km)	38	9,463	20,316
Forest area share of total land area (%)	8.0	39.6	36.2
Annual deforestation (% change, 1990–2000)	0.0	–0.1	0.1
Biodiversity			
Mammal species, total known	103		
Mammal species, threatened	13		
Bird species, total breeding	204		
Bird species, threatened	6		
Nationally protected area (% of land area)	4.2	6.8	7.7
Energy			
GDP per unit of energy use (2000 PPP$/kg oil equiv)	1.4	2.5	4.1
Energy use per capita (kg oil equiv)	3,465	2,697	1,227
Energy from biomass products and waste (% of total)	..	2.3	12.3
Energy imports, net (% of energy use)	–223	–23	–22
Electric power consumption per capita (kWh)	1,371	2,808	1,289
Electricity generated by coal (% of total)	..	29.4	42.8
Emissions and pollution			
CO_2 emissions per unit of GDP (kg/2000 PPP$ GDP)	2.0	1.1	0.6
CO_2 emissions per capita (metric tons)	7.5	6.7	2.9
Particulate matter (pop. weighted average, µg/cu. m)	68	33	49
Passenger cars (per 1,000 people)	..	138	28
Water and sanitation			
Internal freshwater resources per capita (cu. m)	206	11,128	8,397
Freshwater withdrawal			
Total (% of internal resources)	2,380.0	7.4	5.9
Agriculture (% of total freshwater withdrawal)	98	57	74
Access to improved water source (% of total population)	71	91	82
Rural (% of rural population)	54	80	71
Urban (% of urban population)	93	98	94
Access to sanitation (% of total population)	62	82	60
Rural (% of rural population)	50	64	41
Urban (% of urban population)	77	93	80
Under-five mortality rate (per 1,000)	102	36	39
National accounting aggregates, 2003			
Gross national savings (% of GNI)	..	21.9	30.6
Consumption of fixed capital (% of GNI)	9.4	10.7	9.8
Education expenditure (% of GNI)	..	4.1	3.2
Energy depletion (% of GNI)	108.9	11.6	8.1
Mineral depletion (% of GNI)	0.0	0.1	0.4
Net forest depletion (% of GNI)	0.0	0.0	0.1
CO_2 damage (% of GNI)	7.4	1.9	1.6
Particulate emission damage (% of GNI)	0.3	0.6	0.7
Adjusted net savings (% of GNI)	..	1.1	13.2

Uganda

Environmental strategy/action plan prepared in **1994**

	Country data	Sub-Saharan Africa	Low income
		Group data	
Population (millions)	25.3	705	2,312
Urban population (% of total)	15.3	36.5	30.4
GDP ($ billions)	6.3	439	1,103
GNI per capita, *Atlas* method ($)	250	500	440
Agriculture and fisheries			
Land area (1,000 sq. km)	197	23,596	30,456
Agricultural land (% of land area)	62	43	43
Irrigated land (% of crop land)	0.1	4.2	26.7
Fertilizer consumption (100 grams/ha arable land)	18	145	654
Population density, rural (people/sq. km arable land)	410	352	509
Fish catch, total (1,000 metric tons)	223	5,191	16,410
Forests			
Forest area (1,000 sq. km)	42	6,435	7,939
Forest area share of total land area (%)	21.3	27.3	26.1
Annual deforestation (% change, 1990–2000)	2.0	0.8	0.7
Biodiversity			
Mammal species, total known	345		
Mammal species, threatened	20		
Bird species, total breeding	243		
Bird species, threatened	13		
Nationally protected area (% of land area)	24.6	8.7	7.7
Energy			
GDP per unit of energy use (2000 PPP$/kg oil equiv)	..	2.8	4.1
Energy use per capita (kg oil equiv)	..	667	493
Energy from biomass products and waste (% of total)	..	57.5	49.4
Energy imports, net (% of energy use)	..	−56	−6
Electric power consumption per capita (kWh)	..	457	312
Electricity generated by coal (% of total)	..	68.2	47.4
Emissions and pollution			
CO_2 emissions per unit of GDP (kg/2000 PPP$ GDP)	0.1	0.4	0.4
CO_2 emissions per capita (metric tons)	0.1	0.7	0.8
Particulate matter (pop. weighted average, µg/cu. m)	16	54	63
Passenger cars (per 1,000 people)	..	..	..
Water and sanitation			
Internal freshwater resources per capita (cu. m)	1,543	5,546	3,583
Freshwater withdrawal			
Total (% of internal resources)	0.5	1.8	11.5
Agriculture (% of total freshwater withdrawal)	60	85	92
Access to improved water source (% of total population)	56	58	75
Rural (% of rural population)	52	46	70
Urban (% of urban population)	87	82	89
Access to sanitation (% of total population)	41	36	36
Rural (% of rural population)	39	26	24
Urban (% of urban population)	53	55	61
Under-five mortality rate (per 1,000)	140	171	123
National accounting aggregates, 2003			
Gross national savings (% of GNI)	17.6	16.9	23.1
Consumption of fixed capital (% of GNI)	7.3	10.6	8.9
Education expenditure (% of GNI)	1.9	4.7	3.4
Energy depletion (% of GNI)	0.0	8.0	5.8
Mineral depletion (% of GNI)	0.0	0.5	0.3
Net forest depletion (% of GNI)	6.9	0.7	0.8
CO_2 damage (% of GNI)	0.2	0.9	1.2
Particulate emission damage (% of GNI)	0.0	0.4	0.6
Adjusted net savings (% of GNI)	5.2	0.6	8.9

Ukraine

Environmental strategy/action plan prepared in **1999**

	Country data	Europe & Central Asia	Lower middle income
Population (millions)	48.4	472	2,655
Urban population (% of total)	68.2	63.8	49.8
GDP ($ billions)	49.5	1,403	4,168
GNI per capita, *Atlas* method ($)	970	2,580	1,490
Agriculture and fisheries			
Land area (1,000 sq. km)	579	23,868	56,103
Agricultural land (% of land area)	71	28	35
Irrigated land (% of crop land)	6.8	10.9	20.8
Fertilizer consumption (100 grams/ha arable land)	181	344	1,170
Population density, rural (people/sq. km arable land)	48	122	497
Fish catch, total (1,000 metric tons)	382	5,527	74,407
Forests			
Forest area (1,000 sq. km)	96	9,463	20,316
Forest area share of total land area (%)	16.5	39.6	36.2
Annual deforestation (% change, 1990–2000)	–0.3	–0.1	0.1
Biodiversity			
Mammal species, total known	108		
Mammal species, threatened	16		
Bird species, total breeding	245		
Bird species, threatened	8		
Nationally protected area (% of land area)	3.9	6.8	7.7
Energy			
GDP per unit of energy use (2000 PPP$/kg oil equiv)	1.8	2.5	4.1
Energy use per capita (kg oil equiv)	2,684	2,697	1,227
Energy from biomass products and waste (% of total)	0.2	2.3	12.3
Energy imports, net (% of energy use)	45	–23	–22
Electric power consumption per capita (kWh)	2,229	2,808	1,289
Electricity generated by coal (% of total)	17.2	29.4	42.8
Emissions and pollution			
CO_2 emissions per unit of GDP (kg/2000 PPP$ GDP)	1.7	1.1	0.6
CO_2 emissions per capita (metric tons)	6.9	6.7	2.9
Particulate matter (pop. weighted average, µg/cu. m)	35	33	49
Passenger cars (per 1,000 people)	108	138	28
Water and sanitation			
Internal freshwater resources per capita (cu. m)	1,096	11,128	8,397
Freshwater withdrawal			
Total (% of internal resources)	49.1	7.4	5.9
Agriculture (% of total freshwater withdrawal)	30	57	74
Access to improved water source (% of total population)	98	91	82
Rural (% of rural population)	94	80	71
Urban (% of urban population)	100	98	94
Access to sanitation (% of total population)	99	82	60
Rural (% of rural population)	97	64	41
Urban (% of urban population)	100	93	80
Under-five mortality rate (per 1,000)	20	36	39
National accounting aggregates, 2003			
Gross national savings (% of GNI)	26.6	21.9	30.6
Consumption of fixed capital (% of GNI)	19.0	10.7	9.8
Education expenditure (% of GNI)	6.4	4.1	3.2
Energy depletion (% of GNI)	6.4	11.6	8.1
Mineral depletion (% of GNI)	0.0	0.1	0.4
Net forest depletion (% of GNI)	0.0	0.0	0.1
CO_2 damage (% of GNI)	5.9	1.9	1.6
Particulate emission damage (% of GNI)	1.0	0.6	0.7
Adjusted net savings (% of GNI)	0.6	1.1	13.2

United Arab Emirates

Environmental strategy/action plan prepared in ..

		Group data
	Country data	High income
Population (millions)	4.0	972
Urban population (% of total)	88.0	79.9
GDP ($ billions)	71	29,341
GNI per capita, *Atlas* method ($)	..	28,600
Agriculture and fisheries		
Land area (1,000 sq. km)	84	31,030
Agricultural land (% of land area)	6	36
Irrigated land (% of crop land)	28.6	12.3
Fertilizer consumption (100 grams/ha arable land)	4,667	1,198
Population density, rural (people/sq. km arable land)	621	202
Fish catch, total (1,000 metric tons)	118	28,712
Forests		
Forest area (1,000 sq. km)	3	7,929
Forest area share of total land area (%)	3.8	25.9
Annual deforestation (% change, 1990–2000)	−2.8	−0.1
Biodiversity		
Mammal species, total known	25	
Mammal species, threatened	3	
Bird species, total breeding	34	
Bird species, threatened	8	
Nationally protected area (% of land area)	0.0	19.5
Energy		
GDP per unit of energy use (2000 PPP$/kg oil equiv)	1.9	5.2
Energy use per capita (kg oil equiv)	9,609	5,395
Energy from biomass products and waste (% of total)	0.0	3.1
Energy imports, net (% of energy use)	−294	26
Electric power consumption per capita (kWh)	9,656	8,693
Electricity generated by coal (% of total)	..	38.2
Emissions and pollution		
CO_2 emissions per unit of GDP (kg/2000 PPP$ GDP)	..	0.5
CO_2 emissions per capita (metric tons)	18.1	12.4
Particulate matter (pop. weighted average, µg/cu. m)	78	33
Passenger cars (per 1,000 people)	..	436
Water and sanitation		
Internal freshwater resources per capita (cu. m)	49	9,479
Freshwater withdrawal		
Total (% of internal resources)	1,050.0	9.7
Agriculture (% of total freshwater withdrawal)	67	42
Access to improved water source (% of total population)	..	99
Rural (% of rural population)	..	98
Urban (% of urban population)	..	100
Access to sanitation (% of total population)	100	..
Rural (% of rural population)	100	..
Urban (% of urban population)	100	..
Under-five mortality rate (per 1,000)	8	7
National accounting aggregates, 2003		
Gross national savings (% of GNI)	..	19.1
Consumption of fixed capital (% of GNI)	..	13.2
Education expenditure (% of GNI)	..	4.6
Energy depletion (% of GNI)	..	0.8
Mineral depletion (% of GNI)	..	0.0
Net forest depletion (% of GNI)	..	0.0
CO_2 damage (% of GNI)	..	0.3
Particulate emission damage (% of GNI)	0.0	0.3
Adjusted net savings (% of GNI)	..	9.2

United Kingdom

Environmental strategy/action plan prepared in **1995**

	Country data	Group data — High income
Population (millions)	59.3	972
Urban population (% of total)	89.7	79.9
GDP ($ billions)	1,795	29,341
GNI per capita, *Atlas* method ($)	28,320	28,600
Agriculture and fisheries		
Land area (1,000 sq. km)	241	31,030
Agricultural land (% of land area)	70	36
Irrigated land (% of crop land)	2.9	12.3
Fertilizer consumption (100 grams/ha arable land)	3,131	1,198
Population density, rural (people/sq. km arable land)	107	202
Fish catch, total (1,000 metric tons)	919	28,712
Forests		
Forest area (1,000 sq. km)	28	7,929
Forest area share of total land area (%)	11.6	25.9
Annual deforestation (% change, 1990–2000)	–0.6	–0.1
Biodiversity		
Mammal species, total known	50	
Mammal species, threatened	12	
Bird species, total breeding	229	
Bird species, threatened	2	
Nationally protected area (% of land area)	20.9	19.5
Energy		
GDP per unit of energy use (2000 PPP$/kg oil equiv)	6.6	5.2
Energy use per capita (kg oil equiv)	3,824	5,395
Energy from biomass products and waste (% of total)	1.0	3.1
Energy imports, net (% of energy use)	–14	26
Electric power consumption per capita (kWh)	5,618	8,693
Electricity generated by coal (% of total)	32.8	38.2
Emissions and pollution		
CO_2 emissions per unit of GDP (kg/2000 PPP$ GDP)	0.4	0.5
CO_2 emissions per capita (metric tons)	9.6	12.4
Particulate matter (pop. weighted average, µg/cu. m)	19	33
Passenger cars (per 1,000 people)	384	436
Water and sanitation		
Internal freshwater resources per capita (cu. m)	2,444	9,479
Freshwater withdrawal		
Total (% of internal resources)	8.1	9.7
Agriculture (% of total freshwater withdrawal)	3	42
Access to improved water source (% of total population)	..	99
Rural (% of rural population)	..	98
Urban (% of urban population)	100	100
Access to sanitation (% of total population)	..	..
Rural (% of rural population)	..	..
Urban (% of urban population)	..	..
Under-five mortality rate (per 1,000)	7	7
National accounting aggregates, 2003		
Gross national savings (% of GNI)	14.3	19.1
Consumption of fixed capital (% of GNI)	11.4	13.2
Education expenditure (% of GNI)	5.3	4.6
Energy depletion (% of GNI)	0.9	0.8
Mineral depletion (% of GNI)	0.0	0.0
Net forest depletion (% of GNI)	0.0	0.0
CO_2 damage (% of GNI)	0.2	0.3
Particulate emission damage (% of GNI)	0.1	0.3
Adjusted net savings (% of GNI)	7.0	9.2

United States

Environmental strategy/action plan prepared in **1995**

	Country data	High income
		Group data
Population (millions)	290.8	972
Urban population (% of total)	77.9	79.9
GDP ($ billions)	10,949	29,341
GNI per capita, *Atlas* method ($)	37,870	28,600
Agriculture and fisheries		
Land area (1,000 sq. km)	9,159	31,030
Agricultural land (% of land area)	45	36
Irrigated land (% of crop land)	12.6	12.3
Fertilizer consumption (100 grams/ha arable land)	1,096	1,198
Population density, rural (people/sq. km arable land)	37	202
Fish catch, total (1,000 metric tons)	5,405	28,712
Forests		
Forest area (1,000 sq. km)	2,260	7,929
Forest area share of total land area (%)	24.7	25.9
Annual deforestation (% change, 1990–2000)	–0.2	–0.1
Biodiversity		
Mammal species, total known	428	
Mammal species, threatened	37	
Bird species, total breeding	508	
Bird species, threatened	55	
Nationally protected area (% of land area)	25.9	19.5
Energy		
GDP per unit of energy use (2000 PPP$/kg oil equiv)	4.4	5.2
Energy use per capita (kg oil equiv)	7,943	5,395
Energy from biomass products and waste (% of total)	3.0	3.1
Energy imports, net (% of energy use)	27	26
Electric power consumption per capita (kWh)	12,183	8,693
Electricity generated by coal (% of total)	51.3	38.2
Emissions and pollution		
CO_2 emissions per unit of GDP (kg/2000 PPP$ GDP)	0.6	0.5
CO_2 emissions per capita (metric tons)	19.8	12.4
Particulate matter (pop. weighted average, µg/cu. m)	25	33
Passenger cars (per 1,000 people)	481	436
Water and sanitation		
Internal freshwater resources per capita (cu. m)	9,628	9,479
Freshwater withdrawal		
Total (% of internal resources)	16.7	9.7
Agriculture (% of total freshwater withdrawal)	42	42
Access to improved water source (% of total population)	100	99
Rural (% of rural population)	100	98
Urban (% of urban population)	100	100
Access to sanitation (% of total population)	100	..
Rural (% of rural population)	100	..
Urban (% of urban population)	100	..
Under-five mortality rate (per 1,000)	8	7
National accounting aggregates, 2003		
Gross national savings (% of GNI)	13.5	19.1
Consumption of fixed capital (% of GNI)	11.8	13.2
Education expenditure (% of GNI)	4.8	4.6
Energy depletion (% of GNI)	1.2	0.8
Mineral depletion (% of GNI)	0.0	0.0
Net forest depletion (% of GNI)	0.0	0.0
CO_2 damage (% of GNI)	0.4	0.3
Particulate emission damage (% of GNI)	0.3	0.3
Adjusted net savings (% of GNI)	4.7	9.2

Uruguay

Environmental strategy/action plan prepared in ..

	Country data	Latin America & Caribbean	Upper middle income
		Group data	
Population (millions)	3.4	533	333
Urban population (% of total)	92.5	76.6	75.4
GDP ($ billions)	11.2	1,741	1,856
GNI per capita, *Atlas* method ($)	3,820	3,280	5,440
Agriculture and fisheries			
Land area (1,000 sq. km)	175	20,057	12,741
Agricultural land (% of land area)	85	39	48
Irrigated land (% of crop land)	13.5	12.5	13.5
Fertilizer consumption (100 grams/ha arable land)	992	892	796
Population density, rural (people/sq. km arable land)	20	210	193
Fish catch, total (1,000 metric tons)	105	17,804	10,082
Forests			
Forest area (1,000 sq. km)	13	9,552	2,427
Forest area share of total land area (%)	7.4	47.6	19.1
Annual deforestation (% change, 1990–2000)	–5.0	0.5	0.6
Biodiversity			
Mammal species, total known	81		
Mammal species, threatened	6		
Bird species, total breeding	115		
Bird species, threatened	11		
Nationally protected area (% of land area)	0.3	11.2	17.3
Energy			
GDP per unit of energy use (2000 PPP$/kg oil equiv)	10.0	6.1	4.3
Energy use per capita (kg oil equiv)	747	1,156	2,232
Energy from biomass products and waste (% of total)	16.7	14.6	4.1
Energy imports, net (% of energy use)	51	–42	–91
Electric power consumption per capita (kWh)	1,834	1,506	2,496
Electricity generated by coal (% of total)	..	5.0	23.9
Emissions and pollution			
CO_2 emissions per unit of GDP (kg/2000 PPP$ GDP)	0.2	0.4	0.6
CO_2 emissions per capita (metric tons)	1.6	2.7	6.3
Particulate matter (pop. weighted average, µg/cu. m)	173	40	29
Passenger cars (per 1,000 people)	..	..	153
Water and sanitation			
Internal freshwater resources per capita (cu. m)	17,455	25,245	10,741
Freshwater withdrawal			
Total (% of internal resources)	1.2	2.0	5.7
Agriculture (% of total freshwater withdrawal)	91	74	71
Access to improved water source (% of total population)	98	89	..
Rural (% of rural population)	93	69	..
Urban (% of urban population)	98	96	96
Access to sanitation (% of total population)	94	74	..
Rural (% of rural population)	85	44	..
Urban (% of urban population)	95	84	..
Under-five mortality rate (per 1,000)	14	33	22
National accounting aggregates, 2003			
Gross national savings (% of GNI)	13.0	19.5	22.1
Consumption of fixed capital (% of GNI)	11.0	10.3	10.7
Education expenditure (% of GNI)	2.4	4.2	5.0
Energy depletion (% of GNI)	0.0	6.4	11.4
Mineral depletion (% of GNI)	0.0	0.7	0.3
Net forest depletion (% of GNI)	0.0	0.0	0.0
CO_2 damage (% of GNI)	0.3	0.5	0.8
Particulate emission damage (% of GNI)	1.9	0.5	0.6
Adjusted net savings (% of GNI)	2.2	5.3	3.3

Uzbekistan

Environmental strategy/action plan prepared in ..

	Country data	Europe & Central Asia	Low income
		Group data	
Population (millions)	25.6	472	2,312
Urban population (% of total)	36.7	63.8	30.4
GDP ($ billions)	9.9	1,403	1,103
GNI per capita, *Atlas* method ($)	420	2,580	440
Agriculture and fisheries			
Land area (1,000 sq. km)	414	23,868	30,456
Agricultural land (% of land area)	67	28	43
Irrigated land (% of crop land)	88.7	10.9	26.7
Fertilizer consumption (100 grams/ha arable land)	1,602	344	654
Population density, rural (people/sq. km arable land)	357	122	509
Fish catch, total (1,000 metric tons)	8	5,527	16,410
Forests			
Forest area (1,000 sq. km)	20	9,463	7,939
Forest area share of total land area (%)	4.8	39.6	26.1
Annual deforestation (% change, 1990–2000)	–0.2	–0.1	0.7
Biodiversity			
Mammal species, total known	97		
Mammal species, threatened	9		
Bird species, total breeding	203		
Bird species, threatened	9		
Nationally protected area (% of land area)	2.0	6.8	7.7
Energy			
GDP per unit of energy use (2000 PPP$/kg oil equiv)	0.8	2.5	4.1
Energy use per capita (kg oil equiv)	2,047	2,697	493
Energy from biomass products and waste (% of total)	..	2.3	49.4
Energy imports, net (% of energy use)	–8	–23	–6
Electric power consumption per capita (kWh)	1,670	2,808	312
Electricity generated by coal (% of total)	4.0	29.4	47.4
Emissions and pollution			
CO_2 emissions per unit of GDP (kg/2000 PPP$ GDP)	3.2	1.1	0.4
CO_2 emissions per capita (metric tons)	4.8	6.7	0.8
Particulate matter (pop. weighted average, µg/cu. m)	83	33	63
Passenger cars (per 1,000 people)	..	138	..
Water and sanitation			
Internal freshwater resources per capita (cu. m)	625	11,128	3,583
Freshwater withdrawal			
Total (% of internal resources)	363.1	7.4	11.5
Agriculture (% of total freshwater withdrawal)	94	57	92
Access to improved water source (% of total population)	89	91	75
Rural (% of rural population)	84	80	70
Urban (% of urban population)	97	98	89
Access to sanitation (% of total population)	57	82	36
Rural (% of rural population)	48	64	24
Urban (% of urban population)	73	93	61
Under-five mortality rate (per 1,000)	69	36	123
National accounting aggregates, 2003			
Gross national savings (% of GNI)	23.4	21.9	23.1
Consumption of fixed capital (% of GNI)	7.8	10.7	8.9
Education expenditure (% of GNI)	9.4	4.1	3.4
Energy depletion (% of GNI)	61.0	11.6	5.8
Mineral depletion (% of GNI)	0.0	0.1	0.3
Net forest depletion (% of GNI)	0.0	0.0	0.8
CO_2 damage (% of GNI)	9.1	1.9	1.2
Particulate emission damage (% of GNI)	0.6	0.6	0.6
Adjusted net savings (% of GNI)	–45.7	1.1	8.9

Vanuatu

Environmental strategy/action plan prepared in ..

	Country data	Group data	
		East Asia & Pacific	Lower middle income
Population (millions)	0.2	1,855	2,655
Urban population (% of total)	22.9	39.1	49.8
GDP ($ billions)	0.3	2,033	4,168
GNI per capita, *Atlas* method ($)	1,180	1,070	1,490
Agriculture and fisheries			
Land area (1,000 sq. km)	12	15,886	56,103
Agricultural land (% of land area)	13	50	35
Irrigated land (% of crop land)	..		20.8
Fertilizer consumption (100 grams/ha arable land)	..	2,297	1,170
Population density, rural (people/sq. km arable land)	531	565	497
Fish catch, total (1,000 metric tons)	27	60,812	74,407
Forests			
Forest area (1,000 sq. km)	4	4,284	20,316
Forest area share of total land area (%)	36.7	27.0	36.2
Annual deforestation (% change, 1990–2000)	–0.1	0.2	0.1
Biodiversity			
Mammal species, total known	..		
Mammal species, threatened	5		
Bird species, total breeding	..		
Bird species, threatened	7		
Nationally protected area (% of land area)	..	9.2	7.7
Energy			
GDP per unit of energy use (2000 PPP$/kg oil equiv)	..	4.6	4.1
Energy use per capita (kg oil equiv)	..	904	1,227
Energy from biomass products and waste (% of total)	..	19.6	12.3
Energy imports, net (% of energy use)	..	–4	–22
Electric power consumption per capita (kWh)	..	891	1,289
Electricity generated by coal (% of total)	..	66.8	42.8
Emissions and pollution			
CO_2 emissions per unit of GDP (kg/2000 PPP$ GDP)	0.1	0.5	0.6
CO_2 emissions per capita (metric tons)	0.4	2.1	2.9
Particulate matter (pop. weighted average, µg/cu. m)	28	69	49
Passenger cars (per 1,000 people)	..	10	28
Water and sanitation			
Internal freshwater resources per capita (cu. m)	..	5,103	8,397
Freshwater withdrawal			
Total (% of internal resources)	..	8.2	5.9
Agriculture (% of total freshwater withdrawal)	..	81	74
Access to improved water source (% of total population)	60	78	82
Rural (% of rural population)	52	69	71
Urban (% of urban population)	85	92	94
Access to sanitation (% of total population)	50	49	60
Rural (% of rural population)	42	35	41
Urban (% of urban population)	78	71	80
Under-five mortality rate (per 1,000)	38	41	39
National accounting aggregates, 2003			
Gross national savings (% of GNI)	..	41.7	30.6
Consumption of fixed capital (% of GNI)	9.5	9.2	9.8
Education expenditure (% of GNI)	5.6	2.3	3.2
Energy depletion (% of GNI)	0.0	3.9	8.1
Mineral depletion (% of GNI)	0.0	0.3	0.4
Net forest depletion (% of GNI)	0.0	0.1	0.1
CO_2 damage (% of GNI)	0.2	1.8	1.6
Particulate emission damage (% of GNI)	..	0.8	0.7
Adjusted net savings (% of GNI)	..	27.9	13.2

Venezuela, RB

Environmental strategy/action plan prepared in ..

	Country data	Group data — Latin America & Caribbean	Group data — Upper middle income
Population (millions)	25.7	533	333
Urban population (% of total)	87.6	76.6	75.4
GDP ($ billions)	85.4	1,741	1,856
GNI per capita, *Atlas* method ($)	3,490	3,280	5,440
Agriculture and fisheries			
Land area (1,000 sq. km)	882	20,057	12,741
Agricultural land (% of land area)	25	39	48
Irrigated land (% of crop land)	17.7	12.5	13.5
Fertilizer consumption (100 grams/ha arable land)	1,230	892	796
Population density, rural (people/sq. km arable land)	130	210	193
Fish catch, total (1,000 metric tons)	435	17,804	10,082
Forests			
Forest area (1,000 sq. km)	495	9,552	2,427
Forest area share of total land area (%)	56.1	47.6	19.1
Annual deforestation (% change, 1990–2000)	0.4	0.5	0.6
Biodiversity			
Mammal species, total known	323		
Mammal species, threatened	26		
Bird species, total breeding	547		
Bird species, threatened	24		
Nationally protected area (% of land area)	63.8	11.2	17.3
Energy			
GDP per unit of energy use (2000 PPP$/kg oil equiv)	2.4	6.1	4.3
Energy use per capita (kg oil equiv)	2,141	1,156	2,232
Energy from biomass products and waste (% of total)	1.0	14.6	4.1
Energy imports, net (% of energy use)	–289	–42	–91
Electric power consumption per capita (kWh)	2,472	1,506	2,496
Electricity generated by coal (% of total)	..	5.0	23.9
Emissions and pollution			
CO_2 emissions per unit of GDP (kg/2000 PPP$ GDP)	1.2	0.4	0.6
CO_2 emissions per capita (metric tons)	6.5	2.7	6.3
Particulate matter (pop. weighted average, μg/cu. m)	16	40	29
Passenger cars (per 1,000 people)	..	..	153
Water and sanitation			
Internal freshwater resources per capita (cu. m)	28,122	25,245	10,741
Freshwater withdrawal			
Total (% of internal resources)	0.6	2.0	5.7
Agriculture (% of total freshwater withdrawal)	46	74	71
Access to improved water source (% of total population)	83	89	..
Rural (% of rural population)	70	69	..
Urban (% of urban population)	85	96	96
Access to sanitation (% of total population)	68	74	..
Rural (% of rural population)	48	44	..
Urban (% of urban population)	71	84	..
Under-five mortality rate (per 1,000)	21	33	22
National accounting aggregates, 2003			
Gross national savings (% of GNI)	22.1	19.5	22.1
Consumption of fixed capital (% of GNI)	7.4	10.3	10.7
Education expenditure (% of GNI)	4.4	4.2	5.0
Energy depletion (% of GNI)	37.2	6.4	11.4
Mineral depletion (% of GNI)	0.4	0.7	0.3
Net forest depletion (% of GNI)	0.0	0.0	0.0
CO_2 damage (% of GNI)	1.0	0.5	0.8
Particulate emission damage (% of GNI)	0.0	0.5	0.6
Adjusted net savings (% of GNI)	–19.6	5.3	3.3

Vietnam

Environmental strategy/action plan prepared in ..

	Country data	East Asia & Pacific	Low Income
		Group data	
Population (millions)	81.3	1,855	2,312
Urban population (% of total)	25.4	39.1	30.4
GDP ($ billions)	39.2	2,033	1,103
GNI per capita, *Atlas* method ($)	480	1,070	440
Agriculture and fisheries			
Land area (1,000 sq. km)	325	15,886	30,456
Agricultural land (% of land area)	28	50	43
Irrigated land (% of crop land)	33.7	..	26.7
Fertilizer consumption (100 grams/ha arable land)	2,948	2,297	654
Population density, rural (people/sq. km arable land)	901	565	509
Fish catch, total (1,000 metric tons)	2,010	60,812	16,410
Forests			
Forest area (1,000 sq. km)	98	4,284	7,939
Forest area share of total land area (%)	30.2	27.0	26.1
Annual deforestation (% change, 1990–2000)	–0.5	0.2	0.7
Biodiversity			
Mammal species, total known	213		
Mammal species, threatened	40		
Bird species, total breeding	262		
Bird species, threatened	37		
Nationally protected area (% of land area)	3.7	9.2	7.7
Energy			
GDP per unit of energy use (2000 PPP$/kg oil equiv)	4.2	4.6	4.1
Energy use per capita (kg oil equiv)	530	904	493
Energy from biomass products and waste (% of total)	54.5	19.6	49.4
Energy imports, net (% of energy use)	–25	–4	–6
Electric power consumption per capita (kWh)	374	891	312
Electricity generated by coal (% of total)	13.6	66.8	47.4
Emissions and pollution			
CO_2 emissions per unit of GDP (kg/2000 PPP$ GDP)	0.4	0.5	0.4
CO_2 emissions per capita (metric tons)	0.7	2.1	0.8
Particulate matter (pop. weighted average, µg/cu. m)	75	69	63
Passenger cars (per 1,000 people)	..	10	..
Water and sanitation			
Internal freshwater resources per capita (cu. m)	4,513	5,103	3,583
Freshwater withdrawal			
Total (% of internal resources)	14.8	8.2	11.5
Agriculture (% of total freshwater withdrawal)	87	81	92
Access to improved water source (% of total population)	73	78	75
Rural (% of rural population)	67	69	70
Urban (% of urban population)	93	92	89
Access to sanitation (% of total population)	41	49	36
Rural (% of rural population)	26	35	24
Urban (% of urban population)	84	71	61
Under-five mortality rate (per 1,000)	23	41	123
National accounting aggregates, 2003			
Gross national savings (% of GNI)	27.1	41.7	23.1
Consumption of fixed capital (% of GNI)	8.0	9.2	8.9
Education expenditure (% of GNI)	2.8	2.3	3.4
Energy depletion (% of GNI)	8.2	3.9	5.8
Mineral depletion (% of GNI)	0.0	0.3	0.3
Net forest depletion (% of GNI)	0.7	0.1	0.8
CO_2 damage (% of GNI)	1.0	1.8	1.2
Particulate emission damage (% of GNI)	0.4	0.8	0.6
Adjusted net savings (% of GNI)	11.6	27.9	8.9

Virgin Islands (U.S.)

Environmental strategy/action plan prepared in ..

	Country data	Group data — High income
Population (millions)	0.1	972
Urban population (% of total)	47.3	79.9
GDP ($ billions)	..	29,341
GNI per capita, *Atlas* method ($)	..	28,600

Agriculture and fisheries		
Land area (1,000 sq. km)	0	31,030
Agricultural land (% of land area)	29	36
Irrigated land (% of crop land)	..	12.3
Fertilizer consumption (100 grams/ha arable land)	1,500	1,198
Population density, rural (people/sq. km arable land)	1,461	202
Fish catch, total (1,000 metric tons)	0	28,712

Forests		
Forest area (1,000 sq. km)	0	7,929
Forest area share of total land area (%)	41.2	25.9
Annual deforestation (% change, 1990–2000)	0.0	–0.1

Biodiversity		
Mammal species, total known	..	
Mammal species, threatened	1	
Bird species, total breeding	..	
Bird species, threatened	2	
Nationally protected area (% of land area)	..	19.5

Energy		
GDP per unit of energy use (2000 PPP$/kg oil equiv)	..	5.2
Energy use per capita (kg oil equiv)	..	5,395
Energy from biomass products and waste (% of total)	..	3.1
Energy imports, net (% of energy use)	..	26
Electric power consumption per capita (kWh)	..	8,693
Electricity generated by coal (% of total)	..	38.2

Emissions and pollution		
CO_2 emissions per unit of GDP (kg/2000 PPP$ GDP)	..	0.5
CO_2 emissions per capita (metric tons)	121.2	12.4
Particulate matter (pop. weighted average, µg/cu. m)	43	33
Passenger cars (per 1,000 people)	..	436

Water and sanitation		
Internal freshwater resources per capita (cu. m)	..	9,479
Freshwater withdrawal		
Total (% of internal resources)	..	9.7
Agriculture (% of total freshwater withdrawal)	..	42
Access to improved water source (% of total population)	..	99
Rural (% of rural population)	..	98
Urban (% of urban population)	..	100
Access to sanitation (% of total population)	..	..
Rural (% of rural population)	..	..
Urban (% of urban population)	..	..
Under-five mortality rate (per 1,000)	..	7

National accounting aggregates, 2003		
Gross national savings (% of GNI)	..	19.1
Consumption of fixed capital (% of GNI)	..	13.2
Education expenditure (% of GNI)	..	4.6
Energy depletion (% of GNI)	..	0.8
Mineral depletion (% of GNI)	..	0.0
Net forest depletion (% of GNI)	..	0.0
CO_2 damage (% of GNI)	..	0.3
Particulate emission damage (% of GNI)	..	0.3
Adjusted net savings (% of GNI)	..	9.2

West Bank and Gaza

Environmental strategy/action plan prepared in ..

	Country data	Middle East & North Africa	Lower middle income
Population (millions)	3.4	312	2,655
Urban population (% of total)	..	59.0	49.8
GDP ($ billions)	3.5	745	4,168
GNI per capita, *Atlas* method ($)	1,110	2,390	1,490
Agriculture and fisheries			
Land area (1,000 sq. km)	6	11,111	56,103
Agricultural land (% of land area)	..	34	35
Irrigated land (% of crop land)	..	38.3	20.8
Fertilizer consumption (100 grams/ha arable land)	..	854	1,170
Population density, rural (people/sq. km arable land)	..	603	497
Fish catch, total (1,000 metric tons)	..	2,840	74,407
Forests			
Forest area (1,000 sq. km)	..	168	20,316
Forest area share of total land area (%)	..	1.5	36.2
Annual deforestation (% change, 1990–2000)	..	–0.1	0.1
Biodiversity			
Mammal species, total known	..		
Mammal species, threatened	1		
Bird species, total breeding	..		
Bird species, threatened	1		
Nationally protected area (% of land area)	..	11.3	7.7
Energy			
GDP per unit of energy use (2000 PPP$/kg oil equiv)	..	3.5	4.1
Energy use per capita (kg oil equiv)	..	1,504	1,227
Energy from biomass products and waste (% of total)	..	1.0	12.3
Energy imports, net (% of energy use)	..	–168	–22
Electric power consumption per capita (kWh)	..	1,412	1,289
Electricity generated by coal (% of total)	..	2.3	42.8
Emissions and pollution			
CO_2 emissions per unit of GDP (kg/2000 PPP$ GDP)	..	0.8	0.6
CO_2 emissions per capita (metric tons)	..	4.2	2.9
Particulate matter (pop. weighted average, µg/cu. m)	..	87	49
Passenger cars (per 1,000 people)	..	..	28
Water and sanitation			
Internal freshwater resources per capita (cu. m)	..	761	8,397
Freshwater withdrawal			
Total (% of internal resources)	..	101.7	5.9
Agriculture (% of total freshwater withdrawal)	..	88	74
Access to improved water source (% of total population)	..	88	82
Rural (% of rural population)	..	78	71
Urban (% of urban population)	..	96	94
Access to sanitation (% of total population)	..	75	60
Rural (% of rural population)	..	56	41
Urban (% of urban population)	..	90	80
Under-five mortality rate (per 1,000)	..	53	39
National accounting aggregates, 2003			
Gross national savings (% of GNI)	–22.8	31.2	30.6
Consumption of fixed capital (% of GNI)	8.1	10.0	9.8
Education expenditure (% of GNI)	..	5.5	3.2
Energy depletion (% of GNI)	0.0	30.7	8.1
Mineral depletion (% of GNI)	0.0	0.1	0.4
Net forest depletion (% of GNI)	0.0	0.0	0.1
CO_2 damage (% of GNI)	..	1.2	1.6
Particulate emission damage (% of GNI)	..	0.8	0.7
Adjusted net savings (% of GNI)	..	–6.2	13.2

Yemen, Rep.

Environmental strategy/action plan prepared in **1996**

	Country data	Middle East & North Africa	Low income
		Group data	
Population (millions)	19.2	312	2,312
Urban population (% of total)	25.7	59.0	30.4
GDP ($ billions)	10.8	745	1,103
GNI per capita, *Atlas* method ($)	520	2,390	440
Agriculture and fisheries			
Land area (1,000 sq. km)	528	11,111	30,456
Agricultural land (% of land area)	33	34	43
Irrigated land (% of crop land)	30.0	38.3	26.7
Fertilizer consumption (100 grams/ha arable land)	75	854	654
Population density, rural (people/sq. km arable land)	903	603	509
Fish catch, total (1,000 metric tons)	142	2,840	16,410
Forests			
Forest area (1,000 sq. km)	4	168	7,939
Forest area share of total land area (%)	0.9	1.5	26.1
Annual deforestation (% change, 1990–2000)	1.8	–0.1	0.7
Biodiversity			
Mammal species, total known	66		
Mammal species, threatened	5		
Bird species, total breeding	93		
Bird species, threatened	12		
Nationally protected area (% of land area)	..	11.3	7.7
Energy			
GDP per unit of energy use (2000 PPP$/kg oil equiv)	3.8	3.5	4.1
Energy use per capita (kg oil equiv)	221	1,504	493
Energy from biomass products and waste (% of total)	1.9	1.0	49.4
Energy imports, net (% of energy use)	–441	–168	–6
Electric power consumption per capita (kWh)	152	1,412	312
Electricity generated by coal (% of total)	..	2.3	47.4
Emissions and pollution			
CO_2 emissions per unit of GDP (kg/2000 PPP$ GDP)	0.6	0.8	0.4
CO_2 emissions per capita (metric tons)	0.5	4.2	0.8
Particulate matter (pop. weighted average, µg/cu. m)	98	87	63
Passenger cars (per 1,000 people)	..	..	..
Water and sanitation			
Internal freshwater resources per capita (cu. m)	209	761	3,583
Freshwater withdrawal			
Total (% of internal resources)	72.5	101.7	11.5
Agriculture (% of total freshwater withdrawal)	92	88	92
Access to improved water source (% of total population)	69	88	75
Rural (% of rural population)	68	78	70
Urban (% of urban population)	74	96	89
Access to sanitation (% of total population)	30	75	36
Rural (% of rural population)	14	56	24
Urban (% of urban population)	76	90	61
Under-five mortality rate (per 1,000)	113	53	123
National accounting aggregates, 2003			
Gross national savings (% of GNI)	19.2	31.2	23.1
Consumption of fixed capital (% of GNI)	8.9	10.0	8.9
Education expenditure (% of GNI)	..	5.5	3.4
Energy depletion (% of GNI)	37.6	30.7	5.8
Mineral depletion (% of GNI)	0.0	0.1	0.3
Net forest depletion (% of GNI)	0.0	0.0	0.8
CO_2 damage (% of GNI)	1.2	1.2	1.2
Particulate emission damage (% of GNI)	0.5	0.8	0.6
Adjusted net savings (% of GNI)	..	–6.2	8.9

Zambia

Environmental strategy/action plan prepared in **1994**

	Country data	Group data Sub-Saharan Africa	Group data Low Income
Population (millions)	10.4	705	2,312
Urban population (% of total)	40.3	36.5	30.4
GDP ($ billions)	4.3	439	1,103
GNI per capita, *Atlas* method ($)	380	500	440
Agriculture and fisheries			
Land area (1,000 sq. km)	743	23,596	30,456
Agricultural land (% of land area)	47	43	43
Irrigated land (% of crop land)	0.9	4.2	26.7
Fertilizer consumption (100 grams/ha arable land)	124	145	654
Population density, rural (people/sq. km arable land)	117	352	509
Fish catch, total (1,000 metric tons)	69	5,191	16,410
Forests			
Forest area (1,000 sq. km)	312	6,435	7,939
Forest area share of total land area (%)	42.0	27.3	26.1
Annual deforestation (% change, 1990–2000)	2.4	0.8	0.7
Biodiversity			
Mammal species, total known	233		
Mammal species, threatened	..		
Bird species, total breeding	252		
Bird species, threatened	11		
Nationally protected area (% of land area)	31.9	8.7	7.7
Energy			
GDP per unit of energy use (2000 PPP$/kg oil equiv)	1.3	2.8	4.1
Energy use per capita (kg oil equiv)	639	667	493
Energy from biomass products and waste (% of total)	81.3	57.5	49.4
Energy imports, net (% of energy use)	5	−56	−6
Electric power consumption per capita (kWh)	583	457	312
Electricity generated by coal (% of total)	0.2	68.2	47.4
Emissions and pollution			
CO_2 emissions per unit of GDP (kg/2000 PPP$ GDP)	0.2	0.4	0.4
CO_2 emissions per capita (metric tons)	0.2	0.7	0.8
Particulate matter (pop. weighted average, µg/cu. m)	73	54	63
Passenger cars (per 1,000 people)	..	..	..
Water and sanitation			
Internal freshwater resources per capita (cu. m)	7,690	5,546	3,583
Freshwater withdrawal			
Total (% of internal resources)	2.1	1.8	11.5
Agriculture (% of total freshwater withdrawal)	77	85	92
Access to improved water source (% of total population)	55	58	75
Rural (% of rural population)	36	46	70
Urban (% of urban population)	90	82	89
Access to sanitation (% of total population)	45	36	36
Rural (% of rural population)	32	26	24
Urban (% of urban population)	68	55	61
Under-five mortality rate (per 1,000)	182	171	123
National accounting aggregates, 2003			
Gross national savings (% of GNI)	15.9	16.9	23.1
Consumption of fixed capital (% of GNI)	8.1	10.6	8.9
Education expenditure (% of GNI)	2.0	4.7	3.4
Energy depletion (% of GNI)	0.0	8.0	5.8
Mineral depletion (% of GNI)	1.2	0.5	0.3
Net forest depletion (% of GNI)	0.0	0.7	0.8
CO_2 damage (% of GNI)	0.4	0.9	1.2
Particulate emission damage (% of GNI)	..	0.4	0.6
Adjusted net savings (% of GNI)	8.2	0.6	8.9

Zimbabwe

Environmental strategy/action plan prepared in **1987**

	Country data	Group data Sub-Saharan Africa	Group data Low income
Population (millions)	13.1	705	2,312
Urban population (% of total)	37.5	36.5	30.4
GDP ($ billions)	17.8	439	1,103
GNI per capita, *Atlas* method ($)	..	500	440
Agriculture and fisheries			
Land area (1,000 sq. km)	387	23,596	30,456
Agricultural land (% of land area)	53	43	43
Irrigated land (% of crop land)	3.5	4.2	26.7
Fertilizer consumption (100 grams/ha arable land)	342	145	654
Population density, rural (people/sq. km arable land)	255	352	509
Fish catch, total (1,000 metric tons)	13	5,191	16,410
Forests			
Forest area (1,000 sq. km)	190	6,435	7,939
Forest area share of total land area (%)	49.2	27.3	26.1
Annual deforestation (% change, 1990–2000)	1.5	0.8	0.7
Biodiversity			
Mammal species, total known	270		
Mammal species, threatened	..		
Bird species, total breeding	229		
Bird species, threatened	10		
Nationally protected area (% of land area)	12.1	8.7	7.7
Energy			
GDP per unit of energy use (2000 PPP$/kg oil equiv)	3.0	2.8	4.1
Energy use per capita (kg oil equiv)	751	667	493
Energy from biomass products and waste (% of total)	59.0	57.5	49.4
Energy imports, net (% of energy use)	13	−56	−6
Electric power consumption per capita (kWh)	831	457	312
Electricity generated by coal (% of total)	55.1	68.2	47.4
Emissions and pollution			
CO_2 emissions per unit of GDP (kg/2000 PPP$ GDP)	0.5	0.4	0.4
CO_2 emissions per capita (metric tons)	1.2	0.7	0.8
Particulate matter (pop. weighted average, µg/cu. m)	61	54	63
Passenger cars (per 1,000 people)	..	..	..
Water and sanitation			
Internal freshwater resources per capita (cu. m)	1,069	5,546	3,583
Freshwater withdrawal			
Total (% of internal resources)	8.6	1.8	11.5
Agriculture (% of total freshwater withdrawal)	79	85	92
Access to improved water source (% of total population)	83	58	75
Rural (% of rural population)	74	46	70
Urban (% of urban population)	100	82	89
Access to sanitation (% of total population)	57	36	36
Rural (% of rural population)	51	26	24
Urban (% of urban population)	69	55	61
Under-five mortality rate (per 1,000)	126	171	123
National accounting aggregates, 2003			
Gross national savings (% of GNI)	..	16.9	23.1
Consumption of fixed capital (% of GNI)	..	10.6	8.9
Education expenditure (% of GNI)	6.9	4.7	3.4
Energy depletion (% of GNI)	..	8.0	5.8
Mineral depletion (% of GNI)	..	0.5	0.3
Net forest depletion (% of GNI)	..	0.7	0.8
CO_2 damage (% of GNI)	..	0.9	1.2
Particulate emission damage (% of GNI)	0.5	0.4	0.6
Adjusted net savings (% of GNI)	..	0.6	8.9

Glossary

Access to an improved water source refers to the share of the population with reasonable access to an adequate amount of water from an improved source, such as a household connection, public standpipe, borehole, protected well or spring, or rainwater collection. Unimproved sources include vendors, tanker trucks, and unprotected wells and springs. Reasonable access to an adequate amount is defined as the availability of at least 20 liters a person a day from a source within one kilometer of the dwelling. (World Health Organization; the data are for 2002)

Access to sanitation is the share of population with access to at least adequate excreta disposal facilities (private or shared, but not public) that can effectively prevent human, animal, and insect contact with excreta. Improved facilities range from simple but protected pit latrines to flush toilets with a sewerage connection. To be effective, facilities must be correctly constructed and properly maintained. (World Health Organization; the data are for 2002)

Adjusted net savings are equal to gross national savings minus consumption of fixed capital, plus education expenditures and minus energy depletion, mineral depletion, net forest depletion, and particulate matter and carbon dioxide damage. In cases where data are not available, adjusted net savings do not include particulate emission damage. (World Bank; the data are for 2003)

Agricultural land refers to the share of land area that is arable, under permanent crops, and under permanent pastures. Arable land includes land defined by the Food and Agriculture Organization as land under temporary crops (double-cropped areas are counted once), temporary meadows for mowing or for pasture, land under market or kitchen gardens, and land temporarily fallow. Land abandoned as a result of shifting cultivation is excluded. Land under permanent crops is land cultivated with crops that occupy the land for long periods and need not be replanted after each harvest, such as cocoa, coffee, and rubber. This category includes land under flowering shrubs, fruit trees, nut trees, and vines, but excludes land under trees grown for wood or timber. Permanent pasture is land used for five or more years for forage, including natural and cultivated crops. (Food and Agriculture Organization; the data are for 2002)

Annual deforestation refers to the permanent conversion of natural forest area to other uses, including shifting cultivation, permanent agriculture, ranching, settlements, and infrastructure development. Deforested areas do not include areas logged but intended for regeneration or areas degraded by fuelwood gathering, acid precipitation, or forest fires. Negative numbers indicate an increase in forest areas. (Food and Agriculture Organization; the data are for 1990–2000)

Bird species, threatened, are the number of birds classified by the World Conservation Union (IUCN) as endangered, vulnerable, rare, indeterminate, out of danger, or insufficiently known. (World Conservation Monitoring Center–IUCN; the data are for 2002)

Bird species, total breeding, are listed for countries included within their breeding or wintering ranges. (World Conservation Monitoring Center–IUCN; the data are for 2002)

Carbon dioxide (CO_2) damage is estimated to be $20 per ton of carbon (the unit damage in 1995 U.S. dollars) times the number of tons of carbon emitted. (World Bank estimates; the data are for 2003)

Carbon dioxide (CO_2) emissions per capita are those stemming from the burning of fossil fuels and the manufacture of cement divided by population. They include carbon dioxide produced during consumption of solid, liquid, and gas fuels and gas flaring. (Carbon Dioxide Information Analysis Center; the data are for 2000)

Carbon dioxide (CO_2) emissions per unit of GDP are carbon dioxide emissions in kilograms per unit of 2000 GDP in purchasing power parity (PPP) terms. PPP GDP is gross domestic product converted to international dollars using PPP rates. An international dollar has the same purchasing power over GDP as a U.S. dollar has in the United States. (Carbon Dioxide Information Analysis Center, World Bank; the data are for 2000)

Consumption of fixed capital represents the replacement value of capital used up in the process of production. (United Nations; the data are extrapolated for 2003)

Education expenditure refers to public current operating expenditures in education, including wages and salaries and excluding capital investments in buildings and equipment. (United Nations; the data are extrapolated from the most recent year available)

Electric power consumption refers to the production of power plants and combined heat and power plants less transmission, distribution, and transformation losses and own use by heat and power plants. (International Energy Agency; the data are for 2002)

Electricity generated by coal refers to the contribution of coal, as an input, in the generation of electricity. (International Energy Agency; the data are for 2002)

Energy depletion is equal to the product of unit resource rents and the physical quantities of energy extracted. It covers crude oil, natural gas, and coal. (A wide range of data sources and estimation methods were used to arrive at resource depletion estimates and are described in a 1998 World Bank working paper entitled "Estimating National Wealth;" the data are for 2003)

Energy from biomass products and waste comprises solid biomass, liquid biomass, biogas, industrial waste, and municipal waste, measured as a share of total energy use (International Energy Agency; the data are for 2002)

Energy imports, net, are calculated as energy use less production, both measured in oil equivalents. A negative value indicates that the country is a net exporter. (International Energy Agency; the data are for 2002)

Energy use per capita refers to apparent consumption, which is equal to indigenous production plus imports and stock changes, minus exports and fuels supplied to ships and aircraft engaged in international transport. (International Energy Agency; the data are for 2002)

Environmental strategies and action plans provide a comprehensive, cross-sectoral analysis of conservation and resource management issues to help integrate environmental concerns into the development process. They include national conservation strategies, national environmental action plans, national environmental management strategies, and national sustainable development strategies. The year shown for a country refers to the year in which a strategy or action plan was adopted. (World Resources Institute, International Institute for Environment and Development, World Conservation Monitoring Center–IUCN, and World Bank)

Fertilizer consumption measures the quantity of plant nutrients used per unit of arable land. Fertilizer products cover nitrogenous, potash, and phosphate fertilizers (including ground rock phosphate). The time reference for fertilizer consumption is the crop year (July through June). (Food and Agriculture Organization; the data are for 2002)

Fish catch, total, consists of freshwater diadrom, demersal marine fish, pelagic marine fish, crustaceans, and mollusks, excluding cephalopods and aquatic mammals. Data refer to production (catch and aquaculture) in live weight equivalent, which is the weight of fish and shellfish at the time of removal from the water. (Food and Agriculture Organization; the data are for 2001)

Forest area is land under natural or planted stands of trees, whether productive or not. (Food and Agriculture Organization; the data are for 2000)

Freshwater withdrawals, total, refer to total water withdrawal, not counting evaporation losses from storage basins. Withdrawals also include water from desalination plants in countries where they are a significant source. Withdrawals can exceed 100 percent of internal renewable resources where extraction from nonrenewable aquifers or desalination plants is considerable, where there is significant water reuse, or where there are significant inflows. (World Resources Institute; the data are for various years; for details see Primary Data Documentation in *World Development Indicators 2005*)

Freshwater withdrawals, agriculture, are freshwater withdrawals for irrigation and livestock production as a share of total freshwater withdrawal. (World Resources Institute; the data are for various years; for details see Primary Data Documentation in *World Development Indicators 2005*)

GDP per unit of energy use is 2000 GDP in purchasing power parity (PPP) terms per kilogram of oil equivalent of commercial energy use. PPP GDP is gross domestic product converted to international dollars using PPP rates. An international dollar has the same purchasing power over GDP as a U.S. dollar has in the United States. (International Energy Agency, World Bank; the data are for 2002)

GDP is gross domestic product, which measures the total output of goods and services for final use occurring within the domestic territory of a given country, regardless of the allocation to domestic and foreign claims. GDP at purchaser values (market prices) is the sum of gross value added by all resident and nonresident producers in the economy plus any taxes and minus any subsidies not included in the value of the products. It is calculated without making deductions for depreciation of fabricated assets or for depletion and degradation of natural resources. (World Bank, Organisation for Economic Co-operation and Development, United Nations; the data are for 2003)

GNI per capita is gross national income (formerly called gross national product or GNP) divided by midyear population. GNI is the sum of gross value added by all resident producers plus any taxes (less subsidies) that are not included in the valuation of output plus net receipts of primary income (employee compensation and property income) from nonresident sources. GNI per capita is in current U.S. dollars, converted using the *World Bank Atlas* method; see Statistical Methods in *World Development Indicators 2005*. (World Bank, Organisation for Economic Co-operation and Development, United Nations; the data are for 2003)

Gross national savings are calculated as the difference between GNI and public and private consumption plus net current transfers. (World Bank, Organisation for Economic Co-operation and Development, United Nations; the data are for 2003)

Internal freshwater resources refer to internal renewable resources, which include flows of rivers and groundwater from rainfall in the country, but do not include river flows from other countries. Freshwater resources per capita are calculated using the World Bank's population estimates. (World Resources Institute; the estimates are for 2003)

Irrigated land refers to areas purposely provided with water, including land irrigated by controlled flooding. Crop land refers to arable land and land used for permanent crops. (Food and Agriculture Organization; the data are for 2002)

Land area is a country's total area, excluding area under inland water bodies, national claims to continental shelf, and exclusive economic zones. In most cases the definition of inland water bodies includes major rivers and lakes. (Food and Agriculture Organization; the data are for 2002)

Mammals species, total known, excludes whales and porpoises. (World Conservation Monitoring Center–IUCN; the data are for 2002)

Mammals, threatened, are the number of mammal species classified by the World Conservation Union (IUCN) as endangered, vulnerable, rare, indeterminate, out of danger, or insufficiently known. (World Conservation Monitoring Center–IUCN; the data are for 2002)

Mineral depletion is equal to the product of unit resource rents and the physical quantities of minerals extracted. It refers to bauxite, copper, iron, lead, nickel, phosphate, tin. gold, silver, and zinc. (A wide range of data sources and estimation methods used to arrive at resource depletion estimates are described in a 1998 World Bank working paper entitled "Estimating National Wealth;" the data are for 2003)

Nationally protected areas are totally or partially protected areas of at least 1,000 hectares that are designated as national parks, natural monuments, nature reserves or wildlife sanctuaries, protected landscapes and seascapes, or scientific reserves. (World Conservation Monitoring Center–IUCN; the data are preliminary, and they are for most recent year reported in 2003)

Net forest depletion is calculated as the product of unit resource rents and the excess of roundwood harvest over natural growth. If growth exceeds harvest, this figure is zero. (Food and Agriculture Organization, World Bank estimates of natural growth; the data are for 2003)

Particulate matter refers to fine suspended particulates less than 10 microns in diameter that are capable of penetrating deep into the respiratory tract and causing damage. It is the population weighted average of all cities in the country with a population in excess of 100,000. (World Bank estimates; the data are for 1999)

Particulate emission damage is calculated as the willingness to pay to reduce the risk of mortality attributable to particulate emissions. (World Bank estimates; the data are for 2003)

Passenger cars refer to road motor vehicles, other than two-wheelers, intended for the carriage of passengers and designed to seat no more than nine people including the driver. (International Road Federation; the data are for 2002)

Population includes all residents who are present regardless of legal status or citizenship—except for refugees not permanently settled in the country of asylum, who are generally considered part of the population of their country of origin. The values shown are midyear estimates. (World Bank, United Nations; the data are for 2003)

Population density, rural, is the rural population divided by the arable land area. Rural population is estimated as the difference between the total population and the urban population. (United Nations; the data are for 2002)

Under-five mortality rate is the probability that a newborn baby will die before reaching age five, if subject to current age-specific mortality rates. (United Nations, United Nations Children's Fund; the data are for 2003)

Urban population is the share of the midyear population living in areas defined as urban in each country. (United Nations; data are for 2003)